Diversity in the Workplace

THE PROFESSIONAL PRACTICE SERIES

Working with Organizations and Their People:
A Guide to Human Resources Practice
Douglas W. Bray and Associates

Diversity in the Workplace:
Human Resources Intitiatives
Susan E. Jackson and Associates

Diversity in the Workplace
HUMAN RESOURCES INITIATIVES

Susan E. Jackson and Associates

Foreword by Eli Ginzberg

THE GUILFORD PRESS
New York   London

A Publication Sponsored by
the Society for Industrial and Organizational Psychology, Inc.
a Division of the American Psychological Association

© 1992 The Guilford Press
A division of Guilford Publications, Inc.
72 Spring Street, New York, NY 10012

Printed in the United States of America

This book is printed on acid-free paper.

Last digit is print number: 9 8 7 6 5 4 3 2 1

Library of Congress Cataloging-in-Publication Data

Diversity in the workplace: human resources intitiatives / Susan E.
  Jackson (ed.) ; foreword by Eli Ginzberg.
      p.   cm. — (The Professional practice series)
  Includes bibliographical references and index.
  ISBN 0-89862-476-2
  1. Minorities—Employment—United States.   2. Personnel
management—United States.   3. Organizational change—United States.
I. Jackson, Susan E.   II. Series: Professional practice series.
  [DNLM: 1. Personnel Management—methods.   2. Race Relations.
3. Staff Development—methods. HF 5549 W926]
  HF5549.5.M5W67   1992
658.3'041—dc20
DNLM/DLC   92-1422
for Library of Congress   CIP

The Authors

CLAYTON P. ALDERFER is professor of organizational behavior at the Yale University School of Organization and Management and the Graduate School of Arts and Sciences, the author of two books and more than 70 articles in the area of organizational behavior and organizational change, and a member of the editorial boards of the *Family Business Review* and the *Journal of Organizational Behavior*. He was coeditor of Wiley's series *Advances in Experiential Social Processes*, and he is editor of the *Journal of Applied Behavioral Science*. With J. Richard Hackman, he won the 1972 Cattell Award for creative research design from the Division of Industrial and Organizational Psychology of the American Psychological Association, and with Charleen Alderfer, Robert Tucker, and Leota Tucker he won the 1979 McGregor Award from the *Journal of Applied Behavioral Science* for the best article combining theory, practice, and values in planned social change. His areas of interest include human needs, group and intergroup dynamics, organizational diagnosis, race relations, board-management relations, personality and leadership, and education leadership. He has served as an organizational development consultant to numerous private and public institutions. He obtained a PhD from Yale University in 1966.

EDEN B. ALVAREZ is a doctoral student in industrial/organizational psychology at New York University. In addition, she is currently working as a human resources consultant for Manufacturers Hanover Trust. Previously, she worked for Catalyst, where she was involved in research investigating corporate child-care options. Her research interests include group dynamics, gender issues in the workplace, and international human resources management.

JOEL M. DeLUCA is director of human resource planning in the national office of Coopers & Lybrand, a company he joined in 1989. He is responsible for the design of advanced management processes in the areas of organization design, change, and human resources. DeLuca began his career as a scientist in the U.S. Air Force with assignments in solar energy power systems, aircraft hydraulics, and fuels development. At the rank of captain he made a career shift into the behavioral sciences. He then worked as an internal organization consultant with the Federal Aviation Administration. Prior to joining C&L he was at SUN Co., a Fortune 20 organization, for 8 years and was the manager of organization planning and executive development. He has also been an external consultant to a variety of public and private organizations. He has a BS degree in physics from Bowling Green State University, a MS in physics from Ohio State, an MBA from the University of Dayton, and a PhD in organization change from Yale University. He has served on the faculties of New York University and the Wharton Business School.

JOHN R. FULKERSON is vice president of organizational and management de- velopment for Pepsi-Cola International. He started his career working for an internationally focused branch of the U.S. government where he was responsible for the assessment and development of high-ability staff officers. He then was a principal in a Dallas-based consulting firm that offered a wide range of organiza- tional psychology services. Subsequently, he was the vice president of personnel for a Texas bank holding company. In his current role, he is responsible for the coordination of programs and organization effectiveness interventions for the International Beverage Division of Pepsico. He directs Human Resource and Orga- nization Development activities that impact organizations and people managing Pepsi-Cola business in some 150 countries. His PhD is from Baylor University.

LINDA S. GOTTFREDSON is professor of educational studies at the University of Delaware and codirector of the Delaware–Johns Hopkins Project for the Study of Intelligence and Society. She conducts research on job aptitude demands, test fairness, and the societal consequences of individual and group differences in intelligence. Previously, she was employed at the Johns Hopkins University, where she conducted research on vocational assessment and differences in career development by ethnicity, gender, and physical handicap. She is editor of "The *g* Factor in Employment" and coeditor of "Fairness in Employment Testing," which were two special issues of the *Journal of Vocational Behavior*. Her PhD in sociology is from Johns Hopkins University.

MARILYN K. GOWING is assistant director for personnel research and develop- ment, a senior executive service position with the Office of Personnel Management in Washington, DC. The Personnel Research and Development Center conducts basic, applied, and innovative research in every area of human resources manage- ment (e.g., staffing procedures, workforce quality, training, and career develop- ment). Previously, Gowing held managerial positions with Laventhol & Horwath, Morris & McDaniel, and the International Personnel Management Association. She has been a national officer of the Society for Industrial and Organizational Psychology and is a past president of the Personnel Testing Council/Metropolitan

Washington. She has received awards for her achievements from the Internal Revenue Service, the U.S. Department of Housing and Urban Development, and the American Society of Association Executives. Her PhD is from George Washington University, which honored her in 1990 with a Distinguished Alumni Award "For exemplary achievement in research, public service, and service to the discipline and profession" of psychology.

NANCY C. GUTIERREZ was appointed director of the Fair Employment and Housing Department by California Governor Pete Wilson. The department administers state civil rights laws and is charged with protecting Californians from unlawful discrimination (based on sex, age, race, religion, national origin, physical handicap, marital status, or cancer-related medical condition) in housing, employment, services, and public accommodations. Prior to her appointment, she was an independent consultant specializing in diversity issues. She spent 31 years with Pacific Bell, retiring as director of management recruitment and assessment. While at Pacific Bell, she supervised company recruitment programs throughout California; developed testing, assessment, and selection programs; and was responsible for maintaining Pacific Bell's community liaison activities, which involved her in numerous educational and volunteer activities. She is a member of the Board of Directors of the National Network of Hispanic Women, the Society of Hispanic Professional Engineers Foundation, Leadership America, and the Los Angeles Girl Scout Council.

WILLIAM C. HANSON is vice president of logistics at Digital Equipment Corporation, which he joined in 1967 after receiving both his BS and MS from Stanford University in industrial engineering. He was made an officer of Digital and promoted to vice president, volume manufacturing in 1976. During this period, he began a drive to enable senior manufacturing line managers to address their understanding of racism and sexism and their implications on personal and work life. In 1979, he was appointed vice president, manufacturing personnel. He brought Barbara Walker into Digital to begin to move the traditional programs of equal employment opportunity and affirmative action into new areas, and later sponsored the initial Core Group, which became a critical part of Digital's larger model of Valuing Differences. He became systems manufacturing vice president in 1980 and in 1983 was made vice president of worldwide manufacturing with responsibility for 35 plants throughout Europe, Asia, and North America. He is a member of the Governing Board of Directors of the Massachusetts Institute of Technology Leaders for Manufacturing Program and the Board of Directors of Carnegie Group Incorporated. He also serves as an industrial executive for the Stanford Integrated Manufacturing Association. He has continued the work of Valuing Differences both within Digital and through writings and presentations to organizations and institutions outside the corporation. He was appointed to his current position as vice president of logistics in 1990.

JOYCE MARDENFELD HERLIHY is director of worldwide employee relations for American Express Travel Related Services Company (TRS), where she is responsible for policy development, survey strategy, and work and family issues. During her 7 years with TRS, she has also held positions in international human resources and compensation planning. Her PhD in industrial/organizational psychology as well as her undergraduate and masters degrees are from New York University.

SUSAN E. JACKSON is associate professor of psychology at New York University. Her research interests include strategic human resources management, organizational consequences of workforce diversity, and the dynamics of strategic issue processing within top management teams. She has written numerous articles on these and related topics. She is an active member of the Academy of Management and the Society for Industrial and Organizational Psychology and she is a Fellow of the American Psychological Association and the Society for Industrial and Organizational Psychology. She currently serves as consulting editor for the Academy of Management Review and is a member of the editorial boards for the *Journal of Applied Psychology, Personnel Psychology,* and *Human Resource Planning.* She received her PhD in organizational psychology from the University of California, Berkeley.

DENNIS M. MARINI is vice president of human resources for Harris Corporation's Semiconductor Sector. Harris Corporation, headquartered in Melbourne, Florida, is a $3 billion worldwide company focused on four major businesses: electronic systems, communications, office equipment, and semiconductors. Marini has 7 years with Harris following a 16-year career in employee relations with General Electric. He is certified as a leadership instructor by the Center for Creative Leadership. His MBA is from Xavier University in Cincinnati, Ohio.

ROBERT N. McDOWELL is a partner and national director of personnel management and recruitment of Coopers & Lybrand. He has been with the firm for 17 years and a partner for 9 years. He has held several positions within the human resources function firmwide, and in addition, has held positions as office director of finance and administration, and staff assistant to the chairman, deputy chairman, and vice chairman. He is a member of several professional associations, some of which include the Human Resource Planning Society, Center for Effective Organizations, American Society for Training and Development and the American Accounting Association. He received his BA from Juniata College and his MA degree from the University of Maryland.

ELIZABETH WOLFE MORRISON is an assistant professor of management and organizational behavior at New York University's Stern School of Business. She conducts research on socialization, information seeking behavior, and organizational citizenship. As a doctoral student, she received several awards and honors, including a Unisys Doctoral Fellowship and a National Science Foundation Dissertation Grant. She also received the 1991 Academy of Management Award for the Best Competitive Paper Based on a Dissertation. She received her BA in psychology from Brown University in 1984 and her PhD in organization behavior from Northwestern University in 1991.

SANDRA S. PAYNE heads the Organizational Effectiveness and Analysis Division of the U.S. Office of Personnel Management's Office of Personnel Research and Development. She is responsible for the Quality Assessment Program, a multiphased series of studies designed to monitor the quality of the federal workforce. The results of these studies are used to recommend human resources management policies across the federal government. Previously, she held positions with the responsibility for federal examining policy, and for all federal written test development and operations. She has received numerous awards for her achievements, including the Director's Award for Distinguished Service in 1991. This is the highest award bestowed by the Office of Personnel Management. She has written a textbook chapter on fire department human resources management, and has served as a private consultant at the local, state, and international levels.

J. RUSSELL RIDLEY, JR., is the director of management development and training for the Harris Corporation. In this capacity he is responsible for corporatewide management development initiatives as well as for providing training services in the areas of leadership, team development, business ethics, sales, and sales management. Prior to his assignment on the corporate staff, he was the director of organizational development for Harris Semiconductor. Before joining Harris, he held positions with the Mead Corporation and Rohrer, Hibler and Replogle. He is a member of the editorial review board for the *Human Resource Planning* journal. His PhD is from the University of Tennessee in industrial/organizational psychology.

LORIANN ROBERSON is an associate professor of psychology at New York University, where she has been a member of the faculty since 1984. She conducts research on motivation, work attitudes, and performance appraisal and has published several articles on these topics. She has also consulted in organizations concerning selection and performance appraisal issues. She is a former winner of the S. Rains Wallace Dissertation Award given by the Society for Industrial and Organizational Psychology. She received her PhD in psychology from the University of Minnesota.

RANDALL S. SCHULER is a research professor at the Stern School of Business, New York University. His interests are international human resources management, human resources strategy, quality enhancement, entrepreneurship and the interface of competitive strategy and human resources management. He has authored or edited over 25 books including the recently published *Quality and the Middle Manager, International Dimensions of Human Resource Management, Human Resource Management in the Information Age, Personnel and Human Resource Management,* and *Managing Human Resources.* In addition, he has published numerous chapters and articles in professional books and journals. Presently, he is associate editor of the *Journal of Business and Economic Studies and Management,* and is on the review boards of *Organization Science, The International Journal of Human Resource Management, Asia Pacific Human Resource Management, Organizational Dynamics,* and *Journal of High Technology Management Research.* He is a Fellow of the American Psychology Association and the Society for Industrial and Organizational Psychology and was editor of the *Human Resource Planning* journal. He received his PhD in management from Michigan State University.

DAVID M. SCHWEIGER is professor and director of the PhD Program in Management in the College of Business Administration at the University of South Carolina. Earlier he was a member of the faculty at the University of Houston. Prior to his academic career he was an engineer with the Sperry Rand Corporation. He has written and consulted extensively in the area of mergers and acquisitions, and is completing a book on this topic for senior executives. Currently he is editor of *Human Resource Planning.* His DBA in management is from the University of Maryland.

VALERIE I. SESSA is a doctoral student in industrial and organizational psychology at New York University and is currently working on her dissertation, titled "Conflict in Decision-Making Groups: A Process Model." She has worked as an adjunct instructor at New York University. In addition, she has 5 years of consulting experience in human resources and organizational research in organizations such as Bellevue Hospital, Ciba Geigy Pharmaceutical Corporation, Citicorp, and the Xerox Corporation.

R. ROOSEVELT THOMAS, JR., is founder and president of the American Institute for Managing Diversity, a research, training, and management consulting enterprise with the objective of fostering effective management of employee diversity. The institute, which is affiliated with Morehouse College and located in Atlanta, Georgia, was founded in 1983. Previously, Thomas served as dean of the Atlanta University Graduate School of Business Administration, assistant professor at the Harvard Business School, and instructor at Morehouse College. He has been active for several years as a consultant to numerous corporations, professional firms, nonprofit organizations, and academic institutions. He is the author of the books *Beyond Race and Gender: Unleashing the Power of Your Total Workforce by Managing Diversity* (AMACOM, a division of the American Management Association, 1991) and *Differences Do Make a Difference* (forthcoming), as well as the article "From Affirmative Action to Affirming Diversity," which appeared in the

Harvard Business Review (March–April 1990). He holds a BA degree in mathematics from Morehouse College, an MBA in finance from the University of Chicago, and a DBA in organizational behavior from Harvard University.

BARBARA A. WALKER is the key architect of "Valuing Differences"—a theory-based model widely used in the corporate world to help people deal with the complex issues created by all kinds of differences. Her approach to diversity work was copioneered with managers and employees at Digital Equipment Corporation, which she joined in 1979. At Digital, she led the development of small dialogue groups as the primary instrument of the Valuing Differences work. In 1983 she became the company's affirmative action/equal employment opportunity/valuing differences manager. She is an attorney, having received degrees from both Howard University and Georgetown Law School in Washington, DC. Prior to joining Digital, she spent 17 years working in the area of civil rights in the Department of Commerce and the U.S. Department of Health, Education, and Welfare. She served in a wide range of legal management positions, including deputy assistant general counsel and national training director for the Office of Civil Rights.

Foreword

I was particularly pleased to have been invited to write this foreword because the invitation came about as a result of my longtime professional and personal friendship with Dr. Douglas Bray. It is only a slight exaggeration to say that he and I, in coauthoring *The Uneducated* (Columbia University Press) in 1953 made an early contribution to the theme that dominates this volume, namely, how a large organization (in our case the U.S. Army in World War II) coped with the inflow of about 300,000 new recruits who did not fit the traditional army model. In this case, the problem was the new recruits' low levels of literacy (about fourth grade, on average). The solution was to use special training units to turn about 85% of them into effective soldiers.

We didn't think of our work as an exercise in organizational diversity. And indeed today a low education level is not the type of difference most organizations are worried about when they puzzle over how to cope with increased diversity. But like Molière's would-be gentleman who had been speaking prose all of his life without realizing it, most of my work as a researcher in human resources and as a policy adviser to all the presidents from Franklin Roosevelt to Ronald Reagan has been highly focused in and around the theme of this book.

My acquaintance with the term *diversity* dates only from about the spring of 1990, when I needed some information from Dean Barbara Black of the Columbia University Law School. She explained then that she would have to get back to me because there was a sit-in in her office resulting from a conflict over diversity. The law students wanted more women and minorities appointed to the faculty. I was reminded of my first experience with what is now subsumed under the term *diversity*, which occurred when I was making some early career decisions. The School of Business at Columbia University was founded in 1916, but by the time I was appointed to the lowest rank on the academic totem pole in 1935, a Jew had yet to be appointed to a tenured position. Nevertheless, I decided that the game was worth the candle and that I would see whether the past might not fore-shadow the future. World War II and its aftermath brought a great many changes in academic appointments. It was not all that long after the war that one of my students—a Jew, born in Stalin's home town, brought up in Palestine, and a member of the British Navy—became dean of our school.

Another illustration from the World War II era makes the point that we are dealing with an old theme, at least to some extent. In the weeks following our entrance into World War II (December 1941) I recommended to the Committee on Scientific and Specialized Personnel in the Executive Office of the President that it consider the immediate registration of all women college graduates between the ages of 20 and 44. Based on my knowledge of what was happening in the United Kingdom, I believed we would soon exhaust our male resources and become increasingly dependent on women workers in a full-scale mobilization.

My proposal was rejected without consideration. We never registered any females. Nevertheless, in the industrial sector women became a major resource in all-out mobilization, and their large-scale participation in World War II was the prime factor in their altered relationship to the world of work, some dimensions of which still remain to be solved about a half century later.

Like issues of gender, race relations have a long history in this country. We went through World War II with *totally* segregated armed forces. Then, as his second administration was nearing its end, President Truman ordered the secretary of defense to initiate desegregation. I played a role in conveying the message on behalf of the secretary of the army to General Thomas T. Handy, the commanding general of the U.S. Armed Forces in Europe. I was told by his senior staff that desegregation would require a minimum of a decade, some said two decades. But General Handy, having ascertained that the secretary of the army was determined to implement the president's directive, accomplished the complete integration of his forces, including housing, recreation, and all social amenities, as well as troop and command structures, in less than 12 months. President Truman's successful initiative to desegregate the armed services has given us 40 years later a black army general as chairman of the Joint Chiefs of Staff. Even more importantly, it has made the armed services the most thoroughly integrated sector in the United States.

As a transition from the past to the future, let me call attention briefly to some of the other major "macro" developments in the last half century that played a significant role in adding to the diversity of the U.S. labor force in all three sectors of the U.S. economy—the private sector, the nonprofit sector, and government. In addition to Truman's initiative, I would single out the following.

First of all, the full mobilization of the workforce that occurred in World War II, when unemployment dropped to below 2%, created greatly expanded opportunities for employment and even modest promotion opportunities for the two groups most discriminated against—women and blacks.

The Civil Rights movement of the 1960s was another potent contribution, the more so because of the substantial pressure exercised by legal and administrative actions and the belated recognition of many corporations that a broadened recruitment and promotion policy made sense on both moral and economic grounds.

Then, once the baby-boom generation was behind us, younger women opted for delaying marriage and having fewer children. They not only increased their labor-force participation, they further decided to pursue career objectives similar to those of their fathers, brothers, and husbands (see Eli Ginzberg et al., *Life Styles of Educated Women*, Columbia University Press, 1965). This most fundamental revolution in American life in the 20th century was greatly aided and abetted by the longtime substantial participation of women in higher education and reinforced by the substantial expansion in public financing in the post–World War II era of higher education in both 4- and 2-year colleges.

The two major immigration acts of the mid-1960s and mid-1980s, plus illegal immigration from south of the border, have made further important contributions to greater diversity.

Another macro development that acted to restrict, not expand, the diversity of the U.S. laborforce needs to be mentioned. The substantial improvements in the Social Security system and the indexing of its benefits for inflation in 1972, together with the substantial growth of private pensions, have resulted in the ever earlier retirement of persons aged 55 or older and more particularly aged 62 or 65. Today no more than a few men and women over age 65 continue to work, and many of them who do so are in transitional part-time work prior to full-time retirement status.

One more macro factor that needs to be identified because of its impact on the demand for labor in the postwar decades is the growth rate of the economy, more particularly the extent to which the nation approached or fell short of full employment. Although the economists have differing views on the issue, few would argue with the generalization that except for the latter 1960s during accelerated hostilities in Vietnam, the economy's slow growth rate failed to produce employment opportunities for all who were able and willing to work. The conservatives will argue that those who could not find a job in nonrecession periods suffered structural handicaps such as inadequate education or other disabilities, but theory aside, there were more job applicants than jobs, which made it easier for organizations to keep operating as they always had, or at least to slow their openness to greater diversity.

These highly selective observations about the micro and macro aspects of diversity in the post–World War II era are a potent reminder that much that happened was hidden from view, even to farsighted researchers at the war's end. What about the years and decades immediately ahead? Some directions are clearly visible; others less so.

The approximately three-quarters of a million legal immigrants and refugees that the United States accepts each year, together with an unknown number of illegal immigrants, assures that the population and the laborforces of the major coastal cities from New York to San Francisco as well as inland cities such as Phoenix, Chicago, and Atlanta are becoming steadily more diversified. A few illustrations: In 1980 New York City's foreign-born accounted for just slightly over 25% of the population. The best projections for the year 2000 point to a figure of 57%. It is doubtful that any other large city in the history of the world has ever experienced such a rapid growth in its foreign-born population as is suggested by the foregoing projection.

One must quickly point out that the present and prospective large immigrant inflows foreshadow a greater need for employer organizations to respond to diversity in the middle and longer term because so many of the newcomers make their initial linkages to the laborforce and employment via immigrant networks, whether joining compatriots in a taxi drivers' group, or going to work in a factory or store owned and operated by a relative, friend, or fellow immigrant who had arrived some years earlier.

But one must quickly add that other organizations—government, nonprofit, and profit—have need to broaden and deepen their knowledge of how to interact with the large numbers of immigrants, the vast majority of whom are not literate in English when they arrive. Probably the biggest challenge is the one facing the public educational authorities. In Queens, New York, the newspapers reported that over 100 different languages were spoken at home by the pupils enrolled in a single public school.

Within a single generation, and often sooner, increasing numbers of recent immigrants will account for a larger proportion of the total laborforce, particularly in the areas of the country where they are concentrated. The private sector has no time to lose to develop the knowledge, skills, and flexibility it will need to operate effectively with a much more diversified laborforce.

Important as the newcomers will be in the transformation of the U.S. laborforce, we need to increase our efforts to do a much better job than we have been doing to improve the access, recruitment, training, retention, and promotion of the two dominant minorities who have been residents in this country for centuries or at least decades—blacks and Hispanics who together account for one-fifth of the population, a proportion that will increase in the years ahead.

This challenge of stronger bridges from school to work has come very much to the forefront of current policy, but in my view, neither the educational authorities nor most local employers have been able to design effective vocational education-training mechanisms that are responsive to the needs of the predominant numbers of minorities who are not interested in or capable of going on to college—as well as correspondingly large numbers of white students who have similar needs for improved transitional mechanisms into the world of work.

My reading of the situation is that although many business leaders are aware of the challenge, they have not yet found the mechanisms required to work with the educational authorities to achieve the reforms, or, as some would call it, the revolution, in secondary schooling that have been delayed much too long. Although countrywide efforts involving a leadership role by the business community in broadening the pool of properly qualified young minority persons to enter the workforce should be a high priority, employers still face many challenges to improve the utilization of the increasing numbers who are currently in their workforce.

There are two further challenges facing the nation that stem from the increasing diversity of its population and workforce and that need to be identified and at least briefly explicated. The first involves the unattended consequences of the women's revolution, which has brought the number of women in the workforce to within striking distance of male workers. The other is the almost completely neglected phenomenon of the older worker, who has been leaving the laborforce at an ever younger age, often before age 60 and almost always before or at age 65.

As far as women are concerned, relatively little attention has been paid to the facts that one-half of all mothers (with husbands present) in the workforce have children under age 1 at home and almost two-thirds have children between ages 1 and 6. Almost three-quarters of working mothers have children under age 18. Although a small number of employers have sought to accommodate this striking transformation in the American workforce, it would be difficult to challenge the generalization that most employers have paid little or no attention to this truly revolutionary transformation in the national scene.

Once again one must not single out employers for all, or even for most, of the blame. The children, many of whom are at risk, are in no position to make their voices heard; most of the mothers who work, especially those with very young children, have no way of knowing what the costs or benefits of such an arrangement will be for their children, their husbands, and themselves. And our governmental structure, which seeks to avoid entanglements with the family (except for the welfare population), has for the most part kept its distance from the problems of working mothers and closely related issues.

The time is surely coming—in my view it is long overdue—when our society needs to take a hard look at the current structure of work, particularly as it relates to working mothers with young children, and I would be inclined to define "young" up to puberty, or even to adolescence. Adjustments in the hours and conditions of work that characterized our society when men dominated the full-time workforce cannot meet the needs of a society in which women with primary responsibility for child-rearing and housekeeping are increasingly career workers holding down full-time jobs. Accordingly, I believe that the single largest challenge on the diversity front is for all of the interested parties—the public sector, employers, and households—to focus on the long-neglected facets of this issue. Second, they must explore and put in place new societal arrangements that over time could be absorbed at a sustainable cost. These would include longer maternity leaves, a reduction in the length of the work week, increased flexibility in arrangements to work at home, expanded and improved preschool facilities, and a host of related adjustments. The one approach that a self-respecting society concerned with its future cannot afford to take is to do nothing and to continue to avoid addressing the issue.

This brings us to the last macro issue that looms ahead, an issue that to date has attracted at best only marginal attention. One can call it the issue of the older worker. My preference is to define it as the extension of working life. Whatever it is called, there are certain key facts that define the issue. The typical work life of an American worker has been roughly 40 years, from about age 20 to age 60. Because a higher proportion of all males in earlier generations lived only to their early or mid-60s, their working life accounted for perhaps as much as two-thirds of their total lifespan. Current projections point to an elongation of life for the average American to age 80, with a potential productive life close to 60 years, or 50% above what it was earlier. When one adds the important fact that physically exhausting work has declined, while office work has come to dominate the economy, the scope for adaptations for older persons to continue working full or part time has been further increased.

Why then have we been moving in the opposite direction? The principal answer is close at hand. Our society has made considerable gains in assuring that older persons will have adequate income to maintain their standard of living. Further, employers have sought to encourage, even to bribe, many long-term employees approaching retirement age to accept early retirement, and many employers have offered enticing inducements to gain their agreement.

Some employers have miscalculated, but most of them knew what they were doing. Many confronted the need to downsize, and the least disturbing to employee morale is the tactic of encouraging "voluntary" retirement. Further, older employees tend to be better paid, so that their early retirement not only reduces the pressure on the wage structure, but opens up positions higher on the ladder for able younger people.

But all of these sensible explanations for what has been happening must not ignore the strong bias in American society in favor of the young; or reformulated, a prejudice against the old. No sector, whether government, employers, or older persons, has addressed alternatives for continuing to make productive use of the potential of the ever-larger number of older persons, a high proportion of whom will have 20 additional years of productive life ahead of them.

Admittedly, some prospective older persons will be unable to work because of chronic illness and disability; others will not want to work more than part time; but still others will be able and interested in continuing to work.

In light of the foregoing, I would not pretend that if all of the elderly opted to work until their 80th year that we would obtain a 50% increase in the nation's effective laborforce, but I could conceive a significant 15% to 20% increase in the decades ahead. And that translates into an additional $1 trillion of GNP. Next to the adjustments that we need to make about women in the workforce with young children at home—my first priority—I would place the elderly on a par with the improved integration of immigrants and minorities.

In sum, the United States has great potential to make significant gains by learning to deal more effectively with a much more diverse laborforce and population. The diversity has been a major source of the nation's accomplishments in the past, and it holds great promise for its future progress.

A serious organizational effort at diversity requires both the unequivocal commitment of those at the top as well as the introduction of accountability measures that leaves no margin of doubt that those at the top are fully committed to the new policy. In the absence of such leadership and commitment, things will move, if at all, very slowly and haltingly, for the simple and obvious reason that most individuals have all sorts of prejudices based on gender, race, religion, language, age, educational credentials, family background, and still other characteristics that in most instances have little, if anything, to do with the individual's ability to perform effectively. But, although they are basically unrelated to the ability to perform, they can nevertheless have an impact on performance. Because most work is performed in larger or smaller organizations and requires on-going interactions among the individual worker, co-workers, supervisors, and managers, deep-seated and widespread hostility toward persons with characteristics and qualities that differentiate them from the others can assure that any "outsider" so seriously handicapped will fail.

ELI GINZBERG, Director
Eisenhower Center for the Conservation of Human Resources
Columbia University, New York

Preface

This is the second volume in the Professional Practice Series sponsored by the Society for Industrial and Organizational Psychology (SIOP). This series, decided upon by the SIOP Executive Committee of 1987–88, is intended to stress the second term of the "scientist-practitioner model," an important ideal of industrial-organizational (I/O) psychology. The scientific emphasis was, and is, being served by the society's Frontiers Series launched in 1986.

Although approximately three-quarters of I/O psychologists are involved at least to some extent in practice, whether in a consulting or in-house capacity, there has been little attention in the professional literature to the process of practice itself. Practitioners say that research reports in the literature are replete with technical details but are of limited help in learning how to solve organizational problems. This series attempts to provide some relevant assistance.

Although the series is sponsored by SIOP, it is addressed to all human resources practitioners, not just I/O psychologists. I/O psychologists have wide influence, but they constitute only a small percentage of the very large number of human resources practitioners. It is believed that these other practitioners will benefit from the series and that, hopefully, human resources practice may be improved generally.

In 1988, Daniel R. Ilgen, then president of SIOP, invited me to become the editor of this series, an invitation I gladly accepted. My first task was to recruit an editorial board. This effort went well. The members of the board are all leading psychologists with extensive experience in human resources practice.

The board quickly decided that the first volume in the new series should be a general one focused on the process of practice in major areas of practice and in major practice settings. They also unexpectedly decided that I should edit this first book. The result was *Working with Organizations and Their People: A Guide to Human Resources Practice*, published in April 1991 by the Guilford Press, which the board selected to publish the series.

Another important decision at the first editorial board meeting was that the next two or three publications should be made up of case studies. Each volume would center on a particular type of organizational problem and detail the various ways in which different organizations were attacking it.

Among the topics listed as possibilities for these next volumes was that of workforce diversity, and this was selected to be the focus of the first set of case studies. Although, as Eli Ginzberg points out in the Foreword, some aspects of diversity have long engaged human resources practice, the term itself has now gained currency to cover a wide range of activities. Diversity has come to be seen as multifaceted, subsuming characteristics of groups of individuals, the life circumstances in which individuals find themselves, the relationships among groups, and many other aspects.

The breadth of these issues suggests that a wide variety of human resources interventions may be stimulated by diversity. The editorial board was convinced that a volume illustrating a range of interventions would be highly worthwhile. This book is the result.

We were very fortunate in persuading Susan E. Jackson of New York University to assume the editorship of this volume. She is the author of many publications in a wide variety of human resources management areas and serves on the editorial boards of several of the most respected journals in human resources research and practice. Of late, she has studied the effects of diversity on decision-making teams and strategic planning activities. This interest has broadened to encompass diversity at all levels of the workforce. As a result of her efforts this book offers a detailed picture of the varied ways in which organizations are responding to such diversity.

DOUGLAS W. BRAY
Series Editor
Tenafly, New Jersey

Acknowledgments

The seed from which this book grew was a research project stimulated by the interests of several doctoral students in New York University's psychology program in industrial and organizational psychology. Special thanks are due to Eden Alvarez, Valerie Sessa, and Karl Peyronnin, who worked with me as we surveyed New York corporations to learn about how they were responding to the growing diversity of their workforces. The cooperation of all of the human resources managers we interviewed are also gratefully acknowledged.

When Doug Bray asked me to undertake this project, I am certain neither he nor I knew how many difficult decisions would have to be made during the course of it, or how much learning would occur. As a seasoned scientist-practitioner, his guidance throughout this project has been invaluable. In addition, the authors of the case studies presented in this volume benefited from the advice they received from all members of the editorial board for the SIOP Professional Practice Series. Special thanks go to Ann Howard, whose timely and thoughtful comments improved each chapter.

The lion's share of this project's secretarial burden has been carried by Elina Dobin, at New York University. She spent uncountable hours shepherding me, my coauthors, and our manuscripts through numerous revisions. I am especially grateful to her for the dedication and patience she showed throughout this project.

Finally, this project would not have been possible without the support and cooperation of the many employees—named and unnamed—who were involved in the cases described in this book, including the executives who agreed to the publication of these cases and the employees who shared their experiences with the case writers. Their stories are offered here for the benefit of others who seek to successfully work through diversity.

SUSAN E. JACKSON
New York, New York

Contents

Diversity in the Workplace

PART I

THE CHALLENGES
OF WORKPLACE DIVERSITY

CHAPTER 1

Preview of the Road to Be Traveled

SUSAN E. JACKSON

During the past 5 years, concern over the implications of the increasingly diverse nature of the workforce has grown. In the wake of Hudson Institute's influential reports titled *Workforce 2000* (Johnston & Packer, 1987) and *Opportunity 2000* (Bolick & Nestleroth, 1988) newspapers and business magazines have focused our attention with stories about ambitious new "managing diversity" programs being implemented by many organizations. Examples of such programs include nontraditional work arrangements, such as flextime and home work stations; education and training programs intended to reduce stereotyping, increase cultural sensitivity, and develop skills for working in multicultural environments; career management programs, designed to promote constructive feedback to employees, mentoring relationships, and access to informal networks; and new employee benefits, such as parental leave and dependent-care assistance.

Surveys of business leaders confirm the perception that interest in managing diversity successfully is widespread. For example, in one study of 645 firms, 74% of the respondents were concerned about increased diversity, and of these about one-third felt that diversity affected their corporate strategy. Why are companies so concerned? The two primary reasons cited were a belief that supervisors did not know how to motivate their diverse work groups, and uncertainty about how to handle the challenge of communicating with employees whose cultural backgrounds result in differing assumptions, values, and even language skills (Towers Perrin & Hudson Institute, 1990).

Concerns about workforce diversity are not always matched by actions, however. Despite recognition of the importance of diversity, most firms are just beginning to evaluate and adjust policies and practices of human resources management designed for yesterday's more homogeneous workforce. The large-scale organizational changes attracting attention from the press are laudable exemplars of what *can* be done, but they attract attention precisely because they are the exceptional cases. Indeed, most programs are so new that it is too soon to judge just how effective they will be. Nevertheless, the goals these firms are pursuing represent a vision of the future that many other organizations should contemplate.

The case studies presented in this volume explain why and how various organizations are addressing a wide range of diversity issues. The cases are themselves diverse. Manufacturing companies, service companies, and the federal government are all represented. The initiatives described include recruitment and promotion activities, facilitation of personal and team development, performance management, and smoothing the interface between employees' work and nonwork lives. Most of the cases deal with responses to the demographic diversity of the U.S. workforce, but this is not their exclusive focus. Also illustrated are the challenges associated with merging diverse corporate cultures and the challenges of managing the global workplace.

Because diversity is a people-related business issue, human resources departments are often involved, and the cases we present reflect this reality. Some cases describe how internal human resources professionals and managers shaped their organizations' agendas and activated change processes intended to improve the effectiveness of the organization and the people it employs. In other cases, line managers were the proactive agents of change, and the involvement of the human resources department followed subsequently. Regardless of the impetus for action, members of the human resources departments in these cases often worked in partnership with external consultants.

OBJECTIVES FOR THIS VOLUME

Clearly, not all organizations approach the issue of diversity in the same manner, nor would this be desirable. A wide range of options is available, and different options are best suited to different organizational circumstances. Therefore, this book does not attempt to provide cookbook recipes that contain all the ingredients for success in working through diversity. Indeed, the cases presented cover only a fraction of the full spectrum of changes organizations may undergo as they deal with diversity-related issues. Rather than offering a full description of available off-the-shelf solutions, this book seeks to clarify the strategic importance of issues related to diversity and to illustrate the dynamic changes activated in organizations when these issues are identified and addressed. It is intended to stimulate all those who are active in addressing human resources management issues to consider how their activities could be and/or should be influenced by the increasing diversity of organizational workforces. By describing in detail the experiences of a few organizations, we hope to alert readers to the complexity and breadth of workplace diversity issues and provide information that can be used to develop new and unique approaches that fit the specific needs of particular organizations.

THE CONTEXT FOR CURRENT HUMAN RESOURCES

To provide a context for the case studies, Chapter 2 describes the changing economic and organizational environments that are pressuring organizations to address issues of diversity in new ways. It provides a brief look at changing business conditions, highlighting three trends that have made working through diversity a necessity for many organizations. These are the growing service economy, globalization, and the changing nature of the workforce. Chapter 2 shows how these trends converge to suggest that working through diversity successfully may be a strategic imperative for many organizations.

If working through diversity is a strategic issue, why have some companies been slow to head down the road to change that will help make diversity work to their advantage? Interviews with human resources (HR) managers in New York City suggest two reasons for why some firms have been slow to respond even though the human resources department staff believes action is needed.

Some HR managers said their firms had not acted yet, because their top-level line managers were insulated from the changing world that surrounded them. The diversity everyone was talking about was "out there," not "in here." The people they were managing (mid-level employees) were still mostly from traditional American families, mostly white, and most often male. Although the corporations they worked in operated internationally, foreign activities were viewed as peripheral and most managers were not drawn into any international exchanges. As one person explained, the line managers considered their firm to be among the best in its industry, which meant it would be able to keep hiring "the cream of the crop." These managers were right about their ability to hire the best, but they were blind to the fact that the crops they would be harvesting were grown from a new variety of seed.

In other companies, the HR managers we interviewed believed that some top executives were aware of diversity in their workforce, yet admitted that the issue had sparked no new initiatives. This was particularly surprising to hear from one firm with an excellent reputation for being employee oriented. Did they have plans for anything in the near future? No. Were they actively studying whether they should address the issue? No. Why? The interviewee responded, "I don't really want to raise awareness of an issue until I have solutions—I'm looking for solutions first."

These examples suggest that some firms have not yet considered how increasing diversity might impact their organizations, because top-level line managers simply do not see the diversity of their workforce, or if they see it they do not recognize its strategic importance. In other firms, the strategic importance may be recognized, but those who could be guiding the process of organizational diagnosis and change are unsure about what to do and/or how to do it. The cases and commentaries appearing in this volume suggest a third reason, namely, disagreements about the objectives to be achieved and disagreements about the best ways to achieve agreed-upon objectives.

These and other circumstances may explain why many organizations are not actively attending to issues of workplace diversity, but they tell us little about why a few organizations have been proactive in finding new ways to work through diversity. The cases in this volume illustrate how issues of workplace diversity have worked their way into the strategic agendas of a few organizations, and they describe several different approaches to creating change.

The cases are intended to illustrate what the path to change can look like, to illuminate some of the impediments discovered by others, and to suggest routes that facilitate progress. The envisioning of a destination worth traveling to is a task organizations must tackle for themselves, however, having thoroughly considered their organizations' objectives and the context in which they strive to achieve them. Admittedly, the case studies may not uncover every barrier, pothole, and banana peel along the path, so reading this book does not guarantee that those who set out on the path to working through diversity will be saved from slipping or even falling. Nevertheless, after seeing how a few companies are working through diversity and the roles played by HR managers, consultants, and professionals, readers should be better prepared for the journey.

CREATING AND ASSESSING A DIVERSE WORKFORCE

Efforts intended to address issues of diversity in organizations often grow in part out of a concern about how organizations treat women and members of nonwhite ethnic groups. Because of this, people are likely to associate current efforts to manage diversity with programs that have been used to intentionally create more diversity in organizations. However, as the term *managing diversity* implies, the organizational interventions that fall within the realm of this label focus on ensuring that the diversity of talents and perspectives that already exist within an organization are well utilized. Many organizations communicate the distinction between activities that create diversity and those related to managing diversity by assigning responsibility for the latter to diversity managers.

Just as it is inaccurate to equate managing diversity with creating diversity, it would be inaccurate to assert that these two types of activities are completely separate. Historically, they are intertwined, as the cases presented in Part II illustrate. Several organizations whose expertise at managing diversity is now being recognized were stimulated to develop that expertise primarily because of their previous success as equal employment opportunity/affirmative action employers. That success resulted in organizations characterized by greater gender-based, racial, and ethnic diversity. The lessons learned about managing these types of diversity are now being adopted and adapted for working through diversity of all types. Nevertheless, the training ground was not today's diverse workplace—it was the newly integrated workplace of the 1970s and early 1980s, when relations between men and women and between African-Americans and white Americans were the focal concern.

Unless diversity exists within an organization, it obviously needs no attention. Less obviously, the process by which diversity is created has important implications for the issues that arise when working through it. In many organizations, workplace diversity is evolving gradually as a natural consequence of doing business in a changing environment, but in some organizations diversity also exists partly because it has been intentionally engineered through aggressive equal employment opportunity(EEO) and affirmative action (AA) programs. Xerox (Chapter 3) and Pacific Bell (Chapter 4) are examples of companies where this is true. Their experiences illustrate the crisscrossing paths taken by organizations to create diversity and to manage it successfully.

The federal government is another example of an organization with a diverse workplace that was shaped, in part, by EEO/AA programs. These programs achieved some of their objectives, but there was a negative side effect—people are now questioning whether those programs produced a workforce of civil servants with questionable job qualifications. Chapter 5 describes the government's response to these critics: the Quality Assessment Program. This chapter highlights a key hurdle in the race to build competence in managing diversity, namely, convincing skeptical supervisors, managers, and policymakers that "different" is not equivalent to "deficient." Until this hurdle is cleared, efforts to mine the potential of a diverse workforce are probably doomed to failure.

MANAGING WORKPLACE DIVERSITY THROUGH PERSONAL GROWTH AND TEAM DEVELOPMENT

The cases in Part III illustrate how three companies addressed diversity using interventions designed to improve interpersonal relations between members of different groups. In all three cases, workshops and group activities were used to surface issues, exchange points of view, and discuss possible alternatives for resolving differences that might threaten the ability of people to work together effectively to achieve organizational objectives.

The general approach used in these organizations is often referred to as organization development (OD). As a specialty area, OD is historically associated with sensitivity training, team-oriented work designs, and the use of survey feedback methods. The cases in Part III illustrate how these methods of intervention can be used to improve the functioning of organizations characterized by diversity.

The objective of OD efforts is large-scale organization change. The introduction of OD-type interventions is often stimulated by a desire to make changes in the structure, procedures, and systems of an organization. Such changes may be required to facilitate the introduction of new technologies, to effect a new business strategy, and to respond to competitive pressures, among other things. Regardless of the impetus, however, achieving the desired change often requires changing the corporate culture (see Burke, 1991). Consequently, many OD specialists have relevant experiences they can draw on to assist organizations in adapting corporate cultures to increasing levels of workplace diversity.

The cases in Part III illustrate three OD-based interventions launched to encourage corporate cultures to be supportive of the types of workplace diversity faced by the companies involved. Although similar in general intent, the target of the development efforts in the three companies described were not the same.

At Digital Equipment Corporation, the initial impetus for action was a desire to address the debilitating stereotypes white males had about women, African-Americans, and Puerto Ricans, but over the years the Valuing Differences philosophy has developed to recognize that personal differences stem from many other aspects of individual experiences as well (Chapter 6).

At XYZ Corporation (a pseudonym), intervention efforts focused narrowly on improving relations between blacks and whites (Chapter 7). Although XYZ had a more narrow focus, its 15 years of effort are particularly noteworthy for two reasons: Their activities were guided by a formal conceptual model for understanding relations between members of different racial groups, and they conducted a systematic evaluation of their progress.

At Harris Semiconductor, team development activities were designed to unite the top management teams from two merging corporations (Chapter 8). The Harris case illustrates how many of the same dynamics that influence relations between people from different social backgrounds surface to influence relations between members of firms brought together in a merger. It also illustrates well the point that working through merger-generated diversity is a critical task, which must be successfully managed to realize the full potential of the newly created enterprise.

USING STRATEGIC INITIATIVES TO MANAGE WORKPLACE DIVERSITY

Unifying the cases included in Part IV is the recognition that successfully working through diversity is a strategic imperative. In the case of American Express (Chapter 9), the focus is on gender diversity. At Coopers & Lybrand (Chapter 10), rapidly increasing gender diversity was the initial spark that drew attention to diversity as a concern, but the organization's response recognizes that this is only one small piece of a much larger diversity pie. Finally, at Pepsi-Cola International (Chapter 11) the strategic imperative was to discover ways to effectively manage the diversity of national cultures represented in a truly global corporation.

The cases in Part IV illustrate several issues that arise when HR managers adopt a strategic perspective for working through diversity. The American Express and Coopers & Lybrand cases illustrate two quite different approaches to introducing organization change, each of which can be successful. At American Express, the economic consequences of ignoring the needs of the large number of female employees were assessed and addressed head-on by a large-scale centralized change in organizational policy, with the approval of the female employees. At Coopers & Lybrand, however, female employees were apparently concerned that their careers might suffer if special attention was directed toward them as a group, reflecting an organizational climate in which career commitment is highly valued. Rather than ignore their own data showing the need to address issues of workplace diversity out of fear of a negative backlash from the workforce, the human resources group at Coopers & Lybrand developed a business-oriented conceptual framework for discussing the issue of diversity and prepared the organization for grass-roots experimentation with new approaches to managing their human resources.

In any large organization that has both a corporate HR staff and local HR staff for subunits of the firm, the question arises of how to apportion responsibility for designing and implementing HR policies. For many HR activities, location-specific practices evolve with little or no guidance from corporate headquarters. This is becoming even more common as corporate

staff is reduced in the interest of running "leaner and meaner" organizations. When HR issues are treated as strategic issues, however, corporate
HR is necessarily involved.

The cases in Part IV reveal three alternative models for corporate HR
involvement: At American Express, the corporate HR group developed a
centralized policy with the expectation that local units would implement
it uniformly throughout the company. At Pepsico International, corporate
HR develops general policies that local units are expected to adopt and
serves as a resource, but both the corporate and local HR staff agree that
local conditions should heavily influence the specifics of policy implementation. In contrast, the Coopers & Lybrand case illustrates a bottom-up
approach. In this model, corporate HR explicitly gave local HR staff the
responsibility for developing initiatives. Rather than issue directives, here
corporate HR adopts a stewardship role: They prepare the organization to
support experimentation and learning, facilitate the exchange of information among local HR staff, assist in evaluating new initiatives as they are
developed, and ensure that lessons learned locally are disseminated corporatewide.

PERSPECTIVES FOR VIEWING THE CHALLENGES OF
DIVERSITY IN THE WORKPLACE

A close reading of the cases contained in this volume reveals many common themes as well as many divergent approaches to working through
diversity. The three chapters appearing in Part V offer commentaries about
issues raised by ongoing efforts to work through diversity effectively.

Chapters 12 and 13 both comment on the relationship between workforce diversity and EEO/AA programs. Chapter 12 retraces some of the
history of the civil rights movement in order to shed light on current
criticisms being directed toward policies and programs designed to eliminate discrimination in the workplace. Linda Gottfredson, professor of
educational studies, warns those involved in activities intended to help
organizations work effectively through diversity to proceed with caution,
and identifies several dilemmas that must be carefully analyzed. The appropriateness of some hiring practices used to eliminate racism in the past
are now being hotly debated in the press, in Congress, in the Supreme
Court, and in the workplace (e.g., see "Affirmative Action," 1991; "Race in
the Workplace," 1991). These debates suggest several lessons for those
whose objective is to help organizations work through the diversity of
today's workforce.

Chapter 13 extends the discussion begun in Chapter 12. R. Roosevelt
Thomas, Jr., founder and president of the American Institute for Managing

Diversity, presents a conceptual framework for sorting through and comparing many types of human resources management activities related to the issue of workplace diversity. He identifies three different approaches to working through diversity: traditional affirmative action programs; initiatives to facilitate Understanding Diversity; and initiatives for Managing Diversity. After describing the characteristics of each approach, the author argues that Managing Diversity initiatives hold the most promise. Only these, he argues, offer the possibility of sustainable, fundamental change in the way organizations approach their task of effective human resources management.

Finally, Chapter 13 identifies several questions to be addressed by those who wish to consider whether a particular organization should alter its current approach to workplace diversity. Primary among these is the question: "What objectives would be served by changing the organization's current model for dealing with diversity?" Implied by this question is the assumption that every organization has in place systems and practices that reflect and communicate an organizational stance regarding diversity of many sorts. Before contemplating any change efforts, these should be analyzed for the purpose of understanding the messages they communicate. Furthermore, the reasons behind the use of current practices need to be considered and understood in light of a particular organization's current objectives and criteria for effectiveness. From this base of understanding, new initiatives for improving the organization's approach to working through diversity can then be developed, if needed. For those who conclude that change is called for, Chapter 14 highlights several additional questions to ask when designing the change effort, and suggests a few principles that should guide sustained change efforts.

CONCLUSION

As this brief preview suggests, the chapters in this volume contain several important messages. Among the most central ones are these: First, workplace diversity of many types is increasing. Although few organizations are likely to be experiencing significant changes in every important type of diversity, most organizations are probably experiencing significant changes in some types of diversity. Second, the implications of these changes are broad and potentially very important. They can impact a variety of human resources management activities. Therefore, workplace diversity is an issue that every employer and every human resources professional should be thinking through. Third, the issue of workplace diversity is not a simple one. It takes different forms in different organizational situations. Consequently, there is no single approach to working through diversity that can be prescribed for all situations. Instead, responses should be tailored to address specific objectives and the environments in which those objectives are being pursued. Finally, because pre-formed solutions with guaranteed results are unavailable, those who recommend action plans for responding to workplace diversity should also take responsibility for ensuring that the results of the change efforts are evaluated against the desired objectives. These and the many other messages communicated in this volume are offered to stimulate both new thoughts and new actions among readers.

REFERENCES

Affirmative Action: A great leveler—or destroyer? (1991, August 5). *Business Week*, pp. 6–8.

Bolick, C., & Nestleroth, S. (1988). *Opportunity 2000: Creative affirmative action strategies for a changing work force*. Washington, DC: U.S. Government Printing Office.

Burke, W. W. (1991). Practicing organization development. In D. W. Bray & Associates (Eds.), *Working with organizations and their people: A guide to human resources practice* (pp. 95–130). New York: Guilford Press.

Johnston, W. B., & Packer, A. E. (1987). *Workforce 2000: Work and workers for the 21st century*. Indianapolis, IN: Hudson Institute.

Race in the work place: Is affirmative action working? (1991, July 8). *Business Week*, pp. 50–63.

Towers Perrin & Hudson Institute. (1990). *Workforce 2000: Competing in a seller's market: Is corporate America prepared?* Valhalla, NY: Towers Perrin.

CHAPTER 2

Working Through Diversity as a Strategic Imperative

SUSAN E. JACKSON
EDEN B. ALVAREZ

Organizations that attack the diversity issue with full force do so because they believe that taking action is a strategic imperative. For most organizations, simply knowing the facts about workforce diversity—which are now parading as headlines in our daily newspapers—does not stimulate major changes in management practices. The facts about the nature of the workforce are important, but their significance is most obvious when they are considered in the context of the changing business environment.

One hundred years ago, as the 19th century drew to a close, Americans in every major urban center were experiencing the industrial revolution, which dramatically altered the nature of their work. Small, home-based businesses closed their doors, and fathers and sons headed out to work in the factories. Independent artisans who offered customized goods and services to their local communities traded in their life-style to work on assembly lines, where work was divided into simple tasks performed by man-and-machine teams. With the industrial revolution, the social intimacy and personalized business relationships that characterized work were replaced by isolation, mass production, and impersonal bureaucracy.

Now, as we approach the beginning of a new millennium, another revolution is transforming our work lives. The economic forces shaping this new revolution are many and varied, but two are particularly relevant to the topic of workforce diversity: the shift from a manufacturing-based economy to a service economy and the globalization of the marketplace. These changes are bringing more and more people from diverse backgrounds into contact with one another, and, at the same time, mean that businesses are becoming more reliant on person-to-person contact as a way to get things done. Add to these trends the changing demographics of both consumers and the workforce, and the stage is set for diversity to emerge as a strategic business issue.

THE SERVICE ECONOMY

As of May 1991, 78% of all U. S. employees (74% of employees in the private sector) worked in service-based industries (Bureau of Labor Statistics, 1991), and projections for the future show a continuing upward trend. However, these figures underestimate the true importance of services in our economy. Manufacturers also know that service is important, and they woo customers by providing it for their products. Services hidden within the manufacturing sector of our economy include activities such as maintenance and repair of automobiles, household appliances, computers, and industrial equipment; customer training; customized design work; and deliveries. Also hidden from these figures are the myriad internal service exchanges that occur within companies.

Defining services is difficult, but capturing the essence of them is easy. As one person put it, "Services is something which can be bought and sold but which you cannot drop on your foot" (Gummesson, 1987, p. 22). That is, services are intangible. More importantly for the topic of diversity, a service is produced and consumed on the spot, during an exchange that involves both the provider of the service and the customer. During a service encounter, production, marketing, and quality control all occur simultaneously.

Bell (1973) described service work as a "game between persons." For companies to win at this game, they need employees who can read their customers and interact with them in a nearly flawless manner. Employees must be able to understand the customer's perspective, anticipate and monitor the customer's needs and expectations, and respond sensitively and appropriately to fulfill those needs and expectations. In the service game, "customer literacy" is an essential skill. But achieving customer literacy is an illusive goal. As some companies are beginning to realize, employing a workforce that mirrors the customers is one step in the right direction. Maryland National Bank in Baltimore discovered this when it studied the customer retention records for its branches. The best branches recruited locally to hire tellers who could swap neighborhood gossip. Of the 20 branch managers, one of their best—located in a distant suburban— was described as dressing "very blue-collar . . . she doesn't look like a typical manager of people. But this woman is totally committed to her customers" (Sellers, 1990, p. 60).

As service activities gain in importance, so do issues of diversity. In a service economy, interactions between people are pervasive, and effective communications are essential to business success. Similarities between people help smooth these basic processes, whereas differences between people can interfere. Ironically, having discovered they can communicate more effectively with their customers by hiring employees who are similar to those customers, employers soon realize they have increased their internal diversity and must find ways to counter the resulting internal communication difficulties among employees plus the challenge of effectively managing and retaining their new, diverse workforce.

GLOBALIZATION SPURS ORGANIZATIONAL RESTRUCTURING

The globalization of business activities is another environmental force that pushes issues of diversity into the foreground as firms envision their strategic objectives. A recent *Harvard Business Review* survey of 12,000 managers from 25 different countries documented how common international expansion has become. Worldwide, 45% of larger companies (10,000 or more employees) had experienced some international expansion in the past 2 years. In the United States, about 26% of all respondents indicated that their company had recently expanded internationally (Kanter, 1991).

As trade barriers fall, foreign sourcing becomes more attractive and new growth opportunities are created. For example, for U.S. pharmaceutical companies, the portion of annual sales coming from foreign markets was recently estimated to be 40% (Business International Corporation, 1991). To capture large shares of foreign markets, licensing agreements and joint ventures with non-U.S. firms are often desirable and sometimes necessary. For large companies, these alliances may require coordinating activities in 100 or more countries. Smaller companies may have alliances involving only one or two foreign locations, but these are critical if corporate survival hangs on their ability to manage them successfully.

For managers, experiences with new international partners can be like a slap in the face that forces them to realize the value of employees with cross-cultural sensitivities, as well as the need for organizational systems that knit multiple cultures together to form a seamless whole. When perfected, such systems will enable organizations to fully utilize the talents of employees from all parts of the world with no interference due to the static created when cultures clash.

But globalization has more subtle consequences, as well. These affect companies that are not even reaching out for a share of the global market. For example, globalization means U.S. firms now compete with companies from around the world for customers who were once a safely isolated home market. With more options to choose from, all consumers of goods and services have more power to insist that their needs and preferences be satisfied. Successful U.S. firms have learned how to get close to their customers, regardless of whether those customers are individuals or businesses, internal or external customers, in the home market or in foreign markets.

As they struggle to get closer to customers abroad and at home and to win their loyalty, many firms are changing their organizational structures. Some of these changes, such as increased use of work teams, merely highlight the importance of working through domestic demographic diversity. Other changes, such as new strategic alliances, reveal new types of diversity that must be managed, including differences in corporate cultures and differences in the cultures that host a company's foreign operations.

New Business Strategies Require More Teamwork

In response to the increased pressure created by global competition, many U.S. businesses focused first on articulating a competitive strategy and then began adapting themselves to fit that strategy. For many, increasing the quality of products and services became a high-priority strategic objective. Indeed, quality enhancement strategies have become pervasive since the federal government legitimized and institutionalized such efforts by launching the Malcolm Baldrige National Quality Award. Other companies focused on innovation—a tactic U.S. firms had historically exploited successfully. To succeed at beating the competition through innovation, more creative products and services had to be developed and speedily made available to consumers.

What is clear now is that use of work teams can facilitate the pursuit of quality and the drive for innovation. For example, since Ford Motor Company adopted its "Quality Is Job One" philosophy, it has engaged in a massive program of organizational change. To produce quality products, Ford believes that employees must be involved in and committed to their jobs and that team-based work engenders this commitment, so teams have proliferated throughout the organization (see Banas, 1988). The same philosophy prevails at Corning Glass, where employees are organized into some 3,000 teams (Dumaine, 1990) and is gaining favor with a growing number of service companies ("Work Teams," 1988).

Besides improving quality, teams facilitate innovation by bringing together experts with dissimilar knowledge bases and perspectives and providing an environment for creative thinking. Armed with more creative ideas, companies can also shorten the cycle time from product inception to production by using concurrent engineering, which is a design process that relies on multifunction teams of experts from design, manufacturing, and marketing.

To ensure that new ideas are successfully transferred from the research and development lab to the marketplace, both suppliers and the intended customer may become team members as well. A Nobel Prize winner at Bell Labs described this new order as follows: "Five years ago managers here didn't even use the word `customer.' Now each of us has two jobs; working in corporate research and serving on a team connected to one of AT&T's product areas" (Bylinski, 1990, p. 72).

Together, multifunction teams plus liaisons with suppliers and customers should speed technology transfer, which is essential for high-technology U.S. firms trying to regain their competitive positions. There is nothing high-tech about the process of managing these technical teams, however. According to a senior vice president at Texas instruments: "You delude yourself if you think that the emphasis in technology transfer is on technology. It's a humanistic task, not a technical one" (Bylinski, 1990, p. 73). Stripped to its core, the task is to make sure that the right people are in contact with one another and supporting one another's efforts. In addition to listening to their customers, the members of successful multifunction teams must break through the walls that have long separated their organizational departments and learn to cooperate.

Teams may not cure all of a company's ills, but many American business leaders apparently agree with Texas Instrument's chief executive officer (CEO) that "no matter what your business, these teams are the wave of the future." A survey by the American Productivity and Quality Center found that half of the 467 large firms in their study planned to be relying significantly more on self-managing teams (Dumaine, 1990). When teams are formed, diversity is inevitable—sometimes it is intentionally designed into teams to stimulate creativity, and sometimes it is simply a natural by-product of drawing team members from a diverse employee population. Either way, it is inescapable.

Mergers and Alliances Require Managing
Diverse Corporate Cultures

Employees are not the only ones teaming up with one another. Companies are teaming up, too. Although the rate of corporate merging has eased since the mid-1980s, it remains high. And, in addition to the traditional merger, where two companies are joined into one, there are a host of minimergers occurring between organizations. As Kanter puts it, companies that were once adversaries are now becoming "PALs"—pooling, allying, and linking together in order to improve their competitive capacity (Kanter, 1989). These are the alliances formed by firms as they tighten their relationships with suppliers and customers. Such alliances often require that two units from two different organizations meld together to act as a linking pin between the firms involved. As in full-fledged mergers, participants in minimergers must learn to cope with diverse corporate cultures.

Working through corporate culture diversity is a major challenge: Respondents to the *Harvard Business Review* survey mentioned earlier were asked to report on the problems their companies had with customer and client alliances. The *most* frequently cited source of problems was differences in corporate cultures. "Different corporate cultures" created problems in 59% of the companies with such alliances, making it considerably more troublesome than "coordinating plans," which was the next most common problem (experienced by 43% of the companies).

Anyone who has experienced a merger, or has simply left a company to take a another job, probably knows that organizational cultures can differ in terms of which ideals are most valued, customs and rituals, the shared expectation employees have for how they should behave, and the way members of the organization interpret events. Like national cultures, corporate cultures serve as unobtrusive backdrops, often going unnoticed except between changing scenes. But when scenes change, as during a merger, the textures of the corporate cultures that must be knit together become apparent. For example, in the aftermath of the merger between Delta Airlines and Western Airlines, the informal, intimate, "Californian" culture at Western Airlines could be appreciated more fully by some employees when they saw how it contrasted to the "Southern" culture at Delta (Kanter, 1989). Similarly, the corporate cultures that dominated U.S. auto companies a decade ago became more salient after Japanese transplants and joint ventures exposed auto workers to radically different corporate environments.

Melding diverse corporate cultures is not a topic typically associated with the issue of managing diversity. However, it is included in this book (see Schweiger, Ridley, & Marini, Chapter 8) to illustrate that many of the same principles are relevant to managing a fusion between diverse corporate cultures as are relevant to working through other types of diversity.

As this discussion of the new business environment shows, in the 21st century communications and the people they connect will be the lifeblood of business. Regardless of who is doing the communicating, and regardless of whether people are connecting with one another face-to-face, fax-to-fax, or phone-to-phone, high-fidelity transmissions will be essential. Through effective communications, businesses will assess customers' needs and desires, create new products and services, market their products and services to a global audience, and manage the production and delivery of products and services across borders of all types, including geographic, economic, cultural, and organizational.

THE CHANGING LABOR MARKET

The shift to a service-based economy and increasing global competitiveness should make the importance of excellent workforce management practices obvious. These should be reason enough for business leaders to list continuous improvement of human resource management (HRM) as a top priority in their strategic agenda. And, given the current environment, it seems inevitable that any organization looking for ways to improve human resources management will see the management of diversity as one issue with broad implications. But for those who have let other priorities distract them from continuous HRM improvement, a third change in the environment should help focus their attention—a tightening of the supply of qualified employees. As one CEO put it, "We're used to competing for customers, but now we'll be faced with a growing need to compete for our workforce" (Sellers, 1990, p. 59).

In the recent past, the labor market could be characterized as a buyer's market. Labor was in abundant supply and therefore it was relatively cheap and easy to acquire. When "traditional" employees were abundant, employees did not need to recruit from the pool of "nontraditional" workers whose differences may have required organizations to make adaptive changes. However, in the near future the labor market will become more and more of a seller's market. The shortage of appropriately skilled labor will force employees to compete to attract, retain, and effectively manage all available employees.

Many companies are already feeling the pinch. According to one survey (Towers Perrin & Hudson Institute, 1990), shortages of technical, secretarial/clerical, professional, and supervisory/management skills make recruiting difficult now for at least half of U.S. employers, and the problem is expected to worsen in the near future. Particular types of labor shortages are slightly worse in some geographic regions and in some industries, but regional and industry variations are relatively minor—the problem is pervasive.

To cope with the scarcity of potential employees, employers are responding with a number of initiatives: They are developing new recruiting strategies designed to find new sources of labor, such as students, immigrants, and retirees; they're devising new benefits packages that better fit the needs of the new workforce, hoping to make their organizations more attractive to job applicants; and they're becoming more flexible regarding employment conditions, for example, by allowing employees more input in the determination of the length and scheduling of their work weeks, offering opportunities for extended leaves of absence, and arranging for job sharing. Such initiatives help companies attract talent from a broader and larger labor pool, buffering the company from the tightening labor market.

Increased employee diversity is a natural consequence of such initiatives. Colleagues working together in the future will be less alike with respect to gender, cultural background, and age. These differences are important because they are associated with differences in perspectives, life-styles, attitudes, values, behaviors, and thought patterns.

Gender Diversity

In the late 1950s, when many of today's CEOs were entering the labor force as young professionals, they were being joined almost exclusively by other men. Back then, men were receiving 95% of the MBA degrees awarded and 90% of the bachelor's degrees in business. As these men are finishing their careers, 30 years later, the picture is dramatically different. In 1990, women received approximately 31% of the MBA degrees awarded, as well as 39% of the law degrees, 13% of engineering degrees (Butruille, 1990), and half of all undergraduate degrees.

Today, females are better educated than ever before *and* more are choosing to be in the active labor force. By the year 2000, the workforce is expected to be almost completely balanced with respect to gender (Human Capital, 1988). Furthermore, gender-based segregation within organizations is gradually decreasing. By 1987 women represented 35% of the population of the executive, management, and administrative workforces (Selbert, 1987), although in 1990 women held less than one-half of 1% of top jobs in major corporations (Fierman, 1990).

Working through gender diversity offers two major challenges to organizations. Ensuring that women's talents and abilities are fully utilized on the job is one challenge. Because women represent such a large portion of the workforce, maximizing their level of productivity is essential to achieving competitiveness. This often requires attacking the artificial barrier of a male-dominated corporate culture. As the CEO of Avon Products has noted, "Cultural discrepancies can come out in little ways. We used to have a lot of white male traditions at Avon. We bought season tickets to sporting events, and we called the annual management outing President's Golf Day. Our first two women officers complained . . . We realized these activities were no longer appropriate. They were too male-oriented and unwittingly made others feel like outsiders" (Edwards, 1991, p. 60). According to one recent survey, 60% of women executives in larger firms feel that their firm's male-dominated corporate culture is an obstacle to the success (i.e., productivity) of women ("Welcome to the Woman-Friendly Company," 1990). These women may be underestimating the problem, however. A poll of 241 Fortune 1000 CEOs found that nearly 80% of these CEOs said there were barriers that kept women from reaching the top. And of those who admitted that barriers exist, 81% identified stereotypes and preconceptions as problems women face (Fierman, 1990).

Many of the obstacles in corporations can be traced to society's stereotypes about men and women, which can create a catch-22 situation for women seeking advancement. A recent New York Times article describing the treatment of male and female politicians vividly depicted the situation:

> In 1987, she [Pat Schroeder, the Colorado Democrat] was denounced for reinforcing the stereotype that women are unable to coolly make tough decisions because she cried as she announced she would not run for President. When President Bush misted up as he addressed the Southern Baptist Convention in Atlanta a couple weeks ago, and confessed to crying when he made the decision to send Americans to war, *Time* magazine gushed over "his new expansiveness," his "more confiding" tone and his "new human dimension." (Dowd, 1991)

Adjusting to the fact that women in our society shoulder a disproportionate share of the responsibility for family care is a second challenge employers face. Failure to adjust to the differing needs of women (vs. men) with family responsibilities interferes with the ability of a company to fully utilize the talents of many of its female employees. When the family responsibilities of these women combine with outdated organizational norms that assume families put few restrictive demands on talented employees, artificial constraints block their promotion into jobs that could make full use of their skills and abilities. By adjusting to the differing family needs of various employees, employers will be better positioned to utilize more fully the talents of all employees. In addition, because the children in the families of today's workforce are the workforce of tomorrow, helping parents be both good family members and productive employees represents an investment in the future. As Peter Lynch, former head of the Magellan Mutual Fund, put it upon retiring at the age of 46 to spend time with his family, "Children are a great investment. They beat the hell out of stocks" ("Managing Generational Diversity," 1991).

Cultural Diversity

After gender diversity, cultural diversity is the second most frequently noted change in the workforce. *Workforce 2000* projections indicate that during this decade, only 58% of new entrants into the labor force will come from the "majority" population of white native Americans, with 22% of new entrants expected to be immigrants and the remainder being mostly African-Americans and Hispanic-Americans. The figures for new entrants contrast sharply with the status quo. Of the 1985 workforce, 83% were white native Americans. By the end of this decade, it is likely that less than 75% of the workforce will be white native Americans (Kutscher, 1989).

However, national figures do not tell the whole story. Regional differences are substantial. For example, our Hispanic population is concentrated in four regions: Mexican-Americans reside mostly in California and Texas, Puerto Ricans favor New York, and a majority of Cuban-Americans live in Florida. Our Asian population, which doubled in size during the 1980s, tends to be located in California, New York, and Hawaii. Our African-American population is more dispersed throughout the country, yet residential statistics for the cities they populate reveal greater segregation of African-Americans than that experienced by the more recently established Asian-American and Hispanic populations (Jaynes & Williams, 1989).

Use of broad labels such as *immigrant, native white, African-American, Hispanic-American,* and *Asian-American* conceals part of the story also, for within each of these broad categories hide many distinct ethnic cultures and subcultures. For example, the 1980 U.S. Census included 10 different categories for Asian-American respondents to use to describe their ancestry, 4 categories for native respondents of Spanish origin, and 16 categories for white native respondents. And several more categories were added to assess the country of origin of foreign-born respondents.

Cultures have consequences that are easily experienced but more difficult to describe. For many people, the concept of culture conjures up images of the exotic customs, religions, foods, clothing, and life-styles that make foreign travel—as well as trips into the ethnic enclaves in our local cities—both stimulating and enjoyable. These aspects of a foreign culture can be experienced without ever engaging in conversation with someone from that culture. It is also easy for businesses to accommodate these aspects of cultural diversity—the cafeteria can offer a variety of ethnic foods and flexible policies can allow employees to observe whichever holidays they choose.

However, the deeper consequences of culture—such as values and ways of interpreting the world—cannot be handled merely by changing menus and policies. And it is these deeper consequences that organizations are struggling with today. When people with different habits and world views come together in the workplace, misunderstandings and conflicts inevitably occur as a result of dissimilar expectations and norms. Employees who behave according to the cultural adage that "the squeaky wheel gets the grease" may be viewed as offensive and undesirable teammates by employees who were taught that "the nail that sticks out gets hammered down." Employees behaving according to the latter adage may be viewed as ineffective by the former group of employees. Such misunderstandings can mean that valuable feedback about problems and successes is poorly transmitted or never becomes available for the organization's use and improvement.

Some readers might question whether cultural diversity is anything new. Skeptics might point out that the proportion of our population who are African-Americans has been relatively stable and the number of immigrants entering our country in recent years is only slightly higher than it was at the beginning of the century, when Europeans were the predominant newcomers (Richman, 1990).

Several factors seem to account for employers' current recognition that cultural diversity requires active management. First, although the proportion of African-Americans in this country has remained stable, their employment patterns have changed considerably during the recent affirmative action era, during which substantial integration occurred for clerical, technical, and skilled crafts jobs (see "Race in the Workplace," 1991). Although often overlooked, education levels of African-Americans have risen during this time, also, providing another stimulant for workplace integration. Second, although the number of immigrants entering this country each year is relatively small, over the years the number of employees with strong ties to another national culture grows due to the continuing impact of nationality on second- and even third-generation citizens (e.g., see Fugita & O'Brien, 1991; Mydans, 1991). Third, the variety of the immigrant population has itself increased, as Asians and Latins from dozens of countries join the European immigrants. Fourth is the changing nature of the work, which requires that employees interact continuously with one another, with customers, and with suppliers. Fifth, and finally, global competition means that cultural diversity among working Americans is only part of the challenge. Insightful business leaders recognize that the common cultural experiences Americans share with one another make it easier to develop multicultural competence at home than abroad. Thus, they can use their multicultural domestic workforce as an educational resource and training ground for learning some of the tough lessons associated with conducting business internationally.

Age Diversity

Age diversity has received relatively little attention to date. Instead, attention has been directed to the implications of a graying workforce. In developed countries such as the United States, the median population age has been increasing. Along with this comes the bulging ranks of "older" employees trying to climb the corporate ladder, which creates havoc for traditional, hierarchical organizations. Such organizations are structured to accommodate large cohorts of entry-level employees and smaller cohorts of employees at more advanced career stages. These organizations tend to segregate employees by age. Organizational elders supervise the cohort that will soon replace them, who in turn supervise their own replacements. In such organizations, higher-ranked managers seldom rub elbows with the incoming generation of employees. As Mark Pastin put it, "You find CEOs who think the best thing about being CEO is that they don't have to mix it up with the riffraff" (Farnham, 1989). For managers who consider isolation from the lower ranks a perk, the ideal form of "contact" with lower-level employees may be sending them a memo or preparing a video for them to view.

But these old hierarchies are a dying breed. Competitive pressures have forced organizational restructuring and modern organizations to sport a new profile. At the same time that walls between organizational subunits are being torn down, the structure is being flattened. As layers of hierarchy are removed, previously segregated generations of employees find themselves working together and even rotating jobs amongst themselves.

Other factors contributing to greater intergenerational contact in the workplace include the entry (and reentry) into the workforce of middle-aged women, who often work in positions dominated by younger employees at the early stages of their careers; employment among former "retirees," who discover that their savings, Social Security checks, and other retirement benefits are inadequate to sustain their life-styles; and programs designed to capture more younger workers, such as internships and apprenticeships that permit high school students to work while earning academic credits.

In addition, in many organizations, the higher education levels of younger employees are considered more valuable than the experience accrued by older employees. Often, the result of all of these forces is an unfamiliar reversal of roles. As one restaurant manager put it, giving orders to older workers "is sort of like telling your grandma to clean the table." If younger generations find this uncomfortable, it is easy to imagine that their grandparents' generation does as well. As one working retiree explained: "For 30 years I was a supervisor, and then one night I step out of one role and into another . . . . When you're being supervised by someone younger, you see a lot of things that aren't going to work, but you have to bite your tongue" (Hirsch, 1990, p. B1).

The combination of changes in the age distribution of employees and new flatter organization structures mean that four generations of workers can find themselves working side by side: the swing generation (1910–29), who survived the Great Depression and World War II and are now over 60 years old; the silent generation (1930–45), which is a relatively small cohort that includes most of our current business and political leaders; the baby boomers (1946–64), whose large size gives them substantial social and economic clout; and the baby bust generation (1965–76), which has been characterized as distinguished by the wide schism that separates the haves and the have-nots ("Managing Generational Diversity," 1991). Even if employees from these four generations were all native Americans, they would differ fundamentally in their values and attitudes about work (see Elder, 1975; "Work Attitudes," 1986), their physical and mental functioning (Rhodes, 1983), and the everyday concerns that reflect their stages in the life cycle. Of course, within each generation, gender and cultural variety also abound, yielding a workforce that reflects the complete palette of human potential.

THE CHALLENGES OF WORKING THROUGH DIVERSITY

By now it should be clear that diversity is important to everyone in today's business organizations. In the longer term, effectively working through diversity is a strategic imperative for success in a highly competitive, global environment. More immediately, diversity is simply a fact of life that influences the recruitment, retention, motivation, and performance of employees. Short-term and long-term responses to diversity must address three challenges: availability, fairness, and synergy.

The Availability Challenge

In the past, employers often dealt with diversity by minimizing it where they could and by trying to ignore it when they couldn't get rid of it. As DeLuca and McDowell (this volume) describe, this approach fits the efficiency mind set that has dominated the industrial era. When the supply of labor was abundant relative to demand, employers could control the diversity in their workforce by using selective hiring practices and by imposing standard operating procedures. From a position of relative power, companies could refuse to hire employees who were unable to work the standard workweek and punish those who were too often absent or tardy, or who just simply didn't fit in. Any negative side effects of such practices, such as lower morale or higher turnover, were treated as justifiable costs paid to ensure a smooth-running organization.

But as qualified employees become more scarce, employers must become more flexible. They can no longer say, "This is when and where you must be available for work, and this is the way we will treat you while you are here." Now they must adapt to potential employees who say: "This is when and where the work must be available for me to do it, and this is the way I must be treated if you want me to stay."

The Fairness Challenge

Flexible policies and practices help employers solve the availability issue created by a tight supply of diverse labor and inevitably bring them face to face with a second challenge, namely, ensuring that all employees and potential employees are treated fairly and feel that they are treated fairly. Employers who fail to meet this challenge squander their hard-won human resources.

During the past quarter century, concerns about fair employment practices were often driven by fear of the repercussions associated with discrimination lawsuits. Whether a company treated employees (and job applicants) fairly was, ultimately, judged by the courts using technical criteria, which were negotiated by attorneys, psychologists, and psychometricians. In this context, fair treatment came to mean equal treatment. Supervisors and managers were admonished to act as if they were blind to differences among employees, especially if those differences might be linked to sex, race, ethnicity, age, or national origin.

Ironically, in this context employees stimulated battles over fairness, but once those battles began, employees' evaluations of fairness were not the stakes companies sought to win. The stakes were money, reputation in the community (perhaps), and freedom to continue conducting business as usual. Times are changing, however. Now, regardless of whether employers find themselves fighting legal battles over fair employment practices, they must take employees' perceptions of fair treatment seriously.

From the perspectives of employees, issues of fairness are not constrained to sex, cultural background, age, or other legally protected attributes. Many other aspects of personal orientation are deemed worthy of tolerance and respect as well, including political views, sexual orientations, family situations, and various personal idiosyncrasies. Employers who appear to favor some personal orientations and stifle others risk paying the price of low productivity due to a restricted pool of applicants, employee dissatisfaction, lack of commitment, turnover, and perhaps even sabotage.

The Synergy Challenge

The third challenge in working through diversity is unleashing and taking full advantage of the latent potential of groups. Groups are powerful motivational tools. When running effectively, work teams can be both more productive and more creative than individuals working alone. But when they function poorly, groups can have disastrous consequences for organizations, because the same social forces that push people to reach their fullest potential can also push people into unproductive and even destructive behavior patterns.

It is the potential for positive synergy that attracts employers to group-based organizational structures. For this potential to be realized, relationships among team members must be relatively positive. A long history of psychological research shows that excessive group conflict interferes with productivity (see Jackson, 1991). Conflict can close down communication channels, waste group energy, and create excessive amounts of turnover. This is not to say that all conflict should be squelched. To the contrary, constructive conflict must be encouraged to stimulate creative problem solving. Too little conflict may be a sign of complacency or stale, routine approaches to addressing new problems. The challenge for employers is to ensure that destructive conflict, which often arises when group members are unable to get along on a personal level, is minimized while ensuring that people with diverse ideas and perspectives are challenged to find resolutions to problems that everyone can endorse.

THE ROLE OF HUMAN RESOURCES MANAGEMENT PROFESSIONALS

Tackling these three challenges of workforce diversity is a key responsibility of modern human resources management professionals. They are the ones who are best able to educate business leaders about the strategic importance of working through diversity and to mobilize them to take immediate actions. And they are the ones with the knowledge and skills needed to analyze what their organizations need to do to respond to simultaneous changes in the nature of competition and the labor market. Finally, human resources professionals have available to them a wide range of tools for changing the attitudes and behaviors of their organizations' employees. These tools include recruiting and selection methods, performance evaluation and appraisal, compensation and reward systems, training and development techniques, and models for redesigning both jobs and the organization within which jobs are performed.

To organizations that succeed in meeting these challenges will go the rewards of greater workforce productivity and improved organizational health. At the same time, employees in successful organizations will reap the benefits of employment conditions that are congruent with their individual needs and aspirations.

REFERENCES

Banas, P. A. (1988). Employee involvement: A sustained labor/management initiative at the Ford Motor Company. In J. P. Campbell & R. J. Campbell (Eds.), *Productivity in organizations: New perspectives from industrial and organizational psychology* (pp. 388-416). San Francisco: Jossey-Bass.

Bell, D. (1973). *The coming of post-industrial society: A venture in social forecasting.* New York: Basic Books.

Bureau of Labor Statistics. (1991, June). *Employment and earnings.* Washington, DC: U.S. Department of Labor.

Business International Corporation. (1991). *Developing effective global managers for the 1990s.* New York: Author.

Butruille, S. G. (1990, April). Corporate caretaking. *Training & Development Journal,* 25, 49-55.

Bylinski, G. (1990, July 2). Turning R&D into real products. *Fortune,* pp. 72-77.

Dowd, M. (1991, June 30). When men get a case of the vapors. *New York Times,* sect. E, p. 2.

Dumaine, B. (1990, May 7). Who needs a boss? *Fortune,* pp. 52-60.

Edwards, A. (1991, January). Special Report: Cultural diversity in today's corporation. *Working Woman,* pp. 45-60.

Elder, G. H., Jr. (1975). Age differentiation and the life course. *Annual Review of Sociology,* 1, 165-190.

Farnham, A. (1989, December 4). The trust gap. *Fortune,* pp. 56-78.

Fierman, J. (1990, July 30). Why women still don't hit the top. *Fortune,* pp. 40-62.

Fugita, S. S., & O'Brien, D. J. (1991). *Japanese American ethnicity: The persistence of the community.* Seattle: University of Washington Press.

Gummesson, E. (1987). Lip services—a neglected area of services marketing. *Journal of Services Marketing,* 1, 1-29.

Hirsch, J. S. (1990, February 26). Older workers chafe under young managers. *Wall Street Journal,* pp. B1, B6.

Jackson, S. E. (1991). Team composition in organizational settings: Issues in managing an increasingly diverse work force. In S. Worchel, W. Wood, & J. A. Simpson, (Eds.), *Group process and productivity* (pp. 138-173). Newbury Park, CA: Sage.

Jaynes, G. D., & Williams, R. M., Jr. (1989). *A common destiny: Blacks and American society*. Washington, DC: National Academy Press.

Kanter, R. M. (1989). *When giants learn to dance*. New York: Simon & Schuster.

Kanter, R. M. (1991, May–June). Transcending business boundaries: 12,000 world managers view change. *Harvard Business Review*, pp. 151-164.

Kutscher, R. (1989). Projections, summary and emerging issues. *Monthly Labor Review, 112*(11), 66-74.

Managing generational diversity. (1991, April). *HRMagazine*, pp. 91-92.

Mydans, S. (1991, June 30). For these Americans, ties to Mexico remain. *New York Times*, p. L12.

Race in the Workplace: Is Affirmative Action working? (1991, July 8). *Business Week*, pp. 50-63.

Rhodes, S. R. (1983). Age-related differences in work attitudes and behavior: A review and conceptual analysis. *Psychological Bulletin, 93*, 328-367.

Richman, L. S. (1990, January 29). Let's change the immigration law—now. *Fortune*, p. 12.

Selbert, R. (1987, November 16). Women at work. *Future Scan, 554*, pp. 1-3.

Sellers, P. (1990, June 4). What customers really want. *Fortune*, 58-68.

Towers Perrin & Hudson Institute. (1990). *Workforce 2000: Competing in a seller's market*. Valhalla, NY: Towers Perrin.

Welcome to the woman-friendly company where talent is valued and rewarded. (1990, August 6). *Business Week*, pp. 48-55.

Work attitudes: Study reveals generation gap. (1986, October 2). *Bulletin to Management*, p. 326.

Work teams can rev up paper-pushers, too. (1988, November 28). *Business Week*, pp. 64-72.

PART II

CREATING AND ASSESSING A DIVERSE WORKPLACE

The three cases in Part II illustrate the linkage between workplace diversity issues and equal employment opportunity (EEO) activities. It should be clear by now that working through diversity involves much more than recruiting and promoting "minority" groups, as they are defined by EEO regulations. Nevertheless, years of proactive EEO policies and practices have significantly increased the amount of workforce diversity in some organizations. These organizations are now learning how to take full advantage of their diverse workforces, a task that sometimes includes dealing with a backlash of concern about the appropriateness and consequences of some practices used to eliminate and/or reverse unfair discrimination in the workplace. The three cases that follow illustrate how EEO-related activities can shape the organizational context in which subsequent diversity work will be carried out.

XEROX CORPORATION

The first case describes Xerox Corporation's widely recognized progress in creating a productive and demographically balanced workforce. Many of the events described in the case unfolded during the tenure of David Kearns, recently retired chief executive officer who joined Xerox in 1971, became president and chief operating officer in 1977, and stepped up to the CEO position in 1982. Kearns aggressively supported human resources initiatives aimed at eliminating discrimination against minority-status employees at the same time he was fighting a major battle to rescue the company from being battered by Japanese competitors (see Kearns, 1990). The value of strong leadership from those at the top is clearly visible in this case.

During the 1960s and 1970s, racial tension rocked U.S. cities, including Rochester, New York, home of Xerox's headquarters. As early as 1966,

Xerox responded by establishing a program called Step Up to train and hire African-Americans for permanent positions. In the 25 years since then, many initiatives have followed, and the exclusive focus on African-American employees has been replaced with a balanced concern for all groups, including white males.

The case describes the most successful intitiatives as well as some of the less successful. Included are discussions of caucus groups, training programs for managers, career planning tools, performance appraisal systems for holding managers accountable for achieving affirmative action goals (which are treated as business objectives at Xerox), and procedures now being used to ensure that all employees develop to their potential and are appropriately recognized and rewarded with promotions into and through the upper ranks.

Although it is not highlighted in the case description, it is worth noting that Xerox has also been at the leading edge of team-based work designs, which are used to support their strategy of competing on the basis of high-quality products. To implement its strategy, Xerox relies extensively on internal problem-solving teams. In addition, it is involved in a number of external alliances with suppliers, competitors, and even the education system in the city of Rochester (see Gabor, 1991). These team-based work technologies are partly responsible for the fact that Xerox won a Malcolm Baldrige National Quality Award in 1989.

PACIFIC BELL

As is often true, the future is already here for the bellwether state of California, which employs more than 10% of U.S. workers. California is one of the most ethnically diverse states, and companies located there are quickly learning that yesterday's mode of operating has become outdated. Changing demographics are one obvious indicator of how different the workforce of the 21st century will be. Many Americans are accustomed to thinking about "majority" and "minority" ethnic groups. Such thinking will soon be outdated in California, where rapid growth in the Asian and Hispanic populations is projected to yield a population in which there are no clear "majority" groups by the year 2000. The largest ethnic group, non-Hispanic whites, will represent less than half of the workforce, giving all groups "minority" status. To survive in this new environment, organizations must quickly develop their expertise in recruiting and developing members of ethnic groups who in the very recent past were a relatively small minority.

Pacific Bell is one company with several years of learning already behind it. Its intensive and focused efforts for recruiting Hispanic employees for managerial positions are described in Chapter 4. A California-based company, Pacific Bell's customer base already includes nearly 8 million people of Hispanic decent (Mydans, 1991), which is over 20% of the state's population. Of these, only about 3.5 million are currently in the workforce, reflecting the population's relative youthfulness and its importance as a future source of labor.

As the most rapidly growing segment of the U.S. workforce, Hispanic-Americans are seeing their presence have an impact. In the 1988 presidential election, candidate Michael Dukakis vied for votes by speaking fluent Spanish. His efforts were countered by George Bush's portrait of a family that includes a Mexican-American daughter-in-law and grandchildren with a Mexican heritage. Business too is vying for the attention of Hispanic-Americans, both as customers and as employees. As they do, they are discovering that gains in the labor market can facilitate gains in the consumer market.

Employees who share the cultural heritage of potential customers have a better understanding of customers' needs and preferences, can remove language barriers that would otherwise hinder communication, and can offer customers a familiar face to turn to. For all of these reasons, hiring employees who mirror the consumer market makes good sense. However, under conditions of rapidly changing consumer and labor markets, achieving this objective can be difficult. It requires a commitment to organizational change and focused efforts designed to create the change. The Pacific Bell case illustrates how one company met the challenge successfully.

It should be noted that although the case description that follows focuses on Pacific Bell's recruiting efforts for Hispanic-Americans, its efforts at working through diversity are not limited to the activites described in the case. Examples of other innovative changes at Pacific Bell include satellite work centers located in suburban areas near employees' homes, telecommuting from home using personal computers supplied by the company, flextime, and staggered work shifts (Smith, 1989). As these examples illustrate, Pacific Bell includes flexible employment conditions as well as recruiting strategies among the solutions it uses to manage its diverse workforce. Here, however, we are able to focus on only some of their efforts.

THE FEDERAL GOVERNMENT

The first two cases describe numerous activities that organizations engage in as they attempt to recruit, assess, train, develop, evaluate, and reward the people who ultimately make up the workforce that will design, produce, and deliver the products and services offered by the organization. Although neither case *proves* that paying attention to workforce diversity brings productivity gains or increases organizational effectiveness, the two cases clearly suggest that the effectiveness of an organization is partially determined by its ability to use the resources of a diverse workforce effectively.

Both cases also hint at a problem that can arise as organizations develop a more diverse workforce. This is the problem of skepticism and even resentment among majority members of the workforce. A natural tendency shared by all individuals is to react more positively to those who are similar than to those who are different. This is one of the most well-documented principles of human behavior. Given our tendency to judge those who are dissimilar somewhat harshly, the problem of skepticism is easy to understand. In fact, it will be an inevitable consequence in organizations as they change from being relatively homogenous to being more diverse.

Chapter 5 describes how the federal government is dealing with the skepticism that exists about the quality of its workforce. Over 2 million civilians are employed by the U.S. government. During most of the past two decades, government employment activities have been conducted in the context of clearly defined affirmative action objectives. Consequently, the civil service workforce is probably more diverse than the workforce of most other large employers. In addition, the government's use of some employment practices during the past several years, such as race-based norms for scoring employment tests, is now being publicly criticized, and even suspended. These circumstances may explain why some management-level government employees have expressed concerns about the quality of current federal employees.

Like most organizations in the service sector of the economy, the effectiveness of the federal government depends largely on the quality of its workforce and its management system. If quality is declining, as some perceive it is, then effectiveness can be expected to decline as well. How can the quality of a workforce or management systems be assessed, especially when the workforce includes over 2 million people, who work in hundreds of different jobs, and when management systems are spread out across thousands of locations? This is the question now being tackled by the federal government.

Chapter 5 describes the Quality Assessment Program currently under way through the U.S. Office of Personnel Management. The progam began in 1988 and is expected to continue for several years. Progam activities are guided by a conceptual model for understanding workforce quality, which is described in the chapter. The chapter also describes the process that led up to the development of the conceptual model and the process used to guide Quality Assessment Program activities. The key principle underlying these processes is constituency involvement.

Among the constituencies interested in the Quality Assessment Program are private sector employers; unions; professional human resources management associations; numerous government agencies; congressional agencies; academics who specialize in areas such as psychology, economics, and public administration; and, of course, government employees themselves. Thus, one objective of this case is offering lessons about how to ensure that diverse constituencies are involved, informed, and supportive of major programs relevant to their concerns.

Although the Quality Assessment Program was developed to respond to those who expressed concerns about declining quality, the data generated by this progam can be used for much more than simply responding to the skeptics. Like many employers, the federal government continually introduces new human resources intitiatives. And, like most employers, these intitiatives often continue without the benefit of systematic evaluation. With the Quality Assessment Program in place, this situation should change in the near future. An enormous amount of empirical data will now be available for evaluating the effectiveness of new initiatives and change efforts, such as training programs, new procedures for screening and testing job applicants, new work schedules, and so on. The types of data sytematically collected and stored will include skill levels, performance measures, and job-related attitudes. Such data are essential to any organization that is as concerned about the quality of its workforce as it is about the quality of the products and services it offers.

REFERENCES

Gabor, A. (1991, July–August). Rochester focuses: A community's core competence. *Harvard Business Review*, pp. 116–126.

Kearns, D. T. (1990). Leadership through quality. *Academy of Management Executive*, 4, 86–89.

Mydans, S. (1991, June 30). For these Americans, ties to Mexico remain. *New York Times*, p. L12.

Smith, S. (1989, September 25). At Pac-Bell, 9-to-5 if it "works for the individual." *Business Week*, p. 154.

CHAPTER 3

Managing Diversity at the Xerox Corporation: Balanced Workforce Goals and Caucus Groups

VALERIE I. SESSA

Managing diversity arose as a natural extension of the affirmative action process initiated within the Xerox Corporation. As a result of the influx of minorities and women into the Xerox workforce, two events occurred. First, on the assumption that attitude changes in employees will grow from daily experience with genuine diversity, Xerox corporate management developed long-term Balanced Work Force (BWF) goals. Second, minority and women employees formed caucus groups that serve as vehicles for employee involvement in managing diversity. To manage diversity effectively, a corporation must value diversity; it must have diversity; and it must change the organization to accommodate diversity and make it an integral part of the organization. This case demonstrates why Xerox values diversity, how Xerox created its diverse workforce, and how Xerox has started to manage diversity through BWF goals and minority and women caucus groups.

The information regarding this case was gathered through interviews with minority and nonminority men and women employees and ex-employees of Xerox, throughout all levels of the corporation. Particularly extensive interviews were held with Theodore E. Payne, the manager of corporate affirmative action and managing diversity. He has worked for Xerox in affirmative action since 1972. His cooperation and assistance on this project are especially appreciated. Other sources of information for this case include memos, letters, corporate publications, corporate records, caucus records, and articles published in the popular press.

THE XEROX CORPORATION

Although the Xerox Corporation is a multinational Fortune 100 company in both the document-processing and the insurance and financial services markets, this case study will emphasize the document-processing organization. Xerox is perhaps best known as the developer of the first plain paper copier. Today, it is a leading supplier of equipment for automating the office. Employees take pride in the fact that through the use of teamwork to improve quality, Xerox won the prestigious Malcolm Baldrige National Quality Award in 1989.

Employing over 100,000 people in its workforce, Xerox has one of the most diverse workforces in the United States. Figure 3.1 compares the ethnicity of the Xerox workforce to the U.S. laborforce. Table 3.1 uses sales and technician job categories to compare the Xerox workforce to the U.S. labor force by affirmative action status and gender. Although these exhibits suggest that Xerox is more diverse than the U.S. laborforce, it should be kept in mind that no one company exactly mirrors the U.S. laborforce; many factors, such as location and type of industry, affect the appropriate balance for each company. In these exhibits the U.S. labor force should be interpreted only as a baseline comparison. Xerox is considered one of the top places for African-Americans[1] ("50 Best Places," 1989; "In Good Com-

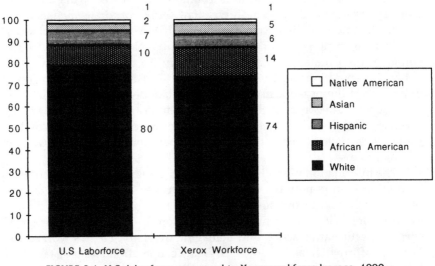

FIGURE 3.1. U.S. laborforce compared to Xerox workforce by race, 1990.

[1]The term *African-American* is the author's choice in denoting people of African origin. However, within quotations the original term used has been retained.

TABLE 3.1. Diversity of Selected Job Categories: Xerox
Workforce Compared to the U.S. Laborforce 1990

	Percentage of Xerox	Percentage of U.S. laborforce
Sales		
Minority Females	9	2
Majority Females	30	18
Minority Males	12	6
Majority Males	49	73
Technicians		
Minority Females	2	1
Majority Females	6	4
Minority Males	23	13
Majority Males	69	82

pany," 1986) and women (Konrad, 1990) to work, as well as for Hispanics in the technical arena (Ferrey, 1990).

VALUING DIVERSITY

As one Xerox employee explains, "If you don't value diversity, you can't manage it." The first step in managing a diverse workforce is to value diversity. The value of race and gender diversity has been evident throughout the history of Xerox, and it is evident today in the culture of Xerox and in management attitudes toward affirmative action and managing diversity.

Valuing diversity can be traced to Chester Carlson, the inventor of xerography, which led to the development of the Xerox copier. Carlson, a philanthropist who gave liberally to African-American causes, made the first xerographic image in 1938. Earning over $150 million from his invention, Carlson gave $100 million to various foundations and charities before his death in 1968. After his death, his wife quoted him as saying that the reason he had done this was because "America could never repay the Negroes for what it had done to them."

Although Carlson was not an employee of the Xerox Corporation, he may have had an influence on Joseph C. Wilson, the founder of Xerox Corporation. Like Carlson, Wilson was known for having a personal belief in fairness and for being morally committed to affirmative action. Wilson became the chairman of the Haloid Company, a small company specializing in making and selling photographic paper following in the footsteps of his father, who founded the company after World War II. Learning of Carlson's invention in 1947, Wilson began negotiations for a license to commercialize the process. In 1958, the Haloid Company changed its name to Haloid Xerox, and in 1961, the company became Xerox.

The personal philosophies of both Carlson and Wilson have remained a part of the culture and business philosophy of Xerox. Xerox prides itself in caring for and making use of its people as well as its financial resources. It is committed to social responsibility and community involvement and demonstrates this by providing a social service leave policy under which selected employees can take fully paid leaves of absence (up to 12 months) to work on community projects of their choice. Examples of projects worked on during such leaves include building a model classroom for retarded children and providing legal aid to the poor. Xerox also sponsors community involvement programs in which groups of company employees, often backed by corporate seed money, work on problems that they have identified in their communities. Typical examples include renovating a teen center and raising funds for a day-care center. It also works to stimulate education and growth of minorities and women through various grants and programs.

The value Xerox places on social responsibility is reflected in its approach to affirmative action and managing diversity. Xerox does not simply have an affirmative action program, it has an affirmative action process. In 1987, David Kearns, then chief executive officer (CEO), said in a statement on equal employment opportunity (EEO), "At Xerox, affirmative action is not a platitude, nor is it a special program. It is a clear cut, plainly stated corporate business objective." Speaking of this value, one minority employee said, "This company has always tended to be very people oriented. The philosophy is inbred here, and it has a positive effect not only on our minority population, but on Xerox as a whole." The Xerox affirmative action process has been recognized by other Fortune 500 firms that use the process as a benchmark in evaluating their own affirmative action programs.

CREATING DIVERSITY

The second step in managing a diverse workforce is to create one. Before managing diversity, a company must have diversity. When the first copier was introduced in 1959, the Xerox Corporation was dominated by white males. Like most corporations, Xerox did little in the area of affirmative action until required to by law and changes in the social environment. To its credit, however, it responded relatively early and decisively.

Galvanizing Events

How did Xerox become aware of the need for change? Payne speaks of six "galvanizing events" that occurred during the 1960s and the early 1970s. Those galvanizing events were crises occurring outside and within the corporation that signaled to Xerox the need for change. Senior management responded to the crises in a manner suggesting that the crises were viewed as opportunities to change the organization instead of as threats to the organization. These events were the beginning of the learning process through which the corporation progressed as it began creating diversity. Table 3.2 shows a time line of the six galvanizing events.

Race Riots in Rochester

The first galvanizing event was a series of race riots that occurred in Rochester, New York, in the summer of 1964. These riots started after the arrest of an African-American at a street dance and lasted several days. Although similar race riots hit many U.S. cities, Rochester was the home of the Xerox Corporation, so senior managers responded by working with civic and religious leaders to seek solutions to the city's problems.

The Civil Rights Act of 1964

Soon after the race riots, the second galvanizing event occurred. The Civil Rights Act of 1964 was enacted into law. Title VII of the Civil Rights Act outlawed employment discrimination on the basis of color, race, sex, religion, or national origin. Xerox responded by starting to hire African-Americans.

TABLE 3.2. Galvanizing Events Leading to
Xerox's Concern for Diversifying Its Workforce

1964	First set of race riots in Rochester.
	Civil Rights Act of 1964.
1965	Executive Order 11246.
	First black caucus established.
1966	
1967	Second set of race riots in Rochester.
1968	
1969	
1970	
1971	Class action suit.

Executive Order 11246

The third galvanizing event took place in 1965 when President Lyndon B. Johnson issued Executive Order 11246. The order prohibited discrimination on the basis of race, color, religion, or national origin by federal agencies, contractors, and subcontractors. In 1967, sex discrimination was added as well. Each agency, contractor, or subcontractor with contracts of $10,000 or more was required to establish and maintain a program of equal employment opportunity in every facility of 50 or more people. It included employment, upgrading, demotion, transfer, recruitment or recruitment advertising, layoff or termination, rates of pay or compensation, and selection for training. To enforce these plans the Office of Federal Contract and Compliance Programs (OFCCP) was established. Xerox was required to comply with the order or risk losing its government contracts.

In response to these mandates, Xerox introduced the Step Up program in 1966. Thirteen African-Americans considered to be "hard-core" unemployables were trained and hired into permanent positions. With the collaboration of the National Alliance of Business, the program was expanded and almost 300 African-Americans were recruited, trained, and placed into jobs. Another expansion, Project Booster took place later. This program sought to establish a relationship between field marketing people and members of the African-American community for sales, technical, and clerical positions.

Second Set of Race Riots in Rochester

The fourth galvanizing event was a second set of race riots occurring in Rochester during the summer of 1967. Payne stated, "I think that the galvanizing events, like having riots right on the doorstep, are more dramatic than any laws." Xerox again responded to the community by actively helping solve the city's problems. They joined with FIGHT (Freedom, Integration, God, Honor, Today), an African-American organization, to create a manufacturing plant that would be owned and run by minorities in Rochester's ghettos. In addition, they sponsored television programs such as *Of Black America, The Autobiography of Miss Jane Pittman,* and *I Will Fight No More,* among others, to raise awareness of racial problems.

Within the company, Wilson as chairman of the board and then-president Peter McColough sent a letter to all Xerox managers declaring affirmative action as a corporate commitment. They committed to intensive recruitment of minorities, charging managers with the responsibility for hiring and training minorities, and stated that they planned to increase the availability of training for unqualified African-Americans and other minorities. They ended the letter with the following words:

> *We are fully aware of the progress that Xerox has already made in assisting the civil rights movement. But it simply hasn't gone far enough. We must do more because Xerox will not add to the misery of the present condition of most Negroes. It will not condone the waste of a great national resource. It will not compromise the conviction on which the success of this enterprise and of the nation depends.*

Black Caucus Groups

In spite of the progressive external image of Xerox and its efforts to hire African-Americans, the internal environment was nonsupportive and hostile in the late 1960s. During this period, African-Americans recognized that they were not expected to participate fully and they started to form groups to raise issues. Receiving little help from the lower-level managers, they went straight to the new CEO, who was now McColough. McColough realized that many of the concerns expressed by African-American employees were no different from those of white employees. Like white employees, they were not being managed well, and they were neither being promoted nor included. This realization was important because it led to the belief that many problems could be attributed to managers who did not know how to manage anyone, let alone people different from themselves. This belief would later affect attitudes toward integrating minorities and women into the workforce.

At that time, management was against the formation of caucus groups inside the corporation. One African-American employee recalled, "People in those days, when they saw two or three black people standing in the hallway together talking, they thought it was about a revolution. It couldn't be we were talking about business. We had to be very careful, Xerox was anti-caucus groups—they were not to be entertained."

Soon, however, African-American groups started to gain respect and recognition by management. The caucus groups formed because African-Americans recognized the need for self-help and support. Perhaps more importantly, the early groups helped white male managers become accustomed to dealing with people of diverse backgrounds. When local management failed to deal effectively with the African-Americans, the groups turned to top management, which then brought its concerns back to the local managers. Thus, while the company concentrated on recruiting and selecting African-Americans, African-Americans developed a social support system to help maintain affirmative action and maximize their own success after being brought into the organization.

Class Action Suit

The final galvanizing event occurred in 1971. A class action suit charging discrimination was brought against Xerox by African-American employees. One issue raised was that because African-Americans were selling in lower-volume territories that relied on cheaper copiers, they received lower commissions and less pay than their white counterparts. Another issue raised was the low rate of promotions into management positions. Senior management took immediate action and conducted an internal investigation. They assigned David Kearns (who would later become the president and CEO of Xerox) to survey the situation. He found that the concerns were legitimate, and that very day he revised the policy to end discrimination in sales territory assignments, promoted three blacks whom he felt were prepared for managerial positions, and ordered all sales representatives to be paid at the same commission rate as the white sales representatives. The checks correcting the differences in commission rates were written and paid that afternoon. As a result of these actions, the suit never went to court. This immediate attention signaled to African-Americans and white managers that senior management took equal employment opportunity seriously.

The Next Decade

Due to these galvanizing events, senior management realized that serious change was warranted; Xerox had begun its journey toward having a diverse workforce. During the 1970s and early 1980s, the corporation continued to develop its affirmative action process. An era of trial and error ensued due to the lack of companies with programs to benchmark. Some attempts worked while others did not. Table 3.3 summarizes the time line of these events.

Decentralized Affirmative Action Plan

Prior to 1972, Xerox attempted to use a centralized affirmative action plan. Numerical targets based on eight availability factors defined by the federal government were developed to represent minorities and women at vari-

TABLE 3.3. Attempts at Xerox to Create Diversity in the 1970s and 1980s

1972	Decentralized affirmative action plan to district level. Made affirmative action a line manager's responsibility. Designated $1 million to start affirmative action in operations. Developed Management Awareness Training and Education Seminar. Formulated Pivotal Job concept.
1973	Turned focus to women, designated female affirmative action officers.
1974	Accepted caucus groups.
1975	Developed Management Practices Program. Added affirmative action to manager's performance appraisals.
1978	HAPA, the Hispanic caucus, starts.
1980	Tied affirmative action to executives' bonuses. Women's caucus groups start to appear. Incorporated Human Resources Strategic Plan into Xerox Business Plan.
1981	Maintained representation during layoffs.
1984	Assessed affirmative action process. Moved to Balanced Workforce strategy.

ous levels in the organization (see Table 3.4). The OFCCP would not approve of this plan, however, because it required a decentralized plan.

In 1972, the personnel staff, at the direction of the president, decentralized the affirmative action plan to the district level, again using the eight availability factors. At this point, affirmative action became a *business priority*. Every manager would be held accountable for progress toward affirmative action goals. This strategy was without precedent among major employers at that time.

McColough designated $1 million of corporate money to be used by operating groups for initiating affirmative action programs in operations. In addition, he sent a letter to every manager reasserting that affirmative action at Xerox was a commitment and, more importantly, that it was the responsibility of the line managers. Transforming affirmative action into a business priority and designating a substantial amount of money to the program again demonstrated to lower-level managers that senior managers were taking affirmative action very seriously.

Training and Education

In 1972, the training and development staff, in conjunction with a minorities relations specialist, instituted the Management Awareness Training and Education Seminar (MATES), which was a training program designed

TABLE 3.4. Eight Availability Factors Defined by the Federal Government

Employable population	People age 16 and over residing in the state.
Unemployment	The number of unemployed people in the state.
Total labor force	People who are either employed or seeking employment in the local area.
Requisite skills available locally	People in the local labor market who have the required skills to perform a given job.
Requisite skills recruitable	People in the recruitable labor market who have the required skills to perform a given job.
Available internally	Xerox people in the specific internal "feeder" job group.
College enrollment	People enrolled in college or professional school programs that will equip them with the required skills.
Available internally through training	Xerox people enrolled in Xerox training programs related to a given job.

to sensitize managers regarding how to deal with people who didn't look like them, or who were from a different background or culture. An informal evaluation revealed that the training program met with only moderate success because the training did not go far enough. Although it did sensitize managers to their biases, it did not provide them with the necessary tools and information they needed to deal with these biases.

In 1975, a new training program, the Management Practices Program (MPP), was developed using a needs analysis. It was a behavior modeling-based management skills program. Using videotaped scenarios and role-playing methods, the program taught managers listening and communication skills, coaching and counseling, and how to work with employees on compensation, performance improvement, and career development. Managers received step-by-step guidebooks on how to interact with employees, how to talk and listen, and how to cover key points in meetings about compensation, performance, career development, affirmative action, and reverse discrimination. An evaluation of the program revealed that improvement occurred in the performance results of teams. For example, sales teams showed a 10%–15% improvement in their results. This training program served as the prototype for such programs existing in Xerox today. Although not labeled as such, this training was in essence the corporation's first formal attempt at managing diversity because managers were taught skills and given tools that helped them to interact with all employees regardless of their race, culture, or gender.

Pivotal Job Concept

In 1972, senior management noticed that minorities and women were not very upwardly mobile. They realized that a vehicle for moving people into higher levels of the organization was needed, and the simplest way to do this was to use what had worked in the past. When the resumes of 50 senior people in divisions such as U.S. Sales were reviewed, senior management realized that there were between two and five key positions that were almost always part of the career paths of senior managers. Examples of these pivotal positions are first-line sales manager, branch manager, and a regional-level job. If a person had not held these pivotal jobs, he would not have reached a high-level position at Xerox. As a result, the company started to target these jobs for minorities and women. Payne explained, "The theory was that if you develop and put enough people into the pool of prospects, some of them will get through, some of them will rise to the top." Today, the pivotal job concept is still being used as a career planning and placement tool.

Focus Turns to Women

In 1973, management turned its attention to women. Unlike African-Americans, whose cause was supported by the momentum of the galvanizing events and the Civil Rights movement, the company voluntarily took the first step in recognizing women's issues. This step showed growth in top management's attitudes toward affirmative action. Women affirmative action officers were put into place at all organizational levels to address women's concerns, such as upward mobility, inhospitable environment, and nonsupportive company policies.

Senior Management Accepts Black Caucus Groups

In 1974, Kearns initiated a meeting with African-American leaders within Xerox requesting the caucus groups to abandon plans to hold a national meeting. Senior managers were concerned that there was a potential for a union based on race, and they thought that this precedent would cause more harm than good. During the meeting, African-Americans convinced Kearns that the groups were meeting to support and develop themselves, not to create problems or unionize. Kearns realized that this could benefit both the African-American employees and the Xerox corporation and should not be seen as threatening. Kearns and the African-American leaders worked out a compromise. The African-Americans would create separate regional caucus groups to which African-American leaders would travel as needed to disseminate information. To this day, the regional caucus groups remain independent. As one African-American caucus member related, "We don't have a national association. We are very careful about that. We don't want to be recognized as a national association which could border on trade unionism." It is interesting to note that unionization based solely on race was not a realistic concern, because there is no basis for this in the labor relations legislation. In addition, race in this case was not the appropriate bargaining unit.

Affirmative Action Added to Performance Appraisals

Because line managers were to be held accountable for their progress in affirmative action, as with any other business objectives, it was necessary to measure each manager's performance in affirmative action. One alternative for measuring each individual's performance is the performance appraisal. Like many companies, Xerox derives managers' merit increases from their performance appraisals. In 1975, the personnel staff added a section on affirmative action to each manager's performance appraisal. Up to 15% of a manager's appraisal depended on the actions he or she had taken to hire and promote minorities and women. During this period of time, there were no standardized guidelines regarding what the correct representation should be. The emphasis was on bringing large numbers of minorities and women into the workplace. It was up to each manager to figure out the numbers and the strategies to achieve these goals. According to Payne, this worked very well.

Because of the success with performance appraisals, the personnel staff later attempted to link the affirmative action performances of upper-level executives to the size of their bonuses. This did not work, however, because many executives hesitated to say their subordinate managers were having trouble in such an important area. Performance on affirmative action was later dropped as a determinant of bonuses.

The Formation of the Hispanic Association for Professional Advancement

In 1978, Hispanics formed their own caucus group, the Hispanic Association for Professional Advancement (HAPA). Hispanic employees felt that there was a discrepancy between the number of Hispanics living in California and the number of Hispanics working for Xerox in California. Although this group was originally located only in California, it later became a national organization with different chapters across the nation.

Because Xerox had realized that caucus groups could be beneficial to the corporation, it was no longer concerned with unionization based on race or ethnicity. This allowed HAPA to become one national organization instead of several regional organizations.

Women's Caucus Groups Start to Appear

In the mid-1970s, management attempted to start a women's caucus based on what it had learned from the African-American caucus groups. It did this by holding round tables, allowing women to express their ideas and concerns regarding women's issues with the hope that these women would coalesce into support groups. This attempt did not work and would not work until the 1980s, when women started caucus groups themselves. Why the caucus group did not work until the women started the groups themselves is unclear. However, the many different types of women's caucus groups that have risen within the company may offer a clue.

Currently there are at least ten different women's caucus groups at Xerox. Some groups are national and some are regional; some were developed solely for minority women; some are based on a specific organization; and some groups are for exempt women, whereas others are for nonexempt women. This stratification is interesting because it reflects the fact that women themselves are a highly diverse group. Not only do women belong to all race and ethnic groups, but by the early 1980s, they held positions in most levels of the organization. This diversity might explain why the women's caucus group did not take hold when management first attempted to get it started. The issues of concern to women at different levels of the organization and to women of different racial and ethnic groups may have been too diverse for one caucus group to handle. Therefore, each caucus group developed due to specific circumstances, as opposed to having formed as a result of an overall plan or strategy. These women's caucus groups are currently exploring ways of joining together to maximize their ability to communicate women's issues to management. This suggests that (at least at Xerox) the most effective support groups must be employee initiated and maintained to succeed. However, at other corporations, such as Tenneco and Polaroid, management has successfully initiated women's caucus groups (Deutsch, 1990).

Human Resources Strategic Plan Is Incorporated into the Business Plan

During the early 1980s, management became aware that competition was moving into the Xerox marketplace and beating it in price and technology.

To cut costs and remain competitive, the company needed to downsize and redeploy many employees. During this crisis, Douglas M. Reid, the corporate vice president of personnel, and his team took the opportunity to convince the president that human resources should have an integral role in developing the company's business plan. The strategy, developed in 1980, was to incorporate human resources issues into the business planning process so that human resources would match the needs of the business. Within the plan that was developed were six platforms including affirmative action, competitive compensation, benefits and policies, employee communications, workforce preparedness, and support to Leadership Through Quality. Five affirmative action objectives were established to support the human resources plan. These objectives focused on defining and achieving a balanced workforce; aggressively pursuing upward mobility for minorities and women; integrating affirmative action into the everyday process of doing business, both within the company and with external customers and suppliers; and communicating the role of affirmative action to all employees. Incorporating the Human Resources Strategic Plan into the Business Plan achieved three objectives. First, it caused the Human Resources planning process to change from being reactive to the Business Plan to being a part of the Business Plan. Second, it forced the company to forecast its future human resource needs and to plan for how to meet those needs. Third, explicitly mentioning the importance of human resources and affirmative action to the organization in its Business Plan fostered the mindset that affirmative action was an opportunity and not a problem.

Layoffs

In 1981, the company was forced to lay off many people in order to cut costs and remain competitive in the marketplace. For example, the manufacturing laborforce was cut in half. In making the layoffs, senior management decided to maintain the representation it had built over the past 10 years and possibly risk a reverse discrimination suit. This decision, it felt, was a conservative one.

Assessment

In 1984, the personnel staff evaluated the progress of affirmative action over the previous decade using numerical representation of women and minorities at the different levels of the organization as well as survey results. It found that the goals that had been set for both minorities and women in nonexempt jobs and entry-level positions had been achieved.

For minority males, a number of goals in middle- and upper-level grade bands had been achieved. And affirmative action had been established as a manager's responsibility. However, goals had not been achieved for upper-level and executive positions for women. And some employees perceived that affirmative action was going overboard, limiting the opportunities available to white males.

There were also three strengths of the affirmative action process so far. First, top managers were committed to affirmative action and realized the necessity of changing. Because of this orientation, top managers had taken three important steps: (1) They adopted a long-term process, not a quick-fix program; (2) they allocated the resources necessary to make the change; and (3) they made affirmative action a business priority, not a staff function. A second strength was that minority and women caucus groups were accepted and encouraged as employee involvement programs to support the change. And third, top managers realized that the issues and concerns raised by the minorities and women were really concerns of all employees. For this reason, no special training programs were developed targeting minorities and women. Instead, training emphasized developing managers to better manage their employees.

There were also three weaknesses with the affirmative action process. First, when a minority or woman was promoted, it was considered an "affirmative action move" even though the person fully deserved the move. Management needed to find a way to remove the stigma of affirmative action. Second, majority males felt that they were being neglected and hurt in the process—they felt that minorities and women were getting all the attention. Management needed a system that would give equal attention to all employee groups. Third, the process was too simplistic. Managers were given rudimentary goals and little guidance in deciding how many minorities and women to hire. They were just ordered to "do it," hire minorities and women. Better goals and guidance were needed to help the managers hire minorities and women.

MANAGING DIVERSITY

Xerox management realized that it needed to further improve the process of bringing minorities and women into the organization and up through the levels. It shifted to a process that emphasized managing diversity, currently accomplished in two ways: (1) on the assumption that attitude changes will grow from the daily experience of genuine workforce diversity, the corporation focuses on managing diversity through its BWF goals; and (2) the caucus groups contribute to the management of diversity through employee involvement.

Balanced Work Force

In 1984, the company changed to the BWF process emphasizing organizational development to continue its transformation from a white male workforce to a fully diverse workforce. BWF means achieving and maintaining equitable representation of all employee groups, majority females, majority males, minority females, and minority males—at all grade bands, in all functions, and in all organizations.

Development of the Plan

The strategy was developed by John L. Jones, the director of corporate affirmative action and EEO, and his staff to correct the weaknesses of the previous affirmative action process. The BWF process gives attention to all employee groups including white males. In the past, a manager's affirmative action goals were met if he or she was at or above the goals that had been set for hiring minorities and women. Now, overachieving in one category means that goals in other categories are not being met. Because of this attention to all employee groups, the stigma of affirmative action was lessened. Finally, managers receive more guidance because they are told how many majority females, majority males, minority females, and minority males they should have.

Both long-term goals and short-term targets were necessary to change the structure of the workforce. Ten-year end-point goals were established. Annual targets were developed to create gradual changes in percentage representation, so that the end-point goals could be achieved over a number of years. Table 3.5 shows an example of how such targets are set. The process for developing the goals and targets was based on the same eight availability factors defined by the federal government and used in developing the first affirmative action plan (shown in Table 3.4). Xerox uses U.S. Census data and internal Xerox headcounts to calculate goals for each job category and grade band. The original goals were developed from the 1980 Census data and updated using an estimate from the National Planning Data Corporation. In 1993, Xerox will be changing to the 1990 Census. One problem using the Census data is that, even as Xerox receives the data, they will be out of date.

For an entry-level position, corporate staff considers each of the eight factors to decide which are appropriate for a particular job. No change was made in the recruiting and selection process. Employees are still recruited and selected into the organization in the traditional manner, which includes recruiting from many different areas, a screening interview, a test battery, and a focused interview.

TABLE 3.5. Goals and Yearly Targets for a Hypothetical Operating Unit

Grade band	Employee group	Head count	Current rep (%)	10-year BWF goal (%)	Annual BWF* target (%)
15-18	Majority female	10	5	23	8
	Majority male	168	77	57	N/M**
	Minority female	4	2	7	2
	Minority male	36	16	13	N/M
	Total	218	100	100	
13-14	Majority female	38	8	20	10
	Majority male	377	76	58	N/M
	Minority female	9	2	7	3
	Minority male	71	14	15	15
	Total	495	100	100	
10-12	Majority female	126	9	18	11
	Majority male	954	69	60	N/M
	Minority female	38	3	6	3
	Minority male	265	19	16	N/M
	Total	1,383	100	100	
07-09	Majority female	326	19	23	21
	Majority male	821	49	57	57
	Minority female	150	9	7	N/M
	Minority male	391	23	13	N/M
	Total	1,688	100	100	
01-06	Majority female	164	29	16	N/M
	Majority male	169	30	67	35
	Minority female	96	17	4	N/M
	Minority male	138	24	13	N/M
	Total	567	100	100	

Note. From *Agenda: 28: A Journal for Xerox Managers*, p. 13. Copyright 1988 by Xerox Corporation Corporate Communications. Reprinted by permission.
*BWF indicates Balanced Work Force.
**N/M indicates no measurement; BWF goal has already been achieved.

Because the company subscribes to a policy of promotion from within whenever possible, it must depend on the lower exempt categories as the primary feeder base for movement into higher-level positions. The lower-level population is used to generate goals for the upper levels. Management recognizes that constant monitoring and progress must be made at the lower levels of the organization to provide the necessary feeder base for the upper levels and that because of management's commitment to using the lower levels as a feeder base, movement of minorities and women into the upper levels of the organization will remain slow.

The responsibility for achieving BWF goals and targets remains with the operating units, although the corporate personnel staff manages these goals at a global level. Managers are responsible for balancing their work groups, and they are evaluated in this area on their performance appraisals. In addition, managers are responsible for developing their subordinates' skills and giving them the opportunity for upward mobility to maintain the feeder base. Although not formally part of BWF, there are several procedures that managers and employees may use to support achieving the BWF goals. First, most job openings are posted throughout the organization to enable employees to apply for these jobs.

Second, employees who are not managers, but who would like to move into the managerial ranks, may request a Panel Interview. Each employee is given a checklist of areas that a manager must know or be able to do (e.g., a sales manager must know how to configure sales territories). When the employee feels that he or she has met these requirements, a Panel Interview is held with the employee and three managers (a district manager, a personnel manager, and another manager). The panel of managers asks the employee a set list of job-relevant questions. At the end of the interview, the panel decides whether or not the employee is qualified to move into a management position using the employee's answers to the interview questions. The Panel Interview was developed in the 1970s by Harold J. Tragash, manager of human resources planning, to provide an alternative to assessment centers used by other companies to promote individuals into management positions. (Assessment centers are used at Xerox as development tools.) The process was validated by a member of Tragash's staff.

A third procedure, the Management Resources Process (MRP), primarily a succession planning tool, can be used as a career development tool for middle-level managers. Each manager fills out a personal history form and indicates career development goals. Then managers participate in a group assessment consisting of themselves, their supervisor, and their peers. From this assessment, the manager receives feedback and develops an action plan with his or her supervisor.

BWF is a key human resources objective and is considered a sound business practice with both short-term and long-term effects. In the short term, it will help achieve revenue and profit plans because many major accounts require a demonstration of EEO and upward mobility of all employees, including minorities and women. In the long term, because growth in the size of the U.S. workforce is slowing, staying competitive demands being able to take advantage of all human resources, regardless of race, age, or sex for all positions from entry level to senior management.

Evaluation

Progress is now measured three times a year. Operating units review current representation with respect to the year's targets and the long-term goals. At this point, recovery plans are instituted if they are necessary. Recovery plans include possible promotions, transfers from other operating units, or hiring from outside to adjust representation in the correct direction. Corporate personnel continuously reviews the balance among the majority men, majority women, minority men, and minority women within each job category (sales, personnel, finance, data processing, engineering, service, etc.). In addition, it is shifting to a system that will also review the balance among the different minority groups (African- , Hispanic- , Asian- , and Native-Americans) within each job category to ensure balance among the minority groups as well.

This evaluation is an improvement over the previous evaluation for two reasons. First, strategies to achieve balance have become more sophisticated. Managers at all levels of the organization now receive specific goals or targets to achieve, and they are given frequent feedback. Second, because of the frequency of evaluation at all levels of the organization, the pressure is taken off individual managers and their performance appraisals. Since its implementation, the BWF strategy has achieved significant results. Managers are developing and moving their employees, leading to upward mobility for all employee groups.

Problems with the BWF Goals

Although the process is logically very simple, it does have two problems. The first problem is targeting in terms of particular locales. Targeting is easy to do on a macro basis, but more difficult to do within each regional area. For example, although Xerox management may want a certain percentage of Hispanics across the corporation, there are proportionately many more Hispanics located on the West Coast than in the Midwest. The company is currently developing a system that enhances the localization of targets. The second problem lies in the implementation of the process. Managers must continuously consider BWF goals when hiring, developing, and moving their employees. This requires commitment to a sometimes complex process, and commitment is not always strong.

The Caucus Groups

Xerox has allowed for the development of a unique system of caucus groups. The caucus groups serve as a vehicle for employee involvement in the company's effort to manage the diversity of its workforce. One minority member related, "The existence of caucus groups is really one of Xerox's leading edge approaches to how it manages diversity in the work place. Xerox supports them [caucus groups] and works with them to help the minorities or women that they serve."

Currently, there are three types of caucus groups: five regional black caucus groups, HAPA, and the many women's caucus groups. In addition, Asian employees are currently deciding if they need their own caucus group. These caucus groups are not an official part of the company, although all members are company employees. In fact, many of the caucus groups are incorporated and are established as separate corporate entities. The caucus groups meet on their own time, and they set their own rules and agendas. Membership in the caucus groups ranges from only a few members to as much as 40% to 50% of the population they represent. To date the black regional caucus groups, HAPA, and the women's caucus groups have not collaborated on any projects. However, caucus groups that have worked together in other companies on various issues have been successful (Deutsch, 1990).

The caucus groups serve several functions: (1) They serve as a communication link between the caucus population and upper management; (2) they are used for personal and professional development; (3) they are used for networking and support within the caucus population; (4) members serve as role models to majority employees for managing diversity; and (5) they are often the vehicle through which the corporation serves the community. In fact, one minority manager said, "Senior management has very high expectations of caucus groups to do much of the managing diversity."

Communication Link

Caucus groups serve as a communication link between groups that they serve and all levels of management. A minority caucus member exemplifies the Xerox open door policy, "Xerox is a peculiar organization among Fortune 500 companies. If I have a problem, I can pick up the phone at any time and call Paul Allaire (the current president and CEO). That's not necessary because I can also call the region manager, the district manager, or Ted Payne. I can call anybody I feel can really address the issue."

Since the first time African-Americans approached Peter McColough with their concerns in the late 1960s through today, the caucus groups have served as a pipeline between minorities and women and management to address problems and negotiate solutions. A HAPA member spoke of the caucus groups as being in a "partnership" with the company, "Xerox basically asked HAPA to work with management to review the BWF process."

Personal and Professional Development

Another function of the caucus groups is self-improvement to help the minority or woman employee compete for jobs. A black caucus member described a training program in one of the black caucus groups, "We run the Management Studies Program [a training program] every year. People come every Saturday for 16 weeks so they can better prepare themselves to understand and to meet the challenges of management." The black caucus groups hold regional conferences, and, recently, a national conference. Both HAPA and the women's caucus groups have started holding national conferences. One section of the conference consists of seminars directed toward self-development.

Networking and Support

The caucus groups and the conferences are used as a vehicle to unite and support the populations they serve. The caucus groups provide an informal communication channel for disseminating information across the organization. Valuable information about the organization or even how members should act are passed through this network. In addition, caucus members at high levels in the organization provide models for lower-level caucus group members. The positive influence of meeting a high-level African-American, or Hispanic, or woman at a conference may influence or motivate lower-level employees to establish higher career goals and seek out higher-level positions. And third, networks empower the employees who are members through employee involvement. The minority and women's caucus groups can and do make a difference.

Role Modeling

Minority and women caucus members also serve as role models in managing diversity to other employees. One minority manager explained, "We practice managing diversity on a daily basis." The use of minority members as role models for other employees is exemplified by the following example:

When I started at Xerox, I was in a sales organization that had 46 men and 4 women. I was 1 of only 2 minority women. Today, the organization I manage is 50% male and 50% female. I have Asians, Hispanics, African-Americans, all tied into the targeting mentality. As you begin to role model and develop a diverse workforce, everyone can start to value everyone else's contribution in a team setting. That begins to break down the barriers that existed in the past.

Community Work

The caucus groups often serve as the link between the corporation and the general minority communities. Many caucus members, because of their own personal interest, work with the outside community. When the caucus groups participate in events such as fund-raisers for scholarships or college funds, Xerox matches the funds raised. There are also one-to-one mentorship programs in which minority students are brought into the company through an intern process. Through socialization of the student to the company, and the company to the student, the student is subsequently able to take a full-time job at a higher level than he or she might have gotten had the internship not taken place.

Changes to the Corporation Made by the Caucus Groups

There are many examples of changes initiated by the caucus groups. The caucus groups have gained the acceptance and respect of management at all levels of the organization. In fact, managers at all levels have regular meetings with minorities and women about issues concerning them.

The caucus groups have caused the company to review its BWF goals. For example, the sourcing patterns using the eight government factors have been changed from the communities in which most of the workers live to include the communities they service. In addition, the caucus groups have influenced the categories used when the BWF goals are set. Previous BWF goals had been broken into four groupings: majority female, majority male, minority female, minority male. HAPA worked with the company to develop targets and plans that break out each separate minority group (e.g., African-, Asian-, Hispanic-, and Native-Americans) for evaluation.

Recruiting measures have been changed in three ways. For example, at one time, job openings were heard about only after they were already filled. Now job opportunity listings are posted throughout the company on a more timely basis. Second, the three-manager Panel Interview process was developed as a more objective way to move people into management positions. Third, the Management Resources Process was changed from being a confidential list of promotable people to a public document. Employees now know whether they are on the list as well as how they are rated. The job opportunity listings, the Panel Interview process, and making the Management Resources Process public bring more fairness to the recruitment and promotion processes. These changes were the result of actions taken by the caucus groups to ensure more objectivity and fairness in these procedures.

EVALUATION

At Xerox, managing diversity can be categorized into four areas. These categories are culture, training and development, evaluation of individuals, and organization development and change.

Culture

The first and most important area of managing diversity is the culture. Affirmative action and managing diversity are very important to the people within the corporation. Affirmative action is a business priority, not a staff function. It is part of the business plan that is included along with traditional areas. And it has been developed as a long-term process, not a quick-fix program. The culture has also allowed for the rise of the minority and women caucus groups that allow employees involvement in affirmative action and managing diversity.

Training and Development

Training and development encompasses the company's first attempts at managing diversity. In 1972, a sensitivity awareness program for managers was introduced (MATES). The program met with only moderate success because, although it made the managers aware of their biases, it did not give them any guidance on how to change these biases. In 1975, the Management Practices Program was introduced; it focused on teaching managers how to manage through behavioral modeling. This time a needs analysis was used to develop the training program. In an evaluation of the program it was found the MPP worked well because the training gave managers actual tools and procedures for managing everyone. The company continues to use this type of training today.

Xerox elected not to give special training to minorities and women, because management realized that many "minority" and "women" concerns were no different from the concerns of the white male majority population. However, some minority groups felt a need for such training and started to train themselves. As already noted, one of the main functions of the caucus groups is the personal and professional development of caucus group members to give them an edge in competing for jobs.

Evaluation of Individuals

This area encompasses the evaluation of managers and executives using performance appraisals and bonuses. Using performance appraisals to evaluate managers on the basis of their performance on affirmative action and later BWF has worked very well. However, in other corporations that have tried this, human resources professionals suggest that it may not work well for two reasons. The main issue is a legal one. If a manager is evaluated poorly in affirmative action, this suggests that he or she is discriminatory and the organization is aware of it. Thus, in the event of a legal action concerning discrimination, the organization can be held accountable if no corrective action has been taken. Although Xerox recognizes the risk, the company believes the benefits of evaluation in this area outweigh the risks. A secondary issue is that it simply looks bad for the manager if he or she ranks a subordinate as doing poorly in this area. However, evaluating subordinates as satisfactory, when in fact they are not, may reinforce unacceptable behavior as meeting the company's standards. This was an issue at Xerox when executives' bonuses were tied to performance on affirmative action. In this case, affirmative action was dropped from executives' bonuses.

Organizational Development and Change

From the middle of the 1960s through the present, Xerox has continued transforming its workforce from one that is primarily white males to one that is highly diverse. In fact, both the BWF goals and the caucus groups can be seen as mechanisms for change. Although the company acknowledges that it still has a long way to go, many employees believe that it is probably one of the better companies in managing diversity. How is it making this change? Beckhard (1987) has analyzed the conditions needed to facilitate successful organizational change. These ten conditions are listed below with how they relate to the conditions present at Xerox.

External Conditions

There must be a set of external conditions that makes it difficult or impossible to maintain the status quo. The six galvanizing events or crises caused Xerox to recognize the need for a change and to start the process of change. Two situations have led to the maintenance of the process. First, Xerox is a federal contractor; therefore, the company is held accountable by the Office of Federal Contract and Compliance Programs for its progress in affirmative action. Second, in the early 1980s, the company was confronted by competition in its marketplace. Traditional procedures for dealing with employees were no longer sufficient. The corporate vice president of personnel and his staff used this crisis as an opportunity to make human resources a part of the overall business plan. Without these events' causing pressure on the organization, it might not have started the change process nor maintained its progress.

Champions of Change

There must be committed champions of change amongst the organization's top leadership. Unless key executives are willing to make real changes, most changes will be ephemeral at best. The commitment to change the make up of the organization has been evident in senior managers, beginning with the creator of xerography, Chester Carlson, and the founder of Xerox, Joseph Wilson. This commitment has continued through Peter McColough, David Kearns, and now, the current president and CEO, Paul Allaire.

Key People

There must be key people at all levels of the organization who will guide and support the change throughout the organization. Key players include people in personnel who designed and implemented much of the affirmative action and managing diversity processes. These key people come from a variety of educational backgrounds. Many people have doctorates in industrial/organizational psychology. Other educational backgrounds include degrees in business administration, economics and industrial and labor relations. Also included are the past and present caucus group members who relentlessly pushed for change from the bottom of the organization.

Belief That Change Is Necessary, and a Willingness to Provide Resources

There must be a conviction that the transformation is necessary, so that an experimental attitude will operate, the organization will stay with the effort, and resources will be provided. The conviction that there was a need for a change is evident from the letter Wilson and McColough sent to all managers in 1968 stating that they believed that the change was necessary for both social and economic reasons. To initiate the change, $1 million was allocated to start affirmative action programs across the corporation. A later sign of this conviction was seen in 1980 when the Human Resources Strategic Plan was incorporated into the Business Plan. Xerox has used an experimental approach in developing its processes of affirmative action. Some ideas such as the pivotal job concept worked, and are still being used today. Other procedures, such as the first training program (MATES), did not work well, so they were redeveloped until they did work. Other ideas, such as attaching performance in affirmative action to bonuses, were recognized as flawed and were dropped. This experimental attitude has been used at Xerox for two decades and continues to be used for managing diversity.

Time Perspective

Organizational development takes time. A medium- to long-term perspective must be used to change the organization. A long-term perspective is evident in both the decentralized affirmative action process put in place in 1972 and the BWF 10-year end-point goals. There has always been the realization that the change would take years.

Description of the Organization

The company must state in behavioral terms what the changed organization will look like. In the early 1970s, top management knew it wanted affirmative action to be a business priority, not a staff role. However, no description of what the workforce should look like in terms of race and sex was developed. In time, the company learned that it would be difficult to diversify the workforce without these goals. Thus, when the BWF goals were developed, top management expressed a goal of what it wanted the entire workforce to look like over the next 10 years.

Information Flow

There must be a commitment to maintaining an information flow among all parts of the organization. Xerox has an open-door policy that allows employees to communicate with whomever they think could best help them. The caucus groups helped open these lines of communication from the bottom of the organization all the way to the top.

Need for Training

There must be an awareness of the need for education. Xerox management quickly discovered that simply giving employees goals without skills and tools to accomplish these goals would not work. Managers now receive basic skills training on how to manage. The caucus groups also realized that training is important. Although the company never specifically targeted minorities and women to receive special training, some of the caucus groups saw a need for self-development. On their own time, minorities and women go through training programs to give them an edge as they compete for jobs.

Resistance

Change leaders must be aware that they will encounter resistance. During the 1970s, many stereotypes needed to be changed regarding the capabilities of minorities and women. Xerox senior management used an interesting approach. It did not attempt to change attitudes; it changed behavior by saying, "You *will* have a certain number of minority managers and a certain number of women managers by next year." Managers who were unable to comply were held accountable.

PLANS FOR THE FUTURE

Beyond the culture, training and development, evaluation of individuals, and organizational development and change, Payne believes that Xerox has done little toward managing diversity. In fact, he considers managing diversity to be the next step to be added to the affirmative action process. According to Payne, there is a danger in focusing too heavily on managing diversity. He cites as evidence other organizations that have shifted their attention from affirmative action to managing diversity and have subsequently lost minority representation in their workforce and are experiencing stagnation of upward mobility. Thus, maintaining goals in affirmative action is necessary because it causes the organization to continue focusing on developing a diverse workforce. Managing diversity is a natural extension of the affirmative action process, which recognizes the value of "optimizing diversity." "Optimizing diversity" means harnessing the heterogeneity of the workforce in a synergistic manner. With respect to optimizing diversity, Xerox plans to continue with the same strategy as it has used with affirmative action—taking one small step at a time. Some examples of steps taken in managing diversity include: (1) use of the *Valuing Diversity* videotapes, which Xerox and several other companies developed in conjunction with Copeland and Griggs, as well as the *Bridges* videotape series developed by BNA Communications; and as a supplement (2) an interactive theater program on managing diversity designed by Cornell University's theater department that allows executives to ask questions after each short play.

In summary, this case study has demonstrated that there are three things needed to manage diversity in terms of race and sex. First, a company must value diversity; a company cannot manage diversity unless diversity is valued. Second, a company must have diversity and continue to focus on affirmative action goals. Although the Xerox workforce is not yet fully diverse, it is one of the most diverse workforces in the United States, because the company has spent the previous two decades creating diversity using affirmative action processes and BWF. Finally, the organization must be changed or transformed to manage and optimize that diversity and make it an integral part of the organization.

REFERENCES

Beckhard, R. (1987). The executive management of transformational change. In R. Kilmann (Ed.), *Corporate transformation* (pp. 89–101). San Francisco: Jossey-Bass.

Deutsch, C. H. (1990, December 16). Putting women on the fast track. *New York Times*, p. 25.

Ferrey, M. E. (1990, Spring). Twenty great places to work. *Professional*, pp. 18–33.

The 50 best places for blacks to work. (1989, February). *Black Enterprise*, pp. 73–91.

In good company: 25 best places for blacks to work. (1986, February). *Black Enterprise*, pp. 88–100.

Konrad, W. (1990, August 6). Cover story: Business Week's best companies for women. *Business Week*, pp. 49–55.

CHAPTER 4

Beyond Good Faith: Commitment to Recruiting Management Diversity at Pacific Bell

LORIANN ROBERSON
NANCY C. GUTIERREZ

Affirmative action programs are supposed to involve a good-faith effort on the part of the organization to seek out, recruit, and encourage minority applicants to apply for jobs. Yet in many organizations, this translates into placing the words "We are an equal opportunity employer" at the bottom of advertisements, and running those ads in some selected "minority publications." Such efforts certainly do not discourage minority applicants, but they do little to encourage them either.

This case study describes an approach to minority recruiting that goes beyond the perfunctory good-faith effort described above. The recruitment program for increasing diversity in management positions at Pacific Bell has been in existence for 10 years. Pacific Bell, a telecommunications company located in California, employs approximately 59,000 people statewide (as of late 1990). Before 1984, Pacific Bell was Pacific Telephone, one of the operating companies of AT&T. Since 1984, the company has been independent as a result of the divestiture. During the 10-year period to be described, both AT&T and the Bell Operating Companies were involved in numerous activities concerning management recruitment, selection, and development. This chapter focuses only on management recruiting at Pacific Bell. Although Pacific Bell was once part of AT&T, the recruiting program to be described was and is specific to Pacific Bell—it was not an AT&T initiative. Rather, it was initiated and developed by Pacific Bell staff, in response to its unique environment.

In this chapter we first present some relevant historical background on the organization's experiences with minority recruitment and the events that led to the program's development. We then describe the program's components in detail. The next sections present both internal and external reactions to the program and its consequences. As will be shown, the successful recruitment of minorities brought more changes to Pacific Bell than just better-looking utilization statistics. Finally, we describe factors contributing to the program's success, as well as challenges the program and the company need to meet in the future.

AT&T'S HISTORY OF MANAGEMENT RECRUITMENT

The history of Pacific Bell's management recruitment activities is part and parcel of that for the whole Bell System under the leadership of AT&T. A coordinated plan for recruiting on college campuses was established as early as 1922. This was developed, improved, and utilized until the time of divestiture. Campus visits were made by a Bell System team made up of representatives of AT&T, the Bell Telephone Laboratories, the Western Electric Company, and one or more operating telephone companies. The telephone company in whose territory the colleges and universities visited were located served as the host and coordinator of the team.

Employment standards included rank in college graduating class and extracurricular achievement, particularly of a leadership nature. A mental ability test was added in the early 1960s. This was dropped temporarily by about half of the telephone companies during later testing controversies.

Campus recruiting was the source of most of the management trainees employed. Additional numbers came from those whose campuses were not visited and who applied by mail or walked into the employment office. It was not unusual for the telephone companies to hire as many as 2,000 college graduates a year. Until more recent years, nearly all of these were white males.

The aim of this recruiting was to employ people who had the potential to reach at least the third level of management (out of seven). To enhance the likelihood of this, there were special development programs in place. In the 1960s the existing program was sharply revised to emphasize job challenge and named the Initial Management Development Program.

Noncollege employment activities provided the hundreds of thousands of individuals needed to perform the many nonmanagement tasks essential to the telephone business. Most men joined the plant department, which installed and maintained telephone equipment. Women became telephone operators, clerks, or service representatives. Advancement into first-level management was frequent. The male plant foreman and the female chief operator were the backbone of the business.

Advancement above first level was much more difficult for these noncollege people. Women amounted to only 1% of those at third level. Men fared better, but only about one-third of those who had been promoted to first level from the ranks ever reached third level, and only 3% made fourth level. As compared to this, as many as 80% of college graduates hired into first level reached their target of third level, and about a third of them went to fourth level or higher.

Although the difference in progress between noncollege and college males might be expected, the difference between males and females in advancement to third level was striking. In addition, few members of minority groups were present in either group or in the college graduate group.

The extent and severity of these problems were formally recognized in 1973. The consent decree between AT&T and the federal agencies responsible for employment discrimination regulation (Equal Employment Opportunity Commission, Department of Labor, Department of Justice) enabled women and minorities to move into jobs not previously available to them. Although AT&T was not required to admit any guilt in discrimination, it did agree to award back pay to affected individuals and to adopt an affirmative action plan with strict hiring goals and preferential hiring. This substantially raised the number of women and minorities hired and promoted in many job categories.

By 1979, the results had been so successful that the decree was ended. AT&T then initiated its Model Affirmative Action Program, in which the company reaffirmed its commitment to achieving statistical parity (the employment of various race and sex groups in accordance with their representation in the labor force). Numerical objectives for protected groups would continue to be set, and each operating company would monitor its own progress toward the goals.

The new affirmative action program was voluntary and did not involve preferential hiring. It was assumed that the new ways of recruitment, selection, and promotion practiced during the decree had become self-perpetuating and that the gains made in minority employment would be maintained. However, the company returned to a greater reliance on internal sources of applicants for upper management jobs, in part because workers had expressed great dissatisfaction with the extent of external hiring during the consent decree years.

THE FORMATION OF THE MANAGEMENT
RECRUITMENT DISTRICT

At Pacific Bell, evidence began to accumulate that this assumption was incorrect. In early 1980, all management recruitment efforts were headed by the Management Employment Office. Its major form of outreach was recruitment at college campuses, and few special efforts to locate minorities were made. The minority population in California was rapidly increasing, yet a very small percentage of this group attended college. This led to fears in minority communities that statistical parity could not be met. It was clear that if Pacific Bell's recruiting was limited to the college and university campuses, employment levels for minorities could not be kept at levels comparable to their laborforce representation. This was an issue for Hispanics, in particular, because their population was growing at the fastest rate. A more competitive recruitment program would have to be implemented in order to yield positive results. The human resources staff realized that some outreach was needed to augment existing efforts, and this was one impetus for change.

A second impetus for change was the realization that existing recruiting methods would be inadequate in terms of meeting the human resources needs that would arise as a result of the company's rapid growth. In 1979, company planners predicted that the largest growth in management jobs would be in the high-technology areas of engineering, marketing, and data systems. This growth would require large numbers of managers with higher levels of technical skills and formal education. Whereas the company was relying heavily on promotion to fill upper management positions, planners realized that this method could not produce the number of skilled people needed in the near future. Something extra was needed.

In recognition of these staffing needs, in June of 1980, the assistant vice president of human resources authorized the formation of a special new subunit, called the Management Recruitment District, to augment existing recruiting and affirmative action efforts. At the time, the human resources department consisted of several groups. The Management Employment group had two independent offices (and two directors): one for northern California and one for the southern part of the state. Management Employment was responsible for all processing of management candidates. It recruited candidates, tested them, and made recommendations for hire. In 1980 Management Employment was using cognitive ability tests as part of its procedure for selection. These multiple choice tests, developed by the AT&T research staff, assessed verbal, math, and problem-solving skills related to managerial performance. Another test used only with entry-level programmers tested the individual's ability to learn the programmer job by teaching a simulated computer language and then having the applicant apply it. A second human resources group, Employee Placement, provided selection services for all nonmanagement positions, including testing for upgrades and transfers. A third group relevant to recruitment and hiring was Assessment. In 1980, this group was responsible for conducting the assessment centers used to select sales candidates and managers. Other human resources groups included the Management Resource Center, which handled transfers of internal managers; Health and Human Services, which handled benefits; Labor Relations; Management Compensation; and Equal Employment Opportunity/Affirmative Action Compliance.

The new Management Recruitment District was to be an extension of Management Employment, which would engage in recruiting only. All qualified candidates would be referred to the Management Employment Office, where screening would be conducted and hiring decisions made. However, the Management Recruitment District was a statewide district, and so would conduct operations in both the North and South. The second author, Nancy Gutierrez, was chosen to head the district. Gutierrez was a longtime Pacific Bell employee. Following company tradition, she had joined the organization as an operator and over the years had been promoted up through the ranks into management. She had moved into the human resources area just prior to being named the management recruitment district director. For the previous 14 months, she had been responsible for reorganizing the employment and placement centers for nonmanagement applicants, where all testing for clerical and craft jobs was conducted. However, Gutierrez had no other experience and no formal education in human resources. She was chosen for the district position because of her extensive field experience and her administrative, organizing, and management skills.

Gutierrez began by formulating a charter for the Management Recruitment District (see Figure 4.1). Concerned that the new district not be

---

CHARTER

This district was formed to organize a competitive recruiting program with the objective of attracting high quality applicants for management and identified nonmanagement positions. Emphasis will be placed on reaching best qualified minority candidates with potential for upward mobility in Pacific Telephone. The intent will be for this district to promote continuity in the employment field by coordinating its efforts with the existing management and nonmanagement placement districts.

The underlying themes in the recruiting effort are the following:

- Creating a positive corporate image.
- Communicating the availability of varied job assignments and indiviually tailored career paths.
- Establishing productive recruiting sources.
- Publicizing the rapid changes occurring in the telecommunications industry.
- Meeting corporate affirmative action objectives.

FIGURE 4.1. Management Recruitment District charter.

perceived as window dressing, designed only to placate minorities, she sought agreement from top management on the purpose of the new district. With their support, a charter was formulated that gave the director of the Management Recruitment District freedom to design and implement a competitive recruiting program.

Although the program was initiated with a primary focus on Hispanics, the charter broadened this to a concern for all minorities. It stated that the primary objective of the district was obtaining high-quality applicants in general, regardless of their ethnic background. Unfortunately, one of the by-products of the consent decree, with its focus on preferential hiring, seemed to be the widespread feeling within the company that minority hires were not the most qualified. People tended to associate the word *minority* with "lower standards." One of the primary goals of the Management Recruitment District would be to break this association, a task that began with the wording of the charter.

DEVELOPMENT OF THE MANAGEMENT RECRUITMENT DISTRICT

Staff Selection

The first step in developing the Management Recruitment District was the selection of staff. Recruiters who could help identify candidates were needed. A high priority was putting together a district staff that reflected the diversity of those being recruited and who themselves understood and valued diversity. Internal candidates were sought, with the objective being to find staff from varied ethnic and gender backgrounds who had experience in those departments that would be the focus of the recruiting efforts. People were needed who had been effective line managers themselves—people who could serve as role models to potential applicants. Excellent communication skills were essential. Eventually seven qualified people were hired to staff the new district: a male and female Asian, a male and female black, a male and female Hispanic, and a white female engineer. Two came from employee placement, and the others came from marketing, engineering, and data systems. In their new positions, all would be second-level managers.

Staff Education

The whole district staff was new to this field of work. Although they themselves constituted a diverse group, they were not experts on diversity issues. They were not recruiting experts either. Few of the staff had a background in human resources or had worked in any human resources office. Thus, they needed to learn about both areas to be able to put together and run an effective program. So the next 3 months were devoted to staff education. The primary objective was to learn what the competition was doing: Who had an effective recruiting program, and what did it entail? Together they attended workshops and symposia across the country, and spoke with recruiters in other organizations to find out their approaches to recruiting. In addition, the staff devoted time to learning more about Pacific Bell. Upon joining the district, each staff person had a narrow perspective on the company, based mostly on his or her own department. However, to recruit effectively, greater peripheral knowledge was needed: knowledge about the entire company, about all departments and how they interrelated, and knowledge about the company's external market and the changes that were occurring. Gaining this knowledge was an important part of the education process. One critical piece of information concerned Pacific Bell's management selection process. The staff's job was to recruit applicants who could perform effectively in this process; thus, it was important that they understand exactly what it involved, especially given that many minorities had difficulty passing the tests. A human resources director responsible for assessment was asked to give a workshop for the Management Recruitment District staff. The workshop informed the Management Recruitment District staff about the testing procedures, how they were developed, what they were designed to assess, and their validity for predicting performance. Similar internal presentations helped the staff learn about the other human resources groups and how they fit together.

RECRUITMENT PROGRAM COMPONENTS

The next step was the development of the recruiting strategy that the Management Recruitment District would use to achieve its objectives. During the previous 3-month education phase, the staff had begun to evaluate existing recruitment sources for their ability to yield high-quality candidates and to develop new ideas for sources. The result was a multi-faceted strategy, which we describe next.

Internal Networking

One component of the Management Recruitment District strategy involved establishing internal networks. A major objective of these networks was to generate employee referrals. Consistent with past AT&T strategy, the Management Recruitment District staff felt that successful employees might know of other individuals who possessed the skills needed for success. The staff contacted recent management hires to communicate their staffing needs and to solicit direct referrals. They also established networks with employees who had contacts in the minority community or in targeted areas within the company, such as marketing. Besides being a source of direct referrals, these individuals could provide guidance on recruiting strategies and they could identify important community contacts.

Networking also helped to improve the company's image in minority communities. For example, because Management Recruitment District staff were able to provide Pacific Bell's Corporate Contributions group with information about which educational institutions and organizations served minority and focus group clientele, they were asked to evaluate contribution requests. This ensured that the company's contributions were effectively distributed.

Internal networking served other purposes as well. It was used as a means to determine the particular recruiting needs of various departments. Rather than just attempt to fill requisitions blindly, Management Recruitment District staff met directly with departments to identify and discuss the departments' specialized staffing needs. At the same time, they could communicate their goals, describe their programs, encourage participation, and gain commitment. The primary strategy was to focus on those departments or groups that had identified staffing needs (such as engineering) and then to gain access to these groups through existing channels. For example, the Management Recruitment District might seek to get on the agenda of regular department staff meetings, or it might accompany equal employment opportunity representatives when they held their regularly scheduled meeting with the departments. In these meetings, line managers were told about the expected changes in the diversity of the workforce, and they were educated about the importance of filling openings with ethnically diverse people. The Management Recruitment District's developmental programs, to be described below, were also promoted. In addition, employees were identified who could contribute by serving as panelists or guest speakers for external presentations. The staff especially valued those employees who could serve as role models for their target population. Thus, they sought out minority employees who had been recently hired, and who were alumni of the colleges or institutions where they did the majority of the recruiting. Employees with strong ties to their alumni groups or other professional organizations were usually eager to help with the recruiting effort. It gave them a chance to renew old ties and was seen as a way to contribute.

Advertising

Advertising was another important element of the recruiting strategy. Traditionally, the Management Employment Office had placed advertisements in newspapers and campus publications. The Management Recruitment District staff decided to expand the use of advertisements. First, they developed "focused advertising"—advertisements directed specifically toward the ethnic groups they wished to reach. Advertisements were developed internally for marketing, engineering, and the fast-track general management positions—all showing a diverse group of people employed in those jobs. These were placed in national and local publications serving minority communities. They were also placed in campus publications to stimulate interest in information sessions and interview schedules. Advertisements were placed continually, regardless of short-term openings, to show a consistent interest and the value placed on employee diversity.

In the third quarter of 1981, the Management Recruitment District contacted an advertising firm specializing in the Hispanic market to develop a media plan designed specifically to locate Hispanics for marketing positions. The result was a series of advertisements presenting personal invitations to the Hispanic professional community to join Pacific Telephone Marketing. In 1982, these advertisements received the El Cervantes media award from Hispanics in communication.

A second type of advertising used was publicity and press coverage of the activities of the Management Recruitment District. For example, a 1981 issue of *Hispanic Business* featured a story on Gutierrez and the aggressive actions her staff was taking to locate and hire Hispanics. Stories such as this gave the group exposure and projected a positive image to the public.

Educational Institutions

A third critical program component involved educational institutions. Previously, colleges and universities had been the major focus of Management Employment when it identified and prioritized schools for campus recruiting. Management Employment had limited its efforts to large, well-known private and public universities and campuses in the state. The Management Recruitment District expanded these efforts and established contacts with many smaller colleges and universities that Management Employment had considered "secondary." Many of these schools were in the California State University system, which tended to enroll higher proportions of minority students. Schools were investigated carefully before deciding whether to establish contact. Schools offering majors or degrees in targeted fields (engineering, science, and business) were preferred, as were schools with a high proportion of minorities and a rich network of student organizations. Also considered were the admission standards of each school, such as the average standardized test scores and high school grades of the freshman class. These indicated the probability of graduates being able to pass the Management Employment Office's testing procedures, which had the highest pass scores of all the Bell Operating Companies.

On the campuses selected, the Management Recruitment District participated in a variety of activities. Following the strategy of Management Employment, they established relationships with campus placement centers, conducted interviews, gave presentations on career opportunities, and participated in campus job fairs and career days.

The district staff made special efforts to establish contacts with campus minority communities. They contacted minority faculty and staff to identify issues and offer support. They also got involved with minority student groups, particularly those identified with business or technical fields. They made presentations to these groups on career opportunities and gave speeches at banquets and luncheons. They also conducted educational workshops on such basic topics as writing resumes, interviewing techniques, and job hunting. With these workshops, the staff specifically addressed minority concerns. Often, minority professional students did not have many role models in their home or community. Because of this they were less likely to pick up job skills typically acquired by modeling, for example, informal networking skills. The Management Recruitment District staff directly addressed such issues.

The staff also informed students of their career options. For example, they discovered that colleges tended to train engineering majors solely in technical skills. Such students believed their career options were limited to research and development positions. The district staff developed a video, "Engineering Your Management Future," to tell engineering majors about career paths in management.

In addition, district staff assisted campus groups in their activities. For example, at California State University in Los Angeles, they worked with the Black Support Group to set up a mentorship program. This gave students a chance to work closely with a business person who would serve as a role model. At San Jose City College, they helped faculty develop a special course for Hispanic students. The objective of this course was to raise the self-confidence of the students and motivate them to continue their education.

Although most college recruiting efforts were limited to California, contact was made with some out-of-state schools as well. Given the staff's initial concern with Hispanics, their first targets were the other southwestern states, which have large Hispanic populations. A study of educational institutions identified the two schools with the largest Hispanic enrollments: Arizona State University and the University of New Mexico. Activities there paralleled those on the California campuses: formal presentations and meetings with faculty and student groups. Later out-of-state recruiting efforts targeted other employment groups, such as MBAs, blacks, and so on.

Networking with Other Organizations

A fourth program component was networking with community-based and professional minority organizations on both local and national levels. The district staff attended meetings and job fairs, arranged for advertising in key publications, gave presentations, and assisted by giving other support where possible. For example, they helped some organizations cover printing costs, and they donated funds for special events. This kind of involvement facilitated recruitment and hiring, disseminated information about Pacific Bell, and enhanced Pacific Bell's corporate image.

In those organizations with the greatest potential for developing and producing management candidates, the staff sought leadership or advisory roles. One example of this was the National Hispanic Council for High Technology Careers. This group formed as a by-product of the National Hispanic Engineering and Science Symposium held in 1980, which the Management Recruitment District attended. During the symposium, many of the participants became aware of the alarming underrepresentation of Hispanics in the sciences and engineering. Solving this problem, they knew, would take the coordinated efforts of industry, education, government, and the community, so the Management Recruitment District hosted a 2-day conference for leaders to address these issues. The National Hispanic Council for High Technology Careers was formed during this conference to facilitate coordination, and Gutierrez was asked to serve as a chairperson. In 1981, the council held its own conference and developed action plans for junior and senior high schools as well as colleges for the promotion of science and engineering. By taking on a leadership role in the council, Gutierrez demonstrated Pacific Bell's commitment to minority employment and advancement.

DEVELOPMENT PROGRAMS

The recruitment programs described above sought to attract applicants who could be immediately hired into management positions. In contrast, the goal of the development programs was to identify promising individuals and prepare them to take future management jobs. Two major development programs were initiated: the Summer Management Program and Management Potential Identification.

Summer Management Program

The Summer Management Program was a summer internship for college students in their junior year who could be placed into first-level management positions. The program was developed to meet several objectives. First, it was an excellent way to attract highly qualified and highly sought after students. The management potential of students could be evaluated prior to their graduation, high-quality talent could be developed for employment in the telecommunications field, and long-term relationships with students could be established. Upon their graduation, student interns might be more likely to choose Pacific Bell as a place to work.

Second, the program advertised Pacific Bell's career opportunities by creating "student ambassadors." Those who had positive experiences in the program spread the word on campus. This helped increase the applicant pool.

A very structured program was developed to achieve these goals. The Management Recruitment District staff, in conjunction with department managers, identified summer jobs. These positions had to be challenging and meaningful, and they had to meet a real management need in the organization. Summer supervisors, or "bosses," were also chosen. A summer boss had to be at least a second-level manager and have a strong commitment to developing others. Bosses would coach and mentor the students during the program and evaluate them at the end of the program. All bosses participated in a half-day orientation program (conducted by the Management Recruitment District staff), which reviewed the objectives of the summer program and the elements and activities involved. The high quality of the students and the importance of the program were stressed, as were the roles and responsibilities of a summer boss.

Like supervisors, student participants were carefully selected. Applicants were actively recruited through key contacts, student groups, and other campus sources. They were screened via interviews and testing, using the same selection criteria used for direct management hires. Typically, each candidate needed to have at least a 2.8 grade point average and also needed to pass a written test. In addition, all candidates had to pass a structured interview. The interview was scored on three dimensions: negotiation skills, leadership skills, and initiative. Those recommended were then matched to the positions based on interests and skill levels.

Besides the work experience, the Summer Management Program offered a series of workshops throughout the summer. Because of the fierce competition for these students, even for summer positions, the Summer Management Program had to be more than just a summer job. Workshops included overviews of the company and industry trends, discussions with senior managers about career paths, meetings with recent college hires to hear about their experiences with the organization, and management skills training. The capstone event was a 1-day conference at which students were introduced to all top officers of the company.

At the end of the program, several evaluations were conducted. Supervisors assessed the work performance of the students, and rated them on Pacific Bell's management performance dimensions. Students evaluated the quality of the program and their own work assignment, as well as their supervisors. This gave the Management Recruitment District staff sufficient feedback to structure the next year's program.

The 1988 student feedback results provide an example of this process. Overall, results were overwhelmingly favorable. On a general question asking students to indicate their overall rating of the program, 64% of students labeled it excellent, and 36% considered it good. However, another question on the feedback survey asked students to list the strengths and weaknesses of the program. The most frequently mentioned weakness concerned the few opportunities for summer interns to meet with one another. As a result of this feedback, the 1989 program featured a new component, Summer Mixers. These were two informal social gatherings of summer interns, supervisors, and middle managers scheduled early in the summer. The purposes of the mixers were to improve interns' interpersonal ties and to give them more opportunities to network.

Management Potential Identification

During the 1980s, all external candidates for Pacific Bell's management positions needed a 4-year college degree. This requirement posed a serious problem for recruiting minorities, many of whom did not pursue higher education, or who attended 2-year junior or community colleges instead of 4-year colleges. However, for internal management candidates, there were no degree requirements. People were promoted into management based on their work history and relevant experience. The Management Potential Identification (MPI) program was developed to exploit this difference in standards. The program sought to recruit individuals with 2-year degrees or their equivalent and move them into higher-level, nonmanagement jobs (such as senior clerical or technical positions). Hopefully, within a 2- or 3-year time frame, they would be ready to be considered for management positions. Thus, the MPI program provided an alternate route for minorities to move into management. The MPI program also was intended to be an extra resource for the company to use to replenish its pool of internal candidates for promotion.

Activities at schools offering 2-year degrees paralleled those at the 4-year colleges. The district staff contacted faculty and student groups, attended job fairs, and conducted interviews. Recruiters looked for candidates with good grades in any field of study, good interpersonal skills, and some related work experience. The staff realized that the MPI program would not be easy to implement, because of the many restrictions imposed on nonmanagement positions (i.e., concerning seniority and work rules). Thus, they had a lot of work to do internally as well. The program was promoted so departments would request MPI hires, and strong managers with whom to place MPI hires were identified, because the success of the program depended heavily on each candidate's rapid development.

Other Recruiting Sources

Two final recruiting sources used by the Management Recruitment District were the military and career transitions. The military was seen as a valuable source of personnel with technical and supervisory experience. It also has a fairly large proportion of minorities. Contacts were established with nearby military bases and veterans' employment representatives to get referrals, and the district staff attended veterans' job fairs.

The career transitions activities involved trying to attract experienced individuals who were in some sort of transition—changing organizations, recently laid off, or seeking a career change. To identify these individuals, staff appeared as panelists for minority and women's organizations assisting with career changes, participated in job fairs, and joined professional organizations to facilitate career transition networking.

RESULTS OF THE RECRUITING AND
DEVELOPMENT PROGRAMS

The results for the program's first year of operation were impressive: The Management Recruitment district staff reviewed 3,649 applications and hired 179 individuals. Of those hired, 32% were female and 54% were minority. Table 4.1 shows the growth in the percentage of minorities in Pacific Bell's management over a 10-year period. As Table 4.1 shows, there was a steady increase in minority representation. The long-term strategy—that of developing networks and potential applicants—was beginning to

TABLE 4.1. Number and Percentage of Minorities in Pacific
Bell's Management Workforce

Year	Total number of managers	Number of minority managers	Percentage of minority managers
1980	28,927	5,055	17.5
1981	30,968	5,894	19.0
1982	28,435	5,934	20.9
1983	25,151	5,614	22.3
1984	21,134	4,867	23.0
1985	19,668	4,767	24.2
1986	20,657	5,036	24.4
1987	18,795	4,751	25.3
1989	17,519	4,763	27.2
1990	17,098	4,822	28.2

Note: 1980–1983 refers to Pacific Bell and Nevada Bell. 1984–
1990 refers to Pacific Bell and Directory.

pay off. Note that the growth in the percentage of minorities does not mean
a similar growth in their absolute numbers. Pacific Bell experienced
significant downsizing after the AT&T divestiture. Yet the table shows that
despite the overall decrease in the number of employees at Pacific Bell,
minority representation continued to grow.

LESSONS LEARNED ALONG THE WAY AND CHANGES MADE

During this time, the staff learned a great deal about which strategies were
more or less successful and how to improve their results. Gutierrez's
philosophy toward the program was that one should be flexible: A fluid
approach will make it easier to change things if they did not work out.
Thus, throughout the first years of the program, the staff continued to
monitor their results, identify important issues regarding recruitment, and
consider the implications for action. As a result, changes in the program's
operation were made continually.

One major change was the elimination of the Management Potential
Identification program. This program failed to live up to expectations. One
problem was the lack of support from the organization in placing MPI
hires. Departments simply failed to earmark positions for the program. In
addition, there was less flexibility in dealing with nonmanagement employees due to labor contract concerns. For example, supervisors couldn't
provide extra training for MPI hires over other employees with greater
seniority. Another problem was the failure of managers to develop the MPI

hires as needed in the appropriate time frame. The development aspect of the program had always been rather vague—there were no *specific* development plans or training experiences provided. It had been left to the individual manager to determine what each candidate needed and then to provide the training. According to one Management Recruitment district staff member, this may have been the program's downfall.

A second change was to put more emphasis on increasing the number of minority applicants. As Gutierrez stressed, "We're not here to grab at the end of the pipeline, but to develop it." For example, the district originally selected universities for campus recruiting based on the percentages of minorities enrolled. The staff soon discovered, however, that the total percentage enrolled was a poor indicator of the number of minorities who graduated. The dropout rate for minority students is very high, particularly for Hispanics. This was a problem, for in order to keep increasing the applicant pool, large numbers of minority graduates were needed. One response to this problem was to get more involved with student organizations and to take a greater role in helping these groups develop. Rather than just give financial support, more advising and counseling were offered. A second response was to develop fellowship and scholarship programs. These lessened financial burdens, increased student motivation, and provided more minority role models in academia, because some funds were directed toward those who intended to teach at the college level. Several scholarship programs were initiated in 1985. In the academic year 1988–89, grants were awarded to more than 17 universities and colleges.

Another aspect of developing the pipeline involved influencing the major fields selected by college minority students. Minority students (and women) tend to go into the social sciences/social services rather than the hard sciences, which poses a problem when an organization needs applicants with backgrounds in technical fields such as math or science. Yet by the time students are being recruited for jobs, they are typically in their junior or senior year and the damage has already been done, so to speak. Therefore, developing the pipeline means influencing the career choices of minority students. Recruiters started meeting not only with juniors and seniors, but also with freshmen, who had not yet chosen a major. They told them of industry needs, and what the future looked like for particular jobs. The message was: "If you want to be in the mainstream, if you want to be successful, you have to be in a field that will be in demand."

The Management Recruitment District's strategy and the responses described above certainly benefited Pacific Bell. It helped them to increase the size of their applicant pool and to improve the company's image so that minorities would be more interested in working there. But these actions also benefited minority students in general. The development strategies (scholarships, workshops, work with organizations, and information sessions) helped minority students to succeed, regardless of whether they ended up working at Pacific Bell. This, in fact, was the message the Management Recruitment District recruiters explicitly wanted to send: "We want you to be successful, even if you don't join the company." This philosophy lent to their credibility. As the program continued, evidence accumulated that Pacific Bell was well thought of in minority communities and respected for its commitment to diversity. The staff was asked to serve in advisory roles for numerous student groups. In addition, it received many recognitions, honors, and awards. Table 4.2 displays a partial listing of the groups that have recognized the Management Recruitment District's activities. Such awards clearly helped to improve the corporation's image.

PROBLEMS ENCOUNTERED

As we have mentioned, testing was an integral part of the management selection procedure at Pacific Bell. All testing procedures were conducted by the Management Employment Office, using procedures developed by the AT&T research staff. Minimum cutoff scores for each test had been determined through research and were used to decide whom to select and whom to reject.

Applicants recruited by the Management Recruitment district staff were treated no differently from applicants recruited through the Management Employment Office. They went through the same procedures and were judged by the same standards. The minority recruiting program was an affirmative action program focused on outreach; it was not a preferential hiring program. The staff made every effort to locate the highest-quality minority applicants and give them opportunities to apply for jobs. Whether these applicants were hired depended on whether they met the selection criteria.

TABLE 4.2. Groups that Have recognized Pacific Bell's minority recruitment activities.

Society of Hispanic Professional Engineers
National Society of Black Engineers
Asian American Business Association of University of Southern California and California State University, Northridge
Minority Engineering Program, California State University, Los Angeles
Society of Mexican American Engineers and Scientists
Office of Career Planning and Placement, California State University, Northridge
The Mexican American Engineering Society
College of Medicine, University of California, Irvine
Mexican American Alumni Association of Loyola Marymount University
National Black MBA Association Inc., San Francisco/Bay Area Chapter

The program was *not* a quota system. Nonetheless, the program had to battle quota stereotypes and negative feelings about minority hiring, which had lingered since the consent decree. Gutierrez was aware of such attitudes when she accepted the job. As she said, "I knew I had to bring in the best and the brightest. Quality in, quality up was my motto." Her way of dealing with skeptics was demonstrating the quality of minority hires, rather than arguing for their competence or attacking others for unenlightened attitudes. For example, in one instance, a department's top managers were reluctant to accept the new hires they had requested because the individuals were minorities. The managers were concerned that they wouldn't be getting "high-quality people," given that the new hires had been recruited by the Management Recruitment District. The Management Recruitment district staff responded by letting the quality of the new hires speak for itself. They brought in a group of ten candidates and introduced them to the officer of the department and the other top managers. The group was then given an exercise to work on—a real business project for the department that would demonstrate their ability to work as part of a team. The managers were asked to watch as the group attacked the project and worked through the issues. They could judge each individual's "quality" for themselves.

When the group interaction was completed, the managers were asked whom they wanted to hire. Although the department managers had listed only three openings, after this demonstration they enthusiastically requested seven people. This strategy resulted in more than the hires being placed—these new hires were welcomed into the department with open arms as being real contributors to the group. Their qualifications were not doubted; they didn't have to prove their worth. Instead, they began their jobs with mentors and the top support needed for success.

Such outcomes would not have been realized if top managers had been chided for their attitudes. The demonstration of actual skill was enough to override concerns due to ethnicity. The district's overarching goal was to position diversity to emphasize *talent*, making ethnicity transparent.

SUMMARY OF THE MANAGEMENT RECRUITMENT DISTRICT PROGRAM

This description of the Management Recruitment District's activities shows that there were several major strategies involved. These are summarized below.

1. *Cast a wide net*. The Management Recruitment District staff tried to locate as many qualified minority applicants as possible. It used a variety

of tactics to achieve this goal. As we discussed earlier, the Management Recruitment District significantly expanded the sites for college recruitment. It went specifically to campuses with large numbers of minorities, even when these were out of state. Its networking with local and national organizations also helped them find minority applicants. The description of the components of its recruiting program shows the large number of sources it considered and used.

2. *Develop the pipeline.* The Management Recruitment District staff also sought to increase the size of the future applicant pool by creating qualified applicants. We have seen that one part of the Management Recruitment District's strategy was developmental—seeking to increase and enhance the job-related skills of minority individuals. Thus, an individual who is not now a qualified applicant might become one in the future. The Management Recruitment District's educational activities with student organizations, its efforts to influence career choice, and its scholarship and fellowship programs all fall into this category. This strategy helped to build a steady supply of qualified applicants for the future.

3. *Build internal acceptance.* The Management Recruitment District built enthusiasm and commitment to its program within Pacific Bell. We have seen that the staff met directly with departments to educate them on diversity. It also personally investigated department staffing needs and then responded to them with high-quality hires. The support of top management was also critical. For example, the involvement of officers in the Summer Management Program was integral to the program's success.

4. *Directly address selection standards.* The Management Recruitment District didn't ignore the fact of testing at Pacific Bell. Instead, one of the staff's first tasks was to learn as much about it as possible. This helped it to target its recruitment efforts toward those most likely to pass the tests and also helped it prepare candidates for the selection process to increase chances of passing. For example, many candidates felt that the paper-and-pencil testing procedures in use were irrelevant, bearing little or no relation to the job in question. This belief did not enhance motivation to do well on the test. Part of the Management Recruitment District's educational efforts involved encouraging applicants to understand the value of the testing procedures and the importance of succeeding.

ORGANIZATIONAL CHANGES MADE AS A RESULT OF MANAGEMENT RECRUITMENT DISTRICT RESULTS

As this chapter shows, the Management Recruitment District's efforts were quite successful in bringing minorities into the organization. Its success stimulated other changes at Pacific Bell. Some of these changes are described below.

Efficacy Seminar

As the number of minority managers increased, so did the need for programs to serve this population. One of the first new programs introduced was the efficacy seminar. This seminar grew out of the concern of an assistant vice president who realized that the minorities in the organization needed to be developed if they were to become competitive candidates for promotion. The efficacy seminar is a 6-day, off-site, training program designed and conducted by external consultants to encourage minority professionals to take responsibility for developing their skills. The program stresses self-development, but also addresses the unique obstacles faced by minorities. It teaches participants how to set goals that take into account real-world constraints on advancement. It also gives participants a place to talk about issues like covert racism and prejudice, which are not likely to be discussed in the work setting. The seminar provides minorities with a safe place to talk about such issues.

Minority and Women's Advisory Boards

A second change that occurred partly as a response to the successful minority recruiting programs was the formation of the minority and women's advisory boards. In 1985, the executive vice president of operations concluded that, in order to develop an understanding of how increasing ethnic diversity would impact the organization, input from women and minorities was needed. So he initiated the first minority and women's board, which consisted of both management and non-management employees. The role of the board was to identify issues and concerns and provide suggestions to management about what the organization could do. Similar boards were soon initiated in other departments.

In operations, two issues emerged as particularly important to the board. First, the board felt that the organization lacked an ability to develop its managers. Few structured programs or processes were in place to help managers improve their skills. Second, there was limited promotion of minority managers beyond the lower levels. Very few minority managers reached the middle-management level or beyond. These two issues were seen as interrelated, for the lack of developmental experiences might most severely affect minorities, whose advancement would then be retarded.

A special task force was appointed to study these issues. It concluded that several conditions were important in facilitating management success: help and support from an older mentor at some time in the career; exposure to the "right" people; appropriate training and education when needed; an organizational investment in them; and a written plan for long-term goals.

Accelerated Development Process

From this research, the Accelerated Development Process (ADP) was born. ADP incorporates the elements listed above into a 2-year program for minority managers. At the core of the program is the development action plan. Each trainee works with his or her immediate supervisor to develop a plan and set long-term career goals. In addition, trainees are assigned (or may select) an executive mentor, a person who is at least two levels above the trainee. The mentor has input into the development plan and meets frequently with the trainee to discuss issues and provide feedback. The program also allows trainees to take classes or other training programs not otherwise available to them. For example, if indicated on the action plan, a trainee could attend a class normally limited to those managers at or beyond the district level.

Reorganization

A fourth organizational change was the reorganization of the human resources departments. In the mid-1980s, after the divestiture, Pacific Bell began to downsize. In the effort to streamline its operations, some of the inefficiencies due to the existence of many human resources groups became apparent. In particular, the functions performed by the Management Employment Office and the Management Recruitment District were scrutinized. There appeared to be many redundancies between these two groups, with both running college recruiting programs. In addition, the need for two separate directors of the Management Employment offices (north and south) was questioned. Eventually, a decision was made to merge these three groups into one statewide organization, which was called Management Recruiting, Employment, and Assessment. The fact that Gutierrez was asked to serve as the director of this entity was a visible indication that the activities of the Management Recruitment District had been successful and deserved to be institutionalized.

THE EVE AWARD

In 1990, Pacific Bell received the Exemplary Voluntary Efforts (EVE) award from the Department of Labor's Office of Federal Contract Compliance Programs. The EVE awards were started in 1983 as a way to honor and reward federal contractors and subcontractors who created successful voluntary affirmative action programs and demonstrated a commitment to equal employment opportunities. In presenting the award, the secretary of labor noted two of Pacific Bell's programs as particularly praiseworthy: the Efficacy Seminars and the Accelerated Development Process. Both of these programs attempt to groom minorities for upper-level management. As we have shown in this chapter, the development of both programs was stimulated by the activities of the Management Recruitment District. Without the Management Recruitment District's successful infusion of minorities into management positions, programs to enhance further minority advancement would not have been needed.

CONCLUSIONS

The Management Recruitment District's program of activities was successful in several ways. First, it was successful in terms of numbers. As a result of its outreach activities, Pacific Bell significantly increased the number of minority management hires. Second, it was successful in increasing organizational awareness of minority issues, and this awareness stimulated further changes at Pacific Bell. The success of the Management Recruitment District's programs in changing attitudes toward minorities, one of Gutierrez's original objectives, is less clear. Whereas hiring statistics were monitored, attitudes were not. Thus, identifying attitude change is difficult. Nevertheless, there seems to be some consensus among current recruiters that there is now little resistance to hiring minorities for entry-level management positions.

In many ways, the recruiting program we have described was quite traditional. For the most part, the methods and sources of recruiting used can be found in any introductory human resources management textbook. However, we believe there were three key aspects of the program that were primarily responsible for its success, and these are often not emphasized in traditional recruiting efforts.

The first is that the Management Recruitment District staff truly valued minorities and was interested in the general issue of minority opportunity and advancement; it was not interested merely in attracting minorities to Pacific Bell. Thus, the primary goal was to help minority individuals succeed. Hiring was the secondary goal. This may seem like a minor distinction, but we believe it is a crucial one. The primary goal of helping minorities succeed led to activities that didn't directly result in new hires. Workshops on job hunting, fellowships, and relationships with many organizations were initiated out of a general concern for minority development. Yet these were very useful activities in terms of meeting the secondary hiring goal. Showing a general commitment to minority success increased the Management Recruitment District's credibility in the community and improved the image of Pacific Bell as a place to work.

The second important factor contributing to the program's success was that activities were continuously evaluated and recalibrated. As the staff learned more about the factors affecting minority success, it changed its strategies to address those factors.

The third important factor was the diversity of the staff. The diversity among the staff brought informed sensitivity to the work. Staff members could check among themselves to see if an approach used with one ethnic subgroup would be equally successful with another. Also, because most staff members had college degrees, they could think back to their own college days and identify things that would have helped them (and others) succeed. The staff's diversity meant that a number of different perspectives on strategy could be utilized.

Some might argue that not every organization can copy this approach and achieve successful results. They would argue that Pacific Bell skimmed the "cream of the crop" from its applicant pool, and there's simply not enough "cream" to go around. The pool of qualified minorities is finite and insufficient to meet every organization's hiring goals.

To make such an argument misses the point of this chapter. The Management Recruitment District's strategy was not to just attract the most qualified minorities; it also involved increasing the number of qualified minorities available. This development strategy for increasing the size of the applicant pool can and should be implemented by every organization.

FUTURE CHALLENGES AND DIRECTIONS

Pacific Bell's minority recruiting programs have been in existence now for 10 years, and they have become somewhat institutionalized. For example, the relationships forged with minority organizations and schools are ongoing, guaranteeing a steady stream of applicants. Minority scholarships are an established part of the corporation's contributions. Pacific Bell has obtained national recognition for its expertise in recruitment and outreach and has been publicly rewarded numerous times, and it is likely these activities will be sustained.

Thus, the biggest challenge for the future is not recruitment. Instead, we believe it is the retention and *advancement* of minority members already in the organization. Due to the Management Recruitment District activity, many minorities and women entered management during the past 10 years. Unfortunately, most of these people are still clustered in first-level and second-level positions. Programs like the efficacy seminars and Accelerated Development Process were developed to address this problem, but their effects are unknown. The efficacy seminars were initiated in 1986, and since then more than 700 minority managers have attended. The program is so popular that there is a waiting list for those wishing to participate. Yet no data on the upward mobility of past graduates are kept. At the time of this writing, ADP is still too new to assess the results—only one class has completed the process, but there is some encouragement. Of the initial group of 75 participants, 9 have been promoted to middle management.

The issue of advancement is crucial. Minorities are initially attracted to Pacific Bell with expectations of advancement. If this is not forthcoming, and appears to be limited, many of those recruited will leave the organization. Given the projected changes in the labor force it will be harder than ever to replace these individuals. Evidence suggests that skill levels among high school and college graduates are declining. Thus, it may not be possible for an organization to replace those it loses with employees of equal quality. In addition, word of limited advancement could spread. Pacific Bell could then gain a reputation for not promoting minorities, and its ability to recruit would be seriously diminished. Thus, the issue of advancement must be addressed and resolved to ensure the continual success of the recruiting program.

This challenge faces any organization that decides to expand its recruiting efforts. When an organization moves beyond good faith and succeeds in recruiting minorities, it must be ready for the payoff. Successful recruiting will bring minorities into the organization. Yet to ensure that these individuals are retained and that they advance, additional programs and *continual* top management support are necessary.

CHAPTER 5

Assessing the Quality of the Federal Workforce: A Program to Meet Diverse Needs

MARILYN K. GOWING
SANDRA S. PAYNE

INTRODUCTION

For the past several years, the press, elected representatives in Congress, the general public, and federal government managers and supervisors have had the general impression that, on balance, the quality of applicants for federal civilian jobs has declined. Impressive public bodies, such as the National Commission on the Public Service, chaired by Paul Volcker, former chairman of the Board of Governors of the Federal Reserve System, contributed to this impression. Its report (National Commission on the Public Service, 1989) used the term *quiet crisis* to describe its conclusion that the public service was facing serious recruitment and retention problems.

Given the direct impact of the federal government on the services provided to the American people (e.g., housing, Social Security benefits, air traffic control, environmental protection), a decline in federal employee quality is an issue of considerable importance. In 1988, elected and appointed officials began to request data to evaluate the extent of this decline, but only anecdotal evidence was produced. There was a clear need for hard data, but none existed. Thus, the federal government's Quality Assessment Program was born. The objective was to gather data on the

---

[1]The thoughts expressed in this chapter are those of the authors and do not necessarily reflect the position of the U. S. Office of Personnel Management.

quality of applicants and employees in all occupations in all agencies and departments of the federal government. The data would be used to track and assess changes in the quality of the workforce in the 1990s, at the year 2000, and beyond.

Given the sheer size and geographic dispersion of the federal government, the scope of this assessment program was unparalleled, creating a real design and implementation challenge. To further add to the challenge was the diversity of interests that needed to be considered for the program to be successful. This was not a research issue that belonged only to federal bureaucrats, or even to the Washington, D. C. community. The constituency is far broader. Whether it is a rocket going into space, or a Social Security check being mailed, the quality of the workforce behind the effort is of fundamental importance either to the American public at large, or to particular subgroups. Businesses, educators, elected officials, the press, unions, professional groups, and others all have their particular concerns and perspectives on the issues and outcomes of research done in the area. There will also be multiple and diverse users of the resulting data base, for example, academic researchers and policymakers. Each group has different needs, and, often, different expectations about what the results of the research will be. For the program to be successful, all of these different perspectives and needs had to be considered and met to the degree possible. Thus, what would be considered a complex undertaking under any circumstances, became even more so.

Viewed in this context, the design and implementation of this program become a case of interest to other human resources management professionals, whether in the public or private sector. The processes used to respond to the needs of diverse groups and to gain consensus may be applied in many other situations. The solutions to logistical difficulties may also be of use in any large data collection effort, and will be of particular interest to large corporations that have widely dispersed offices nationwide. This case is therefore presented as a discussion of the factors contributing to the complexity of the program, including the size and scope of the federal government as an employer, the diversity of and interactions among the various stakeholders, the methods used to respond to this diversity, and the specific events that shaped the program. We then present the multiple phases of the program, including the results to date, and a summary of the lessons learned.

The Federal Government Workforce

The federal workforce includes nearly 2.2 million civilian employees in over 900 occupations (from accountant to zoologist) in over 50 agencies and departments. These organizations vary greatly in size and mission. Nearly half of the federal workforce is employed by Defense departments. Other large departments include Agriculture, Health and Human Services, Justice, Treasury, and Veterans Affairs.

The federal government is the largest employer in the United States, hiring more than 300,000 people in most years, and always several hundred each day to replace those lost through attrition. Almost 98% of federal employees work in the executive branch of the government (i.e., for the president), with the remainder in the legislative (congressional) and judicial (court) branches.

Although Washington, D.C., is the center of the federal government, only 14% of the workforce is located there. Government employees work in all 50 states; 6% are employed overseas. Federal employees also work in a variety of ways: 93% work full time; the remainder work part time, or on intermittent schedules.

Federal employees have a diverse background. In 1990, 57% were men; 27.4% were minority group members (16.7% black, 5.4% Hispanic, 3.5% Asian/Pacific Islander, 1.8% Native American); 7% had disabilities; their average age was 42.3 years old; 35% had college degrees.

The broad diversity of the federal workforce just described is only beginning. Projections are that this diversity will continue to grow, as is happening in the rest of the U.S. laborforce.

The publication of *Workforce 2000* (Johnston & Packer, 1987) captured the attention of the country with its dramatic predictions regarding the future nature of the national workforce. The projections of *Civil Service 2000* (Hudson Institute, 1988), a parallel document, were equally startling:

> The national decline in the numbers of new young workers and the slower growth of women entering the workforce promises to make hiring and retention much more competitive in the years ahead.... Federal employers in locally tight or expensive labor markets must be able to compete for workers on a par with private employers if they are to continue to fulfill their responsibilities.... The Federal government will become, like the rest of society, increasingly an employer of women. While seniority and increasing education will substantially reduce concerns over equal pay by the year 2000, it will not alleviate pressures for benefits, leave time, day care, and other policy changes related to women's dual roles as breadwinners and family managers ... the continuing aging of the Federal workforce that will result as large numbers of baby boomers move toward retirement presents a major challenge to Federal managers seeking to respond to change. Toward the end of the century, the median age of Federal workers is likely to reach an all-time high. (p. 27)

The prospect of intense competition for scarce workers led the federal government to create new programs to attract, hire, and retain the increasingly diverse workforce. The introduction of these programs underscored the importance of developing hard data for their evaluation. Federal managers and executives need real data about workforce quality changes in order to make informed decisions about the effectiveness of these programs. This is particularly important given the scarcity of resources during times of shrinking budgets and the need to make every dollar count.

Federal Personnel Responsibilities

The U. S. Office of Personnel Management (OPM), which is the federal government's central personnel agency, was the logical choice to create the needed data base. OPM has data collection facilities, systems, and procedures in place, as well as a staff of personnel research psychologists. The program could not be designed or implemented, however, without coordination with the other federal agencies that have a role in the personnel process.

Personnel responsibilities in the federal government are handled in a variety of ways. Individual departments and agencies have personnel offices to recruit, hire, and manage their workforces. However, all personnel activity is operated under a government-wide merit system administered by OPM. OPM provides policy direction, advice and assistance, and oversight of agency personnel activities. OPM also has direct responsibility for recruiting and examining for the many occupations that are found across agencies, such as clerks and computer specialists. Created by Presidential Executive Order 12107, OPM received many of the functions of the former Civil Service Commission. OPM duties and authorities are specified in the Civil Service Reform Act of 1978 (5 U. S. C. 1101). Those duties are summarized as follows:

> The Office of Personnel Management administers a merit system for Federal employment that includes recruiting, examining, training, and promoting people on the basis of their knowledge and skills, regardless of their race, religion, sex, political influence, or other nonmerit factors. The Office's role is to ensure that the Federal Government provides an array of personnel services to applicants and employees. Through a range of programs designed to develop and encourage the effectiveness of the Government employee, the Office supports Government program managers in their personnel management responsibilities and provides benefits to employees and to retired employees and their survivors. (National Archives and Records Administration, 1990, p. 676)

Oversight of personnel activities, including recruitment and selection, is conducted by two other agencies also, one in the executive branch, and one in the legislative branch. The Merit Systems Protection Board (MSPB) was also created by the Civil Service Reform Act of 1978, receiving the functions of the Civil Service Commission not assigned to OPM. MSPB protects the integrity of the federal merit system by hearing and adjudicating appeals by federal employees and by reviewing federal personnel regulations. It also conducts special studies and employee surveys on federal personnel issues. MSPB regularly issues reports on the recruitment, selection, and retention of federal employees, and published one of the earliest reports of declining quality in the federal service. (This report is discussed in the next section of this chapter.) Because of the importance of this issue, MSPB has initiated a series of special studies on the quality of the federal workforce.

The General Accounting Office (GAO) is an arm of the legislative branch. It performs evaluations of government programs and activities at the request of individual congressional members and committees. It also initiates some studies on its own, to meet legislative requirements, or to provide supplemental information. The GAO developed a strong and early interest in the quality of the federal workforce, and has created a special group to prepare studies and issue reports in this area.

Quality Assessment Program Beginnings

The first systematic report of the perceptions of declining quality was issued by MSPB in 1986. Every 4 years, MSPB surveys government managers and employees for their opinions and experiences on a variety of relevant issues. The 1986 Merit Principles Survey was administered to a sample of 21,620 employees throughout the government, with a response rate of 77%. The survey included questions on their general impression of applicant quality. The survey respondents felt that the quality of applicants for federal government jobs had declined slightly over the previous 4 years for all types of jobs, and most clearly for clerical jobs.

In August 1986, Congressman William D. Ford requested the GAO to determine if hard data were available, and if not, to evaluate the feasibility of collecting such data, to support or refute the perceptions of declining federal workforce quality. Two years later, the GAO (U.S. Government Accounting Office, 1988) concluded that

> only a few aspects of its definition of quality could be measured from existing records. Automated files contain a few indicators pertinent to workforce quality, chiefly on education. These are, however, not up to

date. Apart from scattered surveys of small groups, no data exist that could shed light on other parts of the definition of quality such as attitudes, values and motivation or the match of capabilities to the needs of the job. Some relevant information might be found in official personnel files, but would be costly to retrieve. There appear to be significant barriers to expanding agency personnel data systems to add routine collection and storage of additional data. (pp. 3-4)

The GAO report went on to recommend that "new data be gathered chiefly by surveying samples of employees in selected occupations . . . [to] permit generalized answers to many of the major questions that have been raised about quality . . . ." (p. 3).

Thus, the GAO report underscored the need for building a data base to answer fundamental questions about workforce quality, instead of continuing to rely on anecdotal/survey data. The GAO proposed collecting quality indicators (i.e., information such as education, grades, experience) and job performance data for samples of employees in a selected group of occupations, repeating the studies at 4-year intervals for trend analyses. The report also recognized that the definition of quality was a critical step in any measurement process and offered a model of individual quality measurement.

The publication of the GAO's report coincided with the birth of OPM's Quality Assessment Program. OPM had met with the GAO staff several times as their report was developed, and OPM was confident that a broad program of data collection was feasible. OPM's program was planned to include the GAO's recommended approach of using employee samples to collect quality data, but went several steps further. First, OPM planned to collect data from applicants too; second, OPM planned to cover all white collar occupations (400+). OPM believed that the problems seen by the GAO for such broad data collection could be overcome by taking advantage of the multiple data collection systems and research staff available for OPM's other programmatic responsibilities. Consequently, in June 1988, the program was officially begun.

Responsibility for the design, implementation, and evaluation of the Quality Assessment Program was given to OPM's Office of Personnel Research and Development (PRD). The PRD staff are primarily industrial/organizational (I/O) psychologists, who are responsible for the research and development for improved selection and management of federal employees. The PRD staff prepares the tests used for entry into many federal occupations, and regularly conducts government-wide test validation projects, involving major data collection from federal applicants and employees, across a variety of occupations and agencies. In fact, the first source of data considered for answering questions about changes in workforce quality was the accumulated research data on test scores. However, because the test score data in each study are from different (new) tests, it is not possible to make direct comparisons of scores. Also, because studies are done only when new tests are introduced, the data are sporadic rather than systematic. Thus, it was quickly apparent that these studies, although useful sources of information, would not meet the long-range needs of the Quality Assessment Program. Once this was determined, the PRD staff moved quickly to design and implement a series of studies that would specifically collect and evaluate data on the quality of the federal workforce.

Initial Program Design

From the beginning, OPM recognized the importance of meeting the needs of the many and diverse constituencies interested in the Quality Assessment Program. As a first step, in November 1988, OPM convened a meeting of key agency human resources management officials, union leaders, congressional staff, and professional interest groups to solicit suggestions and obtain support for the OPM program. Representatives from MSPB and the GAO were included. At this meeting, OPM presented the initial framework for the Quality Assessment Program, and the general consensus was that the program should begin.

The initial framework for OPM's program included five parts: (1) building a data base of information from job applicants to support a series of longitudinal studies; (2) conducting studies of incumbent employees in critical occupations to begin answering questions about quality while the longitudinal data base matured; (3) collecting quality data from the private sector to use for benchmark comparisons; (4) planning for the use of quality study data in the evaluation of human resources management programs; and (5) fostering the exchange of information among federal researchers and managers.

THE MODEL OF WORKFORCE QUALITY

Ideally, the first step in a program of this scope and importance would have been to define a model of quality to underpin the research program. However, given the total absence of quality data and the strong interest of management in beginning the Quality Assessment Program quickly, the PRD staff began data collection with only a tentative model in place. This initial data collection is decribed in the next section, on program implementation. However, before beginning those descriptions, we will discuss the evolution of the model OPM has now adopted for the Quality Assessment Program, and the process used to ensure that the model is responsive to the concerns of the various interested constituent groups.

Initial Formulation

Several events shaped the Model of Workforce Quality that is used in the Quality Assessment Program. Early discussions among OPM researchers led to the recognition that "quality" is a complex, multidimensional concept that would lead to new measurement challenges. In February 1989, the senior author was chosen to head PRD. She suggested that the program model be expanded from its initial focus on individual assessment, and proposed that it play off of the traditional I/O models for understanding behavior in work settings.

Input from Interested Constituencies

Further development of the model took place as the result of direct feedback on the Quality Assessment Program from representatives of the interested constituent groups. In May 1989, OPM and MSPB took the unusual step of jointly sponsoring an invitational meeting of public and private sector leaders to gain a broad perspective on the issues surrounding workforce quality assessment. A key recommendation of the participants was to expand the assessment of workforce quality to include the measurement of the quality of service provided to the public. They also emphasized the impact of the work situation on the provision of this service. This focus fit nicely with the expanded approach to quality assessment being developed by OPM.

Because of the continued, intense public scrutiny of the Quality Assessment Program and the usefulness of the suggestions received at the two public meetings held in 1988 and early 1989, OPM and MSPB established a joint national Advisory Committee on Federal Workforce Quality Assessment. Selected to represent the primary constituencies, the advisory committee includes 23 members, who represent the private sector, government agencies, congressional agencies (the GAO), academia (I/O psychologists, economists, public administrators), unions, and professional human resources management associations.

The committee's functions are to:

1. Review the various workforce quality assessment efforts under way or contemplated within the federal government; advise on the

adequacy of those efforts; suggest alternative approaches or additional initiatives; and provide links between federal assessment efforts and those outside the government.

2. Review the data gathered as a result of assessment efforts and advise on the interpretation of those data.
3. Advise on strategies or interventions in response to the end results of workforce quality assessment efforts, especially where problems are identified or where a need for workforce quality improvement activities is found.

The advisory committee was convened specifically as a strategy to ensure that the diverse constituencies for the Quality Assessment Program would be heard at an early stage. This strategy can be effectively applied in any project that must satisfy diverse needs, even those that are much smaller in scope than the case described in this chapter. For example, when an organization designs and implements a new policy that will affect employees, a committee of employees, managers, union representatives, and staff from the personnel office can be established. To be effective, this committee should be chosen to represent all affected interests, and should also be drawn to represent the constituencies in broader terms of diversity, for example, by sex, race, educational background, occupation, and geographic location.

The advisory committee played an important role in the development of the Model of Workforce Quality finally adopted by OPM for use in the Quality Assessment Program. At its first meeting, early in 1990, it strongly affirmed the need to assess situational factors and organizational outcomes in addition to individual characteristics. In later meetings, after the model had been adopted by OPM, it worked in subcommittees to focus on the measurement of the different variables in the specific parts of the model. The subcommittee reports will provide guidance to OPM and MSPB regarding refinement of current quality measures or the addition of new measures.

Model of Workforce Quality Currently in Use

Using all of this information, Dr. David Dye, an I/O psychologist on the PRD staff, prepared a model that integrated what was known about how individual characteristics and organizational conditions relate to performance, turnover, and provision of service. Based on his report (Dye, 1990), OPM adopted the Model of Workforce Quality as shown in Figure 5.1.

This model presents workforce quality as an equation. It demonstrates that workforce quality is not easily defined or simply measured. Quality

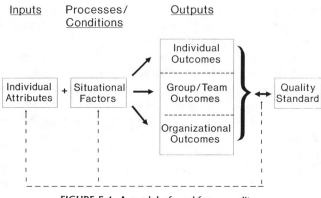

FIGURE 5.1. A model of workforce quality.

can be assessed by focusing on any part of the equation—on individual characteristics (shown as the input side of the equation); on the situation or organization in which the individual is working (shown in the process part of the equation); or on the quality of performance—individual, team, or organizational (shown as the outcome side of the equation).

Individual characteristics are those fixed and dynamic qualities that individuals bring to the organization or develop while within the organization. Examples are education level and grades, specific skills and abilities, job experience, and interests. Many of these characteristics are very stable; others are more likely to change over time.

Situational factors are the circumstances surrounding the existing work situation that can affect quality. They include organizational policies, practices, and conditions, such as culture and climate, strategic objectives, availability of resources, work environment, and skill requirements for performing the work.

Individual outcomes refer to the behaviors and attitudes of particular employees. They include job performance, training success, job progression, awards and commendations, job satisfaction, and job turnover. Team outcomes refer to behaviors and attitudes at the level of the work group. Examples are awards given to work units and employee survey results. Organizational outcomes refer to output and effectiveness at the level of the organization. Examples include quality and quantity of delivered products and services, surveys of customer satisfaction, and productivity indices.

The model uses arrows to illustrate the natural progression from individual input plus the impact of the processes and conditions present in the work situation to the three levels of outputs that result. It also introduces the concept of a Quality Standard. Any assessment of quality must take place against benchmarks. These benchmarks can be absolute standards, such as the minimum level of skill needed to perform a job, or they can be referential, such as comparisons against standards of performance set in previous years or against standards set by customer feedback. Finally, the model includes feedback loops, designed to illustrate the continual assessment of each of the variables in the model, and the feedback of information in order to improve the quality present in each variable.

IMPLEMENTATION OF THE QUALITY ASSESSMENT PROGRAM

The Quality Assessment Program began as a five-part program, but expanded quickly to include seven parts. In addition to the five original parts, which were described earlier, are the following program areas: (1) an assessment of workplace literacy; and (2) development of new selection tools, called Quality Profiles, based on Quality Assessment Program data. Given the dynamic nature of the issue, and the wide variety of interests the program is designed to serve, it will not be surprising if it continues to grow.

Part 1. Data Base and Longitudinal Studies

It would not be possible to track and assess changes in the quality of the federal workforce over time without the systematic collection of uniform data. The OPM Quality Assessment Program incorporates the collection of such data into the job application and selection process. Applicants are asked questions about their previous education and experience, skills, interest in public employment, and other background information. In most cases, the questions are contained in a short, machine-scannable form designed for the Quality Assessment Program. The form is given to job applicants with other application materials. In some cases, the questions have been incorporated into the automated forms used to apply for particular federal jobs. Completion of the questions is voluntary, and applicants are assured that their responses are not included in their job application and examination process. Forms are processed at OPM's central automation facility in Macon, Georgia, and the data are accumulated into data files organized by occupational groups. When a written test is used in the selection process for the occupation, the applicant's test scores are added to this data base.

The questions included in the applicant forms came from two sources. OPM researchers used the list of individual characteristics proposed by the GAO in 1988 as possible "indicators" of workforce quality. This list was supplemented by our own experience with collection of background data as part of OPM examination development studies. As studies are conducted using the data, the quality indicators will be reevaluated, and questions may be added and changed over time. However, a core of questions will remain the same, to provide the longitudinal data base.

Recently, OPM completed the first revision of the basic data collection form. New questions were added, to better reflect the expanded Model of Workforce Quality, and the instructions were improved to make it more "user friendly." The new form was introduced in August 1991.

Systematic data about the quality of the applicants for government jobs were first collected in May 1989. Because of the scope of the needed data base—covering applicants and employees in more than 400 white-collar occupations in over 50 federal agencies—researchers and OPM management recognized that this ambitious undertaking had to be phased in over time. The first quality applicant data were collected on a limited number of occupations to test the feasibility of the forms and the procedures used. The first occupations covered included more than 60 clerical job titles, computer specialists, and several administrative jobs (e.g., contract specialist). In 1990 and 1991, the occupational coverage expanded greatly and now includes nearly 200 occupations.

The data base now includes nearly 4 million pieces of information, on more than 160,000 job applicants. Baseline reports have been prepared for internal use on the 1989 applicants. As the data base continues to grow, trend reports will be prepared, comparing the quality of applicants for each occupational group over time. These trend reports will be available to the public. We plan to prepare reports for at least two occupational groups each year, beginning in 1992.

In the fall of 1991, OPM began the first longitudinal study, using the clerical occupational group. Automated personnel records from 1990 and 1991 will be searched for matches with the 1989 applicant group. Data for the applicant group will be compared against the data for those hired. Data for 1989 hires who have already left government employment will also be compared. These comparisons will tell us how successful we have been at hiring and retaining the best qualified of our applicants. This report will be completed in 1992. We plan to do at least one trend study each year.

Part 2. Incumbent Studies

Purpose

Because of the need to answer questions about quality now, without waiting for the longitudinal data base to mature, OPM is conducting a series of studies of incumbent employees. The focus of the studies is on occupations that have been identified as having potential quality problems because of high turnover, reported difficulties in recruiting, evidence of large disparities in public and private sector pay, or rapid technological changes that may increase the level of skills required to perform the work. In 1990, OPM conducted studies of scientists, engineers, and computer specialists. In 1991, studies began on economists and statisticians. OPM focused on these occupations for initial studies because of their critical importance to federal government activities, and well-documented difficulties in recruiting and retention. Future studies will focus on lower-level jobs, such as clerical and technical occupations, which demographic projections have identified as potential problem areas. We expect to conduct incumbent studies in two different occupations each year.

Design

The incumbent studies are designed to obtain data describing the quality, characteristics, and attitudes of the workforce in the specific occupation studied. In each study, incumbent employees are given machine-scannable questionnaires covering their educational and work histories. Included are questions similar to those used in the applicant questionnaires as quality "indicators," as well as questions tailored to the occupation under study. Examples of general items are major field of study, grade point averages (GPAs), awards received, special training, and length of directly related experience. Examples of tailored questions, as used in the scientist and engineer study, are the number of articles published in professional journals and the number of patents acquired. The questionnaires also include questions on the incumbents' perceptions of quality among their peers (and, in the case of incumbents who are supervisors, their perceptions of the quality of their subordinates). Finally, some questions are included that ask the incumbents for opinions on organizational factors that affect their ability to produce high-quality work, such as the amount of red tape, and support for training.

The incumbent studies also collect a second measure of quality, this one assessing employee job performance. The employees' supervisors are asked to fill out special performance appraisal forms to serve as a direct measure of quality. In addition to these research performance ratings, the annual performance ratings that are given for operational use are also collected from central personnel records.

The incumbent studies also provide some information on changes in quality over time by comparing data from employees who have different decades of entry into federal service (e.g., those entering in the 1950s, the

1960s, and so on). Of course, this method of analysis is not sufficient for definitive conclusions regarding the changes in quality over time, because the data base does not include those employees who left the government.

The incumbent studies will contribute to our understanding of the usefulness of individual characteristics as quality indicators. By comparing the answers to the background questions to the research performance ratings that are collected from supervisors, we can learn which questions are good indicators of quality job performance. (We have used research performance appraisals rather than operational performance ratings to counteract the frequent problems documented in the I/O literature when performance ratings are used as criteria. Also, an unexpected benefit of the Quality Assessment Program has been the creation of a data base of both research and operational performance appraisals on a large number of people. PRD researchers are using this data base to develop a better understanding of performance appraisal as a criterion measure.)

For each occupational group, the incumbent study will be repeated over time, probably at 5-year intervals. Comparison of the longitudinal results will again provide direct data for assessing change in the quality of the workforce.

Initial Programmatic Results

OPM has completed the first studies of incumbents, in the scientist/engineer and computer specialist occupations. Both research samples were randomly drawn and stratified to represent employees at all grade levels, from a cross section of government agencies, nationwide. The scientist/engineer study sampled 14,490 employees in 37 non-Defense agencies (the Department of Defense is currently conducting a separate study of their scientists and engineers, which is still under way). The final study sample was 8,637, a 60% return rate. The computer specialist study sampled 6,700 employees from 41 agencies, with 4,007 in the final sample (again, a return rate of 60%).

One interesting result is that these studies indicate that some of the actions taken by the federal government to respond to difficulties in recruitment and retention of scientists and engineers appear to have been effective. The data collected and used in the cohort comparisons do not show the drop in quality that some people had predicted, at least for the indicators studied. In most cases, the data collected show either stability or increases in the quality indicators when the samples are analyzed by year of entry. For example, among scientists and engineers, GPA, class standing, and highest degree obtained have not been lower in recent years in comparison with earlier years; nor have such indicators as number of publications and patents.

In the case of the computer specialist cohort analyses, some increases are noted in the quality indicators. For example, there is a 38% increase in undergraduate degrees for computer specialists from 1950 to 1990, and a small, steady increase in average GPA from 1970 to 1990. There is also a significant increase in the number of employees receiving work-related awards (82% in recent years, compared to 44% in prior years). These results are likely due to the fact that the computer specialist occupation was an emerging field in the 1960s and early 1970s, however, and few new job entrants were as well educated as those entering the field today.

Results for performance ratings were mixed across the studies. Average performance ratings given by the supervisors to scientists and engineers did not decrease; in the computer specialist study, operational ratings and one type of research rating decreased, whereas the other research rating stayed the same.

The perceptions of quality reported by the study participants differ from the quality indicator data. In each case, the managers included in the study perceived the quality of new recruits in the 1980s to be lower than for the 1970s. They also perceived the quality of those who left the government in the 1980s to be higher than the quality of those who left in the 1970s.

Interpreting the Results

Of course, these data must be interpreted with caution, as the studies only include employees who have remained on the job. It may be that employees who left were of higher quality, as the supervisors perceive.

The quality indicator data in these studies also somewhat contrast the data reported by MSPB (U.S. Merit Systems Protection Board, 1990). The 16,000 MSPB survey respondents reported that the quality of employees who joined their work units during the past 4 years was somewhat lower than the quality of those who left the government. Moreover, for vacancies at all levels, supervisors rated the quality of applicants less favorably than did supervisors in its earlier survey (U.S. Merit Systems Protection Board, 1986).

The contrast between hard data and managerial perceptions is one of the possible pitfalls of a research program of this type. When expectations have been clearly established and data do not conform, the researchers must be very clear about the strength of the data. In these studies, the data can be viewed only as preliminary; the next step is to track a particular set of incumbents over time, and compare the quality characteristics of those who actually leave with those who stay. It is also very important for the research staff to ensure that all constraints on the data collection are presented, before erroneous conclusions are drawn. The long-term success of the research program will depend both on the ability of management to accept and understand the research findings, and on the ability of the researchers to present the findings accurately and completely.

Part 3. Private Sector Comparison Data

An important part of the Quality Assessment Program is the collection of comparison data on quality of applicants and employees in the private sector. It will be difficult to interpret properly any quality changes discovered in the studies conducted as part of the program without these comparisons. For example, a study could find that quality has declined over a certain period of time. If, however, quality has also declined in the private sector, a different set of conclusions and recommendations for action would be drawn than would be the case if quality in the private sector went up in the same period of time.

A pilot study of direct private sector data collection is currently under way. Ronald C. Pilenzo, a member of the advisory committee, and president of the Society for Human Resources Management in 1990, wrote personally to executives in several major private sector firms noted for their excellence in products and service, asking them to consider participation in this project. His letter described the challenge facing the federal workforce and the nation, and underscored the importance of this issue to corporate executives. Four major private sector companies—Federal Express, Walt Disney World, Textron, and TRW—have indicated their willingness to participate in this trial data collection effort. The agreement of these impressive corporations was in large part due to Pilenzo's support, but also reflects the recognition by the executives of those companies of the importance of good government and the role business could play in reaching that goal.

Each of these companies has a strong reputation for high quality, and their participation should provide a real marker for comparison of government quality. The plans call for a sample of their employees in computer specialist occupations to complete the same questionnaires as in the federal incumbent studies. If the effort is successful, direct data collection will be expanded to other occupations, and to applicants as well as employees.

Part 4. Program Evaluations

The data collected in the Quality Assessment Program will be useful in answering the general questions about changes in quality that are facing the federal government as an employer. However, the data are also useful for direct evaluations of human resources management programs being introduced to meet the changing needs of a more diverse workforce. The quality studies will provide data on the quality of the workforce immediately prior to and following the implementation of each new program to see whether the intervention produced the desired change in quality.

For example, Congress recently passed legislation to increase pay for certain occupations and geographic areas in order to address serious recruitment difficulties. Our data will tell if the pay changes are working. The data we are collecting now, which is before the pay reform, will serve as the baseline. The data collected after the pay reform will provide the change information. By comparing the quality of applicants and hires before and after, OPM can determine if quality improved, remained the same, or declined. As with the other quality studies, the data will need to be interpreted in comparison with changes that take place at the same time in the private sector. For example, the job market for new college graduates in 1991 is markedly different from the job market even 1 year ago. With a tighter job market, there are increased numbers of applicants for all jobs, including federal jobs. This could result in higher quality, but the impact may be only temporary. When the change data are analyzed, all such factors must be carefully taken into account.

Another application of the Quality Assessment Program data in program evaluation is for the innovative Federal Flexible Workplace Pilot Project. Under "Flexiplace," employees can work at home, or at other alternate work locations. Flexiplace arrangements could serve to make the government a more attractive employer to high-quality individuals, including the disabled. The federal government began an 18-month study of Flexiplace in 1990, and 12 agencies are currently participating. In this pilot study, data will be collected and analyzed pertaining to productivity, performance, satisfaction, cost, and other factors associated with working at remote sites. A sample of nearly 1,000 employees is expected, across the participating federal agencies. A wide variety of data will be collected from the study participants and compared against a similar group of employees who are not in the Flexiplace pilot. Among the instruments will be measures of the quality of service provided by the organization and of individual performance. The instruments will be used with both groups, before and after the pilot project begins, and at intervals during the project. Also, whenever there are quality study data for occupations that are included in large numbers in the Flexiplace pilot project, comparisons of employee quality will be drawn. The comparisons will be used to evaluate the impact of the Flexiplace program on workforce quality.

In addition to use by OPM researchers, some agencies and departments have also indicated an interest in receiving a breakdown of the government-wide quality data for their own organizations. They intend to evaluate specific management practices, and revise those practices that do not result in the retention of their top performers.

Part 5. Information Exchange

OPM recognized the need for both collecting and disseminating information on quality assessment initiatives as being integral to the usefulness of the program. As a first activity, OPM established a network of researchers with an interest in workforce quality. This network has over 450 names and is continually growing. Although the majority of the members are federal researchers and managers, the network is open to the state and local government and private sectors as well. As reports in the Quality Assessment Program are completed, they are announced to the network. In addition, OPM staff collect information from the federal participants each year and prepare an annual report of agency activities.

Part 6. Workplace Literacy Assessment

One aspect of individual workforce quality is workplace literacy. This subject is receiving serious attention from the Departments of Education and Labor. They are sponsoring an assessment of basic skills literacy among American adults, with the purpose of identifying the education and training needs of the national workforce. The federal government is also interested in workplace literacy, particularly as federal jobs are becoming more complex, increasing the need for basic verbal and mathematical skills.

To measure the basic literacy skills of the federal workforce, OPM is developing a multiple-choice, machine-scored test. The test will be introduced in 1992 to assess literacy levels of a sample of federal employees in various grade levels and occupations nationwide and will be readministered in future years to assess trends. This basic skills test is an additional measure of the quality of individual attributes in the Model of Workforce Quality.

The test will also serve as the core of a diagnostic battery that will be used to plan training for employees based on their individual needs. Rapid technological change and a smaller entry-level workforce will make it important for employers to retrain their existing workforce to meet new organizational needs. Training, which can be designed at the most appropriate level of the trainees and which develops all workers to their fullest potential, will be a necessity. The diagnostic test battery will have a major role in this effort.

Part 7. Quality Profiles

A very recent addition to the Quality Assessment Program has been the direct use of the studies to develop a new selection tool, the "Quality Profile." Leonard Klein, OPM's associate director for career entry, suggested this further expansion of the program after seeing our initial study reports. His idea was that PRD could use quality study data to identify the indicators that would help us to select applicants who would both perform well on the job and stay with the organization for a certain period of time (e.g., 3 years). These indicators would then be used as the basis for objectively scored, self-report questionnaires, to be completed by job applicants. PRD staff have designed Quality Profiles for nine occupations, using data collected from various quality studies, and will continue to develop new Quality Profiles in the future.

Future Quality Assessment Activities

The development of the Model of Workforce Quality emphasized the need for the design of additional quality measurement tools to assess the other variables in the model. One new measure OPM is preparing will be used to assess situational variables. OPM's Federal Quality Institute (FQI) has created a list of organizational criteria that describe the extent of commitment to "Total Quality Management" in an organization. From these criteria, OPM researchers developed a "Total Quality Survey" to assess the presence of those same criteria in an organization (i.e., Top Management Leadership and Support; Strategic Planning; Focus on the Customer; Employee Training and Recognition; Employee Empowerment and Teamwork; Measurement and Analysis; Quality Assurance; and Quality and Productivity Results). This questionnaire will be available for agency use, and questions from it will also be included in the incumbent studies that OPM is conducting for specific occupations.

Other measures will probably be suggested by the advisory committee when the subcommittees complete their review of the Model of Workforce Quality. Preliminary indications are that measures of service quality and team performance will be needed. PRD staff will incorporate new suggestions into their work plans for 1992.

KEY LESSONS LEARNED

Our involvement in this major federal government-wide program has highlighted a number of key lessons that should guide others managing programs of similar scope and complexity. These lessons learned are sum-marized below.

• *Gain the support of top management in your organization and in other organizations affected by the program to ensure commitment of adequate per-sonnel and monetary resources.* The Quality Assessment Program received a major boost in 1989 with the arrival of OPM Director Constance Berry Newman. She incorporated the quality studies into President George Bush's management-by-objectives (MBO) system, which gave the pro-gram higher priority for resources and a basis for commitment by agency leaders throughout the government. Newman also expanded the scope of the program from the provision of *data* to the provision of *solutions.* The MBO goal is to monitor whether the government is attracting and retain-ing top performers and, if not, to devise solutions to reverse the loss of talent.

• *Involve others in problem definition, program implementation, and evalua-tion.* The inclusion of representatives from the public and private sectors, the unions, the professional associations, academia, and others at public meetings and on the national Advisory Committee on Federal Workforce Quality Assessment resulted in the expansion of the definition of quality. The advisory committee was particularly supportive of expanding the model to include situational measures and measures of team and organiza-tional outcomes, including products and services. The advisory committee also recommended that, although centralized measurement of individual attributes would work across the federal government, the measurement of the quality of products and services should be decentralized to specific agencies and departments. Further, the advisory committee suggested that the organizational outcome variables should include both customer sur-veys of perceived satisfaction with the products and services and other measures of organizational productivity. The clear lesson here is that our definition of quality will be evolving for some time based upon vital information from others.

• *Do not underestimate the problems in communicating the importance of a given program to the operational level, even if the program has high visibility and top management commitment.* While the importance of the Quality Assess-ment Program was clearly identified and communicated from the top of the federal government, we found some difficulties in getting this message across to the lower operational levels of the organizations responsible for the actual data collection (i.e., the distribution of the data collection forms to the applicants for federal government jobs). Because of the distributed nature of the federal hiring process, quality data must be collected from many sources, including OPM's regional examining offices and federal agency personnel offices. Initial instructions for data collection were sent out through written Operations Letters and Bulletins, a routine method of communication used across the federal government. During the first year, the quality of the data received varied considerably across sources, with some of the staff assigned responsiblity for direct data collection, apparently not understanding the instructions, or perhaps not giving sufficient importance to the task.

To rectify this problem in communication, we asked each regional director of OPM to appoint specific Regional Quality Contacts in the examining offices. These contacts will be our representatives in ensuring that the quality data are collected from applicants applying through OPM. Further, these quality contacts have responsibility for briefing the operating offices of agencies and departments within their geographical areas to emphasize the importance of collecting the data from applicants for the quality program. We have also established an Agency Working Group to advise us on the best procedures for requesting and monitoring data collection, and for marketing the Quality Assessment Program. To assist in these activities, we have prepared posters and slide shows on programmatic objectives.

• *Be prepared to deal with management reactions to the inconsistencies between anecdotal data and empirical data.* Preliminary results that the quality of the employees in two occupational categories—computer specialist and scientist/engineer—is not declining are encouraging. However, it is recognized that many factors led to these results, and they must be further studied in the context of the longitudinal research. Further, management must always be given all of the information needed to interpret the results correctly. For example, although the studies are finding little support for a nationwide decline in quality, this may not be true for specific geographical areas or for certain grade levels.

• *Be prepared for great change in programmatic direction, and remind team members of these possibilities.* The Quality Assessment Program has expanded dramatically into new and unanticipated directions. These changes were partially due to the suggestions from the advisory groups and from management, but were also due to review of the early study results and our own urging. Key examples were the expansion of the Model of Quality Assessment, the plan to assess workplace literacy, and the idea to develop Quality Profiles.

• *Remember that it is possible to begin a complex project without the luxury of enough time to create a complete plan.* Although not ideal, the need for immediate action on a major initiative frequently precludes conducting an ideal study. In this case, data collection began before the instruments could be perfected and a model developed. Fortunately, changes to the original instruments and study plans have primarily been additions, rather than corrections, and valuable baseline data were collected without undue delay.

IMPACT OF THE QUALITY ASSESSMENT PROGRAM

In 1990, OPM and the federal personnel community incorporated the goal of workforce quality assessment into their *Strategic Plan for Federal Human Resources Management*. The plan states:

> The goal of the federal human resources management system is to create a responsive system that enables each agency to attract, develop and retain a quality and representative workforce needed to accomplish its unique mission. . . . This goal statement compels us to adopt the 'quality' candidate and the 'quality' employee as our primary points of perspective. . . . (U.S. Office of Personnel Management, 1990, p. 8)

Thus, OPM and the federal personnel community have reaffirmed a commitment to define and measure quality; to determine whether quality is changing over time in conjunction with the changing diversity of the workforce; and, if declining quality is found, to take steps to reverse the loss of talent. This commitment resulted in no small way from the influence of I/O psychology practices on program planning.

To our knowledge, no other organization is undertaking a quality assessment effort of the scope and complexity of the Quality Assessment Program. The program is unique in that it collects data on both applicants and incumbents across all federal government occupations, while simultaneously providing for private sector comparisons for comparable occupations. The program provides a wonderful opportunity to build a rich data base to support or refute perceptions of changing workforce quality over time.

REFERENCES

Dye, D. (1990). *An explication of a model for assessing the quality of the federal workforce*. Washington, DC: U.S. Office of Personnel Management.

Johnston, W. B., & Packer, A. E. (1987). *Workforce 2000: Work and workers for the 21st century*. Indianapolis, IN: The Hudson Institute.

Hudson Institute. (1988). *Civil service 2000*. Washington, DC: U.S. Office of Personnel Management.

National Archives and Records Administration. (1990). *The United States government manual, 1990/91*. Washington, DC: Author.

National Commission on the Public Service. (1989). *Leadership for America: Rebuilding the public service*. Washington, DC: Author.

U.S. Government Accounting Office. (1988). *Federal workforce: A framework for studying its quality over time*. Washington, DC: Committee on Post Office and Civil Service, House of Representatives.

U.S. Merit Systems Protection Board. (1986). *1986 merit principles survey report.* Washington, DC: Author.

U.S. Merit Systems Protection Board. (1990). *Working for America: A federal employee survey.* Washington, DC: Author.

U.S. Office of Personnel Management. (1990). *Strategic plan for federal human resources management.* Washington, DC: Author.

PART III

MANAGING WORKPLACE DIVERSITY THROUGH PERSONAL GROWTH AND TEAM DEVELOPMENT

Many of the activities described in the first three cases took the form of human resources policies and programs for assessing individuals and for staffing the organization. Emphasis was given to changing the rules and systems of the organizations, and assessing the consequences. Changes in the rules and systems were expected to change behavior, but few of the activities described were *directly* targeted at changing the attitudes or understandings of people in the organizations involved.

The cases presented in Part III put relatively more emphasis on changing the individuals who populate the organization, instead of the larger system itself. The activities described include informing individuals about the factual similarities and differences between themselves and others, attempting to change attitudes about those who are similar and dissimilar to oneself, and trying to change the ways people behave toward one another. The primary vehicles for creating these changes are education programs and group discussions.

DIGITAL EQUIPMENT CORPORATION

The concept of "valuing differences" is now a familiar one to anyone who has read even a little about current responses to workforce diversity. But when Digital first articulated its Valuing Differences philosophy a decade ago, it was breaking new ground as a pathfinder. When most organizations were still trying valiantly to be color-blind and gender-blind, Digital chose to acknowledge and even celebrate differences. Its success with this initiative has won Digital numerous awards from organizations such as the Department of Labor and the American Society for Training and Development and from publications such as *Working Mother* and *Black Enterprise.*

Today, Digital's Valuing Differences philosophy is supported by several types of activities, including training programs, leadership groups, and a full calendar of cultural events. But at its inception, the Valuing Differences approach was no more than a few small Core Groups of executives getting together to discuss their attitudes and prejudices about employees in their inner city and Puerto Rican plants. Chapter 6 describes the experiences of Digital's first Core Group participants—top-level managers—and chronicles the grass-roots proliferation of Core Groups throughout the organization. It tells how a small effort to "do the right thing" by confronting destructive stereotypes developed into a powerful substructure that changed the organization's culture. Now the issues discussed are not limited to ethnic biases; among others, they include gender, physical ability, sexual orientation, and even the surprisingly pernicious differing perspectives held by employees who work in the sales and manufacturing subunits of the company.

At Digital, there is a clear focus on changing the attitudes and perspectives of individual employees. Valuing Differences activities are not judged by numerical indicators, such as statistics on equal employment opportunity, turnover patterns, attitude surveys, or summaries of comments made during exit interviews. Initially, the company intentionally avoided measuring the outcomes of Core Group discussions. More than any words from top management ever could, the absence of record keeping about Core Group activities clearly communicated that the primary objective of these groups was personal development.

As a final comment, it is noteworthy that both authors of this case were key players during the intitiation and development of Digital's Valuing Differences philosophy; thus, they were pioneers in working through diversity. In fact, although it is difficult to be certain, it is likely that coauthor Barbara Walker was the first person to hold the new-age title of manager of Valuing Differences.

XYZ CORPORATION

There are some similarities between the experiences of Digital Equipment Corporation and the XYZ Corporation: Both companies began to work on race relations issues at about the same time; both sustained their efforts over several years; in both companies, interventions were stimulated and supported by top-level managers who were committed to change; and both companies relied on external consultants as well as internal support staff to effect change. It is due to these similarities that the cases appear sequentially in this volume. However, the differences in the experiences of the two compaines are as instructive as the similarities.

One of the most exceptional features of the XYZ case is that the corporation's change efforts were firmly grounded in and shaped by academic theory (also notable is the fact that the theory was improved by the interventionists' experiences). Theory-driven interventions are unusual in today's business organizations, especially in the area of human resources management. They are not unheard of, however. For example, quality improvement interventions designed around Edward Deming's statistical control theory begin by first teaching the theory to employees and then helping them implement the theory.

In the XYZ case, the relevant theory is called *embedded intergroup relations theory*. This theory draws attention to the impact our group memberships have on our experiences and attitudes. It also considers the influences of the social context that surrounds us. Most importantly, the theory points out that feelings and behaviors reflect a complex interplay between personal attitudes, which are related to group memberships, and the social contexts in which people find themselves. For example, the theory indicates that race relations cannot be understood by focusing on how members of one group differ from another group. Nor can the relations between men and women be understood by focusing on how they differ from each other. Instead, what must be considered, for example, are the unique dynamics that arise between a black boss and a white subordinate, a white boss and a black subordinate, two blacks, and two whites.

Embedded intergroup relations theory played several important roles in the XYZ Corporation case. First, there was an effort to teach employees of XYZ Corporation about the theory. These educational efforts started at the top, but were eventually offered to employees at all levels. In addition, the theory was used to structure the memberships of a variety of task forces, committees, and workshop groups formed during the intervention. Finally, the theory guided the collection and analysis of data for evaluating the consequences of this long-term attempt to change an organization's culture.

The data-intensive evaluation of changes at the XYZ Corporation represents a second key difference between this case and the Digital case. Results of an evaluation of the project 10 years after it was started showed steady increases in the proportion of black managers serving in positions of power. But perhaps more intriguing are the data showing the attitudes of blacks, whites, men, and women with respect to those aspects of the intervention that emphasized educating people and those that emphasized redistributing power. These are discussed and interpreted in detail near the end of this case.

THE MERGER OF HARRIS SEMICONDUCTOR AND
GENERAL ELECTRIC SOLID STATE

Up to this point, all the cases presented have dealt primarily or exclusively with how companies are addressing demographic cultural diversity. Traditionally, cultural diversity is used to refer to the differing attitudes and behaviors of people who are demographically different (e.g., in terms of race, ethnicity, gender, age). As Chapter 2 pointed out, the increasing number of corporate alliances and partnerships mean that today many businesses must learn to operate in a context of corporate cultural diversity, in addition to working through demographic cultural diversity. The case of the Harris Semiconducor–General Electric Solid State merger illustrates the similarity of issues generated by these two types of cultural diversity.

Chapter 8 begins by describing the business objectives behind the merger. It is clear from this introduction that high stakes were involved. Managing the merger process successfully was a business necessity. The potential benefits of effectively integrating the two corporate cultures could be easily stated and assessed in economic terms. Presumably, then, the context was one in which executives from the two companies were highly motivated to establish a mutually beneficial, synergistic relationship—to create one new corporate culture that would supplant the two establishd cultures of the merging companies.

The merger raised numerous human resources/management issues because the human resource practices (e.g., compensation and benefits, performance appraisals) used in the two companies were not the same, but these isssues are not the focus of this case. Instead, the case focuses on describing how a management team was put together and the team development interventions used to facilitate interactions among its members. The authors also describe how similar interventions helped to create cohesive work units at lower levels in the organization.

Some of the team development efforts were designed to educate members from the two organizations about their new corporate partners. Like demographic cultural awareness workshops, the objective was to help each group understand the facts about the merger, the competencies each company would contribute to the new enterprise, and the perspectives of the new corporate partners. Other interventions were designed to establish new patterns of behavior. For example, creating and sustaining new communication patterns were especially important. In addition, managers from the two companies needed to learn to trust and support one another, and deal constructively with the inevitable conflicts they would experience. Social events and group discussions were used to achieve these objectives.

Readers who have experienced a merger first-hand should recognize the challenges of diversity management created when two corporate cultures must be integrated to function as a unitary whole. Readers with no merger experience are likely to learn a bit about how mergers are carried out, and they should develop a better understanding of how team development activities can facilitate the merger process. Hopefully, both types of readers will also see that many of the challenges faced by organizations working through corporate cultural diversity are similar to those faced by organizations working through demographic cultural diversity.

CHAPTER 6

Valuing Differences at Digital Equipment Corporation

BARBARA A. WALKER
WILLIAM C. HANSON

INTRODUCTION

Digital is a worldwide corporation that sells computer and network solutions. It has 120,000 employees in 64 countries throughout the world. Over 50,000 of these employees are outside the United States. The company has multiple manufacturing sites in Europe and the Pacific Rim, as well as plants in Mexico, Canada, and the United States. Over 50% of the company's revenue is generated outside the United States.

Over the past several years Digital Equipment Corporation has become widely recognized as a leading pioneer of diversity work, a new and fast-growing area of human resources management. Its management approach to dealing with employees and all of their differences, called Valuing Differences, was developed in the early 1980s. This placed Digital at the cutting edge of diversity work well before the Hudson Institute's report, *Workforce 2000*, called national attention to the country's rapidly shifting demographics.

This chapter describes the evolution of Digital's Valuing Differences philosophy and the Core Group model, which the company uses to create, encourage and manage workforce diversity. The principles and concepts underpinning the way the diversity work is done at Digital are described, as are the benefits of this work.

WHAT IS VALUING DIFFERENCES?

Digital's Valuing Differences philosophy focuses employees on their differences. Employees are encouraged to pay attention to their differences as unique individuals and as members of groups, to raise their level of comfort with differences, and to capitalize on differences as a major asset to the company's productivity.

The philosophy is anchored in the conviction that the broader the spectrum of differences in the workplace, the richer the synergy among the employees and the more excellent the organization's performance. It is a belief in the constructive potential of all people. It assumes that each person's differences bring unique and special gifts to the organization. In the early 1980s, when Valuing Differences was first articulated, the approach was regarded as radically different because it is all-inclusive. It goes beyond traditional protected-class issues of equal employment opportunity (EEO) and addresses issues created by all kinds of differences among people in the workplace.

Digital's Valuing Differences work is done in a variety of ways. The company sponsors and supports a wide range of activities such as awareness and skills training, "Celebrating Differences" events, and the development of leadership groups and support groups. But the most exciting aspect of the Valuing Differences approach is the emphasis placed on personal development through small-group dialogue. At Digital these ongoing discussion groups are called Core Groups.

Awareness and Skills Training

External consultants and in-house trainers conduct sessions that help employees raise their levels of awareness about the issues of diversity in their workplace. Some of the sessions are specifically focused on learning about the cultural norms of different geographical groups. Digital's most popular in-house training course is "Understanding the Dynamics of Difference," a 2-day course designed to introduce employees to basic Valuing Differences concepts.

Celebrating Differences Events

Each year, various organizations within the company plan and sponsor a year-long calendar of cultural and educational events. Employees celebrate Black History Month, Hispanic Heritage Month, Gay and Lesbian Pride Week, International Women's Month, and so forth. These events give employees an opportunity to learn, in ways and at times they choose, about different groups at regularly scheduled times throughout the year.

Leadership Groups and Support Groups

Members of "same–differences" interest groups come together regularly to provide one another with needed emotional and career support. Some of these groups are referred to as "Efficacy" groups because their members participated in Efficacy training—a program designed to help minority employees learn how to deal effectively in the dominant culture. In addition, Digital supports task-oriented leadership groups. Sometimes these are also "same–differences" interest groups. For example, white women or black men may form a task force that meets on a regular basis to recommend and monitor changes in company practices that impact Digital climate and culture.

Core Groups

Digital also supports an informal network of small ongoing discussion groups. These are groups of seven to nine employees who commit to coming together on a monthly basis to examine their stereotypes, test the differences in their assumptions, and build significant relationships with people they regard as different. These groups, often described as the "engine" of Digital's Valuing Differences approach, will be discussed in more detail in the following section.

HOW THE APPROACH EVOLVED

The Beginning: Struggling at the Top

Digital Equipment Corporation was founded in 1957 in Maynard, Massachusetts, a small New England town where people grew up with little or no contact with other cultures. In the early years, the company's workforce included very few black and Hispanic employees. Of these only a handful were professionals or managers.

By the mid-1970s, when Digital managers first began sorting through their affirmative action (AA) responsibilities, the company had already established two manufacturing plants in Puerto Rico and an inner-city plant in Springfield, Massachusetts. The plants in Puerto Rico had about 1,500 employees. The Springfield plant had a predominantly black workforce of about 700 employees. In addition, Digital was in the process of developing plans for another inner-city plant in the Roxbury section of Boston.

As the manufacturing organization developed affirmative action plans that increased the numbers of minorities hired in the general workforce, a number of managers believed that Digital had accomplished an affirmative action success story. On the other hand, some managers struggled with a gnawing sense that making the numbers did not accomplish the general intent and spirit of affirmative action.

Some managers were highly skeptical about the plants in Puerto Rico and Springfield, and regarded them as no more than experiments in corporate social responsibility. They thought of them as "minority" plants and assumed that they would produce business results that were lower than results produced by comparable plants. In addition, the majority of the senior managers in the Puerto Rico plants were white men imported from stateside operations. One Puerto Rican manager said that he felt "like a minority in my own country."

These factors combined to create a view among some managers—inside the plants as well as in the headquarters offices—that these plants were "less than" their counterpart plants in other Digital locations. Managers assumed that they would not produce excellently and, therefore, they did not demand excellence. Their lower expectations resulted in patronizing the plants; they protected them by giving them lower standards than they used in other plants. As a result, while the Springfield and Puerto Rico plants were successful in achieving whatever standards had been set for them, they were not given the same opportunities given other plants to achieve excellence.

A number of the managers who thought of the Springfield and Puerto Rico plants as protected plants that produced "less than" business results were reluctant to strengthen Digital's affirmative action program. They considered affirmative action detrimental to the company's business excellence, and resisted learning how to lead a strong affirmative action program. But Digital's culture had always been firmly rooted in a strong sense of core values that focused on employees as the company's most valuable asset. The culture held that it was critical to "respect individuals" and to "do the right thing." As a result there were key leaders determined to do the right thing in affirmative action and equal employment opportunity.

One of these key leaders was the vice president, who was held accountable for business results in the group of manufacturing plants that included Springfield and Puerto Rico. It was his view that accountability for business results demanded that all plants achieve excellence; it was unacceptable that any plant achieve "less than" business results.

He was also especially troubled when he learned that a Puerto Rican manager had been made to feel like a minority in his own country. It was true, he acknowledged, that he and other senior managers were uncomfortable working closely with black and Hispanic managers. They were unable to give minorities direct and forthright feedback.

Clearly company results depended, at least in part, on maintaining effective work relationships with "minorities" in the Springfield and Puerto Rican plants, and with minority employees in other manufacturing operations. He made a practical business-driven decision that the key affirmative action issue was not focusing on the "numbers," but rather trying to identify the obstacles that blocked senior managers from working effectively with black and Hispanic employees. The next step would then be working to remove those blocks.

Management began the work with itself. The vice president and his staff—predominantly white males—met with women and minorities in the organization in 1-day sessions in order to raise their self-awareness about race and gender issues. At best, most of the sessions were regarded as benign because they never got to the "real" issues. The managers, hearing themselves described as racist and sexist, thought they were being accused of being bad people. Hence, they would become defensive and shut down. The women and minority participants, in turn, would at times become enraged and engage in behavior that appeared irrational. Whenever the two sides came close to discussing the critical issues, communications would invariably break down. As a result there was little opportunity for learning on either side.

Breaking the Taboo of Silence

The breakthrough came in 1977, when the manufacturing vice president introduced his staff to a black management consulting firm that dealt primarily with race issues. These consultants took the approach that racism and sexism are so deeply embedded in American culture that it was part of the very air that everyone breathed. They said that, as a result, everyone was racist and sexist. This approach helped managers become less defensive in the sessions as they came to understand that they were not being accused of being bad people.

The sessions became intense and deeply meaningful. Over time a significant consulting relationship developed. Small groups of top-level manufacturing managers started meeting with the consultants in small 2-day workshops. In these groups they talked openly and frankly about the issues of race and the stereotypes they held about blacks.

These dialogues helped senior managers get in touch with a fundamental obstacle to their ability to provide the necessary leadership in AA/EEO. They had regarded open and candid conversation about race and gender issues as taboo. They were reluctant to talk about race and gender differences, and particularly in the presence of minorities and white women for fear that they would be viewed as prejudiced.

The intensive 2-day workshops helped them appreciate the benefits of discussing race and gender differences despite the anxiety and embarrassment they initially felt. It became clear that the taboo, which held them in silence on such important issues, blocked them from learning. If they couldn't talk about the issues, they couldn't learn from one another; nor would they ever be able to learn from people they regarded as different. Their first task as leaders was breaking the taboo. They discovered that, as they became more comfortable, struggling openly with their prejudices, they began to explore other subjects traditionally regarded as taboo in the corporate world, such as bonding, intimacy, forgiveness, and love. They felt deeply enriched by these discussions, and realized there was something in it for them to continue talking about differences.

These top-level managers continued learning together. They continued their self-awareness dialogues in the safety of their own small groups with the consultants who had helped them break through, and with women consultants who focused them on gender issues. By 1979, these top-level managers were ready to spread what they had learned. They encouraged the delivery of self-awareness sessions throughout the manufacturing organization.

Core Groups—the Beginning

In July of that year they hired an external consultant on a full-time basis to help them capture the learnings and to put shape to the work that had begun. As this consultant talked with managers and other participants doing the self-awareness work, she realized that people eagerly sought ways to continue their race and gender dialogues. In October, she brought several of the top-level managers together with blacks and women in a small ongoing discussion group. They committed to working with one another in monthly meetings. They also agreed to keep one another "safe" so that they could openly discuss their thoughts and their feelings about racial, cultural, and gender differences.

Even with all their self-awareness, the work was not easy. Having paid so little attention to the differences of others or even to differences among themselves, the senior-level managers had not learned how to interact easily with women, or with people they saw as racially different. They learned to "slow down" their emotions and suspend judgments that got in the way of hearing one another. This allowed them to explore and sometimes even confront one another about their stereotypes and assumptions. The group, which met at least once a month for 3 years, became known as a Core Group—a "safe place" where managers could struggle openly with their stereotypes and assumptions.

In 1980, the consultant helped form two more Core Groups. By this time the small group dialogues involved about 30 top-level managers, including three vice presidents and a handful of black, Hispanic, and white women managers. Such an air of discovery and excitement built up around these ongoing group discussions that other employees joined with top-level managers to form more groups.

Empowering Everybody

In the beginning, the Core Group work centered primarily on the issues of minorities and women—the people traditionally viewed as the victims of racism and sexism. The original goal was to help white male managers to strip away the stereotypes they held about minorities and women so they could see them as unique individuals. But this focus shifted as Core Group participants discovered that everybody—not just women and minorities—felt victimized by racism and sexism. White men were feeling lonely, left out, and disempowered. They too felt victimized. Making women and minorities the sole focus of the work merely reinforced the prevailing "us versus them" approach to AA/EEO work, which made everyone feel devalued.

At this point the leaders realized that a critical step in pulling together an aggressive program for the recruitment, hiring, and development of minorities and women required building an environment in which everyone felt empowered. And that meant paying attention to everybody's differences, including those of white males. The leaders pushed toward making a formal distinction between the mandatory EEO compliance work, designed to help protected-class groups, and the distinctly different work of empowering all employees.

Participants then began paying attention to everyone's race and culture, not just the racial and cultural issues of women and minorities. This helped white males as well as women and minorities to raise their levels of comfort and trust as they sorted through the issues created by their differences. A powerful slogan emerged, a precursor of the evolving Valuing Differences approach: "Affirmative action is for everyone." It had become important that not one person feel victimized by Digital's affirmative action work.

Initially the work in Core Groups downplayed group differences, which some people pointed to as evidence of inferiority. Yet, although the dialogues led to higher levels of comfort and trust among some individual men and women and among some blacks and whites, on the whole participants still felt devalued. They discovered that the approach of down-playing group differences had contained a built-in contradiction. The very purpose of the work was learning how to work with groups of people regarded as different, yet their work together had failed to take into account the implications of group differences. In a sense, in the effort to see one another as individuals, they had been ignoring their group differences —another important dimension of difference. And when they ignored their group differences, everyone still felt devalued.

Eventually they began to explore their group differences as well as their unique individual differences. They probed for core identity differences among whites and blacks and Hispanics, and between men and women. Despite some fears that the work of identifying group differences ran the risk of reinforcing the very stereotypes they were trying to erase, they felt relatively safe doing this work together because they had learned to confront stereotyping.

This work led them to examine the assumptions that they held as individuals and as members of different groups. Through these discussions, they discovered that they held unexamined and faulty assumptions about their very own groups, which at times led them to faulty assumptions and beliefs about others. For example, white male participants assumed that they were more alike than not; this assumption led to their belief that others in the same racial group were also very much alike.

Their next step was studying the implications of their group differences with respect to such issues as styles of bonding, competition, and power sharing. They viewed this work as an important step in developing effective strategies that could help employees of different race and gender groups work together interdependently.

All Differences

As more and more employees invited others to join in the dialogues, they addressed the full spectrum of the traditional EEO protected-class differences—not just race and gender but physical ability, age, and sexual orientation. Moreover, as Core Groups spread beyond manufacturing to other parts of the company, participants also brought with them their issues as members of different organizations, functions, and geographies. They slowly realized that they returned again and again to the same question underlying their earlier dialogues. No matter what the issue, the question was the same: Whose standard should we apply . . . yours or mine? People's standards were determined by the differences in their assumptions and perspectives on the world. For example, Digital employees in the sales and services placed a heavy priority on clear, discrete, doable tasks. These employees were often at a loss dealing with employees in the manufacturing organizations, who primarily focused on processes. Whenever there was conflict between members of these groups, each insisted that the other was out of touch with reality. Core Group dialogue helped them to understand that they had very different perspectives on the world, and hence different standards.

At this point the work had shifted yet again. The sole focus on EEO differences had been expanded to include all kinds of differences. This broader more inclusive focus provided a way to address difficult organizational issues between such groups as manufacturing and engineering, and between line and staff. As the company became more international, the approach also provided a powerful entry into dialogues about cultural and geographical differences with European managers who had sometimes become confused and even offended by the AA/EEO approach. Affirmative action and equal employment opportunity were strictly regarded as issues relevant only to the United States; on the other hand when issues were discussed in Valuing Differences terms, employees in Europe were enabled to relate in terms of their own experiences.

Core Groups and Valuing Differences

By 1984 there were more that 35 Core Groups with hundreds of participants. The collective Core Group philosophy of paying attention to all differences and learning about differences through small-group dialogue became known throughout the company as Valuing Differences.

The philosophy was written into the company's AA/EEO statement and became policy. A Valuing Differences function was established as an organization separate from the AA/EEO function. Numerous line organizations within the company employed full-time and part-time Valuing Differences managers. Their official job was creating an empowering environment in which diversity was nurtured. Specifically, their tasks included putting Core Groups together and sometimes leading them, as well as designing and developing awareness training. They were also responsible for developing strategies that empowered employees and encouraged interdependence and synergy across all kinds of differences.

Official support of Valuing Differences meant that Core Groups continued to grow. The first few years they grew exponentially; thereafter there was a steady increase as they multiplied and spread throughout the company. Membership in Core Groups is strictly voluntary. Each group meets during the workday at least 4 or more hours a month.

Each participant signs up, in effect, to become a serious student of differences. These small ongoing dialogues, all about differences, help participants do the work of personal growth and development. Although the experience of each Core Group is different, they all focus on helping participants learn how to:

1. Strip away their stereotypes.
2. Probe for differences in the assumptions of others.
3. Build authentic and significant relationships with people they regard as different.
4. Raise their levels of personal empowerment.
5. Identify and explore group differences.

Core Groups are led by employees who have attended a 2-day workshop known as Affirmative Action University, or AAU. The reference to affirmative action in the workshop's name is a reminder that Digital's philosophy of helping employees learn to value all differences began as an attempt to respond to affirmative action legislation. The reference to university is a reminder that the philosophy encourages personal growth and learning.

The AAU workshop was created on the basis of insights developed by the consultant who put together and led Digital's first Core Group, as well as the first 20 or so successive Core Groups. The workshop was designed to help employees from different levels in the organization learn how to encourage and lead open and frank discussion. AAU places a heavy emphasis on helping leaders learn how to "keep people safe" and remain committed to staying with the dialogue.

CRITICAL PRINCIPLES AND CONCEPTS THAT SHAPED THE VALUING DIFFERENCES MODEL

Prior to the publication of *Workforce 2000*, the 1987 report on the country's changing workforce and the growing need to depend on women and minorities as the major source of labor, focusing on differences was regarded as a revolutionary management approach. In effect, traditional management practices treated difference as evidence of inferiority. Anyone regarded as different was thought of as "less than" anyone who was a member of the organization's dominant culture. Consequently the kindest, gentlest approach was to ignore differences and to treat everyone the same.

Today's changing demographics require that corporations develop strategies for integrating workers from highly divergent cultures. There is a growing emphasis on diversity as more and more corporations prepare for the future.

Generally, the term *diversity* is used to refer to at least three separate kinds of work: (1) affirmative action and equal employment opportunity, which focus on hiring and developing people in the nation's protected-class groups; (2) multicultural work, which is usually designed to help people learn about the cultural differences of specific (often geographic) groups (e.g., people living in Japan); and (3) values/empowerment work in which the term *differences* is expanded beyond EEO, to include such differences as lifestyles and learning styles, as well as race, gender, and so on. Programs also differ in the emphasis they place on creating attitude change and behavior change. Furthermore, some programs focus on individual differences, whereas others emphasize group differences.

No matter which basic approach an organization chooses, it is clear that learning how to help people deal with their differences is an extraordinarily complex challenge. The approach ultimately chosen must be tailored to fit and suit the organization's culture and philosophy.

Digital's Valuing Differences model is the sum of incalculable insights and breakthrough learnings that unfolded when Digital colleagues paid attention to the differences among them. The following section describes the fundamental concepts that shape the way the work is done at Digital.

Dialogue Is the Key to Personal Growth and Change

At the heart of diversity work is a fundamental question about the individual's ability to build interdependent relationships with people he or she regards as different. Core Group dialogues gave employees a place to think about the nature of their relationships with others in the company.

True dialogue, that is discussion that does not have as its goal conflict resolution or determining right from wrong, can cause people to question their beliefs. Through dialogue about differences, participants struggle with fundamental questions about their capacity for love, intimacy, risk taking, forgiveness, power sharing, believing in others and, ultimately, their willingness to be interdependent with their colleagues. Dialogue provides a minilab in which employees can examine their views, assumptions, and beliefs, and if they deem it appropriate, change them.

People's unique characteristics and their view of the differences of others usually determine their self-interests. Self-interests arise out of the meaning given to the context in which people find themselves. In other words, differences have no meaning except in terms of the whole. Becoming a member of an ongoing dialogue can be likened to moving away from a reductionist approach to learning, that is, as a separate learner, toward a holistic group process—a way of experiencing wholeness together. Joining a dialogue is the work of becoming and staying connected.

Digital's small-group dialogues gave the participants a way to face and confront their stereotypes and assumptions about one another's differences. Participants were then able to hear different points of view and relate to one another at deeper levels. The discussion itself became a way to change relationships.

Perhaps most importantly, they learned that they can learn from one another. And as they learned, they became motivated to listen. They began to "bond," developing authentic and trusting relationships with people with whom they had never expected to build any relationship at all. Some participants were enabled to build such relationships simply because they had learned how. Others developed relationships with people they had learned to value. In turn, bonding caused them to deepen their investment in thinking and learning about one another's issues.

The work of dialogue helped participants raise their comfort level for taking risks and giving one another feedback. They acknowledged that their new relationships made them vulnerable to one another, and that at times they would "let each other down." They developed critical insights about their ability to forgive one another. They opened up to seeing one another as mentors and precious allies. This is essentially the work of learning to value differences.

To Stay in the Dialogue, People Must Feel Safe

It was early in the work that Core Group leaders observed that whenever people discussed their differences—no matter what the difference—the emotional decibel level would skyrocket. It became clear that the honest and candid exploration of stereotypes and assumptions about people and the groups to which they belong is always highly emotional work.

Often when people talk openly and honestly with others about the differences among them, they feel threatened and challenged. Others' views threaten the individual's own values and beliefs. When people participate in open and honest discussions about differences, many feel— with or without justification—that they are being asked to change to suit the preferences of others.

The realization that the work is always highly emotional and intense led to understanding that there is a critical need to "keep people safe." Hence, these words emerged as an important code in doing the work. There was a recognition that people can hear and learn from one another only when they feel safe. "Keep people safe" was not a reference to maintaining harmony and accord. It referred to a way of working with one another—helping people manage their level of emotion so that they would hang in with one another, that is, stay in the dialogue. The dialogues created a structured situation in which people were asked to suspend the emotional opinions and judgments that get in the way of listening and learning.

In a sense the meaning of "keep people safe" when building relationships with co-workers is the same as it is when building relationships with "significant others." The process of successfully developing a significant relationship—with a friend, for example—requires establishing an environment in which two people can be themselves and still commit to hanging in with one another. When there is disagreement, one is not threatened that the other will turn on his or her heels and walk away from the discussion, never to return! A Core Group replicates just such an environment of commitment and investment in one another. In the course of learning how to establish Core Groups, participants identified a number of ways to help keep one another safe. Generally, except for confidentiality, they agreed that there would be no norms, no upfront declarations about hard and fast rules. In that way people were encouraged to be themselves. They agreed that although the work may be therapeutic, its purpose was not therapy; they committed to keep all their discussions on the subject of differences. Each group was enabled to move at its own pace; hence, safety meant not rushing ahead and moving into discussions for which the group was not ready. At the same time, individual participants were supported if they took risks pushing to discuss any given issue. Still, the sanctity of the implicit contract among them depended on the group moving as a whole.

Because Core Groups met during Digital work time, some participants felt most safe when they took the time to identify "what's-in-it-for-them" to do the personal development work. Others felt safe only when they had taken the time they needed to develop a clear understanding of "what's-in-it-for-Digital," that is, the connection between their personal growth in the area of differences and Digital's productivity and profitability.

There Is No Substitute for the Investment in Time

There is no substitute for time. Time is the organization's most critical resource when it undertakes diversity work.

Although the work began at Digital in the late 1970s, Valuing Differences did not become official company policy until 1984. It took a full 3 years to make the first six core groups happen. Today there are more than hundreds, and probably thousands, of small dialogue groups within Digital. And as they spread, so does the Valuing Differences philosophy.

When the work began, the organization's most senior leaders were sufficiently empowered to keep their eyes on the vision for change, not on a target date for when the vision would be accomplished. They accepted the reality of time as a critical factor of success, and they were willing to give time and space to the managers doing the work. Their leadership made possible the exploration and percolation of new ideas and relationships, thereby enabling managers to experiment with what was best for Digital's culture and environment.

Often the Valuing Differences work is likened to being on a journey. There is a sense of movement, although the destination seems unclear. Organizationally, it is a journey toward building an environment that empowers everyone to learn about the value of differences. For the participants in the work, it is a personal journey. For both the organization and the employee, the journey requires time.

The work does not lend itself to the traditional "fix-it" approach, which is often based on the expectation that the problem will be "fixed" within a short time frame. When people feel pressured to produce results in less time than is needed to do the job, they can end up shortcutting the fundamentals and, paradoxically, ensure the longevity of the work. It may even take them years to identify the problem.

All too often, the time dimension is unwittingly used to narrow the vision. When time is made the bottom line for measuring progress in the area of personal development, there is a danger that timeframes become more important than the quality of the work. Or worse yet, time becomes a pressure that makes everyone involved in the work feel like they are victims. Leaders become their own victims—hostages to an excellent vision made impossible by self-imposed time constraints.

An aspect of "keeping people safe" in the Core Groups was asking them to "slow down the process." In a sense, they were asked to alleviate the pressure created by time by slowing down their emotions. "Slowing it down" was a way of slowing down time.

The willingness to invest in time has been particularly empowering to the evolution of Digital's approach to diversity work as personal development. It is lifelong learning that inures to the benefit of the whole—Digital and its employees. The work must be managed so that people do not establish unreal and false expectations that it will one day be finished. Learning to value and manage diversity is a process of change—in people and in the organization; it is work that is never "done."

People Are Motivated to Learn about Differences When the Work Is Seen as an Opportunity for Personal Development

When Digital managers were first asked to join discussions on the issues created by race and gender, they raised all manner of objections. Some said they felt that the only purpose of the work was to help "them"—the women and minorities—and would not benefit the managers themselves. Others viewed the discussions as "forced guilt trips" intended to show that they were racist, and, as such, constituted an attack on their personal character. They argued that they were being forced to change their values and beliefs and that the work should be limited to behavior and skills training. But organizational leaders felt that mandating behavior was essentially the same as mandating personal values. Instead, they pushed for discussions.

As managers participated in the discussions, they developed a sense that the issues were bigger than "just" race and gender; they realized that there was something to be gained by each of them. They were learning about themselves, and not just about people they regarded as "others." They recognized the benefits of personal development dialogue for themselves as well as for minorities and women.

People are more willing to take on the painful emotional work of dealing with differences when they can learn about themselves, and not only about others. Only when people view the work as an opportunity for self-development—as a personal learning experience—and not as change dictated and forced by the interests of others, are they likely to become invested in the work.

The Pivotal Work in Learning to Value Differences Is Personal Empowerment

Valuing Differences is, in effect, a model for empowerment. Learning to value the differences of others brings into question the ability to be open, to trust in oneself and in the potential of others, the ability to take risks and to forgive, all of which deepens one's sense of personal empowerment. Learning to value the differences of others is essentially the same as learning how to empower oneself and others.

The original purpose of the diversity work was empowering the people traditionally regarded as victims—women and minorities. But the reactions of the white male managers to the early Core Group work on race and sex helped participants to discover that when an organization deals with the issues of one group at the expense of others, everybody feels victimized by racism and sexism. Paying attention to the issues of one group at the expense of others is essentially tantamount to disempowering everyone. When the group traditionally in power—white men—saw themselves as inadequate to deal with the demands and expectations put on them, they too felt like victims. They felt powerless.

Ongoing dialogue gave them an unusual opportunity to rethink and refine their understanding of what it means to be interdependent with their co-workers. It gave them an opportunity to talk about power as the central issue. They learned that their traditional view of power as finite made them feel threatened, and consequently limited their willingness and ability to work interdependently with people they saw as different. But their shift to a view of power as infinite provided an incentive toward building an environment in which everyone feels powerful. Their dialogues helped them to get in touch with the paradox of power: The more the individual shares his or her own personal power with others, the more empowered the individual becomes. They learned that giving away power to others is not the same as becoming their victim. For example, they learned to share information and other resources that they had previously held tight to themselves.

In the empowering environment, the organization pays attention to everybody's differences. Every employee is enabled to address the issues that make them and others feel devalued—whether racism, sexism, or whatever form of generic intolerance. Empowered through a deep internal belief in their own ability to deal effectively with others, they accept the unpredictability of others, and can adapt to change and the nonroutine. They are even able to deal with the unfairness of others, and the inability of others to value them.

Empowered people are charged by a sense of purpose and a vision of what can be, and not solely by their pains and prejudices. By letting go of prejudice, and their hurts and pains, and replacing them with forgiveness, they deepen their personal source of power. As a result, they become expansive, adventurous, courageous, and willing to take risks. They can let go of their own self-interests and act as a member of a team on behalf of the whole.

Trusting in the ability of others to do the right thing empowers people to see themselves as peers. Positioning people as equals is an important step in empowering people. It conveys the message that no one, whether a boss or a subordinate, is more important than anyone else. This is a critical message when building an empowering environment because trusting in people can be the equivalent of valuing them.

Through their dialogue, participants learned that empowering others is not a skill. It is not a technique. It is a way of working with others that conveys a belief in their potential and in the unique skills, perspectives, and gifts that each person brings to his or her relationships. Valuing Differences is a philosophy that encourages people to learn something constructive from everyone and from every transaction. This way of thinking about and seeing the world enables each person to trust and see the potential in others, and learn from the "bad" as well as the "good." This is the essence of empowerment.

THE VALUE OF VALUING DIFFERENCES

This pioneering work is still so new that Digital leaders have yet to learn how to quantify the connection between doing the work and Digital's profitability in precise numerical terms. For the most part the company has relied on anecdotal data, which indicate that the work has had a profound impact on Digital employees. Through the years, the evidence shows that Digital's Valuing Differences work gives the company some specific and concrete advantages:

1. *A solid reputation as one of the best places to work—not just for women and minorities, but for everyone.* Today, "Quality of Worklife" is a number one concern for many employees. The companies known as the "best place to work" will attract and keep the best people—the most skilled, the best educated.

2. *Empowered managers and leaders who empower others.* A core aspect of Digital's culture depends on enabling all of its empoyees to "do the right thing." In an empowering environment where people feel that their differences are valued, employees are enabled to do what they believe is right. The manager is also empowered to share information, and give people the time, space, and freedom to do what they believe to be right. They make distinctions among people, and by doing so, are enabled to get to the heart of a problem instead of wrestling with what it looks like on the outside. Digital's success also depends on the ability of a variety of people at different levels in the organization to demonstrate leadership. The more leaders, the richer the organization. In this empowering environment, the informal leadership multiplies. The organization's formal leaders are in turn empowered by the energy and synergy of the informal leaders.

3. *Greater innovation.* The ability to value differences and move away from traditional "either/or" thinking frees up Digital employees to think creatively. They can, for example, think differently about problems and dilemmas. Traditionally people seek to eliminate dilemmas. They are seen as "either/or" polarities: "I want A, but if I have A, then I can't have B. And I want B too. But then I can't have A." The result is that employees view differing goals as win–lose choices that must be avoided at all costs. The traditional solution is to find ways to make the most acceptable, or least offensive, trade-offs, usually ending up somewhere in between polarized wants.

When people value differences, and can truly value divergent, and perhaps opposing perspectives, they are creatively forced to come up with some different ideas that allow them to have both. The question is no longer: Which must I choose? Instead, it becomes: If I believe that there is value in both, how can I have both? Valuing both leads to other alternatives and other values.

4. *Higher employee productivity.* An organization is the sum of its people. Productivity depends on people's relationships with one another—their promises and commitments, their celebrations, and their ways of resolving conflict. Their ability to build interdependent relationships depends on how they deal with their differences.

The fundamental task of management is to integrate people—no matter where they may be located—so that everybody works seamlessly toward common objectives. In bureaucratic organizations, managers must depend on installing and exercising controls to secure performance. But in companies like Digital, where networks have begun to replace hierarchies and participative management is the goal, the task of managing different people is much more complex. The manager is challenged to deal with the individual as the basic unit of change, and wrestle with the question of how to include everybody in the organization's thinking and decision-making processes. Under this new management paradigm, productivity is the product of the synergy and interdependence created in healthy empowered relationships.

5. *Effective global competition.* Digital employees are enabled to accept the fact that cultures across the world are unique and operate from different worldviews. As a result, employees are willing to take the time to identify, study, and even try to understand specific differences in cultural norms and values.

With employees who have perspectives from cultures all around the world, Digital is enabled to compete more effectively in world markets. Diversity work helps the company better understand and value all of its markets as well as its workforce. This knowledge leads to more effective worldwide products and marketing approaches.

CONCLUSION

The success of an organization like Digital Equipment Corporation depends on its willingness and ability to tap into this country's greatest and most accessible asset: the remarkable diversity among people. People's differences, including even those among people who appear to have the same background, can be an invaluable source of perspectives that add depth, richness, and insight to ways of doing business.

Capitalizing on diversity means helping employees become their very best by learning to accept, trust, and invest in others. An organization's first step is embracing a philosophy that values people by paying attention to their differences. A second is nurturing an environment and a process for dialogue that empowers and enables each employee to find his or her own unique key to learning to value differences. Digital's Valuing Differences philosophy and Core Group model will help organizations convert a kaleidoscope of differences into business productivity and profitability.

CHAPTER 7

Changing Race Relations Embedded in Organizations: Report on a Long-Term Project with the XYZ Corporation

CLAYTON P. ALDERFER

INTRODUCTION AND BACKGROUND

As this paper is being written, the national media regularly remind all who pay attention about the centrality of race relations in our country's present and past. The front cover of *Newsweek* for May 6, 1991 showed a picture of a young black man and a young white man accompanied by the title, "The New Politics of RACE." Approximately 1 month later, the same magazine's cover showed a white female in a close relationship with a black man along with the words "Tackling a TABOO . . . Love and Prejudice."

Even a sample of the events related to race that have been in the headlines during the past several months is impressive. The white male police chief of a major city whose officers were filmed beating a black male suspect was asked to resign by the city's black male mayor. Persistent reports indicate that efforts by white male business leaders and black male civil rights leaders to reach agreement about a new national civil rights bill were being discouraged by white male staff from the White House—reportedly because the Republican party planned to campaign again against "quotas" in the 1992 elections. For only the second time in the 50-year history of the Academy Awards, a black woman received an Oscar for the excellence of her acting. Finally, a black army general, who serves as chairman of the Joint Chiefs of Staff for the Republican administration, returned to his high school in the inner city of New York to speak with students about their aspirations. He did this after repeatedly being praised for brilliant military leadership.

Many other examples could be given to illustrate both the despair and the hope that characterize race relations in the United States today. Indeed, the problems associated with race relations are so difficult and so disturbing that many citizens prefer simply to avoid the topic. Any serious effort to bring about progressive change begins with the widespread reluctance even to discuss the subject.

The present report tells about a project of more than 15 years in duration carried out by the fictitiously named XYZ Corporation. I write about the undertaking as a white man who has been associated with the work from its beginning to the present. Throughout the history of the project, all major activities have been the product of a gender-balanced black and white cooperation. This process began with the formation of a four-person race- and gender-balanced consulting team that, in turn, worked with a 12-person (later expanded to 20) race, gender, and hierarchically balanced Race Relations Advisory Group of corporation members (Alderfer, Alderfer, Tucker, & Tucker, 1980; Alderfer, Tucker, Alderfer, & Tucker, 1988).

In 1988, the original consulting team separated after 12 years of working together, and a new team was formed to continue the work. As a result, I am the only member of the original undertaking whose connection with the project spans the entire history in an uninterrupted fashion. This report, therefore, has the benefits of being written by the one person closely associated with the activities throughout their entire life and the limitations of portraying the project only from the perspective of a white man.

Prior to the start of the project in 1976, the XYZ Corporation had in place several elements that contributed significantly to the continuity and vitality of the project. Formed in 1967 during the Civil Rights Movement, the Black Managers Association is respected by the corporation as a support system for black employees and an interest group speaking influentially about the concerns of black members in the predominantly white organization. Also a key element of the organizational context when the project began was an affirmative action plan, which influenced corporate hiring and promotion policies. Indeed, one of the reasons that the director of human resources gave for contracting for the original diagnosis of race relations in management was that, despite progress in meeting affirmative action goals, both black and white employees expressed dissatisfaction with the changes that were occurring in the organization. Finally, at the time the project began, the chief executive of the corporation was a white man highly respected for his commitment to progressive race relations. In the years following, as the original senior leadership group changed, their successors were nearly all individuals who at one time had had sustained involvement with the project. The result has been a continuity of understanding and commitment to the work that is uncommon in complex corporate organizations. Predominantly white corporations are sometimes known to replace progressive leadership in one generation by individuals with decidedly different values in the next.

ORIGINAL DIAGNOSIS AND GROUND RULES

The project began with an agreement between the consulting team and the corporation to carry out a diagnosis of race relations in management and to form a 12-person Race Relations Advisory Group to assist with that process (Alderfer et al., 1980). Black members of the consulting team established a relationship with the Black Managers Association in order to assure that project activities would not conflict with that organization's objectives. The white male member of the consulting team had a relationship with several of the senior managers of the corporation (including the chief executive officer) prior to the start of the project. When the diagnosis began, the consulting team asked and the management agreed to take seriously the results of the diagnosis. Although in spirit there was an understanding that recommendations and action steps would follow from the results of the diagnosis, there was no advance commitment to particular kinds of changes. It was conceivable—although in spirit unlikely—that no actions would follow after the diagnosis, if changes were not implied by the findings. In short, the parties (both consultants and managers, and within those groups, both blacks and whites) entered the diagnosis with open minds and a willingness to respond to the findings—whatever they might be.

Subsequent experience with other organizations has indicated just how unusual it is to be able to establish these initial conditions. Carrying out a diagnosis of race relations in management turns out to be a way of working that few senior white male managers find comfortable. People seem less nervous enlisting consultants to conduct workshops without attempting to understand the character of race relations in their organizations. This orientation is especially noteworthy, because it is well known that training programs not tied to changes in day-to-day activities generally do not result in sustained change—however well received the training programs might be.

Covering more than 50 pages, the original diagnosis was detailed and covered a variety of topics in order to convey a picture of race relations among the XYZ managers. The data and analysis included both areas of agreement (the company should be certain that both whites and blacks were qualified for the positions they held) and of disagreement (whether blacks or whites had promotion advantages) between black and white managers. Results were first discussed with the Race Relations Advisory Group prior to their being fed back to the individuals who had participated in the study. In the data collection process, during the advisory group discussions, and throughout the feedback sessions, the reaction of people from the organization was that the point of view about their racial group (whether black or white) was accurately conveyed. Another noteworthy fact is that, except for eliminating certain identifying information, the diagnosis was approved for publication by the corporation in essentially the same form as it has been presented to the organization.

Perhaps the two most noteworthy findings pertaining to differences between the racial groups were that (1) on some matters, group membership was a most powerful predictor of perception—even when there were "objective facts" about the issue; and (2) on matters of promotion, each group believed strongly that the other one had an advantage. Among the findings, 82% of white males and 77% of white females in contrast to 14% of black males and 12% of black females agreed with the statement, "Qualified blacks are promoted more rapidly than equally qualified whites." In addition, 95% of black males and 89% of black females in contrast to 9% of white males and 12% of white females agreed with the statement, "Qualified whites are promoted more rapidly than equally qualified blacks." The precision with which these two statements were crafted was a direct outcome of consultation with the Race Relations Advisory Group and with senior white male executives who were not members of the group.

Another finding of considerable significance was the degree to which white women and white men showed similar perceptions and opinions on racial matters. Replicated in other organizations as well, this result shows race to be more powerful than gender in explaining measures of racial attitudes developed directly from people's experience. It also raises empirical questions about the soundness of using the phrase "women and minorities," which implies that the two categories of people are alike or might be appropriately treated in similar fashion on matters that pertain to race and gender. The tendency to treat white women as if, on racial matters, they were more similar to blacks than to white men is also found frequently in scholarly literature—often but not exclusively when the scholars are white women. I believe these sorts of errors arise from consultants and scholars acting tacitly as if we somehow are immune to the phenomena we study (i.e., that our own race and gender do not influence how we collect and interpret data). This is the equivalent of assuming that researchers in role are not subject to the lawfulness of human behavior.

PROJECT FOCUS

At the outset, we decided not to involve the bargaining unit in the diagnosis and to focus primarily on management. When the original recommendations were formed, they became the basis for an ongoing program
of change that continues to the present. Gradual efforts to include bargaining unit people in program activities have been developed. More generally, as events have unfolded, the concrete character of the action program
has been altered periodically to recognize goals that have been achieved
and to take account of the new understandings that have emerged.

Following from the diagnostic results, the program developed three
additional major elements: (1) a strategy to intervene in how the upward
mobility decisions were made in order to alter the balance of power between blacks and whites in the corporation, (2) a workshop to educate
managers about race relations in the corporation and to provide them
with an opportunity to learn race relations competence, and (3) a tradition of evaluating the results of these interventions—both singly and in
combination and both immediately and in the long term—in order to
determine how the program was succeeding and to make adjustments as
needed.

RACE RELATIONS ADVISORY GROUP

The Race Relations Advisory Group, which had initially served as a temporary group to assist the consultants with the original diagnosis, was
established as a permanent structure with monthly half-day meetings to
monitor project activities and to provide a continuing source of advice to
senior management about improving race relations in the corporation. As
a result the Race Relations Advisory Group became the focal unit from
which all project elements (diagnoses, mobility interventions, workshops,
and evaluations) were formed and examined (Alderfer et al., 1988).

Regular meetings of the advisory group also provided opportunities
for periodic reflection about the state of race relations in the corporation.
These observations sometimes led to race- and gender-balanced task forces
from the group looking into circumstances that came to their attention.
One example of this kind of activity occurred in connection with a department especially known for its inability to find qualified blacks for certain
kinds of jobs. An advisory group task force working with the management
of that department provided a way of understanding the issues that otherwise would not have been available to the overwhelming white male
leadership group.

ELEMENTS OF THE PROJECT

The model for changing race relations at the XYZ Corporation consisted of embedded intergroup relations theory, diagnoses conducted with active participation by the Race Relations Advisory Group, educational workshops to teach about race relations competence, power-sharing interventions to adjust the imbalance of power between black and white managers, and systematic assessment of project results. This section describes further these elements and the relationships among them as the project unfolded after the first year. Understanding the interdependency among the several parts of the project is critical for grasping a sense of the work as a whole (see Figure 7.1).

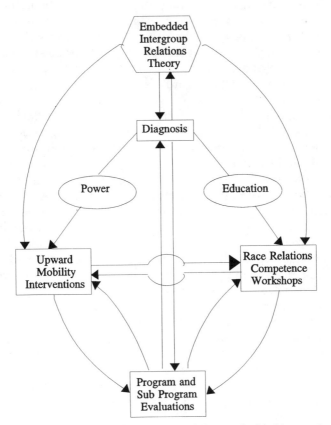

FIGURE 7.1. General model for changing race relations embedded in organizations.

Theory

From the outset, the work was based on embedded intergroup relations theory (Alderfer, 1977; 1986). The theory provides a framework for understanding group relations in organizations—conceptualizing race relations as a special class of group relations. At each step in the project, the theory played a part: in designing and interpreting the diagnoses; in planning and conducting interventions; in assessing the planned changes; in establishing and maintaining relationships with individuals and groups from the XYZ organization; and in shaping how the consulting team worked together.

Unlike many social science theories, which focus only on their subjects, embedded intergroup relations theory takes consultants and researchers as well as respondents as part of its domain. This orientation strives for a disciplined subjectivity (rather than a rational objectivity) based on a consciousness of the professionals' group memberships (rather than on a tacit or explicit denial of group effects on investigators).

Researchers and consultants who work from this perspective recognize that they participate in the same phenomena they study as they examine it. They recognize that regardless of role, they are not immune from what they study and attempt to change. It was in this spirit that I noted that the account I give in this paper is from a white male with a long association with the project. It was this framework that caused the project to deal with white women on their own terms rather than as if they were similar to black men and black women.

In my experience with organizational consultation as a profession, it is unusual for theory to play a central part in projects. An early form of embedded intergroup relations theory, however, was in place, when this project began (Alderfer, 1977). Indeed, most of the actions taken during the work have come about through exchanges between concrete elements of particular situations and interpretations of those events based upon the theory. Moreover, the theory has not remained static as the project has evolved. Rather, it has become more precise and complete as the work progressed (Alderfer, 1986). One example of such a change in theory has been the developing of the concept of embeddedness.

Embeddedness refers to the relationships among a focal system, the suprasystem in which it is partially or wholly contained, and the subsystems that are contained within it. As an example framed to examine race relations, one might take, as focal system, a work group consisting of black and white employees with a black female boss in a predominantly white organization. The department in which that work group is located is the immediate suprasystem. Subgroups of white and black employees in the work group are subsystems of the focal system. The theory then predicts that the nature of race relations in the department will influence the supervisor-subordinate relationships between the boss and his or her subordinates in the work group differently depending on the race of each subordinate. For example, if race relations in the department are conflictual, and the department head is white, then dissatisfied white subordinates in the work group will be more likely to "go around the boss" in appealing up the chain of command than will dissatisfied black subordinates.

Types of Interventions: Education and Power

A conceptual orientation among advisory group members that developed in connection with the original diagnosis and remained throughout the project has been the distinction between interventions focusing on power in comparison to those emphasizing education. The power emphasis stated that race relations problems occurred because whites in the predominantly white corporation had much more formal authority and informal influence than blacks. The education focus stated that race relations problems occurred because people (primarily whites) did not adequately understand race relations. When the relationship between blacks and whites was primarily cooperative in spirit, the separate racial groups usually agreed that *both* power and education interventions were necessary to effect progressive change in race relations. When the relationship between blacks and whites was conflictual, then blacks tended to become advocates for power-based changes, and whites tended to favor education-based changes.

Upward mobility interventions were primarily directed to reduce the power imbalance between blacks and whites, and the race relations competence workshop was aimed mainly at increasing the understanding of race relations among XYZ managers. There was, however, a high order of interdependency between the two kinds of interventions. A significant proportion of managers who worked to improve upward mobility decisions participated in the race relations competence workshop. Workshops proved especially useful in helping managers to understand that individual perceptions of events and people were sometimes importantly influenced by the perceiver's racial group membership. Similarly, factual details learned in the workshops proved helpful in improving the processes by which upward mobility decisions were made. We heard frequently, for example, that white managers found it easier to explain decisions to recommend blacks for promotion in terms of the managers' being forced by "quotas" to make the selection rather than telling a white man that a black candidate was more qualified for the open position. When these kinds of conversations were examined, white men were able to acknowledge that they often found it easier to tell other white men that "quotas" took a recommendation for promotion out of their hands than to say that they found a black person to be more qualified than a white person for an open position.

In the process of these kinds of discussions, white men acknowledged that "before the days of affirmative action," other kinds of explanations (e.g., favoritism, company politics) were used to explain why someone purportedly more qualified did not receive a particular promotion. We see the same kind of argument about "quotas" with all its denials and other limitations being employed nationally by elected and appointed officials of the Republican party. Given the emotional difficulties associated with facing oneself as either promoter or promotee (successful or unsuccessful), it is understandable that such an argument would be appealing.

What this chain of reasoning does not acknowledge and what managers and leaders privately understand (and only rarely state publicly) is that a significant proportion of the variance in any upward mobility decision is highly subjective. For example, assessment centers, one of the most important advances in management assessment, have been "validated" mostly by showing that the assessments predict upward mobility decisions. Yet senior managers in every corporation I know indicate that "the right chemistry" with those already in the group is crucial for a person to be selected for top management.

Taking a strictly operational view of any upward mobility decision, therefore, is recognizing that a person selected is more approved (i.e., more pleasing, less threatening, and perhaps also more competent to do the work) by those with authority to make the choice. Recognizing these dynamics does not deny that the capacity of leaders and managers to work well together is crucial for an organization to be effective, and it also does not provide an easy way out of the dilemmas associated with the ultimate subjectivity of such decisions. What it can do, however, is lead to individuals becoming more open minded about the soundness of their private criteria and to groups being more appropriately composed to balance differing perspectives in determining who, among the available candidates, is most qualified for a given position.

Upward Mobility Interventions

Objectives

When the original diagnosis was completed, there were very few black managers above the second level of management in the corporation. Although the term was not used at the time, this phenomenon has become known as an *invisible glass ceiling*. The aim of the upward mobility interventions was to eliminate the glass ceiling for blacks who were qualified to become middle- and higher-level managers. Given the nature of mobility decisions, we expected the intervention to improve the quality of selections for all candidates.

Conceptual Model

Embedded intergroup relations theory holds that all people have their emotions, cognitions, and behavior shaped by their multiple group memberships (Alderfer, 1986). Group memberships include both identity groups, such as race and gender, and organization groups, such as hierarchical position and functional specialization. In the language of the project, XYZ managers developed the proposition that "Like likes like." To the extent that such a proposition is taken seriously, it has a number of important implications for efforts to eliminate the glass ceiling for promotions. Without indicting people, it implies that any group will have a tendency to reproduce itself unless disciplined efforts are made to correct the natural biases. ("I am objective" or "I try to be unbiased" tend to drop out as acceptable explanations, when the theoretical proposition seriously enters one's consciousness.)

When the project began, corporate personnel committees were overwhelmingly populated by white men. No wonder, then (according to both the academic theory and the managers' theory), that it was difficult to find qualified black managers who could be recommended for promotion. Furthermore, because few high-ranking black managers existed in the corporation, the number of such people who could be appropriately called into mobility decision processes in order to balance the almost exclusively white and male perspectives was limited. Intervention into the upward mobility processes was designed to help the corporation escape from this self-sealing loop.

Special Task Force for Evaluating Candidates

The first step in breaking out was to establish a special race- and gender-balanced task force of highly regarded managers to assess all (i.e., not just black) managers potentially eligible for membership in a newly created upward mobility program. Approximately half of the task force members were closely connected to the race relations improvement project, and the other half were not.

A program of generating new evaluations of candidates was undertaken. This activity was structured to allow both the candidate and the candidate's boss to nominate evaluators of the candidate's managerial potential. These evaluations were then turned over to the special task force, which made recommendations about who should be included in the program. Recommendations from the special task force were then turned back to the departmental committees, who made the final decisions.

As it turned out, the departmental committees selected individuals, on average, who were less qualified by the company's own criteria than those recommended by the special task force. These choices were not conscious, however (i.e., the committees did not say they intended to choose less qualified people). When statistical analyses of the results of the decisions were fed back to senior managers, their comment was that the department committees were more likely than the special task force to take account of political factors in the organization as they made their decisions.

The characteristics that differentiated those black candidates who were selected from those who were not differed from those that separated white candidates who were selected from those who were not. Black candidates who were selected by the departmental committees, for example, tended to be lower on performance stability than those not selected, and white candidates who were selected by the departmental committees tended to be lower on oral communication skills than those not selected. Thus, for black and white candidates viewed as subgroups as well as for the overall group of candidates, the departmental committees selected individuals who were, on average, lower on specific dimensions than those who were not chosen. Finally, analyses showed that black candidates who were selected by the departmental committees were predicted more accurately by ratings of overall managerial potential than white candidates. This supported the black point of view that it was often whites, not blacks, who were less qualified for promotion.

Corporate Personnel Committees

The second portion of the upward mobility intervention was for the corporation to give more careful and disciplined attention to the composition of the standing corporate personnel committees that made promotion decisions. As more black men, black women, and white women moved up in the corporation, they became eligible for membership on these committees after they had experience in jobs one level above those to which promotions were made.

To be sure that the consciousness of racial dynamics was not lost, the human resources department gave regular attention to how the committees were composed and to whether members attended Race Relations Competence Workshops. The Race Relations Advisory Group also received periodic reports about the composition of the personnel committees.

Monitoring Upward Mobility

In addition to analyzing the selection of the departmental committees, the Race Relations Advisory Group played an important role in monitoring the upward mobility interventions over the long term. Approximately once per quarter, the vice president for human resources reported to the group on both the distribution of black and white managers throughout the hierarchy and on how promotion opportunities were utilized.

The decade of the 1980s was an era of considerable downsizing for the corporation. Therefore, regular attention to the distribution of managers by race and gender was an important element in the overall race relations improvement program. Sometimes the difficulties associated with these changes became severe. At one point in the late 1980s, for example, several of the most senior black managers left XYZ for other positions. When the corporation did not immediately replace these people with a comparable number of black managers, the race relations improvement program experienced significant stress. Although black managers did not take the view that they were entitled to certain positions or to a specific number of positions, they did express strong dissatisfaction with the fact that relatively few blacks were viewed as ready for promotion to the vacant jobs. They were also dissatisfied that only a few of the most senior blacks held key line positions. Eventually, more promotions of blacks to upper-level management did occur. However, to date, the number of black managers in positions comparable to those who left is still smaller than prior to the departures.

Race Relations Competence Workshop

Content of Learnings

The stated purpose of the Race Relations Competence Workshop was to provide members of the XYZ management with an opportunity to learn race relations competence as defined in a document written by the Race Relations Advisory Group (Alderfer et al., 1988). The workshop was a 3-day program of lectures, experiential group activities, and one-on-one role playing (Alderfer, Alderfer, Bell, & Jones, in press).

Race relations competence defines understandings and behaviors about race relations that are expected of bosses as a function of the race of boss and subordinate. Some information is similar for all four types of relationships. In other words, whether the boss and/or the subordinate is black or white makes little difference. But some understandings and behaviors do differ depending on the racial composition of the boss–subordinate pair. An example of a behavior that applies to all relationships is black and white "Managers must conform to the corporate policy on race relations and accurately communicate information about this policy to subordinates." An example of an understanding that applies only to blacks supervising whites is, "White subordinates may be devalued by others or feel resentment themselves because they have a black supervisor."

In advance of attending the workshop, managers received an abbreviated version of the original diagnosis written to underline in a straightforward fashion how black and white managers perceived race relations at XYZ. Similarities and differences between blacks and whites both were described. Managers attending the workshop also received a copy of the XYZ statement on Race Relations Competence. In the workshop itself, the competence document was reviewed by the consultants, after the managers had participated in the role plays designed to exemplify key elements of the concepts.

Format

Workshop lectures were spread evenly throughout the 3 days on the topics, which included: intergroup relations and racism, thinking and feeling, dynamics of role playing, and conflict and change. The first and last lectures were about the subject matter of race relations and change, and the second and third were about learning processes inside and outside the workshop.

Semistructured group discussions occurred in race-alike and cross-race groups. Alike groups reflected on their own characteristics and prepared an agenda for cross-race discussions. Cross-race groups discussed the agenda developed in the race-alike groups and examined the here-and-now behavior among participants as it occurred in the room. Each lecture was done by a different consultant. Race-alike work was done in breakout rooms without consultants present, whereas the cross-race discussions took place with pairs of consultants (black male, white female; black female, white male) in the room.

Role plays were based on the four situations defined by the Race Relations Competence Document and described the kinds of events that actually occurred in the XYZ corporation. Race alike role plays (black–

black; white–white) took place in race-alike settings with consultants of the same race. Cross-race role plays occurred in the total groups with the race of the consultant matching the race of the boss in each situation.

Attendance

Throughout the history of the workshop, debate occurred among members of the Race Relations Advisory Group and senior managers outside the group about the appropriate degree of voluntarism among participants. Initially, participation in the workshop began with the most senior managers and moved downward in the hierarchy. The strategy was "top down," and upper-level managers were clearly "expected," although not formally required, to attend.

When the workshops were populated by the upper portion of the hierarchy, there was always a shortage of eligible black managers to maintain a ratio of no more than 2.5 white managers to each black manager. Therefore, some black managers were asked to attend more than once. This open practice sometimes drew criticism from whites, because they felt at a disadvantage to blacks who were more experienced with workshop activities.

As noted above, members of the corporate personnel committees were expected to attend, and periodically reviews were conducted to find out whether this condition was being satisfied. Personnel committee members who did not attend were contacted and asked to participate.

In the passing years, the corporation adopted an increasingly formal management-by-objectives (MBO) program. Some white (never black) managers reported to workshops by announcing that they were there as "someone else's MBO." Needless to say, people who arrived feeling coerced to be present tended to be less receptive to learning, and, in the worst cases, they actively interfered with others' learning. The consultants favored encouraging key people to attend the workshops, but they regularly spoke against requiring attendance.

Evaluation of Workshops

Evaluation of the workshop was carried out regularly and across several time spans. During the workshop itself, the staff provided an opportunity at the end of each day for participants to comment on their experiences and to evaluate the learning. Approximately 4 weeks after each workshop ended, participants received a questionnaire inviting their assessment on a number of dimensions. Then, in 1986 after the project had been under way nearly 10 years, the entire undertaking was evaluated—including specific attention to the workshop (Alderfer, Alderfer, Bell, & Jones, in press).

In response to these evaluations, periodic changes were made in the design and conduct of the workshop. Role plays within the workshop were periodically revised to fit the experience of participants; this was especially necessary as more participants came from lower levels in the hierarchy. At one point, workshop attendees began to include members of the bargaining unit, as racial issues began to be discussed in the corporation's quality-of-working-life program. When that decision was made, group interviews were held with bargaining unit people to enlist their cooperation in designing role plays that would be relevant to their work experiences as well as to those of managers.

As workshop participants were drawn increasingly from middle and lower ranks, the gap in education and authority between participants and consultants also widened. Under these conditions, the consultants tended to be viewed more as similar to authority figures in the organization than as peers from a different profession. To counteract the unfavorable effects of greater social distance, consultants changed their behavior to bring themselves into a closer, more friendly relationship with participants.

THE SOCIAL AND POLITICAL CONTEXT

The events described here occurred during the 1980s. Nationally, it was a time of retrenchment in civil rights policy. Some white male middle managers in the corporation used the ideology and practices of the Reagan administration to criticize corporate policy. Forms of these comments included statements such as "The corporation is doing more than the government requires" or "XYZ may be doing things that are against the law." Whether the corporation was doing more than the government required depended on the government official and the conditions under which he or she spoke. I think it is unlikely, for example, that Edwin Meese or William Bradford Reynolds would have approved of the XYZ race relations improvement program, if they had known about it. During this period, however, a number of white male corporate leaders spoke out publicly against the orientation of Meese and Reynolds, although I do not know whether XYZ was involved in this activity. There were neither formal accusations nor evidence known to me that XYZ violated the law; they did not have a policy of "quotas" (although some within the corporation accused them of having such a policy). They did regularly observe and discuss the distribution of people in departments and throughout the hierarchy by race and gender. Corporate policy did include objectives for increasing the number of black men, black women, and white women who held jobs that at one time were occupied solely by white men.

During this same period, senior corporate leadership asked for a half-day race relations workshop for the XYZ Board of Directors. A modified version of the 3-day event was designed and carried out. In order to provide an adequate number of black participants, as the composition of the board included only one black director, the workshop was also attended by the most senior black managers. Nearly all XYZ directors attended the special workshop, and, in the weeks following, the board passed a resolution affirming the board's commitment to the XYZ race relations policy.

PROGRAM EVALUATION

In 1986, nearly 10 years after the original diagnosis had begun and 2 years after all program elements described above had been established, a systematic evaluation of the XYZ race relations improvement was undertaken. The aims were to determine what changes, if any, had occurred in the profile of black managers throughout the hierarchy of the XYZ organization and how elements of the program were perceived by members of the XYZ management.

The Race Relations Advisory Group played a central role in the design and conduct of this evaluation, and it received the first feedback of results. Then the findings were presented to senior management. After that, all participants in the study who wished to attend a series of voluntary feedback meetings were invited to half-day meetings.

Data Collection Methods

Information about the distribution of black and white managers throughout the hierarchy and on corporate personnel committees was obtained from organization records with the assistance of the personnel staff.

Data pertaining to how the interventions were perceived by XYZ managers were obtained from an organic questionnaire (i.e., a questionnaire written in the language and concepts of black and white XYZ managers) developed in cooperation with the Race Relations Advisory Group and administered to all black managers and to a 10% random sample of white managers in the corporation. At random, half of the potential respondents received the questionnaires in race-gender-level alike groups, just as the original diagnosis had been distributed, whereas the other half received the instrument as individuals by mail. This field experiment

showed that the alike meetings had higher response rates and more trusting reactions to the data collection process than did mailing the instrument
to individuals.

Information about perceptions of program elements derives from
three kinds of questions. First, we asked how much information the re-
spondent had about the element. The results present the percentage of
people who said they had "no information." Second, we asked people who
said they had Vague, Some, Basic, or Detailed information to answer a set
of more detailed questions about the program element. The specific questions are included in exhibits that follow. Answers to each of the questions
ranged on a 6-point scale from "strongly agree" to "strongly disagree." For
analysis and tabulation purposes, we combined the three agree and the
three disagree responses. The exhibits show the percentage in each group
who gave one of the three agree responses. Finally, we asked respondents
to choose a recommendation about the program element among five options: keep and strengthen; keep as is; keep but reduce resources; review
with the expectation to eliminate; and definitely terminate. Because of the
manner in which the responses were distributed, we combined the latter
three options into one, which appears in the tables as "Weaken." Data from
these three types of questions were tabulated by the four race and gender
groups.

We also attempted to determine the distribution of black and white
managers throughout the variety of departments within the corporation
during the same period as we traced the hierarchical patterns. As it turned
out, the organization had undergone several structural changes during the
12 years covered by the time series study. Therefore, it was not possible to
make meaningful comparisons of black and white managers among functional groupings across time, because the departmental configuration
changed in a manner that did not permit sensible comparisons.

In the following subsections, I present the evaluative information in a
manner that parallels the major elements of the model.

Evaluations of Race Relations Advisory Group

Table 7.1 shows how the XYZ managers perceived and evaluated the Race
Relations Advisory Group. On five of the questions, there were differences
between blacks and whites in the information they had about the group
and in how they perceived the group's effects. Black males and black
females reported having more information about the group than white
males and white females.

Black males and black females were more likely to see themselves and
the XYZ organization as benefiting from the group, whereas white males

TABLE 7.1. Statements about Race Relations Advisory Group

		Percentage agree			
		Black males $(n=74)^a$	Black females $(n=92)^a$	White males $(n=207)^a$	White females $(n=111)^a$
A.	No information[b]	36	46	64	68
B.	1. Helps race relations at XYZ	87	88	89	86
	2. Hurts XYZ organization[c]	2	2	12	14
	3. I have benefitted[b]	71	67	31	36
	4. Helps XYZ organization	96	96	85	88
	5. Hurts race relations at XYZ[d]	2	0	11	17
	6. I have been hurt	11	2	11	9
C.	Recommendations[b]				
	1. Strengthen	92	94	27	57
	2. Keep as is	4	2	49	29
	3. Weaken	4	4	24	14

[a] "n" indicates the number of people responding.
[b] Differences significant at $p < .001$, X^2 test.
[c] Differences significant at $p < .05$, X^2 test.
[d] Differences significant at $p < .01$, X^2 test.

and white females were more likely to see the group as hurting the XYZ organization and as hurting race relations at XYZ. On the matter of recommendations, black males and black females were more likely to recommend strengthening the group, whereas white males and white females were more likely to recommend keeping it as is or weakening it. Most blacks and most whites thought the group helped race relations in the corporation, and few whites or blacks reported that they had personally been hurt by the group.

Evaluations of Upward Mobility Interventions

In assessing the upward mobility interventions, we have information from company records and from the managers' perceptions. Data contained in Figures 7.2, 7.3, and 7.4 show the proportion of black managers who held positions at several steps in the XYZ managerial hierarchy and on the personnel committees before, during, and after the upward mobility interventions. We also include mobility data about white women managers during the same period as a comparison.

In observing these data, one is aided noting the following milestones in the history of the race relations improvement project:

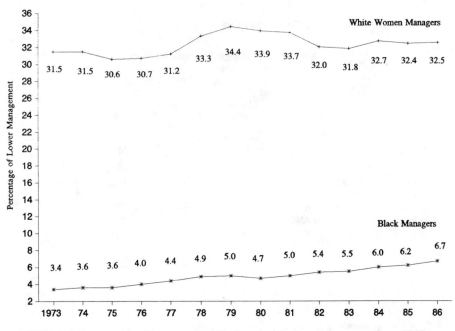

FIGURE 7.2. Percentages of lower-ranking black and white female managers from 1973 to 1986.

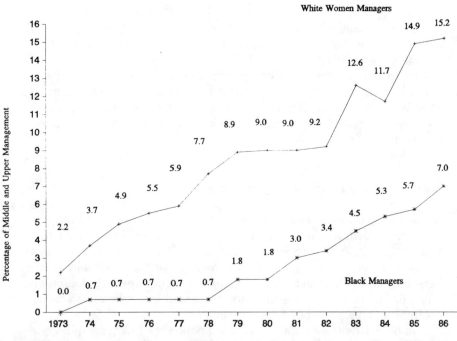

FIGURE 7.3. Percentages of upper-ranking black and white female managers from 1973 to 1986.

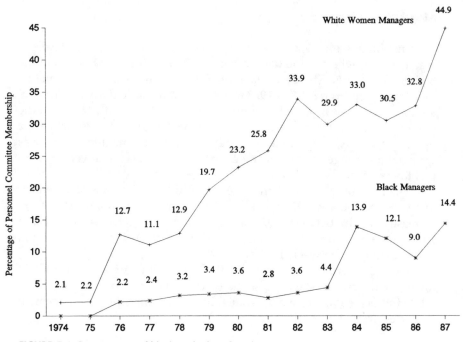

FIGURE 7.4. Percentages of black and white female managers serving on personnel committees from 1974 to 1987.

1976: Race relations consulting team begins diagnosis
1979: Diagnosis fed back to management
1980: Race Relations Advisory Group expands from 12 to 20 members and becomes permanent structure
1981: Design and testing of upward mobility program and race relations competence workshop
1982: Implementation of upward mobility program and race relations competence workshop

Between 1973 and 1979, the XYZ management force expanded by approximately 33%, whereas between 1979 and 1982, the group decreased by approximately 25%. From 1982 to 1986, the group again began to expand. In compiling the information charts, we combined black men and black women into a single group and added the lowest two and highest five levels in the hierarchy in order to have relatively stable numbers to interpret. This method of reporting helps to maintain the confidentiality of the organization and to show certain identifiable patterns of change.

Management Jobs Held

Information in Figure 7.2 pertains to managers in the lowest two levels of management, whereas the data in Figure 7.3 pertains to managers in the highest five levels. The percentage of black managers in lower management increased from 3.4% in 1973 to 6.7% in 1986. Particularly noteworthy are increases of nearly a whole percent between 1976 and 1978 when the diagnosis was occurring, and of 1.7% between 1981 and 1986, when the upward mobility program was designed and implemented. There was virtually no change in the percentage of black managers in lower management between 1978 and 1981.

The percentage of black managers in middle and upper management increased from 0% in 1973 to 7.0% in 1986. Particularly noteworthy were increases of 2.3% between 1978 and 1981 and of 4.0% between 1981 and 1986. There was virtually no change in the percentage of black middle and upper managers between 1974 and 1978.

Over the period of observation, the percentation of white women in lower management stayed essentially constant at approximately 32%, while the percentage of white women in middle and upper management increased from 2.2% to 15.2%.

Representation on Personnel Committees

Figure 7.4 shows the percentage of black and white female managers on personnel committees between 1974 and 1987. There were no black managers on personnel committees until 1976, when the percentage grew to 2.2%. Between 1976 and 1983, the percentage grew to 4.4% in a most gradual fashion. Then in 1984, the percentage jumped markedly to 13.8%, dropped somewhat in 1985 and 1986, and then reached 14.4% in 1987. The year 1984 marked the time when the special task force intervention into the upward mobility system ended, and the process of evaluating managers was completely returned to the existing system as modified by changing the composition of the personnel committees. Elimination of the special task force occurred for a variety of reasons. Maintaining the special task force was expensive, and it generated substantial dissatisfaction on the part of the members of the normal personnel committees, who objected that they were being unfairly accused of not doing their jobs well.

During this same period, the organization was undergoing several kinds of wrenching change pertaining to size, corporate mission, and composition of the top leadership group—as well as that brought on by the efforts to improve race relations. In my opinion, there are limits to how much change any system can take; I believe that the XYZ management eliminated the special task force, in part, to keep within manageable limits the amount of stress the management group had to contain. During the same period, the percentage of white women on personnel committees increased from 2.1% to 44.9%. The years between 1975 and 1977 saw an increase of 10.5% in the percentage of white women on personnel committees, and the years between 1978 and 1986 saw an increase of 34.0%.

The primary objective of the upward mobility intervention was to increase the racial equity of promotion decisions throughout the XYZ corporation and, most especially, at the middle and upper levels of management. The information bearing on whether the "glass ceiling" for blacks moving into middle and upper management was penetrated is seen most clearly in Figure 7.3, where one can see an increase in the proportion of black managers in middle and upper management beginning in 1979 and 1980 and then increasing markedly from 1982 onward. Figure 7.4 shows a similar pattern in the composition of personnel committees from 1984 onward. Both these patterns of change began somewhat before the upward mobility program was completely designed and then accelerated after the program was in place. The delay in acceleration of the black managers' movement toward populating personnel committees reflects the time it takes from when black managers in substantial numbers held more senior positions and when, because of their experience and competence in these jobs, it became appropriate for them to serve on personnel committees that selected others for higher-level jobs.

The information contained in Figures 7.3 and 7.4 strongly suggests that the upward mobility interventions did increase the number of black managers in middle and upper management positions. Because data were not obtained from similar organizations that either had no programs at all or had different kinds of programs, we cannot be sure that causes other than or in addition to XYZ's race relations improvement program explain the observed changes.

I have noted several times throughout this chapter, however, that the kinds of changes attempted and achieved at XYZ were decidedly not in accord with the Reagan administration policies and practices. The organization was not bringing about its changes in the distribution of power by black and white managers in a national political environment that favored such changes. Indeed, a report in the *New York Times* of July 14, 1987, showed that, during the Reagan years from 1980 through 1986, the number of blacks who held presidential and noncareer appointments in the senior executive service was cut in half (Williams, 1987). During the same period, the number of such appointments held by "women" (i.e., race unidentified) increased slightly. The Reagan administration, therefore, showed itself to be less averse to upward mobility for "women" (race unidentified) than for "blacks" (gender unidentified).

The data from XYZ showed that white women moved into middle and upper management positions and onto personnel committees sooner and in greater percentages than did black men and black women. Although this chapter is primarily about race relations, I believe that the changes for white women are significant and do bear on understanding racial dynamics. White women, after all, do have a race. White women as members of the Race Relations Advisory Group from the project's beginning and, in later years, as vice president for personnel played important leadership roles in the changing of race relations at XYZ. The data about the upward mobility for white women indicate that upward mobility for blacks was behind that for white women.

Within XYZ management, there were many more white women than blacks (thousands as compared to hundreds), so the corporation had many more white women than blacks to choose from when making management promotion decisions. The data also indicated that on racial matters white women's perceptions and opinions were much more like those of white men than those of black men or black women, thereby suggesting that white women might be more acceptable as colleagues to white men than either black men or black women. Certainly the white men of the XYZ Corporation were more familiar with white women than with black men or black women.

Perceptions of the Power-based Change Efforts

Information about perceptions of the efforts to change both the race and gender profile of the XYZ management and the composition of the personnel committees that make promotion decisions is contained in Tables 7.2 and 7.3. On the topic of the upward mobility interventions, seven of the measures showed differences among the race and gender groups. Black females and white females reported having more information about the program than did black males or white males. Black males and black females were more likely to perceive the upward mobility program as helping race relations at XYZ, as personally benefiting them, and as helping the XYZ organization, whereas white males and white females were more likely to see the program as hurting the XYZ organization and hurting race relations at XYZ. Black males and black females were more likely to recommend strengthening the program, whereas white males and white females were more likely to recommend weakening it.

On the topic of increasing the proportion of blacks on personnel committees, four of the measures showed differences among the four race and gender groups. Black females and black males were more likely to say that they had personally benefited and that it helps the XYZ organization to

TABLE 7.2. Statements about Upward Mobility Program

	Percentage agree			
	Black males $(n=72)^a$	Black females $(n=88)^a$	White males $(n=204)^a$	White females $(n=109)^a$
A. No information[b]	31	53	35	41
B. 1. Helps race relations at XYZ[c]	70	62	40	41
2. Hurts XYZ organization[b]	8	30	52	39
3. I have benefitted[c]	37	48	14	20
4. Helps XYZ organization[c]	88	82	48	67
5. Hurts race relations at XYZ[c]	19	30	57	45
6. I have been hurt	23	30	29	31
C. Recommendations[c]				
1. Strengthen	90	66	25	26
2. Keep as is	6	5	21	24
3. Weaken	4	29	54	50

[a] "*n*" indicates the number of people responding.
[b] Differences significant at $p < .02$, X^2 test.
[c] Differences significant at $p < .001$, X^2 test.

TABLE 7.3. Statements about Increasing the Proportion of Blacks on Personnel Committees

	Percentage agree			
	Black males $(n=72)^a$	Black females $(n=88)^a$	White males $(n=204)^a$	White females $(n=109)^a$
A. No information	42	53	62	78
B. 1. Helps race relations at XYZ	83	95	84	78
2. Hurts XYZ organization[b]	7	0	17	18
3. I have benefitted[c]	59	67	30	18
4. Helps XYZ organization[b]	93	98	82	82
5. Hurts race relations at XYZ	10	7	16	18
6. I have been hurt	7	12	10	15
C. Recommendations[c]				
1. Strengthen	95	93	36	50
2. Keep as is	0	2	47	42
3. Weaken	5	5	17	8

[a] "*n*" indicates the number of people responding.
[b] Differences significant at $p < .02$, X^2 test.
[c] Differences significant at $p < .001$, X^2 test.

change the personnel committee composition, whereas white females and white males were likely to agree that changes in the committee composition hurt the XYZ organization. In terms of recommendations about changing personnel committee composition, black males and black females were more likely to recommend strengthening this intervention, whereas white males and white females were more likely to say keep it as is.

Perceptions of Race Relations Competence Workshop

Information about perceptions of the Race Relations Competence Workshop is contained in Table 7.4. Seven of the measures show differences between the race and gender groups in how they perceive the workshop. Overall, the evaluation of the workshop by all groups was quite positive. However, more white males and white females than black males and black females said that they had no information about the workshop. In assessing the workshop, black males and black females were more likely than white males and white females to say that it helps race relations at XYZ, that they have personally benefited from it, and that it helped the XYZ organization, whereas white males and white females were more likely than black males and black females to say the workshop hurt the XYZ

TABLE 7.4. Statements about Race Relations Competence Workshop

		Percentage agree			
		Black males $(n=72)^a$	Black females $(n=88)^a$	White males $(n=204)^a$	White females $(n=109)^a$
A.	No information[b]	28	36	58	56
B.	1. Helps race relations at XYZ[c]	98	91	82	85
	2. Hurts XYZ organization[c]	6	2	14	7
	3. I have benefitted[d]	82	88	63	60
	4. Helps XYZ organization[b]	98	98	87	87
	5. Hurts race relations at XYZ[d]	8	0	18	9
	6. I have been hurt	4	0	5	3
C.	Recommendations[b]				
	1. Strengthen	90	96	41	62
	2. Keep as is	8	4	35	20
	3. Weaken	2	0	24	18

[a] "*n*" indicates the number of people responding.
[b] Differences significant at $p < .001$, X^2 test.
[c] Differences significant at $p < .05$, X^2 test.
[d] Differences significant at $p < .01$, X^2 test.

organization and hurt race relations at XYZ. All groups were most likely to recommend strengthening the workshop among the several options, although black females and black males were more likely to give this response than were white females and white males.

Different Effects of Power and Education

In observing the full set of findings about the XYZ race relations improvement program it is apparent that the several program elements received different degrees of support. Even though blacks generally were more favorable than whites to all program elements, some interventions received more general support than others. In some instances, white reactions were predominantly favorable, even if the evaluations were not as positive as those from blacks. This pattern of findings applied to evaluations of the Race Relations Advisory Group and to the Race Relations Competence Workshop, but clearly not to the Upward Mobility Program and less clearly to the Personnel Committee composition intervention. These findings are consistent with the differential orientations of blacks and whites from the outset of the project. Whites tended to favor educational interventions, and blacks tended to favor power strategies. Blacks reported that they had more information than whites.[1] These observations led to an additional inquiry about the possibility of evaluation having a different association with information, depending on whether the intervention was primarily focused on education or power.

Overall evaluation scales were formed by adding the six harm and benefit items (which had high associations among them) for each separate program element. For each race and gender group, the educational interventions (workshop and advisory group) tended to show higher positive

---

[1]I, of course, do not know concretely why whites reported having less information about program elements than blacks. The information was developed from questionnaire ratings, not from interviews. However, from other events connected with the project, I can offer informed speculation. White people who acknowledge a willingness to work for improved race relations face substantial criticism from white peers. Various kinds of name calling (i.e., "Bleeding heart liberal" is a generous form) occur. We even developed a role-playing scenario to deal with these dynamics in the workshop. My hypothesis is that whites connected with the program would be less likely than blacks to tell other whites about their activities in order to save themselves from criticism, and whites not associated with the work might be less likely to inquire for similar reasons. Blacks, on the other hand, would probably face less criticism and more praise from black peers for their efforts and therefore be more likely to provide information to black peers. Conversations between blacks and whites about the program are harder to predict but would be limited in frequency by the comparatively small number of blacks in relation to whites.

correlations between having information and giving a positive evaluation of the program element than the power interventions (upward mobility and personnel committees).

Different Responses to Change by White Women and White Men

It is important also to notice that even though white women's attitudes toward race were similar to those of white men, white women also showed more receptivity to changing race relations than did white men. In all of the four tables, a higher percentage of white women than white men recommended strengthening the specific program elements. In the study of the Race Relations Advisory Group, we observed that white female members of the group changed their racial attitudes more during the first years of the group's existence than did white men (Alderfer et al., 1988). In the later years of the program, white women also led the Race Relations Advisory Group.

CONCLUSION

The work reported here provides an overview and an evaluation of approximately 15 years of black–white cooperation in the service of improving race relations in the XYZ Corporation. The activities began in the 1970s, an era supportive of progressive change in race relations, and continued through the 1980s, a period of regressive change nationally. During this period, XYZ also changed its senior leadership and, with difficulty, maintained its race relations improvement program.

I characterize the results achieved by XYZ as modest and sustained progressive change. Especially notable is the degree of commitment demonstrated by black and white, male and female managers from all levels of the organization to the strenuous work required to bring about significant change. The bias I am most aware of in this paper is that it may understate the degree of struggle associated with the change (and lack of change) that was accomplished.

In this project, there were no magical breakthroughs, although there was clear evidence of discontinuous progressive change. Even as this chapter is being written, the company is putting into place a new action program to address issues uncovered by a recent first-level diagnosis. Many people at the XYZ Corporation worked hard for the goals of the project. Some took significant risks with their careers along the way. Some black women, black men, white women, and white men received rewards from the organization comparable to their contributions, but not everyone did. Many served goals far larger than their own narrow self-interests, or the work reported here simply would not have been possible. No one closely connected to the project and committed to its goals believes that the system can relax its efforts or reduce its vigilance, if the change that has been achieved is to be maintained and the progress that is possible is to be continued. Upon reviewing the results of this study, a senior black member of the Race Relations Advisory Group commented, "I see it on paper, and it looks good. Why don't I feel good?"

One answer to this question is that serious work to effect progressive race relations is simply not easy. Although the current national political leadership is not as regressive as its predecessors, it is not progressive either. Perhaps the fairest characterization is that they are less regressive. The 1988 election campaign included appeals to racist feelings among white Americans, and within recent weeks, administration officials actively worked to impede an effective compromise between white business leaders and black civil rights leaders designed to reverse through legislation some of the regressive Supreme Court decisions of the 1980s. Apparently the Republican party wants to be able to campaign against "quotas" in the 1992 election. At the level of national politics, this strategy is a rough equivalent of a white XYZ manager explaining to a white colleague that a white person did not get a promotion, because "the company had to promote a black person." This kind of political strategy does not help race relations nationally. At XYZ, it would be evaluated as failing to show race relations competence. Neither XYZ nor any organization can remain unaffected by the political climate in which it is embedded. The political climate, in turn, reflects the United States's long-standing, deeply felt ambivalence about how much we want to work on solving versus avoiding or exacerbating our racial problems.

ACKNOWLEDGMENTS

I wish to express my appreciation to the Office of Naval Research, whose Organizational Effectiveness Programs through contract number N100014-82-K-0715 provided support for this research; to Charleen Alderfer, Ella Bell, Jimmy Jones, Robert Tucker, and Leota Tucker for their contributions to the design and implementation of the project; to Jack Gillette, Sharon Rogolsky, and David Thomas for their help with statistical analyses reported in this paper; to the XYZ Corporation Race Relations Advisory Group members for their interest and support for the project; to the senior executives of the XYZ Corporation, who provided a most sophisticated kind of support for this work throughout its 15-year history; and to the Yale School of Organization and Management for 1990 and 1991 summer research grants to Clayton P. Alderfer.

REFERENCES

Alderfer, C. P. (1977). Group and intergroup relations. In J. R. Hackman, and J. L. Suttle (Eds.), *Improving life at work* (pp. 227-296). Santa Monica, CA: Goodyear.

Alderfer, C. P., Alderfer, C. J., Tucker, R. C., & Tucker, L. (1980). Diagnosing race relations in management, *Journal of Applied Behavioral Science, 16*, 135-166.

Alderfer, C. P. (1986). An intergroup perspective on group dynamics. In J. Lorsch (Ed.), *Handbook of organizational behavior* (pp. 190-222). Englewood Cliffs, NJ: Prentice Hall.

Alderfer, C. P., Tucker, R. C., Alderfer, C. J. & Tucker, L. (1988). The race relations advisory group: An intergroup intervention. In W. A. Passmore & R. W. Woodman (Eds.), *Research in organizational change and development* (Vol. 2., pp. 269-321). Greenwich, CT: JAI Press.

Alderfer, C. P., Alderfer, C. J., Bell, E. L., & Jones, J. (in press). The race relations competence workshop: Theory and results. *Human Relations.*

Williams, L. (1987, July 14). For the Black Professional, the obstacles remain. *New York Times*, p. A16.

CHAPTER 8

Creating One from Two: The Merger Between Harris Semiconductor and General Electric Solid State

DAVID M. SCHWEIGER
J. RUSSELL RIDLEY, JR.
DENNIS M. MARINI

INTRODUCTION

I'm confident the employees of both Harris Semiconductor and General Electric Solid State want this merger to succeed. One dimension of that success is how well we manage the integration. (Jon Cornell, president of Harris Semiconductor Sector, August 22, 1988)

When Jon Cornell (hereafter referred to as the president) made this comment as he prepared to embark upon his first major acquisition, he displayed insight that many executives have failed to show in the past. In spite of all the complex negotiations that were occupying his time, he knew that the key to the success of the upcoming merger between Harris Semiconductor Sector (HSS) and General Electric Solid State (GESS) would be his and his colleagues' ability to take two organizations and successfully combine them into one unified organization.

In this chapter we present a detailed examination of the challenges that were faced and the interventions that were used to integrate two companies, each with its own culture, management systems and processes, and organizational structures. The case is primarily based on our collective experiences drawn from the role that each of us played during the integration process. J. Russell Ridley, Jr., was director of organizational development of Harris Semiconductor Sector prior to and during the merger. Dennis Marini became vice president of human resources of the new HSS in January 1989. Prior to this role he had served as director of human resources in other divisions of Harris Corporation and in other companies. Finally, David Schweiger served as an external consultant to the senior management of HSS during the merger. To supplement our memories, we consulted notes we had taken during our numerous meetings and interviews with executives, managers, and employees; archival records; and selective surveys that were conducted during the integration process.

Our description is divided into several sections. The first section describes the events leading up to the merger. Particular attention is given to the strategic situations facing both companies prior to the merger and the major strategy driving the merger. We believe that these were instrumental in determining what the integration process would look like and the diverse challenges that would have to be managed. The second section describes the challenges that were faced and the interventions that were used to manage diversity and facilitate the integration of the companies prior to the closing. The third section focuses on the challenges that were encountered in putting the new Harris Semiconductor together after the closing; that is, the point at which the acquired company is legally transferred to the acquiring company. The fourth section examines an important issue that is rarely considered in discussions of the merger integration process: the impact of external environmental pressures. Too often the merger integration process is discussed as if it occurs in a vacuum. In this section we illustrate how changes in the business environment affected the integration and rebuilding processes. Finally, we summarize key lessons that we learned during the acquisition experience. It is important to note that there are many problems and challenges that transpired during the acquisition that are not covered in this chapter. We have limited our discussion to topics consistent with the diversity theme of this book. Problems and challenges we encountered are discussed only when they affected issues of managing diversity.

THE HSS STRATEGIC SITUATION AND MERGER STRATEGY

HSS, as of 1987, had the lowest revenue and third-highest profit among the five independent business sectors (Government Systems, Communications, Lanier Business Products, Information Systems, Semiconductor) of Harris Corporation. HSS designed and produced standard, semicustom/application-specific integrated circuits and custom circuits for the government (military and aerospace), industrial, electronic data processing (EDP), communications, and consumer segments of the semiconductor industry. The government segment, which utilizes custom and semicustom products, represented by far the largest portion of HSS's business (59%). HSS was the eighth-largest supplier of integrated circuits in the United States and the second-largest supplier to the U.S. government. Due to its primary focus on the government segment, the lion's share of HSS's sales were concentrated in the United States.

Although HSS had been profitable in 1987, certain opportunities and threats were emerging in the semiconductor industry that could affect its profitability in the ensuing years. First, the industry was emerging from its worst recession in history (1985) and was now facing overcapacity, consolidation, increased international and technological competition, globalization, and reduced growth in domestic markets. Second, changes were occurring in important market segments. HSS was heavily focused on the government market, but this market was shrinking.

At the same time, new opportunities were emerging in overseas markets and in selected product lines. To take advantage of the opportunities and avoid being victimized by the threats, the president and his staff decided in their 1987 5-year plan to (1) significantly reduce their dependence on the government segment, (2) increase their focus on the industrial, EDP, and communications segments, and (3) begin to penetrate the European and Japanese markets. What vehicle would best enable HSS to alter its market segment focus and improve its competitiveness? After examining a number of alternatives, the president and his staff decided that an acquisition would be an attractive strategic move.

At this time, General Electric had announced that its solid state business (with annual sales of $470 million) was for sale because it was not consistent with GE's strategic objective and was reported to be marginally profitable. Solid state was just one of many businesses within GE. The availability of General Electric Solid State appeared to be an excellent opportunity for HSS to implement its strategy. As John T. Hartley, chairman, president, and chief executive officer (CEO) of Harris Corporation would later comment:

> *The acquisition of GE Solid State brings Harris to the front rank of world semiconductor competitors, with the size, strength, and resources to compete successfully with the best in the world.*

There was some overlap in the markets served by HSS and GESS, but there were a number of very important differences that would benefit HSS. First, GESS had a much stronger presence in the commercial, industrial, and automotive/consumer markets, and would thus provide an opportunity for HSS to reduce its dependence on the military market, yet still be the largest supplier in that market. Second, GESS had a far greater presence in Europe and South Asia. Thus, the acquisition would greatly increase sales in those markets. Third, the acquisition would afford HSS a new presence in the discrete power market, thus expanding its product offerings.

Not only would the acquisition broaden market focus, it would permit HSS to increase its overall size and presence in all markets and become the sixth-largest U.S. semiconductor company. The increase in size would enable HSS to achieve scale economies from higher volumes in such areas as procurement, research and development (R&D), manufacturing, marketing, and distribution. The combined R&D talents would further provide HSS with opportunities for new-product and other technology programs, such as computer-aided design and process development.

The fit between the two companies looked good and on August 22, 1988, Hartley announced that HSS intended to acquire GESS. After continued negotiations and due diligence investigations (i.e., a process whereby an acquiring company examines a potential acquisition), a definitive agreement was signed on November 7, 1988, whereby HSS would buy GESS for $206 million in cash. On November 30, 1988, the deal was closed and GESS became a part of HSS.

MANAGING THE PRECLOSING INTEGRATION PROCESS

As noted in the opening quote by the president of HSS, the benefits of the acquisition would not be easily realized. He had watched as other semiconductor firms tried their hand at managing major acquisitions. This led him to conclude early on that GESS would not be an appendage. Instead, the goal would be to build a stronger company based upon the strengths of each company.

The merger would more than triple the number of people employed by HSS and significantly increase the geographic scope and complexity of the company. GESS employed about 10,000 people worldwide. Headquarters, engineering, and marketing were located in Somerville, New Jersey, with various manufacturing and assembly operations located in Ohio, California, Pennsylvania, Ireland, India, Malaysia, Taiwan, and Singapore. GESS also had 39 sales offices worldwide. HSS on the other hand employed about 4,000 people worldwide with headquarters, engineering, marketing, and most of its manufacturing operations centrally located in Melbourne, Florida, and Kuala Lumpur, Malaysia.

To add to the complexity, GESS was really three companies. One company was Intersil, which was managed as a subsidiary of GESS prior to the HSS acquisition. Intersil was an entrepreneurial semiconductor firm located in Santa Clara, California (Silicon Valley). It had been acquired by GE in 1981. A second company was RCA Solid State, which had been acquired by GE in 1985. The third company was the GE Solid State organization. According to a number of GESS, ex-RCA, and Intersil managers, neither RCA nor Intersil had been fully integrated into GESS by the time HSS acquired GESS. This was evident in that each company's systems, product lines, and building signs remained independent following the acquisition. Moreover, many managers indicated that they still identified with their pre-acquisition company.

Indeed, combining these various organizations would require a well-managed integration process with many decisions having to be made. As the 18 months following the closing would show, a well managed process would require a great deal of flexibility and an openness to learning on the part of members of both organizations. The most important decision would involve how to manage the integration decision-making process:

- Who would be involved and how would decisions be made?
- Who would staff the new Harris Semiconductor, especially at the senior management level?
- How would the organizations be combined; that is, which units would be consolidated, remain independent, be eliminated, or be reorganized?
- How would differences in systems, policies, procedures, and management processes and philosophies be reconciled?
- How would the new Harris Semiconductor be rebuilt; that is, how would the organization be structured and how would new managerial teams be established?

By the closing date, the HSS management had developed a general integration plan for how the two companies might fit together. The plan established ground rules and time frames for managing the integration process; identified key functional and product areas that would need to be examined for integration; and identified key HSS and GESS managers who would be responsible for implementing the plan. In spite of the plan, many of the integration decisions had not been made. As the president noted on August 22, 1988: "It's still too soon to comment in any level of detail on how the combined organizations will look, but they will be combined."

The inability of managers to specify every integration decision prior to or even just after the closing is typical in many mergers and acquisitions. Executives cannot learn everything there is to know about an acquired firm during negotiations and due diligence (i.e., prior to the closing). Thus, although the president and his staff had laid out an integration plan, it was not possible to simply implement it. Integration decisions were made and adjusted as they continued to learn about how each company operated. Many of these decisions continued to be made long after the closing. Essentially, the integration process turned out to be an incremental process aligned to a basic vision of how the two companies might fit together. We now discuss how the integration of the diverse cultures, management systems and processes, and organizational structures was managed at HSS and the challenges that were faced along the way.

Transition Teams

From the point at which the acquisition was conceived, two decisions had been made by the president. First, all efforts would be given to facilitating interaction, learning, and joint problem solving and decision making among members of HSS and GESS. He believed that only through these efforts could interfirm diversity be effectively managed. Second, integration was going to be completed as fast as possible. He reached these two very important decisions based upon the personal advice of CEOs who he knew and who had been through major acquisitions. The first decision proved to be beneficial, but the second proved to be detrimental. In retrospect, it is clear to us that the speed at which the integration proceeded outpaced the new organization's ability to learn and assimilate the new behavior patterns needed to execute the integration plan.

Staffing the Transition Teams

The first step to facilitate interaction, learning, and joint problem solving took place just after the signing of the agreement in principle (which is an agreement to negotiate a merger or an acquisition formally). GESS and HSS each created separate transition teams, with each team led by an executive from the respective firms. The team was composed of "cooperative" managers who had knowledge of the different functional areas within the respective companies, who could broadly understand the role of the function within the combined firm, and who top management viewed as "high potentials." Leaders and members of the HSS and GESS teams were chosen by their respective presidents. (The GESS president agreed to retire at the closing.) Thus, managers from each company were paired with counterparts from the other company to critically examine the current capabilities of each company.

The Mission

According to the HSS transition team leader, the mission of the teams was "to facilitate the due diligence process and make the integration of these two world-class organizations smooth and, most important of all, *right.*" This would involve joint decision making between managers of both companies. Either they would choose the "best" human resources, marketing, manufacturing, and management practices for the new Harris Semiconductor, regardless of which company the practices came from, or they would create new practices.

Initially, each team learned about the manufacturing capabilities, processes, equipment, staff, policies, procedures, and other organizational matters of the other company. This involved separate deliberations by, and a number of meetings between, each team at each firm's headquarters. Seven functional teams were created to examine specific integration issues such as sales, manufacturing/R&D, management information systems (MIS), quality, legal, human resources, and finance. For example, HR members had to examine issues concerning the integration of compensation and benefits, training and development, and personnel information systems. Members of both teams were given guidelines on U.S. antitrust and procurement laws, which prevented them from discussing some issues related to pricing, customers, and so on.

The Process

To facilitate the transition process, the two team leaders and the team members were temporarily relieved of their normal day-to-day responsibilities. Moreover, the teams were housed in locations away from headquarters to minimize distractions.

During their initial meetings, the transition teams focused on defining their objectives and setting a timetable of events. This turned out to be a very challenging task because none of the members of the HSS team had ever been through a merger or an acquisition, and members of the GESS team had not been involved in the RCA integration process. They had minimal understanding of how related events would unfold. Moreover, the transition teams were uncertain about their purpose and the length of time they would be working together. Were they to disband at the closing (November 30, 1988), or would they continue through the completion of the integration and rebuilding process (maybe several years)? This uncertainty may have been due to the lack of acquisition experience on the part of the entire HSS organization and the limited experience on the part of the GESS organization. Clearly the uncertainty hampered the ability of the teams to resolve a number of integration issues. The teams were also uncertain regarding how much they should focus on short-term versus long-term issues. The teams bounced back and forth between resolving short-term issues, such as getting GESS employees paid with HSS checks on November 30, and longer-term issues such as converting ten separate financial systems into one integrated worldwide system and integrating personnel policies and systems.

Very early in the transition process, the two transition teams met for 2 days. The purpose of the meeting was to permit functional counterparts from both teams to get to know one another and to learn about one another's organizational culture and management practices. Although there were no formal attempts at this or any other meeting to build relationships between counterparts, many "partnerships" (i.e., personal working relationships) developed from the informal interactions. For example, one team member commented that he and his counterpart talked one or two times a day, that they alternated weekly trips between Melbourne and Somerville and that his counterpart assigned two people on his staff to work with him. He further commented that the transition teams' members developed a rapport and generally liked one another, developed a spirit to make the merger a success, and employees of both companies "bent over backwards" to provide support and assistance to the transition teams. The effectiveness of the relationships was likely due to the teams' being staffed and led by cooperative people, and having had ample opportunities to meet.

The transition team leaders were kept informed of progress on the merger and they were given assistance in coordinating their team activities. The functional teams operated pretty much on their own, working freely with other functional teams when coordination was needed.

The team visits to both companies' facilities early in the transition process highlighted some of the diversity and ensuing integration problems that might emerge down the road. In particular, GE's acquisition of RCA illustrated failures to manage diversity and integration. As one of the HSS team members observed:

> *At one old RCA plant, I saw only RCA (and no GE) signs, and a big "Nipper" (the RCA Dalmatian mascot) doll in the lobby. At Intersil I saw a very small GE sign; managers there I observed did not consider themselves a part of GE and certainly not a part of RCA; they were fiercely independent and proud of it. On a visit to another GE facility I was told that their number one concern was that HSS would be taken over by RCA management just like GESS was.*

The functional teams continued to work together effectively until the last week in November 1988, when the deal was closed and the president announced who his top management staff would be. (More will be said about this later.) At that point many of the transition team members put their own personal plans into action (many times undoing transition plans). In addition, the members who did not get key jobs lost motivation and were not as helpful as they had been. Although the transition teams were never formally dissolved, many team members moved out of the separate transition headquarters and into their new jobs. As such the transition process informally shifted from the transition teams to the "post-transition" organization.

Evaluating the Effectiveness of the Transition Teams

Overall, the transition team process helped manage the diversity that was faced during the integration process between HSS and GESS. The process could have been more effective, however, had the purpose and duration of the teams been more clearly addressed at their inception and had the "baton passed" more systematically from the teams to the organization.

The HSS transition team leader also concluded after the closing that more thought should have been given to the question of who would staff the team. In particular, he felt that the individuals selected to be on the team should have been those who would have headed up their respective functional areas, who would have to live with the transition decisions, and who would have the power needed to effect change. In many situations, this turned out not to be the case, even though team members were identified as "high potentials." Some members proved during the transition team process not to have the capabilities needed to run functional areas or product lines. Other members voluntarily left HSS after the closing. More effort to keep them (e.g., financial incentives, stronger signals concerning their future role in HSS) would have been worthwhile. Nowhere was this more evident than in the MIS organization. While it is not certain that the MIS manager was invaluable, a void in leadership in this area has created numerous problems for the new organization. After the closing and to this day the company has struggled with reconciling diverse business systems (e.g., payroll, financial, sales, manufacturing, and planning) and developing one that is usable and unified. This has greatly hampered the management's ability to conduct its business effectively.

The Orlando Offsite Meeting

During 3 days in late September 1988, 63 key managers, directors, and executives from GESS and HSS attended a 3-day offsite meeting in Orlando, Florida. The purpose of the meeting was to create a forum by which these individuals could begin to learn about and develop an appreciation for their counterparts from the "other" firm, to learn about the other firm's history and how it operates, and to be exposed to the strategies, goals, and vision of the new Harris Semiconductor. Included in this meeting were all members of the transition teams, who already had an opportunity to meet and work with their counterparts. It was hoped that this meeting would provide a solid foundation on which a new HSS could be built.

What was particularly valuable about this meeting was its timing. It was conducted only 1 month after the acquisition agreement was reached in principle, and 6 weeks prior to the closing. To this point most of the key managers and executives had not had any contact with their counterparts (exceptions were the executives involved in the negotiations and members of the transition teams). Rather than allowing time for rumors and stereotyping to develop and leaving the first encounter between individuals from both companies to chance, an offsite meeting was scheduled. The president believed that this would create the best conditions for facilitating interaction and learning and managing diversity.

The meeting, which was designed by the president, the HSS director of organization development, the external consultant (this was the point at which he first became involved in the merger), and a number of other HSS staff, consisted of a blend of presentations, small- and large-group discussions, and social activities. Whereas the presentations were used to convey factual information, the group discussions and social activities were used to facilitate social interaction and learning. The social activities were particularly helpful in that they permitted individuals to see one another in "somewhat" of a nonwork situation. Several transition team members commented that this further enhanced the working relationships they had developed.

The Agenda

The meeting opened in the afternoon of the first day with a 1-hour presentation by the president, who outlined major changes that were occurring in the semiconductor industry and explained why the GESS acquisition was taking place. It is important to note that although GESS was acquired, the president described it as a merger. The term *merger* was used to emphasize that GESS management and employees would be fully involved in integration problems and decisions and not be treated as "second-class" citizens. He established several management guidelines for the integration. These included:

- Combining two good organizations into one great one
- Looking for the "multiplicative advantage"
- Integrating the organizations as soon as possible
- Not tolerating the "not invented here" syndrome
- Selecting the right person for the right job
- Balancing employment from both organizations

However, he also emphasized that he would remain in charge of the combined companies and that headquarters would remain in Melbourne. He went on to further discuss the environmental challenges and organizational changes that HSS had to face and what he perceived the HSS culture to be during the years leading up to the acquisition.

At the time of the merger, HSS had two diverse and somewhat contradictory subcultures as reflected by its two major customers: government and commercial. As a government contractor, HSS had some of the characteristics of governmental agencies; that is, propensity for micro management, low tolerance for risk taking, and resistance to change. As a commercial supplier in the volatile semiconductor market, HSS also had cultural characteristics of this dynamic marketplace. As the president remarked, "The semiconductor industry is like living on the last six inches of a bullwhip." To compete effectively in the commercial marketplace, one of the subcultures at HSS promoted innovation, hard work, and personal accountability to achieve results. However, a common set of characteristics that cut across both subcultures and the entire organization was a premium on technological excellence, a strong profit motive, the highest standards of ethical conduct, and an ability to face reality squarely and deal with its implications, either good or bad. Even at the point of the merger, HSS was struggling to integrate the two subcultures, let alone the GESS culture it was merging with.

Following the president's presentation, a brief update was given by the two leaders of the integration team. At this time, there had been very little team activity. Late in the afternoon, organized social activities, which included a number of "friendly" team sporting events, began. Attempts were made to create mixed teams composed of individuals from both HSS and GESS. Again, it was felt by the designers of the meeting that the sporting events would help break down some barriers between individuals from both companies and allow them to see one another in a different light. Moreover, it laid a foundation for a "common organizational history" or shared experience that they could relate to and possibly joke about at a later date. The remainder of the afternoon and evening was spent at an informal cocktail party and dinner where individuals had another opportunity to get to know one another.

The second day of the meeting began with a 3-hour presentation by the external consultant on "Making Mergers Work." The presentation was used to educate the participants about the organizational and behavioral challenges that they all needed to manage if the acquisition was to be successful. Topics presented included managing employee uncertainty, individual and organizational change, intercultural learning and conflict, and staffing (retentions, terminations, and relocations).

For the HSS people, this was their first acquisition. For the GESS people this was their second acquisition (several candid interviews at GESS revealed that GESS never fully digested the first one, however). During the rest of the morning and part of the afternoon, executives from both HSS and GESS provided additional overviews of their respective companies.

The remainder of the work portion of the afternoon and the morning of the second day were dedicated to small group discussions. Four mixed groups of HSS and GESS people were created. Each group, which was assigned an experienced group facilitator who had previously worked with the company, was asked to address the following questions:

- What are the factors that will help us ensure that we have a successful merger, and what are the factors that will hold us back?
- What messages do you want to tell the panel and the other groups?
- When you get home, what are you going to tell your people about this meeting?

Following deliberations, each group reported its findings to the questions back to the larger group and to a panel that was composed of the president, the most senior executive from GESS (who later became part of the president's staff), and the two leaders of the transition team. The purpose of the group discussions was to create an opportunity for people from both companies (1) to interact while working on work-related issues, (2) to vent about issues pertaining to the merger, (3) to realize that many of their colleagues and counterparts shared many of the same concerns, and (4) to legitimately identify for the president and the transition team many of the issues that would need to be managed for the merger to be successful. As time would tell, many of the issues that were identified during this session would become critical during the integration process.

Following the work session on the second day, team sporting events, a cocktail party, and dinner were again held. The meeting was adjourned at noon on the third day.

Evaluation of the Meeting

To assess the effectiveness of the offsite meeting, each of the participants was surveyed about a week later by the director of organization development. Each was asked to respond to five items scaled from a low of 1 to a high of 10 and three open-ended essay questions. Of the 63 people who had attended the offsite meeting, 36 responded. Because the survey was anonymous, no follow-up was attempted. However, the responses were evenly divided between the members of the two organizations. The means and ranges for each of the scale items are shown in Table 8.1.

The open-ended essay questions provided some very useful insights that added to the scaled responses. The first question asked participants whether they were "personally" pleased and/or disappointed with the meeting process and why. Typical responses from people who were "pleased" were:

Provided an open yet structured mechanism and forum for communication and interaction.

It was helpful to talk about issues, fears, and concerns—almost therapeutic. It was not threatening and gave me an opportunity to get to know Harris people as people!

GESS are real people . . . good guys.

Open discussions, removal of barriers, identification of issues, and development of interpersonal relationships.

First opportunity to "touch" the new company and understand its vision.

People who were disappointed commented:

Did not hear enough from GESS executives.

Did not get a schedule for integration actions. (What are we gonna do? When?)

TABLE 8.1. Evaluations of the Orlando Offsite Meeting

Item	Average rating	Range
Openness of discussions	9.3	7–10
Content of discussions	8.0	6–10
Meeting format	8.2	5–10
Effectiveness of facilitators	7.8	5–10
Meeting location	9.5	8–10

Note. Ratings were made on a scale of 1 (low) to 10 (high).

The second question asked whether they thought that the meeting was effective or ineffective and why. Nineteen respondents said there were no negative aspects to the meeting. Typical responses from these people were:

Personalities of cultures were made evident (compatible).

Addressed both groups as equal partners and emphasized people.

Enabled each side to see the strengths of the other.

Gave top management an opportunity to get first hand from their troops their concerns.

Began a very necessary team building rapport effort.

Encouraged open discussion of merger issues and personal concerns.

Clearly set the stage for the vision of the combined company and went a long way toward focusing on the real issues.

Those who felt there were some negative aspects of the meeting commented as follows:

Some of the politics that occurred.

Belief that certain decisions were already made but not announced.

Frustration in not resolving issues.

Would have liked more specifics on the organization.

The final question asked participants whether another offsite meeting similar to the one in Orlando should be held and why. Typical responses included:

Yes, to continue dialogue between top management of the merging companies.

Yes, and submeetings down to the functional level ASAP.

Yes, we have only broken the surface in problem solving. Once the organization is announced, teams should be formed to establish goals going forward.

As the evidence suggests, many of the goals of the offsite meeting were accomplished. Learning and positive interactions between members of diverse management teams were effectively begun. As time would tell, however, one meeting would not be sufficient for establishing all the new relationships that would be needed to build a unified "world-class" organization.

REBUILDING THE NEW HARRIS SEMICONDUCTOR

On November 30, 1988, the deal was closed and GESS became a part of HSS. The major challenges facing the president at this point would be to continue the momentum, to fulfill the expectations that were begun during the transition process, and to realize the benefits of the strategy driving the acquisition. To accomplish this would involve restructuring and staffing the new organization, and developing new management teams throughout the organization.

It became apparent early in the integration process that units within the original firms would have different fates during the rebuilding process. Some units were nonredundant and would remain intact (e.g., several manufacturing plants); some units were redundant and needed to be consolidated (e.g., the top management teams, sales forces, support staff); and many units needed to develop new or different interactions and working relationships with other units.

Thus, the integration process did not simply turn out to be a case where GESS units were combined with old HSS units. Instead, the president began with a virtually blank piece of paper and attempted to build a new and "better" organization from scratch. As it turned out, these activities would take more time and prove to be more difficult than anticipated, as threats to individual goals and careers, technical complexities (e.g., system incompatibilities), and cultural differences between the firms manifested themselves and business conditions changed. Moreover, as is typical in many acquisitions, integration timetables were exacerbated as the president continued to discover new things about the GESS organization and his own organization. For example, he learned that the GESS organization had been underfunded, was losing market share and money, and had excess capacity. Ideally, the due diligence process reveals facts such as these, but in reality it is not uncommon for such facts to be "discovered" after the closing. As we have found in other acquisitions, an incremental learning process about both firms is not atypical. Thus, it turned out that although there were a number of attempts at restructuring the new HSS and in building management teams, problems and impediments continued to arise, resulting in an incomplete process and considerable frustration. In the remainder of this section we will discuss some of the major challenges that were faced and the interventions we used in helping rebuild the new HSS.

Staffing the New Organization

Continuing his focus on the human side of the acquisition, and to convey to the GESS managers that he would not treat them as "second-class citizens," the president and a few key HSS senior managers decided to staff the senior management of the new HSS by using a balanced approach; this came to be known as the "red-dot, blue-dot" approach. Red dots were former GESS managers, and blue dots were HSS managers. Essentially, the top levels of management would be fully integrated through the retention of a "relatively" equal number of GESS and HSS managers. For the most part, neither the capabilities nor the motivation needed to rebuild the organization was systematically considered in the selection decision. A few individuals with experiences and skills from GESS were identified as being indispensable to the new Harris Semiconductor. These individuals included the most senior GESS manager, who understood the commodity business and had a strong employee following; the GESS vice president of sales, who understood the worldwide and auto and industrial markets; and the vice president of human resources, who had responsibility for an organization twice as large as HSS. Thus, during the first week of December 1988 the president announced his key staff assignments. Four out of ten of his direct reports and four out of eight of the next level of management would come from GESS.

Although the balancing was a noble gesture, there were several problems with it. The first problem was that many people, especially those from the old HSS, felt that the approach was not fair or in the best interest of the new organization. In fact, it was perceived to be discriminatory against the best talent available. Many people felt that to achieve the ambitious strategy for the merger would require the best talent available.

A second problem with the red-dot, blue-dot approach was that it underestimated the difficulty of relocating several key GESS managers from Somerville to Melbourne. Coupled with generous retention packages, it was assumed that most people would have few problems moving from a high to low cost of living environment and would welcome an opportunity to work for the new HSS. Although the GESS managers were royally courted and introduced to the Melbourne area, several GESS managers reported that family issues, deep roots in their existing communities, and difficulties in adjusting to the physical climate and culture of Melbourne discouraged them from relocating. It proved very difficult to gauge which managers intended to remain with HSS.

A third problem with the red-dot, blue-dot approach was that it did not sufficiently take into account the different management styles and philosophies of the two companies. During the first few months following the closing, the president's staff met numerous times. Not all of the GESS managers he selected had relocated, so they commuted to Melbourne for the meetings. Some had rented apartments. During this time, both the GESS and HSS managers had opportunities to work together and interact with the president as they rebuilt the new company. As time progressed it became apparent that the management styles and philosophies of the top managers from the two companies differed. (More will be said about this later.)

The staffing approach used to fill senior management positions had negative consequences. First, there were individuals who were assigned to jobs for which they did not have the capabilities needed to perform effectively. Second, during the first year, there were several defections by GESS managers whose desires to remain with HSS were inadequately gauged. For example, within 3 months of the closing, the former GESS vice president of sales, who had been appointed vice president of sales for the new HSS, resigned. Shortly thereafter his replacement, who also came from GESS, resigned, as did the vice president of sales from the old HSS, who was not given the job. This greatly destabilized the sales force and was very traumatic for the whole organization because the sales organization deals directly with customers who can immediately impact the business. Incidents such as these eventually led many GESS managers to question whether the HSS organization was truly interested in learning from them, as it became apparent that few GESS managerial practices would be used in the new organization. On the other hand, several HSS managers felt that many GESS practices and the caliber of their management team were not as good as those at HSS. This perception was further exacerbated over time as it became apparent that the quality of the GESS business was not as good as HSS managers thought it to be during due diligence.

Within 6 months after the closing, only two executives from GESS remained on the president's staff. Although each GESS executive who left had his own motivations, it was clear that a more systematic selection process would have been beneficial. Assessment of managers' capabilities and motivations, and selection based on strategic needs and talent rather than balancing, could have led to an organization that was more stable and integrated in a shorter period of time. Instead of effectively integrating the management of the two organizations, the balancing approach built further barriers between them.

Developing Teams

After the management staffing decisions were first announced, the three of us were charged with the responsibility of helping develop a number of teams within the organization. Time and human resources for accomplishing this were limited, so first priority was given to teams that had the greatest immediate impact on the business. These turned out to be the top management team, the sales managers, and the human resources staff. The human resources organization became particularly important because of its role in helping the line managers deal with postacquisition issues and build their teams. Integration efforts were going on throughout the new HSS, especially in manufacturing, marketing, technology, and finance. Due to space constraints we will focus on the efforts in which we were directly involved.

Top Management Team Development

By March 1989 and after numerous discussions with the president, we decided to begin developing the top management team with a core group from his overall staff. This group of executives was chosen based upon their strategic impact on the business and their spheres of influence on the rest of the organization. The group was deliberately kept small so that candid discussions could take place. The core team was composed of six senior managers, five of whom came from the old HSS organization. The sixth was a former GESS executive.

We felt the initial team development effort should focus on this team because the fate of HSS was in its hands. We also realized that by now members of the entire staff had already participated in numerous acquisition-related meetings, they were tired, and they were under a great deal of pressure. With this in mind, we conducted a series of offsite team development workshops with the smaller core group. The purpose of the offsite workshops was to get the team away from some of the day-to-day pressures and to provide them with uninterrupted time to work together.

The first workshop, which was facilitated by the director of organization development and the external consultant, was conducted during the second week of March 1989. This workshop focused on the team development process itself. At this meeting, the team was first asked to identify the characteristics of an effective senior management team and to rate its effectiveness with respect to the criteria. Even though many of the members of the team had worked together in the old HSS, the group identified a number of areas in which they needed to improve. These included:

• Working together as peers
• Showing one another respect and confidence
• Supporting one another privately and publicly
• Having a sense of humor

- Handling conflict one on one rather than openly in public
- Differing with one another without attacking
- Being decisive, aggressive, and action oriented in a positive sense

As it turned out, this meeting illustrated that the old pre-acquisition HSS team was not fully integrated and that creating a team of individuals with diverse functional backgrounds and managerial philosophies within a firm is just as challenging as creating a new one with members from two firms. The meeting also provided the GESS executive with an opportunity to learn more about the old HSS culture.

Based on the characteristics needed to be an effective top management team, each member of the team identified things that he or she could do differently to help the team improve. Every member then responded in writing to each member's list. Following some rather candid discussions, each member agreed to work on a personal set of objectives for improving team effectiveness. As a symbolic gesture, each person signed his or her respective list of objectives. Following the development of their lists, the members were given an opportunity to discuss what they would need from the other members. This workshop did not lead immediately to a cohesive team, but it did provide a forum by which members of the team could communicate, learn about one another, and attempt to resolve problems.

By April 1989, it became clear that the acute technical challenges of the merger (e.g., reconciling systems and creating usable financial information) and the demands of continuing to run the business in a tough business environment had reduced the core team's discretionary time. Soon they began to prefer using their time to solve technical issues rather than focusing on team process. The core team did decide to set aside time just to themselves by getting together for several hours prior to the president's staff meeting. This helped them to catch up with one another and discuss policy matters. It also helped avoid surprises during the larger staff meeting. In sum, the workshops laid the foundation for building an effective and cohesive team.

Strategic Councils

During the first 2 years after the merger, the new HSS was restructured a number times as the president attempted to define the strategy, structure, and management systems and processes for HSS. The multiple attempts were precipitated by changes in business conditions, staffing changes, difficulties in solidifying the management information systems, and continuous learning about the GESS organization.

At many points during the restructuring, attempts were made to facilitate the horizontal (between firms) and vertical (between management levels) integration of the top two layers of management of both organizations, to continue to build unified teams, and to ensure that the managers responsible for the diverse functional areas and product lines were fully represented in HSS decisions. In many respects, the need to complete the work of the pre-acquisition transition teams kept coming up as a major priority. Again, this was considered to be the most critical factor affecting the future of HSS.

Late in August 1989, the president developed his Strategic Councils concept. Four councils were created. Represented on each were experts in technology, new product development, business development, and organizational development. Thus, the councils broadly represented the various areas of the organization. The president asked these councils to review existing and proposed technologies, products, businesses, and organizational initiatives. Based on their reviews, the councils were asked to make recommendations and submit them to an integrative council (which the president chaired). The integrative council was then to review and integrate the recommendations made by the four other councils.

A 2-day offsite meeting was held in late August 1989 to develop and charter the councils. During the morning of the first day, the Strategic Council concept was introduced by the president and followed by a session on individual differences in decision-making styles and team decision making. The purpose of this session was to help managers (who were primarily from engineering backgrounds) understand and appreciate the importance and challenges of making decisions in a group of individuals with diverse decision-making styles. Many participants felt that the session helped them to understand the importance of diverse styles in effective top management teams. However, they also felt that the session underscored the difficulty of integrating the styles in a fashion that would yield high-quality decisions and team member commitment to them.

In the afternoon, each council, with a facilitator, was charged with developing Council Operating Guidelines. Each council spent the morning of the second day developing council charters, deliverables, time frames, and resource requirements. Following lunch, each council presented the results of its initial deliberations to members of all the councils and then proceeded to develop mechanisms by which they would coordinate with the other councils.

Although the results of the 2-day workshop were not uniform, it was apparent that communication and working relationships among members of some councils improved greatly. Moreover, the workshop and council concept helped members focus on the rebuilding of the new Harris Semiconductor. If there was one downside to the council concept, however, it was that its full potential was never realized. After several months, the councils were eliminated; the president had decided to restructure the organization. This initiative, like many others undertaken during mergers and acquisitions, was eliminated before its full benefit could be realized. While relationships were being developed, personal frustrations with incomplete implementation and multiple continual changes became stressful for individuals.

Summary

In this section we highlighted some of the efforts that were made to rebuild the new Harris Semiconductor after the merger. The major purposes of these efforts were to develop new unified teams, to further break down barriers between managers from the old HSS and GESS organizations, to integrate the top two layers of management, and to focus these managers' efforts on making the new company effective. These efforts were only moderately successful as the organization continued to restructure.

In addition to developing teams, several efforts to integrate operations located at distant geographic sites were undertaken. In the next section we discuss one of the more challenging efforts, the Intersil subsidiary of GESS.

The Case of Intersil

The Intersil subsidiary in Santa Clara, California, proved to be a very interesting management challenge during the integration process; it highlighted the problems that cultural diversity and trust play during an acquisition. The Intersil experience also highlights many of the challenges of managing diversity that were prevalent throughout the new Harris Semiconductor.

Intersil is only one of six major domestic geographical sites of HSS. To some degree, each of the sites experienced the effect of managing diversity during the integration process. From the outset, it was clear that Intersil was very different from HSS. Intersil operated in the heart of Silicon Valley with numerous other semiconductor firms. The labor market was such that qualified, skilled employees could literally walk across the street and become employed by another firm. HSS, on the other hand, was located in Melbourne, Florida, and was the only semiconductor firm in the area. Many managers described the HSS/Intersil encounter as truly a case where East meets West. Moreover, Intersil was one of the first entrepreneurial semiconductor firms in the industry. Despite its acquisition by GESS in 1981, it operated independently whenever possible. HSS was a rather large firm and part of a parent company. Thus, from the outset the challenges of managing diversity were sizable.

The first challenge occurred soon after the closing (January 1989) when the president decided that Intersil did not fit with HSS's future plans and announced that the subsidiary was for sale. Many HSS executives felt that the sale was a good idea. The salaries, benefits, perks, and "corporate culture" at Intersil were way out of synch with those in Melbourne, although they were typical for Silicon Valley. Moreover, Intersil had been managed autonomously while owned by GE and was used to having abundant resources. As such, it was not accustomed to the discipline that would be needed for it to be profitable. Reactions to the news were mixed, but many prepared for the change accordingly. During the ensuing few months there was minimal contact between HSS and Intersil executives with the exception of an HSS executive who was charged with overseeing Intersil.

After several months, HSS decided not to sell Intersil. They decided that it had a role after all in HSS's future strategy. HSS announced in July 1989 that it would keep Intersil, although it was not clear to employees what HSS would do with it.

At this point, many of the managers and employees who remained at Intersil felt alienated and isolated from HSS, and they were unsure about their futures with HSS. During this time many talented people left Intersil. A lack of communication from HSS concerning Intersil's future and the reversal of the sale undermined much of the trust that Intersil people had for HSS. In fact, many of them felt that it was just a matter of time before HSS would shut them down. That this issue was significant became apparent when, in October 1989, we interviewed numerous managers and employees at Intersil to learn more about their concerns. The following are some typical comments made by Intersil managers and employees:

> Explain to us more about the HSS organization; we need a telephone book.

> I do not know who to contact in Melbourne for answers, although it has been better during the last few months.

> There is a lack of direct communication between Santa Clara and Melbourne along functional lines. Information only flows along the grapevine.

> Key functional operating managers from HSS and Intersil need to meet in Santa Clara.

> We get *Harriscope* [the HSS newspaper], but we are not involved in the "wonderful" activities that are described in it.

Where do we fit in the future of HSS? Any information in this regard would help.

We need access to the 1990 HSS manufacturing calendar and access to HSS policies, and we need to learn more about the HSS organization.

HSS needs to help integrate Intersil people—make them feel like they identify with HSS.

After the decision to reverse the sale, a great deal of work was needed to reconcile the different cultures, the uncertainty, and the trust problems. As the previous comments suggest, most Intersil people knew almost nothing about their new owner. Several steps were taken to improve the situation, beginning in early October 1989. First, key managers from Intersil were brought to Melbourne on a regular basis to meet with their functional or technical counterparts. Second, the senior HSS executive overseeing Intersil visited the facilities on a more regular basis and attempted to understand and help resolve differences between the firms and problems that Intersil faced. Subsequent discussions suggest that he indeed made progress. Moreover, he helped provide the subsidiary with much needed direction.

In sum, many of the subsequent efforts were designed to open communications and to signal to Intersil managers and employees that they were indeed part of HSS. However, efforts to do this earlier would have minimized many of the problems that needlessly emerged.

Other Attempts to Rebuild the New HSS

There were many additional attempts to rebuild the HSS organization. The common theme running through all the initiatives was that in areas that needed to be combined, or where new interrelationships among units needed to be developed, communication and intercultural learning would be useful. In this section we discuss three illustrative attempts. The first, involves the use of the company newspaper, the *Harriscope*. The second, involves the use of team development efforts to rebuild units below the top management level. The third was the use of organizational symbols.

Harriscope Updates

Throughout the pre- and post-closing periods, the widely read HSS employee newspaper, published biweekly, dedicated considerable space to merger events. The intent of the newspaper was to keep employees and managers informed about merger-related changes taking place and to facilitate employees' understanding of how both companies operate. Immediately following the closing, considerable effort was made to ensure that GESS employees received the newspaper and were made to feel a part of the company.

The newspaper continued to update employees with a good mix between pieces that attempted to unify the two organizations and pieces that told of changes that were being made. Through the paper, the president made every effort to be honest with employees from both organizations. He shared his enthusiasm and vision for the merger, but he also discussed many of the difficult changes that had to be dealt with, such as shutting down and consolidating facilities and reductions in headcounts.

To help integrate the organizations, there were several continuing features in the newspaper. First, there were biographies and interviews with each of the senior executives. Second, there were pieces on many of the different operations within the new HSS. These included operations from both GESS and HSS. Each piece focused on what the operation does, its history, its geographic area, and background information on some of its employees. Although the newspaper articles were just a small effort, they helped to facilitate intercultural learning between the organizations and to symbolize that management was committed to building a unified, stronger organization with individuals from both GESS and HSS. As importantly, the pieces conveyed that HSS management respected the contributions and history of GESS.

Unit Team Development

As the staffing of the organization solidified, many units engaged in team development activities, with varying degrees of success. One such effort was undertaken in the legal department. In late December 1988 the senior counsel, with the aid of the director of organizational development, conducted a 1-day workshop with his staff, which was made up of lawyers from both companies. The goal of the workshop was to develop a direction for the legal department. The workshop began with a review of the missions, goals, and strategy of HSS. It was felt that the direction of the legal department should be consistent with that of HSS. Following the review, profiles of the GESS and HSS legal departments' cultures and legal practices were developed and discussed. The profiles focused on such issues as the lawyer's role, profit focus, treatment of people, values, and codes of conduct. Based on discussions of differences in the profiles and the needs of HSS, the team attempted to develop its direction; that is, its mission, vision, goals, strategies, and best practices. This workshop was deemed to be effective by participants.

Another attempt to develop a team met with less success. In the middle of February 1989 HSS held its first worldwide sales meeting since the merger. At this meeting, a 1-day workshop with the sales management was conducted. The purpose of this workshop, which included both GESS and HSS sales managers from around the world, was to focus on short-term and long-term issues that needed to be managed in order for the new sales organization to operate effectively. Based upon the success of the Orlando Offsite, and comments from participants that similar meetings should be held throughout the company, we decided to use an abbreviated version with the sales organization.

Although the session seemed to go well, interviews afterward suggested that managers did not feel it was effective. Many of the opinions were influenced by the fact that they now were working for their third vice president of sales since the closing 2 months earlier. Many of the managers were uncertain and confused about the future of the sales organization and did not know whether their new vice president would be permanent. In fact, the current vice president became known as the "vice president du jour."

Whether the workshop would have been effective under other conditions is not known; however, it was apparent to us that stabilization of the leadership position was essential before a unified team could be built. Moreover, during this time a massive consolidation and ensuing reduction in the size of the sales force were taking place, which put a considerable amount of stress on the entire sales organization.

A third effort to develop a team occurred in the human resources organization. Under the leadership of the vice president of human resources (who was new to HSS as of January 1989) it became apparent immediately after the closing that his organization needed to be developed very quickly to serve as an example and a support group for the line organization. A 2-day workshop with the human resources organization was conducted in March 1989.

The purpose of the workshop again was to build an HR team and, as importantly, to equip it with the skills needed to support the line organization. Like the legal department's workshop, the initial HR workshop focused on developing a direction. Actually two directions were articulated for the HR department. One focused short term on helping HSS make it through the merger, and the other focused longer term on building HSS.

During the workshop, the external consultant presented an overview of the challenges that would be faced in the postmerger rebuilding process, such as resolving cultural and systems conflicts, managing staffing and reductions in force, and developing teams. He also discussed skills in areas such as conflict resolution, team building and development, individual counseling, and organizational and human resources systems and policies design, which would be needed by the HR organization to meet the challenges. Following the workshop each member of the HR team went back to that part of the organization (i.e., functional area, plant, product line) to implement the direction.

Several other HR meetings to continue the team development process were held. Based on comments from members of the HR and line organizations these efforts were successful.

In this section we highlighted several team-building efforts. Although the exact formats differed depending upon the nature of the issues faced and the leadership of each group, they all had several things in common: They attempted to facilitate communication, intercultural learning, and joint problem solving among members of both organizations, and they focused on developing a team with a common purpose—the future effectiveness of the new Harris Semiconductor. However, there was one factor that these team development efforts did not all have in common, which played a critical role—namely, leadership. Very early on it became apparent to us that for any team development effort to be successful, the leadership position needed to be solidified. In many cases it did not really matter to members of the team which organization the leader came from so long as that person would be around long enough and have sufficient organizational power to implement the direction successfully. Nowhere was that more evident than in the sales organization.

Symbolic Gestures

There were numerous symbolic gestures that management made to convey to both organizations that their cultural heritage would be a respected and valuable part of rebuilding the new HSS. Thus, rather than trying to eliminate diversity, management attempted to build from it. First, the new logo contained the Harris, GE, RCA, and Intersil names. Second, the first paycheck that employees received after the closing had the HSS logo on it. This was no mean feat, given the challenges that were faced in integrating payroll systems.

Third, signs were changed at several locations to reflect the new company. Sign changes went more smoothly in some cases than in others. At Intersil, for example, there was some degree of resentment to the change. Many people felt that the Intersil name was more respected in Silicon Valley than the HSS name, in spite of the fact that Intersil had lost money for 7 consecutive years. At the old RCA facility, the RCA sign had remained in a prominent place, and a large scale model of the Nipper (the famous RCA dog) remained in the lobby long after GE had acquired the firm. When HSS installed the HSS sign and removed the Nipper, people at the facility did not respond positively. It became clear to HSS management that although the attempts to unify the organizations were noble, some would not be achieved easily or quickly. The Nipper incident was a case of people holding on to their previous identity. It was also clear that GE had made very few attempts during the 3 years that it owned RCA to truly unify the GE and RCA semiconductor operations.

In this section we illustrated the many attempts that were undertaken to combine the diverse organizations. Some met with more initial success than others. A major problem that evolved with all of the efforts was that the initiatives were very difficult to sustain. In many cases, workshops were conducted one or two times when they needed to be ongoing. In the next section we discuss how the environmental context contributed to this problem.

THE IMPACT OF EXTERNAL ENVIRONMENTAL PRESSURES

It became apparent to anyone involved in the merger that the complexity of the integration process was quite challenging. In the spring and summer of 1989, it also became apparent that the integration would not be the only challenge HSS had to face. A merger does not take place in a vacuum. While HSS management was working feverishly to integrate the two companies, and managing the integration process relatively well, external events began to put extreme pressure on them. As time would show, these pressures altered the integration process.

The spring and summer of 1989 were difficult times in the semiconductor industry. Market conditions were not as strong as had been predicted. The president had to find new ways to meet the financial commitments he had made to the parent company in his business plan and to meet the commitments the parent company had made to its stockholders concerning the impact of the GESS acquisition on corporate profitability. In neither case were those commitments going to be relaxed. In addition, shortly after the closing it became apparent during due diligence that HSS had overestimated the sales and profit margin projections for GESS. This problem occurs in many acquisitions.

By the spring of 1989, many people were very tired of the integration process, they felt highly stressed, and they were questioning the value of the merger. The short-term financial pressures exacerbated this. The integration and financial pressures left everyone wondering whether there was a light at the end of the tunnel. What was amazing was that in spite of the pressures, many mobile people stayed with the organization.

The many short-term pressures to meet business plans shifted some of management's focus from integration plans to short-term profitability plans. As a consequence, a number of the rebuilding initiatives were temporarily sidetracked. Moreover, an "us versus them" syndrome began to emerge. Many HSS employees began to point fingers and blame the GESS organization for their woes, often questioning why the GESS managers did not tell the HSS managers about the weaknesses in the GESS organization during due diligence. To the credit of the president and his team, whenever instances such as these were displayed, they were dealt with forcefully. An "us versus them" syndrome would simply not be tolerated by the senior management team. The president's stance on this issue was very effective in eliminating or minimizing the syndrome.

Two years after the closing (the time of this writing), we would like to report that the integration is proceeding smoothly and that financial pressures have disappeared, but this is not the case. Market pressures continue and the restructuring schedules and costs have been exceeded. The latter is due to a combination of undue optimism, underestimation of the task, and some execution and process issues (some of which have been identified in the case). In fact, some analysts and employees continue to question the wisdom of the acquisition and its ultimate success. On the other hand, important learning has occurred and significant benefits will occur from the various consolidations accomplished. One of the major benefits, for example, is that the strategic focus of HSS has greatly improved.

Whether the acquisition is ultimately deemed a success or not will greatly depend on the time frame employed and the patience exhibited by the many stakeholders of HSS. As the president noted:

> *It will depend on whether we run out of corporate and financial community patience (i.e., as Vince Lombardi commented: "I never lost a football game, I just ran out of time") and/or individual and organizational energy. These will be greatly modulated by market conditions. In this regard, the current economic outlook [December 1990] is certainly not a source of encouragement. The other relevant variable is the staying power/burn-out of the organization. We have been running on after-burners for two years. We either run out of fuel and burn up the turbines or we will become renewed by our own success. Corporate actions (obviously), but also perceived corporate attitudes, will influence this outcome.*

WHAT HSS LEARNED

HSS management put it simply: "We learned that merger integration is harder than it looks and takes longer than you think." Although this statement appears rather obvious, it does not always initially register in senior managers' thinking when they undertake a merger or acquisition, especially if it is their first one. Many senior executives have been very successful in other endeavors and underestimate the complexity of the merger implementation process, especially when it is a large-scale integration, as was the case at HSS. We believe that the HSS–GESS merger has been an important learning experience for those managers involved and will serve them well in the future. They have learned a great deal about combining diverse organizations and managing under crisis and stress. These conditions are especially evident when a company buys and integrates another company that is nearly twice its size. HSS's willingness to agree to this case and its willingness to openly share it are testimony to their commitment to institutionalizing that learning.

With respect to the improvement of practice we have gained the following insights from this merger.

• *Successfully merging two firms requires the effective management of many types of diversity.* In this case the organizations involved differed with respect to management philosophy, HR practices and policies, location, information systems, and organizational cultures. In order to manage such diversity, communication, intercultural learning, and joint problem solving among members of combining organizations are essential for an effective merger, especially when the goal is to rebuild a new unified organization.

• *Single-shot interventions are not sufficient for integrating diverse organizations.* Continued communication and learning are necessary. Multiple vehicles for achieving these (e.g., workshops, symbols, newspapers) may be warranted, especially when time and resources are scarce and most people are exhausted.

• *High levels of commitment, tenacity, and patience may be needed by managers of combining organizations, especially when it is an extensive integration.* This may require investing additional time and/or other resources. Certainly, contracting resources during the integration process should be avoided.

• *Rebuilding management teams as early as possible during the integration process is critical.* The company needs teams that can get on with the essential task of running the business. This is a time when senior management leadership is critical if the organization and its employees are to survive.

• *Failure to reconcile and integrate vital management information systems can undermine the companies' ability to conduct business.* Specifically, it makes it difficult for top management to empower managers and to hold them accountable for measured outcomes (e.g., profit margins).

• *Mergers usually prove to be more difficult and take longer than most managers anticipate.*

- *Mergers and acquisitions do not take place in a vacuum.* External conditions must be considered during the integration process. It is important that managers remember that business goes on, in spite of the merger.
- *A careful balance must be struck between perceived fairness and the capabilities of managers in staffing decisions.*
- *Learning as much as possible about the merger partner prior to the consummation of the deal and understanding differences between the combining firms may be the most crucial elements in the merger process.*

REFERENCES

Buono, A. F., & Bowditch, J. L. (1989). *The human side of mergers and acquisitions.* San Francisco: Jossey-Bass.

Chatterjee, S., Lubatkin, M. H., Schweiger, D. M., & Weber, Y. (1989). *Cultural differences and shareholder value: Explaining the variability in the performance of related mergers.* Paper presented at the National Academy of Management meetings. Washington, D.C.

Sales, A. L., & Mirvis, P. H. (1984). When cultures collide: Issues in acquisition. In J. R. Kimberly & R. E. Quinn (Eds.), *Managing organizational transitions* (pp. 107–133). Homewood, IL: Irwin.

Schweiger, D. M., Ivancevich, J. M., & Power, F. R. (1987). Executive actions for managing acquisitions before and after acquisitions. *Academy of Management Executive, 1,* 127–138.

Schweiger, D. M., & Walsh, J. P. (1990). Mergers and acquisitions: An interdisciplinary view. In G. R. Ferris & K. M. Rowland (Eds.), *Research in personnel and human resources management* (pp. 41–107). Greenwich, CT: JAI Press.

ACKNOWLEDGMENTS

We would like to greatly thank Mr. Cornell and the many managers at the new HSS and the Harris Corporation for the cooperation and time that they provided in helping us develop this case. We appreciate their willingness to be written about candidly and their contribution to the improvement of managerial practice.

PART IV

USING STRATEGIC INITIATIVES TO MANAGE WORKPLACE DIVERSITY

We refer to the human resource (HR) activities described in this final set of cases as "strategic initiatives" to emphasize that these chapters describe corporate responses to diversity that are intentionally planned, targeted against business objectives, long-term oriented, *and* involve the entire organization. In all three cases, a corporate-level human resources group took primary responsibility for the planning activities. However, it is interesting to note that despite their status as corporate HR groups, none of these planning groups was in a position to simply dictate changes from above and then watch the organization transform itself. To the contrary, each of the corporations described allows its local subunits a great deal of autonomy. Consequently, any strategic intitiatives created at the corporate level must be designed to meet the diverse needs and constraints of the local constituencies. The cases in this section illustrate several alternatives for coping with a basic paradox posed by decentralized organizational forms, namely, the need to build a corporate culture that unifies different sectors of the corporation without imposing debilitating constraints.

AMERICAN EXPRESS TRAVEL RELATED SERVICES

The Travel Related Services (TRS) subsidiary of the American Express Corporation is the company most frequently associated with the American Express name; its travelers' cheques and credit cards are familiar products. Like many similar firms, TRS depends heavily on a labor force with clerical skills for handling record keeping and customer service tasks. Therefore, in contrast to many manufacturing companies, having a workforce with a large proportion of female employees is nothing new. Nevertheless, TRS management practices have been traditional in many ways; they were not tailored to address the specific concerns of their nontraditional, female-dominated workforce.

An awareness of the potential business consequences of impending labor shortages recently focused the company on the importance of being an employer of choice among people with the skills needed by the company. Signaling their new stance, the president of the North American TRS division announced in 1990, "The workforce challenge is one of the most important issues, if not the key challenge, for service providers in the Nineties" (quoted in Sellers, 1990, p. 59).

Now, TRS is actively engaged in the process of "Becoming the Best Place to Work." In order to achieve this objective, it must carefully consider the needs of its workforce. It has begun to do this already, and the exercise reveals some interesting facts. Chief among these is that the most salient and apparently "constant" characteristic of the workforce—namely, that it is predominantly female—is illusionary. What appears stable is in fact changing rapidly. For example, in addition to being ethnically more diverse, today's female employees are much more likely to be single, compared to the past. Also, now many more employed females have young children who must be cared for. For these employees, the best places to work are companies that are sensitive to the implications of these facts.

Chapter 9 describes the recent events that launched TRS on its new journey to Becoming the Best Place to Work. Key among these were the publication of the *Workforce 2000* report (Johnston & Packer, 1987) and a subsequent internal analysis of the report's implications for American Express. Using data from the reports, the TRS corporate human resources group convinced top management to support a large, long-term investment in its workforce.

This case details the procedures used by TRS to decide which of several possible organizational changes represented the best investments, given the many differences in the workforce characterisitics of the local subunits. The specific new benefits now offered to employees are described, as are the company' analysis of the long-term returns expected from their investment. Finally, Chapter 9 suggests what the road ahead might look like for TRS as it attempts to make deeper changes in its corporate culture.

COOPERS & LYBRAND

As a services-based organization, Coopers & Lybrand, a large public accounting firm, is similar to TRS in that it is heavily dependent on its human resources. Much of the work performed by employees of Coopers & Lybrand is quite technical and requires advanced training to perform. In addition, employees are generally viewed as ambassadors who represent the firm to a wide range of professional clients. Thus, attracting and keeping high-quality talent are essential to the success of the business.

Traditionally, white males dominated the workforce of this accounting firm (as well as others), but change is imminent, for business schools are now graduating nearly as many female accounting majors as male accounting majors. Furthermore, both the men and women now entering the firm bring with them new attitudes about work and a wide variety of situational differences related to their life away from work and their career aspirations. At Coopers & Lybrand, as elsewhere, the current generation of new hires reflects the changing societal conditions that produced the unique cohorts of baby-boomers and baby-busters.

Coopers & Lybrand faces a situation similar to the one in other organizations, but its response to this situation is unique. They have conceptualized the issue of workforce diversity in a way that positions it as parallel to other types of diversity faced by organizations, such as diversity of markets, products and services, professional specialties, management processes, organization structures, and professional subcultures. This positioning helps other managers see that workforce diversity is just one example of a much larger diversity pie.

In addition, Coopers & Lybrand's approach to working through diversity is intentionally nonprogrammatic. Rather than attempting to formulate programs to be disseminated in a top-down manner, the corporate HR group has designed a system that will encourage local HR units to experiment with programs that meet their needs. In this organizational learning model, the seeds of innovation are planted and nurtured at the grass-roots level. Tiny seedlings are expected to flourish initially, but subsequent thinning will ensure that only the most viable will mature. Corporate HR guides the thinning process and broadcasts local success stories throughout the firm, with the expectation that other subunits will adopt programs that fit their needs.

At Coopers & Lybrand, the objective is facilitating organizational learning using a systematic approach. Rather than adopt programs used in other firms, they intend to teach themselves. Although self-teaching may be a somewhat slower approach, there are several benefits expected, as described by the authors of this case.

PEPSI-COLA INTERNATIONAL

The diversity of the U.S. workforce is impressive, but in comparison to the diversity of the global workforce, U.S. employees are relatively homogenous. Working through global workforce diversity is a challenge that today's largest corporations are currently struggling with, and it is a challenge that an increasing number of smaller corporations are to likely to meet soon.

PepsiCo, the parent company of Pepsi-Cola International, is among the world's 50 largest corporations, according to a recent analysis ("The Global 1000," 1991). And according to *Fortune* ("America's Most Admired Corporations," 1991), it is also one of the five that executives, corporate directors, and financial analysts most admire, in part because of its ability to attract, develop, and keep talented people. For the international division of this firm, these human resources management activites must be achieved for a workforce that is spread throughout 150 different countries.

The Pepsi-Cola International case describes how one world-class organization manages the megadiversity of a global workforce. Like decentralized domestic firms, its approach must accommodate widely differing local conditions without compromising the integrity of the whole. Furthermore, it should create and support synergy among the subunits. Success cannot be had simply by exporting human resources management technologies developed for an American workforce and its particular culture.

Pepsi-Cola International seeks to achieve its objectives through the creation of a common corporate culture that knits together its many subunits and has worldwide applicability. The corporate culture is driven by and supports the business objectives of the company, focusing all employees on performance outcomes. Human resources policies and programs communicate the culture to everyone in the company. To be successful, human resources policies must be appropriate for adoption in every local workplace. This requires flexibility as well as reliance on a few basic principles of human behavior.

The basic principles of human behavior that underlie the human resources policies and programs at Pepsi-Cola International are described in this final chapter. The key to the effectiveness of the corporation's approach to human resources management appears to lie in a design that specifies in quantifiable terms what employees are to accomplish in their jobs, rather than the means employees must use to achieve their objectives. The diversity of local country cultures is accomodated by this approach because employees are given the autonomy to approach their jobs in a way that is congruent with country-specific norms and values. Thus, this case echoes a theme introduced by the Coopers & Lybrand case. As the authors of Chapter 11 note, the management challenges created by a diverse work force are similar to the challenges created by differences in raw materials available in different parts of the world. Local managers must have the autonomy to adapt the company's basic company procedures to fit the characteristics of the resources available to them.

REFERENCES

America's Most Admired Corporations. (1991, February 11). *Fortune*, pp. 52–74.
Johnston, W. B., & Packer, A. E. (1987). *Workforce 2000: Work and workers for the 21st century.* Indianapolis, IN: Hudson Institute.
Sellers, P. (1990, June 4). What customers really want. *Fortune*, pp. 58–68.

CHAPTER 9

Becoming the Best Place to Work: Managing Diversity at American Express Travel Related Services

ELIZABETH WOLFE MORRISON
JOYCE MARDENFELD HERLIHY

BACKGROUND INFORMATION ABOUT THE COMPANY

Diversity is becoming a fact of life for most American businesses. This chapter tells the story of one firm's efforts to address the needs of an increasingly diverse workforce. It describes a change effort undertaken by the Travel Related Services (TRS) subsidiary of the American Express Company. This change effort began in 1987 and resulted in a set of four initiatives introduced in late 1990. These initiatives were the first step in an ongoing change effort entitled *Becoming the Best Place to Work*.

Based in New York City, American Express is a holding company consisting of five fairly autonomous subsidiaries: American Express Travel Related Services, American Express Bank, Shearson Lehman Brothers, Investors Diversified Services, and Information Services Company (see Figure 9.1). In addition to marketing the American Express Cards and Travelers Cheques, TRS also provides consumer and business travel, insurance, and publishing services. TRS has a net income of over $800 million annually, and has over 50,000 employees worldwide. Accounting for more than 70% of American Express's net income, and containing more than 50% of its total employees, TRS is the subsidiary that most people associate with the American Express name.

Diversity can be conceptualized in a variety of ways. At TRS it was conceptualized quite broadly as differences with respect to lifestyles, val-

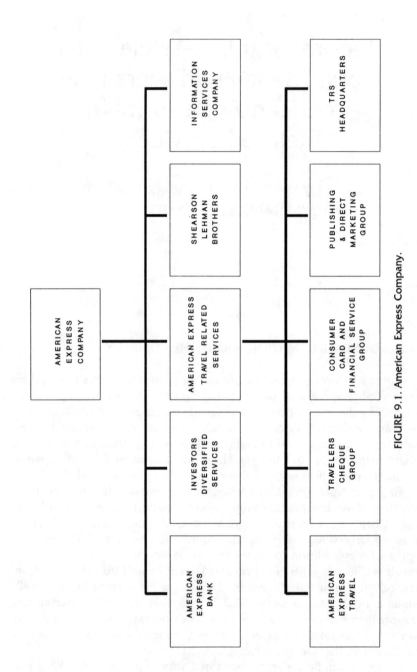

FIGURE 9.1. American Express Company.

ues, and family obligations. Particularly given some of the demographics of TRS's workforce, these were seen as the most pressing diversity issues facing the company. By the end of 1990, over 70% of TRS employees were female, almost 50% were in dual-career marriages, and over 40% had children. Further, 70% of employees held nonexempt customer service positions, where they were responsible for answering telephones, handling billing inquiries, providing credit authorization, or entering data. The inflexible and demanding nature of these jobs made balancing work obligations with family and other lifestyle concerns particularly difficult.

We begin this chapter by describing how the issue of diversity was first brought to the attention of senior management at American Express. We then focus on how the issue was addressed by human resources at TRS, describing the events that occurred throughout 1989 and 1990. Following that, we discuss some of the difficulties encountered in bringing about the change, and we identify what we see as critical success factors. We conclude with a discussion of future actions that TRS has planned.

RECOGNIZING THE WORKFORCE CHALLENGE

The first formal recognition that workforce diversity might be an important issue for TRS, and for American Express in general, occurred within corporate human resources (serving American Express as a whole rather than just TRS). This was consistent with the primary mission of the corporate staff, which is to scan the environment for important trends and to conduct strategic planning. The event that brought diversity to the attention of corporate human resources was the release of *Workforce 2000* by the Hudson Institute in 1987. Detailing the changing nature of the U.S. economy and labor market, the report presented a clear picture of the workforce in the year 2000. It noted that the labor pool will grow more slowly in the 1990s than at any other time in the nation's history, and that it will become increasingly diverse with respect to gender, race, ethnicity, values, and lifestyles.

Forming a Corporate Think Tank

In response to *Workforce 2000*, the senior vice president of human resources for corporate American Express amassed a "Think Tank" to address what was then called the Workforce Challenge. The group was formed to study and discuss the implications of *Workforce 2000*, and to determine the relevance of changing demographics for American Express. The Think Tank consisted of a representative grouping of 25 senior human resources personnel (vice president and above) from across the five subsidiaries and four senior line managers. The inclusion of the latter was seen as crucial for ensuring that line management would be receptive to the group's conclusions.

The Think Tank members heard presentations from outside consultants who were experts in the area of workforce diversity. These provided them with a more detailed understanding of the workforce changes that were occurring. Given the fast-paced and growing nature of American Express's business, which required a large number of new employees each year, the Think Tank members were particularly concerned about the company's ability to attract and retain qualified employees in the face of a shrinking and increasingly diverse labor pool. As such, they decided to focus on the issue of attraction and retention of employees. They selected several key customer service jobs and collected the following data for each: number of persons within that position, average tenure, average training time, average time until competent, and rate of turnover.

In June 1988, the Think Tank released a report with these figures to American Express's senior management. The report highlighted very clearly the high cost of turnover for American Express. It also highlighted the fact that attracting and retaining qualified customer service personnel were critical for American Express, and would become much more critical as the workforce began to grow at a slower rate and as it became more diverse.

Commitment from the Top

Senior management reacted very quickly to the Think Tank's report. At the senior management meeting in October 1988, a 2-day event held once every 18 months, the entire first day was devoted to the Workforce Challenge. The day began with an impassioned speech by the president of American Express. In that speech, he posed the Workforce Challenge as "the most difficult—and most important—challenge facing American Express." He argued that the company needed to attack the changing labor market "with the same dedication we do any other market." As he saw it, "the company's very survival [was] at stake."

The message conveyed was that top management believed changing demographics was a serious business issue, and that American Express needed to address it immediately. In order to attract and retain the workers who would be required to do business in the future, argued the president, American Express needed to create a work environment that would attract and motivate diverse individuals—individuals with their own unique needs, values, backgrounds, and lifestyles.

LAYING THE GROUNDWORK FOR CHANGE

Following the president's speech, the senior managers of each subsidiary were given the task of addressing the Workforce Challenge within their own subsidiaries. Within TRS, the largest of the subsidiaries, the task was handed to the human resources staff at the headquarters in New York. The remainder of this chapter will describe their efforts to address the issue of a changing workforce.

The human resources function at TRS comprises staff human resources at the headquarters in New York as well as line human resources within each of the business units and operations centers. Headquarters human resources is accountable to TRS senior management, with an informal reporting relationship to corporate human resources. Line human resources, on the other hand, is responsible for supporting its local business. As such, it reports directly to its local line management, with "dotted-line" reporting relationships to human resources at headquarters.

The Work and Family Survey

Given the Think Tank's conclusions, senior management of human resources at TRS felt that its biggest challenge was whether it would be able to attract and retain employees in the face of a shrinking labor pool and increasing diversity with respect to values, expectations, lifestyles, and family responsibilities. After careful consideration, senior management decided that the first thing that it would do was to collect data from its own workforce. The managers hoped that by better understanding the needs and concerns of current workers, they could determine the requirements for attracting and retaining workers of similar caliber in the future. They also decided to focus on needs and concerns with respect to balancing work and family. This had been a growing concern within TRS human resources, and the Think Tank's report highlighted the urgency of addressing it. To assist in collecting the data, human resources contracted with an outside consulting group, as it traditionally does when it needs to obtain expertise in a particular area. Because of the concern about diversity with respect to balancing work and family, human resources contracted with a consulting group specializing in that area.

The consulting group administered a survey to a random sample of over 3,000 employees at various levels throughout TRS. The sample was stratified into four categories: exempt men, exempt women, nonexempt men, nonexempt women. The survey assessed (1) the child-care arrangements that employees were currently using, (2) the perceived value of a variety of organizationally sponsored child-care programs, (3) the perceived value of a variety of policies to accommodate work and family (e.g., flextime, part-time work, etc.), (4) difficulties that employees were experiencing in balancing work and family, (5) trade-offs that employees had made to accommodate work and family, (6) the perceived supportiveness of American Express with respect to family needs, and (7) turnover intentions.

The consulting group also reviewed existing policies relating to work and family, observed employees on the job, and examined data on turnover, recruitment, and staffing. In addition, it conducted 16 employee focus groups at five locations, and held interviews with managers and supervisors at one large facility. The focus groups were conducted to provide additional insight into the issues identified on the survey. The interviews were conducted to determine (1) the extent to which managers felt that demographic changes were important, (2) the human resources issues that they saw as most critical to their business, and (3) the kinds of adjustments that they felt were needed to accommodate "the new breed of workers."

The survey and focus groups highlighted three primary issues. First, employees were experiencing significant difficulties balancing work and family responsibilities. Of those with children 60% had had at least one absence from work because of a sick child in the prior 3 months. In addition, more than 40% of employees expressed concern about their ability to find quality child care at an affordable price. Many questioned whether they could successfully combine work and family responsibilities at all.

The second issue identified was that employees were dissatisfied with what they perceived to be a lack of flexibility in their work schedules. Forty-nine percent of employees indicated that they had considered terminating their employment. Of these, 44% had considered doing so to seek a job with greater flexibility. An example of the lack of flexibility that employees were faced with was the rigid policies with respect to attendance and with respect to start and stop times. Employees were expected to be at their workstations during specified periods of time and were penalized for tardiness or excessive absences. These policies had always been seen as essential for TRS's success, because a customer service business requires that workstations be staffed at all times. It appeared, however, that the policies were no longer compatible with the expectations and needs of TRS's workforce.

The third issue highlighted by the survey and focus groups was that 35% of employees with children felt that senior management was not supportive of those with family responsibilities. This perception was shared throughout the ranks, with 47% of exempt women expressing dissatisfaction with the lack of senior management support.

The survey results met with surprise from several members of senior management. In particular, senior managers were surprised to learn that they were perceived as unresponsive to employees' needs. The survey suggested that employees wanted to be treated as whole and unique individuals with legitimate interests and needs outside of the workplace. In order for this to occur, however, a significant departure from the existing culture at TRS would be required. Traditionally, TRS had strived to maintain an exchange-based relationship with employees; a relationship where all employees were treated equally, and where family and personal issues were kept separate from work issues. The survey and focus groups suggested that this was no longer acceptable to many employees.

The survey also suggested that employees wanted a formal statement of management support as well as a range of services and policies to make that support concrete. Based upon the employees' responses, the consulting group suggested that TRS (1) provide some form of child-care support, (2) experiment with greater workplace flexibility, and (3) demonstrate corporate commitment to work and family issues via a formal policy statement.

Developing Specific Initiatives

After having obtained the results of the survey and focus groups, the executive vice president of human resources formed a task force to decide how to respond to employees' concerns. The task force was comprised of human resources managers from throughout TRS, and was chaired by the director of fair employment practices and the vice president of benefits. The group began by contacting a team of work and family specialists at a large benefits and compensation consulting firm. The reason for using outside consultants was to draw on individuals with expertise in designing programs for addressing work and family needs. The task force also felt that outside consultants would be able to provide them with information on what other companies were doing, information that would be difficult to obtain themselves. The task force selected a particular firm because TRS had used it in the past and was very satisfied with its work.

The consultants conducted several employee focus groups to identify specific policies and benefits that employees felt were needed. Each focus group consisted of employees at a similar stage in their lives (e.g., young workers with children, older workers approaching retirement, etc.). Participants were asked the following: "If you were offered an identical job, for the same pay and in the same city, what would it take, in terms of specific benefits and policies, to make you accept the offer?" Based on the employees' responses, 14 possible benefits and policies were identified:

part-time work, job-sharing, child-care centers, sick child care, compressed work weeks, variable time schedules, a school-days work program, expanded parental leave, a child-care voucher program, changes in vacation/sick day policies, education loans, expanded tuition aid, telecommuting, and sabbaticals.

Following the focus groups, the consultants performed analyses to assist the task force in deciding which benefits and policies to adopt. They focused on the 16 firms that TRS human resources considers to be its national competitors in the labor market, and compiled a report on what each was doing with respect to the benefits and policies that were under consideration. In addition, the consultants compiled a report with sample eligibility requirements, administrative procedures, and projected costs for each proposed benefit or policy. Aided by these analyses, by the end of July the task force had four initiatives that they were ready to present to the Office of the Presidents: a child-care subsidy program, improved benefits for part-time employees, a sabbatical program, and flexible work arrangements.

1. *Child-care subsidies.* The child-care subsidy program would provide partial reimbursement for the cost of child-care. After careful consideration, the task force decided not to adopt on-site child-care centers, as suggested by the survey and focus groups. The reason for this, according to the vice president of benefits, was that subsidies were seen as the best way to address the needs of the largest number of employees. "What many people don't realize is that on-site centers do not reach everyone [e.g., employees in small travel or sales offices in geographically isolated areas], and that centers generally cannot accommodate all of the children at a given facility." A subsidy program, it was decided, would be a more *equitable* way to address the child-care needs of employees. In addition, a subsidy program would be *flexible* in the sense of providing assistance regardless of the type of care needed (infant care, full day care, after-school care, etc.); it would allow employees to select a child-care provider that best met their needs. In other words, a subsidy program was seen as the best approach for addressing the *diverse* child-care needs of employees.

The child-care subsidy program was later expanded to cover dependent care as well as child-care, and was entitled KidsCheque (for child-care) and FamilyCheque (for dependent care). The reason for expanding the program was the recognition that a sizable and growing segment of the workforce was caring for aging parents. Thus, elder-care responsibilities were seen as another important component of workforce diversity.

2. *Improved part-time benefits.* The improved benefits initiative would provide part-time employees with benefits comparable to those of full-timers. Previously eligible for medical, dental, and vision coverage for themselves, in addition to long-term care, sick-leave coverage, vacation

coverage, basic life insurance, and flexible spending accounts, part-timers would now be eligible for dependent medical and dental coverage, tuition assistance, short- and long-term disability, group life insurance, family and personal leave, and group legal assistance. As with the subsidy program, the goal was to respond to the needs and concerns of an important and diverse segment of the workforce, with the goal of attracting and retaining employees in the future.

3. *Sabbaticals.* The sabbatical program would provide employees with 10 or more years of service ("career employees"), the opportunity to take an unpaid sabbatical for personal reasons, or a paid sabbatical for community service. The program, discussed for some time but not decided upon until fairly late, developed out of a recognition that many career employees have different needs and concerns from employees with shorter service. The goal of the sabbatical program was to provide career employees an opportunity for time away from work, for relaxation, or for self-development. It was hoped that the time away would reduce the stress and burnout that frequently occur within customer service jobs, curtail the trend toward early retirement, and support TRS's commitment to good corporate citizenship.

4. *Flexible work arrangements.* Flexible work arrangements would allow for all of the options suggested by the focus groups, including flextime, job sharing, gradual return after family leave, compressed work weeks, and telecommuting. Although some of these had previously existed on a local level, they had not been formally sanctioned by TRS management. It was hoped that by formally encouraging such flexible arrangements, TRS would be able to accommodate the diverse needs and lifestyles of employees. For example, job sharing might appeal to full-time students, whereas telecommuting might appeal to single parents.

Unlike the other initiatives, flexibility would be administered on a local basis, at the full discretion of local management. There were two reasons for this. First, there were important differences from one office or operations center to the next, such that it would be difficult or even impossible to mandate across-the-board flexibility policies. For example, a small travel office with six employees had very different constraints from a large operations center with several thousand employees. Second, an important component of the TRS culture is the belief that local managers must be allowed as much discretion as possible in running their businesses. In other words, the task force did not see flexibility as something that it could—or should—mandate.

Although there was clearly a risk that local management would be slow to implement flexibility, this was something that the task force members felt they were willing to accept, at least in the short run. They did not, however, see this as a very likely scenario. The interviews conducted by the first consulting group revealed that many managers wanted to be more flexible and would readily do so once it was sanctioned by TRS senior management. Further, it was felt that once TRS instituted a policy stating that managers *could* be flexible, reluctant mangers would be faced with significant pressures from employees. It was also felt that reluctant managers would feel pressured once other business units began to adopt flexible arrangements (see Table 9.1 and Figure 9.2).

Gaining Initial Commitment

In August 1989, the executive vice president of human resources gained initial approval for the initiatives from the Office of the Presidents. She was able to do so by making a strong business case. She referred back to the turnover data released by the Think Tank and argued that TRS could not afford *not* to institute changes. In order to attract and retain qualified employees, she argued, TRS could no longer provide the same thing for everyone—it needed to be more responsive to the diversity of the work-force. The biggest source of resistance that she encountered was concerns about costs. She was able to counter these concerns, however, by arguing that the costs were important investments (as important as capital invest-ments), and that they were necessary if American Express was to remain ahead of the competition.

MAKING IT HAPPEN

With the Office of the Presidents approving of the proposed plans, the executive vice president of human resources recognized that it was more urgent than ever to fill the vacant position of senior vice president of employee relations and human resources. The incumbent of that position would direct the implementation of the initiatives and the longer-term strategy that they would soon represent. This strategy, known previously as the Workforce Challenge, had just been retitled Becoming the Best Place to Work, with the aim of broadening its focus. The change in title reflected a goal of not just responding to changes in the external workforce, but of creating a more favorable workplace for all employees.

The man who was selected to direct the change process was new to TRS; he had previously been the vice president of employee relations at a large telecommunications company. He was selected for the job for two primary reasons. First, he was seen as a dynamic leader who would be able to create and direct an effective team. Second, and even more importantly, he had extensive line as well as human resources experience. This meant

TABLE 9.1. The Four Initiatives

KidsCheque and FamilyCheque

A. Child-care subsidy for all full-time employees earning up to $40,000 and with family income of up to $80,000[a]
  - Covers children up to the age of 13
  - Pays up to 50% of weekly child-care or dependent-care costs, to a maximum of $25 for one child or $35 for two or more children
  - Employees eligible after 6 months of employment
  - Effective January 1991

B. Subsidy for employees' dependents who are physically or mentally incapable of caring for themselves
  - Same regulations as those governing KidsCheque

Workplace flexibility

A. Flexibility alternatives in scheduling
  - Options for flextime, job sharing, and part-time work
  - Administered on a local basis
  - Effective October 1990

B. Flexible return from family and sick leave
  - Employees may return to work on a part-time basis
  - Family leave or sick leave and flexible return combined may extend up to 20 weeks
  - Allowed one flexible return within any 12 month period
  - Regular benefits coverage continues
  - Effective November 1990

Sabbaticals

A. Paid sabbaticals for community service
  - Up to 6 months for employees with 10–19 years of service
  - Up to 12 months for employees with 20+ years of service
  - Must be used for community service
  - Employees apply through local management, with TRS Sabbatical Board making final selection
  - Same job guaranteed for up to 3 months; comparable job guaranteed after 3 months
  - Effective April 1991

B. Unpaid sabbaticals for personal pursuits
  - Up to 3 months for employees with 10+ years of service
  - Employees apply through local management, with TRS Sabbatical Board making final selection
  - Same job guaranteed
  - Effective April 1991

Improved part-time benefits
  - Benefits comparable to those of full-time employees
  - Eligible after 6 months of employment
  - Effective January 1991

---

[a]By these criteria, 99.9% of nonexempt employees and 85% of employees overall were eligible.

KEY ADVANTAGES

1990 INITIATIVES	ATTRACTION & RETENTION	MARKETPLACE DIFFERENTIATION	INCREASED PRODUCTIVITY	TO MEET COMPETITION	COMMUNITY RELATIONS	PERSONAL DEVELOPMENT
KIDSCHEQUE AND FAMILYCHEQUE	X	X	X			
SABBATICALS	X	X	X		X	X
WORK-PLACE FLEXIBILITY	X	X	X	X		
PART-TIME BENEFITS	X			X		

FIGURE 9.2. Benefits of each of the four initiatives.

that he would be able to relate to the business concerns that would inevitably be raised, and that he would be able to bridge the gap between line management and human resources.

Once hired, the senior vice president did two things. First, he met with as many people as possible—human resources, line management, and senior management—to define the issues that still needed to be resolved and the concerns that needed to be addressed. Second, he selected persons to fill three key positions beneath him: the vice president, the director, and the manager of employee relations. He filled the positions in such a way as to provide a balance of both technical and line expertise. Whereas all three persons had extensive experience in employee relations, the vice president had several years' experience in line human resources, while the director had strong technical experience and a doctorate in industrial/organizational psychology.

Once these positions were filled, Becoming the Best Place to Work began to take shape. In the months that followed, three key activities were conducted. First, an overall strategy for what it would mean to Become the Best Place to Work was articulated. Second, the initiatives were revised, refined, and made operational, and commitment was gained from line and human resources management. Third, a plan was developed for communicating the goal of Becoming the Best Place to Work to employees.

Defining the Vision

One of the most important activities that occurred during late 1989 and early 1990 was defining the long-term "vision" of what it would mean to Become the Best Place to Work. It was the senior vice president of employee relations and human resources who was most responsible for this part of the change effort. The goal that he articulated was to create a work environment in which the diverse needs of each and every employee were respected. The four initiatives were only the first step in reaching this objective. Ultimately, the goal was to alter day-to-day management practices. For example, whereas employees had traditionally been treated equally by their supervisors, it was now seen as necessary that they be treated more as individuals. This represented a significant shift in values for TRS.

Refining the Initiatives and Gaining Commitment

Throughout January and February of 1990, the employee relations staff projected the costs of each of the initiatives and identified specific issues that still needed to be resolved. In March, they held a 2-day meeting with all senior line human resources managers (approximately 30 individuals). The purpose of this meeting was twofold. First, it was aimed at obtaining input from each of the different business units. Second, it was aimed at creating a sense of ownership.

Both of these goals were extremely important. Obtaining input was important because each of the locations had slightly different needs and concerns. For example, employees in Salt Lake City had more children, on average, than employees in other geographical areas. As a result, the Salt Lake facility had more at stake with KidsCheque—both costs as well as benefits—relative to other facilities. As another example, because the operations center in New York City had a larger percentage of students and older workers than the other centers, part-time benefits and sabbaticals were particularly relevant to them.

The second goal, creating a sense of ownership, was also highly important. Part of the TRS culture was the belief that because each location has its own unique needs, line human resources managers should have the discretion to do what is in the best interest of their employees and their local management. As a result, they might be hesitant to support a program that did not seem to address the particular needs of their business group. Because line human resources would be implementing and administering the programs, however, its commitment was vital.

The meeting began with a presentation by the senior vice president of employee relations and human resources, in which he outlined the four initiatives, the objectives behind them, and some initial ideas for marketing the changes. He also outlined all of the issues that were unresolved. Participants were then divided into small groups, and each group was asked to discuss two of the initiatives and to make specific recommendations on the unresolved issues. After their individual discussions, the groups presented their recommendations to the entire group for discussion. Consensus was reached on each initiative, and the following morning, participants were presented with revised versions of the initiatives.

To facilitate the small-group discussions, employee relations provided each group with a detailed packet of information for each initiative. Each of the packets contained the following information: the purpose of the initiative, eligibility requirements, administrative procedures, issues open for discussion, data on the number of eligible employees, projected costs of each of several alternatives, and information on similar programs at other companies.

As an example of the data that group members had at their disposal, the KidsCheque packet contained the following: the number of employees earning less than $30,000, $35,000, and $40,000 annually; the number of employees within each of these groups who had children under age 13; projected costs of the program and projected benefits percentages assuming maximum weekly subsidies of $25, $30, and $35, assuming 25%, 50%, and 75% participation of eligible employees, and assuming eligibility cut-offs of $30,000, $35,000, and $40,000. Issues open for discussion in this case included (1) the salary cutoff for eligibility, (2) the maximum weekly subsidy, (3) whether a limit should be placed on the number of children covered, and (4) the method of payment.

Following the meeting, the planning process progressed to a stage of fine-tuning. Human resources and line management from throughout TRS participated in this fine-tuning process. Volunteers were recruited for four "action teams," one for each initiative. Over the next several months, the action teams identified and resolved all of the issues that needed to be addressed before the initiatives could be implemented. For example, members of the sabbatical team contacted various community service facilities (e.g., schools, shelters, hospitals) to assure that they would be receptive to volunteers, and they interviewed human resources managers at companies that already had sabbatical programs to determine how their programs were administered. Before the initiatives were finalized, the employee relations staff conducted eight focus groups with employees from each of the business units. These focus groups served as a final reality test, and helped the staff to anticipate questions that employees might raise when the initiatives were introduced.

The final part of the fine-tuning process was the creation of an Administrative Task Force, consisting of volunteers from both headquarters and line human resources. The objective of the task force was to discuss, finalize, and document all of the issues that would be involved in administering the initiatives. Its efforts culminated in a detailed reference manual that was distributed to all line human resources. The reference manual covered eligibility requirements, policies and procedures, and sample questions and answers for each initiative. According to the employee relations staff, the task force's ability to anticipate and address many of the issues that would later arise was critical to the eventual success of the change process.

Communicating the Vision

The fourth activity that occurred during the spring and summer of 1990 was the development of a strategy for communicating Becoming the Best Place to Work to employees. The employee relations staff saw this as extremely important, because it felt that a large part of any change effort is marketing it to employees. It was hoped that even before the initiatives were put into effect, the communication materials would set the change process in motion by shaping employee perceptions of TRS.

Employee relations formed a Communications Task Force, consisting of both headquarters and line human resources. In addition, it hired an outside consultant so that it would have a communication expert solely dedicated to Becoming the Best Place to Work. The consultant's role was to help the task force design a step-by-step plan to ensure that an integrated and consistent message would be conveyed to employees. He also helped to design mailings as well as a logo that would be recognized throughout TRS.

Focus groups were conducted to determine employee reactions to different communication tactics. The focus group discussions revealed two things. First, in order to be noticed, communications (mailings, memos, etc.) needed to stand out visually, clearly address employees' interests and needs, and be concise. Second, employees preferred to receive information gradually rather than all at once. Based on this information, the task force decided to distribute several staggered mailings rather than one comprehensive mailing. They also decided to use bright neon colors in order to attract employees' attention.

Introducing the Strategy

In late June 1990, the senior vice president of employee relations and human resources presented the four initiatives and the longer-term goal for Becoming the Best Place to Work to the Office of the Presidents for final approval. He was able to obtain this approval by focusing on the *business* advantages of Becoming the Best Place to Work. That is, he presented the package less like a typical human resources plan and more like a marketing plan: focusing on the goal of differentiating TRS in the labor marketplace and placing TRS ahead of the competition. He emphasized again and again the importance of acting immediately to obtain a first-mover advantage.

Soon after the plan was approved, the employee relations staff held meetings with line human resources in New York, Jacksonville, and Phoenix. Attendees were shown a draft of the Management Briefing that would eventually be presented to line management. The briefing explained the demographic trends leading to the Becoming the Best Place to Work strategy, the philosophy behind the change effort, and the longer-term goals for the future. Attendees were also shown the communications materials and the administrative details for the initiatives. They were encouraged to ask questions and to suggest changes, several of which were used to make minor revisions.

In early September, the official "roll-out" began. A formal announcement from the Office of the Presidents was sent to each employee's home, introducing Becoming the Best Place to Work. This was followed by four other announcements, distributed at work over the next 2 months, each of which introduced one of the four initiatives. In addition, managers received flexibility guidebooks that informed them of different options for flexible work arrangements. During this same time, each of the local operations centers and businesses held their own Becoming the Best Place to Work "kick-off." Several of the centers held fairs, with information booths and promotional materials. One center even held its fair on a weekend so that family members could attend. Another center held a meeting for employees who had been with TRS for 10 or more years, at which the employees were commended for their service and informed about the sabbatical program.

REACTIONS FROM EMPLOYEES

From the beginning of the roll-out phase, most employees appeared to be highly enthusiastic about the four initiatives. This was particularly true for KidsCheque. The vice president of human resources at the operations center in Phoenix described the early responses to KidsCheque as "phenomenal." In weekly lunch meetings with employees, he noted that Kids-Cheque was invariably the first topic of discussion. "They see it as the greatest thing that TRS has ever done . . . . It has been *extremely* positive in terms of how the company is perceived." The vice president of human resources at the operations center in Jacksonville noted that within weeks of introducing KidsCheque, almost 80% of her eligible employees had signed up. In addition, she was receiving resumes from people who had heard about KidsCheque from the local media and who were interested in joining TRS as a result, and telephone calls from human resources managers at other companies who were interested in instituting similar programs.

Employees were extremely favorable in their response to the flexibility initiative as well. By early 1991, management and employees at almost every location were beginning to work together in designing and implementing flexible work arrangements. To elicit ideas, several locations were instituting contests, and others were using task forces. At one location, for example, the human resources department formed a team of nonmanagement employees. The team's mandate was to consider the needs of the business, together with the needs of employees, and to design flexibility proposals that would satisfy both. The group members then had to sell the proposals to management. To assist them, they were provided with training in group facilitation and in selling ideas upward. According to the vice president of human resources at the facility, the program was important in two respects. First, it enabled the facility to identify flexibility options that would meet the needs of both management and employees. Second, it was a source of empowerment for employees.

Overall, employees responded to Becoming the Best Place to Work with enthusiasm. There were, however, some exceptions to this. In particular, many of the professionals within the headquarters functions (finance, purchasing, real estate, etc.) were unimpressed with the changes. The salary level of these employees made them ineligible for KidsCheque or FamilyCheque, and the nature of their jobs made part-time work and flexible scheduling unfeasible. Consequently, the initial four initiatives had little to offer them, and many were cynical about TRS's long-term goal of Becoming the Best Place to Work. It is important to note, however, that the entire headquarters staff represents less than 5% of TRS's workforce.

DIFFICULTIES ALONG THE WAY

As of this writing, the employee relations staff at TRS felt that Becoming the Best Place to Work had been launched with success. Several difficulties, however, were encountered along the way. The first was overcoming resistance by members of senior management who did not feel that change was needed. The second difficulty was overcoming resistance by senior line managers who were concerned about the costs of adopting the initiatives. The third difficulty was dealing with employee disillusionment caused by inflated expectations.

Convincing Senior Management that Change Was Needed

One of the biggest difficulties encountered, particularly during the early stages of the change process, was convincing senior management at TRS headquarters that change was needed. Many took the position of "if it's not broken, why fix it?" The executive vice president of human resources found it extremely difficult to convince such individuals. She questioned: "How does one convince people that something is coming when they cannot see it yet? How could one have convinced the US auto industry, ten years ago, that by the end of the decade the Japanese would own 30% of their market?"

In some cases, she was able to convince management of the need for change by simply making them aware of the demographic changes that were about to occur, the high costs that TRS was already incurring because of turnover (the Think Tank data), and the concerns highlighted by the employee survey. Even after Becoming the Best Place to Work was formally introduced, however, there were still some senior managers at headquarters who failed to see demographic changes as important. They were not purposefully resisting the change, but unlike line management in the field, they had simply not yet begun to "feel the pain" of a shrinking and diverse labor pool.

Dealing with Concerns about Costs

Not only were there managers who failed to see the need for change, but there were also many line managers who questioned the initiatives because of the financial costs that would be incurred. The line managers were particularly concerned about the costs of KidsCheque and FamilyCheque. Because the subsidies would comprise a part of total payroll costs, they would have a significant effect on line managers' bottom-line.

Managing concerns about costs was extremely difficult and required that the senior vice president of employee relations and human resources hold repeated one-on-one meetings with senior line managers. He attempted to assuage their concerns by convincing them that the initiatives should not be seen as costs, but rather as long-term investments that would pay off in the future. He was also able to cite the fact that the Office of the Presidents was firmly behind the initiatives. This support was extremely important in convincing management that Becoming the Best Place to Work was the right thing to do.

In addition to the senior line managers who were concerned about costs per se, there were those who felt that the timing was simply not right. They recognized that the initiatives would be needed *eventually*, but given the huge financial investment that would be required, they felt that it was best to wait until TRS was experiencing true difficulties attracting employees. These opinions became particularly salient in the fall of 1990. The downturn in the economy, coupled with uncertainty about events in the Persian Gulf, caused many managers to question whether it was wise to commit to such a costly program until it was absolutely necessary.

The senior vice president of employee relations and human resources addressed these concerns by arguing that the timing would never be perfect, but that if responding to workforce changes was truly important, then TRS should act immediately to stay ahead of its competitors and to demonstrate its commitment to workforce diversity. He argued that "Becoming the Best Place to Work is not something that you turn on and off like a faucet when business takes a downturn."

Along with the efforts by the senior vice president of employee relations and human resources, line human resources was instrumental in overcoming the resistance of its line management. It located information about benefits and policy changes that the local competition had either recently adopted or planned to adopt, and argued that attracting new employees at a *local* level would become extremely difficult if TRS failed to adopt the initiatives. In general, this tactic was far more effective than appeals to abstract demographic changes. In a few rare cases, however, line managers remained unconvinced. Where this was the case, the initiatives were not promoted wholeheartedly during the roll-out, and flexibility options were not readily adopted. Because of the value placed on management discretion, however, this was something that the employee relations staff was willing to accept in the short term.

Dealing with Employee Disillusionment

A third difficulty that was encountered, and one that may become even more problematic in the future, was employee disillusionment about the longer-term goal of Becoming the Best Place to Work. The primary source of this disillusionment was that some employees expected that significant changes in day-to-day management practices would occur immediately. The executive vice president of human resources found this particularly frustrating.

> *Becoming the Best Place to Work is not a religious conversion whereby everybody will suddenly be treated perfectly. Yet as soon as people saw the Becoming the Best Place to Work logo, many of them thought that things would happen instantaneously . . . . If I was going to do things over again, I would make sure that we emphasized to people right from the start that this is going to be a journey . . . . It's not that your boss is suddenly going to treat you better . . . . In retrospect, we could have done a better job of conveying this.*

KEY SUCCESS FACTORS

Given the above difficulties, one might ask how Becoming the Best Place to Work was introduced with such seeming success. Based on discussions with those involved in the process, several factors come to light. First, the planning process was thorough and systematic. Second, employee relations was able to create a sense of ownership among line human resources. Third, it was able to make a strong business case for Becoming the Best Place to Work. Fourth, there was strong support from the Office of the Presidents. Finally, employee relations was able to articulate a guiding philosophy for what it was trying to achieve.

Systematic Approach

After being alerted to the changing nature of the workforce by American Express senior management, members of human resources at TRS identified whether, and in what ways, the changes were relevant to them. They collected data from their own workforce, and continued to obtain input and verification at several points along the way. The survey, employee focus groups, and meetings with line human resources, all ensured that the problem was accurately defined, that appropriate measures were being taken, and that relevant issues were addressed.

Creation of Ownership

The bottom-up approach that was taken not only provided headquarters human resources with useful information, but it also created a sense of commitment and ownership throughout the organization. For example, by eliciting employee input via the survey and focus groups, and then using that input in designing the initiatives, employee relations obtained support from employees throughout the company. In addition, it created a strong sense of ownership among line human resources by involving it in the process of refining the initiatives. This grass-roots approach was essential in facilitating the change effort.

Presentation of a Strong Business Case

A third factor accounting for the initial success of Becoming the Best Place to Work was the ability of human resources to make a strong business case for the proposed changes. By appealing to the turnover data released by the Think Tank and by arguing for the competitive advantage that would be reaped by acting immediately, it was able to convince the majority of line managers that Becoming the Best Place to Work was a necessary business investment.

Support from the Top

In addition to support from the ranks, another factor accounting for the success of Becoming the Best Place to Work was strong support from the top. At the very beginning, it was the president of American Express himself who defined workforce diversity as an important issue that needed to be addressed immediately. In addition, human resources elicited the commitment of the Office of the Presidents at two key points along the way (August 1989 and June 1990). Becoming the Best Place to Work clearly could not have occurred without this support from above. In particular, the ability to refer to this support greatly facilitated the process of selling the proposed changes to line managers.

A Clear Guiding Philosophy

A final key to success was the fact that there was an overall philosophy guiding the change effort: the goal of Becoming the Best Place to Work. As one of the outside consultants noted, it was not the specific initiatives that would matter in the long run, because other companies would no doubt copy them. Rather, what would provide TRS a competitive advantage was the long-term goal to create a work environment that was more conducive to employees' diverse needs, values, and lifestyles.

WHAT LIES AHEAD

The initiatives introduced in late 1990 were just the first step toward the goal of making TRS the Best Place to Work. The next step is to begin changing day-to-day management practices that are inconsistent with that goal. In particular, changes are needed in the fairly rigid attendance and tardiness policies that TRS management has traditionally seen as prerequisite to quality customer service.

Another change required is management training. Managers cannot simply be told to "treat people better." Rather, they need to be given a clear understanding of what this means, and the skills to actually do so. To accomplish this goal, TRS began a leadership training program in early 1991. By the end of the year, all vice presidents will have attended a 3-day training workshop. An important component of this program is an upward feedback mechanism whereby participants are provided with feedback from their subordinates and colleagues and trained in using that feedback to change their leadership behavior. Beginning in 1992, managers below the vice president level will also participate in the leadership training program. In addition, TRS plans to institute both flexibility training and diversity training for managers. Although the details have not yet been determined, these two programs will be aimed at raising awareness with respect to flexible work options and workforce diversity issues. The programs will also enable participants to develop individualized plans for improving their management skills.

Work–family initiatives that are being considered for the future include an emergency child-care program and a hotline for latchkey children. In addition, TRS human resources plans to begin aggressive efforts to attract, retain, and develop minority managers. Finally, an important plan for the future is to expand Becoming the Best Place to Work internationally. According to the senior vice president of employee relations, this will require a region by region approach, because "what it means to be the best place to work in the Philippines may be very different from what it means to be the best place to work in France."

Monitoring and Evaluating the Change Process

The months and years ahead will involve an ongoing process of monitoring and evaluating the change process. At the time of this writing, a second employee survey is planned for the fall of 1991. This will enable the employee relations staff to assess changes in employee attitudes and perceptions of the workplace. Focus groups will also be used for continuing evaluation. In addition, communication between employee relations in New York and managers in the field will enable an assessment of progress. "My goal," noted the senior vice president of employee relations, "is that in 18 months we could go out to any facility and ask managers what they personally were doing to make this a better place to work, and they would have a response."

To help assure that the change process will remain in motion, senior management incorporated Becoming the Best Place to Work into TRS's 1991 strategic plan. This action demonstrated very clearly senior management's continued commitment to the program. It also set the stage for a situation where managers will eventually be evaluated on their efforts to make TRS the Best Place to Work. In other words, because goals throughout the organization are designed to be consistent with the strategic plan, Becoming the Best Place to Work will eventually "trickle down" and be reflected in managers' yearly goals.

Difficulties Ahead

Despite the ambitious plans for the future, there will clearly be some difficulties in the months and years ahead. A long-term change such as Becoming the Best Place to Work, one that involves new values and norms and a new type of relationship between managers and employees, takes considerable time. Indeed, it may take years to fully work through the longer-term changes that are planned with respect to management practices. It will also take time and effort to implement flexible work arrangements. Even with managers being highly supportive of flexibility, in many cases it will be extremely difficult to provide flexible work schedules while still assuring that the necessary number of customer service lines are covered.

CONCLUSIONS

TRS's story provides several lessons for managers and human resources practitioners who decide to engage in similar broad-based efforts to prepare for diversity. First, it illustrates the importance of engaging in a thorough diagnosis and planning process before actually implementing a change of this scope. Second, companies embarking on change efforts of this type should not overlook the importance of involving as many people as possible. Nor should they overlook the importance of support from the top—support that sends a powerful message throughout the organization. Third, Becoming the Best Place to Work illustrates the importance of articulating a clear guiding philosophy and a vision for the future. Fourth, and perhaps most important, the successful launching of Becoming the Best Place to Work illustrates the importance of human resources planners recognizing the larger business context. Employee Relations recognized the importance of presenting the strategy as a "business imperative" rather than merely a human resources initiative, and it recognized the importance of addressing legitimate business concerns. Although much still lies ahead, American Express Travel Related Services has begun its journey to Become the Best Place to Work. Human resources, together with senior management, sees the change effort as one that will help TRS attract and retain diverse and high-quality employees, differentiate itself in the marketplace, and communicate a new set of values to employees, potential employees, and customers.

CHAPTER 10

Managing Diversity:
A Strategic "Grass-Roots"
Approach

JOEL M. DeLUCA
ROBERT N. McDOWELL

The phrase *managing diversity* grows daily in use throughout the business world. However, it means different things to different people. Some executives see diversity as traditional equal employment opportunity issues popping up again repackaged for the 1990s. Others view it as a broader workforce issue that the human resources (HR) function should address. Still others, although a minority at the moment, see diversity management as a strategic business issue. The latter view frames the context for this discussion.

What follows outlines an overall approach to change that our organization is developing to manage its own increasing diversity. The approach is evolving and is not intended to replace existing initiatives in the organization. It is designed more as a path to follow than as a program to implement.

This chapter first describes the perspective from which the approach originates. It emphasizes our belief that diversity is fundamentally a business issue that may be signaling an end to the "one-size-fits-all" era of management. We then describe the basic blueprint of the approach for which the operational details are being developed as we progress. It emphasizes a related belief that approaches to workforce diversity need to leverage grass-roots forces existing throughout the organization.

BACKGROUND ABOUT THE ORGANIZATION

Coopers & Lybrand was founded in Philadelphia in 1898. Today, it provides professional services around the world. Its core mission is stated as

"Solutions for Business." Client services offered include auditing, tax advice, management consulting, and actuarial and benefits consulting.

In this chapter, we focus on the U.S. part of the firm, which serves a diverse client base that includes companies such as AT&T, Ford Motor Company, Johnson & Johnson, and Goldman Sachs. Over the years, innovations in expert systems, manufacturing technology, and financial services have spurred the firm's growth. In the 1980s the number of partners and staff doubled, while revenues increased by over 350% to exceed $1 billion. The firm now employs over 15,000 people, including approximately 1,300 partners. More than 100 practice offices throughout the country operate within a matrix structure that emphasizes the client service disciplines and geographic locations. The practice office is the basic business unit of the firm. Each practice office is headed by a managing partner and provides a full range of client services to its geographic area.

Structure of the Human Resources Organization

The human resources organization is matrixed in a parallel way to the firm's management structure. At national headquarters, the chief human resources partner works with senior management on firmwide personnel policy. Each client service discipline and geographic region has its own respective human resources director. Each practice office has human resources professionals reporting directly to the managing partner. Human resources directors interact on an as-needed basis, as well as meeting quarterly to discuss emerging human resources issues in the firm and to coordinate the implementation of various human resources initiatives.

The Human Resources Staff

Field human resources professionals in the firm have widely diverse backgrounds and a range of practical experience including recruiting and college relations, staff assignment planning, professional development and career planning, and employee benefits. At the regional level, most directors are also partners in the firm. Most hold advanced degrees in business, accounting, or the behavioral sciences. The roles they play are highly integrated with day-to-day practice office operations and few have experience with managing strategic initiatives.

The corporate HR staff includes the chief human resources officer and the director of human resources planning. Robert McDowell, who is the current (1991) chief human resources officer, has spent the past 17 years in a variety of human resources, operations, and staff roles in the firm. He has worked in line human resources positions, as staff director to an operations vice chairman, and as staff to chairman of the firm. In these various roles he has had experience with firmwide organization planning, budgeting, manpower planning, marketing and business development, and practice office operations in addition to human resources management. His academic training includes an MA with an emphasis in counseling and vocational psychology.

Joel DeLuca, who is the current director of human resources planning, joined the firm in 1989. He began his career as a research and development scientist in the U.S. Air Force. At the rank of captain he made a career shift into the behavioral sciences. He has been an internal consultant with the Federal Aviation Administration and an external consultant to public and private organizations, and headed the organization planning and leadership development function in an energy corporation. His academic training includes a master's degree in business administration and one in physics, as well as a doctorate in organizational behavior.

DIVERSITY: A STRATEGIC BUSINESS PERSPECTIVE

The approach an organization takes toward managing diversity depends on how it frames the issue. Cultural diversity is a hot topic in today's organizations. Yet cultural diversity is just the visible tip of the larger diversity iceberg lurking beneath the surface. Attending to issues of cultural diversity could represent a viable starting point for developing an understanding of the larger diversity issue. But attending to cultural diversity could become a titanic mistake if that form of diversity remains the exclusive focus. Diversity is rapidly emerging as a significant management issue in many arenas, including business markets and organization structures. Consideration of the major pieces in the total diversity pie, shown in Figure 10.1, reveals the need for a broad approach to managing diversity.

Business Diversity

Since World War II, mass production methods predominated in most U.S. businesses. Technological advances created a cornucopia of new products. Basic labor-saving devices such as washing machines, stoves, and refrigerators, and entertainment products such as radios and television sets were sought by a national and even global market. Mass production based upon one-size-fits-all designs made these products affordable to the general populace. Variations in products were small because specialization decreased economies of scale and increased prices.

Business Diversity

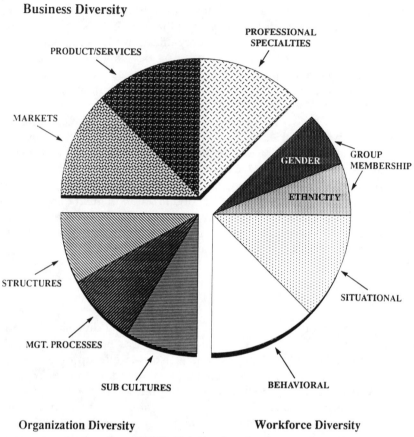

FIGURE 10.1. The diversity pie.

Today, markets are diversifying faster than many companies can keep up. Huge mass production markets have splintered into economic niches. The broad label of *consumer* has diversified into baby-boomers, Yuppies, Dincs, Empty Nesters, and so on. A glance in today's mailboxes reveals a plethora of catalogs, with each catalog designed to appeal to a particular market niche. The more niches, the more catalogs. Globalization brings even more types of diversity to the marketplace. Every country represents unique political and cultural niches. Business success requires a specialized strategy for each niche.

Market niching is a major form of business diversity facing today's managers. It signals a shift away from large homogeneous markets toward multiple specialized markets. "Big is better" has started to give way to "boutique is best." In addition, other constituencies including government and community stakeholders are pressing new types of demands. As a result, today's executives face unprecedented levels of diverse environmental forces.

Organization Diversity

During the reign of mass production, a function-based organizational form was *the* design. The functional form organized work into departments such as manufacturing, marketing, finance, and research and development. It neatly parceled tasks into hierarchical boxes and emphasized unity of command, clarity of boundaries, order, control, and stability. It provided the consistency and efficiency necessary to obtain the economies of scale required for mammoth enterprises. The functional form of organization became the one-size-fits-all design.

The function-based design works well in relatively stable environments. However, responsiveness under conditions of rapid change, which face today's businesses, is not its strong suit. Increased niching of world markets has, therefore, caused many new organizational designs to emerge. The functional form, with its emphasis on a top-down, hierarchical management style, has not been replaced. Instead, it has been joined by other designs, such as the matrix organization and the M-form. These new organization designs often require different management skills. For example, managing a matrix structure in which each person has two or more supervisors requires skills different from managing an organization designed around functions and based on the principle of unity of command.

A large business today may contain a diverse mix of structures under the same organizational roof. Executives may have to manage product-based, market-based, and geography-based organizational forms within a holding company structure that also contains some matrix organizations and some functional designs. Forms of ownership may also differ. Thus, managers may be dealing with franchises, strategic alliances, joint ventures, and employee-owned business units. To add to this diversity, there could be different subcultures, management processes, and subunits organized on emerging network organizational forms. Add even newer forms designated by labels such as clusters (Mills, 1991), stable-core/flexible-ring (DeLuca, 1988), shamrock (Handy, 1989), and flex-firm (Toffler, 1990) designs and the diversity challenge starts to go through the roof. Managing today's organizations is less an issue of searching for the one best form. It's more an issue of learning to manage a diversity of forms, each with different requirements.

People Diversity

By now, most white male workers have heard that they are a species whose dominance is in decline. The demographic shifts point to a multicolor, dual-gender future. However, it would be a mistake to assume that such diversity is the only or even the predominant type of workforce diversity. Besides the diversity due to DNA (race and gender) and culture, situational and behavioral factors introduce additional workforce diversity.

Situational diversity refers to the current conditions of an employee's life. It covers such issues as age, marital status, family stage, economic status, and geographical location. The classic profile of a worker as married with a spouse and children at home, and who desires a 30-year career with one company is far from today's reality. Yet many organizations still have one-size-fits-all benefits packages, retirement plans, and career systems based on a view of the workforce as homogeneous.

Dual-career couples, single-parent families, individuals in their third career and nearing retirement with no pension, and baby-boomers with both young children and aging parents to care for are but a few examples of workforce diversity due to situational factors.

Behavioral diversity refers to the more subjective characteristics of today's workforce. Genetic and situational diversity factors such as race, sex, age, marital status, and parenthood are objective facts about a person. Behavioral diversity, on the other hand, involves more subjective factors such as work style, problem-solving styles, needs, desires, and values. Even if one addressed only the white male segment of the workforce, one would find increasing differences in terms of career intentions, life orientations, and work values.

The traditionally held assumption that most employees are ambitious workers who want to climb their way to the top is no longer valid. Some employees still fit the traditional picture. Others see themselves as having a single career that spans several organizations. Still others envision multiple careers. And a growing number do not view their work life in career terms at all.

Behavioral diversity also includes differences in work style. When highly motivated and creative workers become a competitive advantage, inspirational leadership becomes as important as administrative control. Such leadership implies a better understanding of employee behavioral differences. The need for a diversity of management styles is replacing the single-style approach of "I am the boss." Some people work best within a participative management style, whereas others still prefer the traditional autocratic style. Some people are comfortable with delegation, whereas others prefer close supervision. Effective leadership today requires skills in several management styles.

In addition, from a cognitive standpoint, the creative problem-solving styles of some employees differ fundamentally from the linear problem-solving styles of others. Because both of these distinct styles are equally important to business growth, successful organizations try to support both styles. The list of behavioral diversity goes on and on and isn't really new. What is new is the growing need for leaders who value such individual differences—leaders who can turn the types of behavioral differences that often create conflicts into motivational synergies for the business.

Diversity Summary

Diversity is stretching the one-size-fits-all era of management beyond its breaking point. It affects every aspect of business operation. One-dimensional markets, organizational structures, and workforce profiles are fracturing into myriad differences. Capitalizing on diversity means viewing it as a strategic business issue. However, operationalizing this view is not straightforward. It may require a mental shift on the part of management.

DIVERSITY MENTAL SHIFT

Figure 10.2 summarizes two basic orientations toward diversity. The efficiency mindset fit the industrial age. To maintain the industrial growth engine characterized by mass production and economies of scale, efficiency became the hallmark of administration. The more efficiently products could be produced, the less expensive they would be to the public. Efficiency and homogeneity go hand in hand. The more things are the same, the more a one-size-fits-all solution can be developed that maximizes efficiency.

Traditionally, administrative management in large organizations valued consistency. Catering to individual differences in interpersonal and cognitive styles was avoided. If everyone was not treated the same, equity problems swamped the organization. Management tended to ease out odd ducks and others who didn't fit the corporate mold. Differences in work style were viewed as deviancy rather than as diversity. In addition, differences created inefficiencies. Instead of using one approach for all, management needed multiple approaches that each required separate administration.

As business, organization, and workforce diversity become less the exception and more the rule, a different management perspective becomes necessary. The information/service age is based more on effectiveness, profitability, and change management than on efficiency, cost reduction,

THEN	NOW
Industrial Age	Information Age

Economies of scale and a relatively stable environment made **efficiency** a prime ingredient for success.	Market niches and rapidly changing environments make **effectiveness** a prime ingredient for success.
↓	↓
Efficiency encouraged a **cost** focus. Establishing common rules and a "management-by-exception" approach to **administer stability** were critical.	Effectiveness encourages a **profit** focus. Establishing adaptable processes with a leadership approach to **manage change** are critical.
↓	↓
Differences frequently meant exceptions, creating either inequity or inefficiency or both.	Differences frequently mean diversity, creating challenges or options or both.
↓	↓
The "efficiency mindset" is geared to view differences as **problems** and conflicts needing to be reduced.	The "diversity mindset" is geared to view differences as **opportunities** to generate synergy.

FIGURE 10.2. Diversity: then and now.

and administrative stability. However, moving from an efficiency to a diversity mindset will not be easy for some managers. The efficiency mindset, which served so well under conditions of mass production and economy of scale, does not embrace heterogeneity and diversity.

Shifting to a diversity mindset requires creativity and leadership. It will be difficult for administrators early trained and long rewarded for an efficiency mindset. Such a shift essentially requires managers to reverse their orientations. The one-size-fits-all management orientation reverses to any-size-you-want. Even for managers who desire to make the shift, temptations to develop a programmatic response will be strong. By a programmatic response we mean one that creates a special program for each new diversity issue as it emerges.

RATIONALE FOR A NONPROGRAMMATIC APPROACH

Responding to diversity with diversity is the most straightforward way to manage it. For each diverse need, develop a separate response based on that need.

This approach works up to a point. For example, managers can create major organizational subdivisions to handle large market niches. Ethnic awareness seminars can be developed to address cultural diversity, and job sharing can be instituted to respond to a work-family concern. However, as amounts of diversity increase, this approach can become an administrative nightmare. In the workforce diversity arena, any-size-you-want implies that every time a new need arises, a new program is created unique to that need. Over time, too many programs for too many separate needs conjure up images of confusion, inequity, and inconsistency, bringing both increased costs and potential lawsuits.

Reactive organizations become trapped into either ignoring or controlling each type of diversity as it develops. Ignoring a new type of diversity means losing the opportunity to capitalize on it. Controlling each type as it emerges leads over time to a heap of programs piled on top of each other with little integration among them. Avoiding this trap requires a different approach.

Instead of responding to diversity with diversity, management needs some form of flexible simplicity. A basic illustration of flexible simplicity is any modern paint store. There are thousands of diverse colors each with unique characteristics demanded by customers. If, to implement an any-color-you-want philosophy, the store stocked gallons of paint for each one, inventory costs would soon drive the owner out of business. Fortunately the diversity of colors customers need can be met by blending just three primary colors. The primary colors represent the simplicity beneath the diversity. By stocking only three colors and having the flexibility to combine them, the paint store can handle thousands of unique requests. In the same way, a diversity mindset identifies the full spectrum of diversity issues and looks for creative ways to avoid developing a unique program for every unique need that arises. Flexible simplicity represents an operating principle potentially useful in managing many types of diversity.

The sheer amount of diversity affecting today's organizations and the limitations of an efficiency mindset make responding to diversity with additional organizational programs an insufficient response. Developing many specialized programs does not address the underlying issue of how a business should organize to succeed in an era of diversity. We believe the broad scope and complex nature of the diversity issue require a different management approach. As a beginning, Coopers & Lybrand is evolving a planned, systematic, nonprogrammatic approach to address diversity in the workforce arena. Hopefully, lessons will emerge of value in addressing business and organizational diversity as well.

A STRATEGIC GRASS-ROOTS APPROACH TO CHANGE

In the workforce arena, managing diversity effectively means managing organizational change. Each issue such as increased cultural diversity in the available talent pool signals a need for some change. The change could be in the organization's management processes, such as how it recruits and what benefit programs it offers, or in specific new behaviors that it trains and rewards, or both. Responding to diversity with diversity would lead to a programmatic response. A new program, generally from headquarters, would be established to implement each change.

The number of change needs related to ethnic, situational, and behavioral differences in the workforce is increasing at such a rapid pace that a programmatic response alone will soon reach its limits. Even a quick diagnosis of workforce diversity needs in the firm yields issues such as child care, job sharing, telecommuting, transfer of dual-career couples, part-time work, mentoring for female professionals, elder care, contingent work schedules, fitness programs, minority development paths, phased retirement, flextime, alternate career pathing, compressed work weeks, retiree supplemental workforce, cultural diversity, paid sabbaticals, and so forth. Handling any one or even several of these issues might be possible with a programmatic response. However, to address the full range of this growing list requires a flexible approach for managing change. Developing such an approach must start with the realities of the organization's current situation.

The Organizational Situation

From an organization design perspective, Coopers & Lybrand can be described as a loosely coupled system (Weick, 1986). Firmwide values, strategy, professional standards, and management processes unite practice offices across the country, but these practice offices are given a great deal of operating autonomy. The majority of employees are professionals who spend most of their time away from their offices and out serving clients. The success of the business rests upon their initiative and responsiveness to the changing needs of the marketplace. The professional orientation of employees, the need for quick client responsiveness, and the geographic dispersion of the business make local autonomy a critical trait. Any approach to change must not interfere with this operational flexibility.

A second characteristic of the current situation is a lack of adequate precedent. Little meaningful experience exists in the profession for dealing with the numbers and types of workforce changes affecting the firm. Diversity issues are emerging rapidly, unpredictably, and in ways that make historical approaches for handling them less and less viable. Even successful approaches from industrial settings are not readily applicable to professional service firms. As a result, it is not likely that the headquarters human resources function can quickly develop solutions and give them to the field as a *fait accompli.*

The risk of becoming "programmed out" is a third factor in the current situation. Many changes made in the 1980s were implemented as official programs from headquarters. Each program in itself was seen as valuable. However, when added together and to an already overloaded work plate, separate programs, each requiring its own implementation process, have begun to wear out their welcome.

A special factor in the current situation is the increase in female professionals. Of all the types of workforce diversity the firm experiences, this is the most visible. Approximately 50% of entry-level professionals are now female; this is a dramatic increase from 14% just 15 years ago. Many female professionals express interest in a wide range of work and career orientations. Required work schedules based on tradition rather than client needs and the assumption that employees want 30-year careers with one organization are being questioned more often than in the past. Flexible work arrangements and alternative career paths are issues that a growing number of female professionals are willing to be vocal about. Any approach to workforce diversity within the firm must address this demographic reality.

One approach would be to focus directly on the needs of female professionals. The firm could establish special programs for females, create female discussion groups, and the like. However, the firm has consciously chosen not to emphasize that path for several reasons. One reason is that the female professionals themselves would likely resist it. Many have worked hard not to appear different from their male counterparts. More than a few have expressed desires to avoid approaches that stress how they might differ from male professionals.

A second reason for not establishing special programs for women is to diminish any potential for a backlash effect due to perceptions of special treatment or favoritism. Although, interviews indicate that many males believe management should address issues associated with female professionals, they don't feel females should receive special treatment. This condition creates a paradox that has stalled some efforts in the past.

However, the major reason for not focusing on what are often labeled as female professional issues is the belief that most are not fundamentally female professional issues. Child care, elder care, part-time work, balancing work and homelife, prejudiced treatment because of background rather than talent, and differences in thinking and problem-solving styles are all issues that management believes are relevant to the entire workforce; these are not just female issues. That females seem more willing to raise them is not a reason to address them as female issues. Therefore, any successful approach to workforce diversity must recognize the rising number of female professionals in the firm without magnifying gender issues.

Preserving local autonomy, coping with lack of historical precedent, avoiding too many separate programs from headquarters, and recognizing the paradox of female professional issues are conditions that an effective change approach should address. Under these conditions, learning how to manage diversity requires looking for simple structure that may underlie surface complexities (as in the paint store analogy). Consequently, the firm is developing an organizational learning model. We seek the understanding and deep knowledge that may lead us to elegantly simple solutions that can be flexibly applied.

Strategically Leveraging Grass-Roots Forces

Based on the factors in its existing situation, Coopers & Lybrand is attempting to capitalize on what is normally a dilemma for large organizations. This dilemma is the one created by dual needs for long-term centralized planning and short-term decentralized action. Traditionally, the direction of major change is from the core to the periphery of the organization. That is, after extensive analysis and deliberation, a major programmatic response from headquarters is rolled out to the field.

Given the nature of the diversity issue, however, the firm is developing an action learning approach for dealing with change that reverses the traditional direction. In this approach, the periphery of the organization serves as the learning edge for the firm as a whole. Grass-roots forces throughout the organization, represented by practice office responses to local needs, initiate the firm's change process. The core serves more to guide and facilitate change than to command and control it. Policy development relies more on local internal experience than on global external expertise.

Three growth stages of organizational change characterize our strategic grass-roots approach: plant, prune, and proliferate. The complete details of these stages are still being developed. Below, we outline the structure and intent of each stage.

Plant

The practice offices strongly experience workforce diversity issues. With an average industry turnover rate of approximately 25%, talent flows rapidly through the organization. The pool of talent is shrinking, while client needs are expanding. By necessity, recruiting and retention are pragmatic, immediate issues for the practice offices.

As a result, grass-roots efforts have been occurring informally for some time. In the past, when a practice office had a specific need because of a workforce diversity issue that didn't fit traditional firm policy, it went to national headquarters and asked for a policy change. But, as stated previously, our industry lacks the necessary practical experience upon which to base policy decisions on many workforce diversity issues. Additionally, because policies are interrelated and affect all parts of the firm, the necessary deliberations at headquarters often took longer than the response time needed by the practice office. Therefore, practice offices sometimes developed exceptions to policy. From an efficiency mindset, these exceptions can easily be interpreted as problems. The strategic grass-roots approach is based upon a diversity mindset that tries to see such problems as opportunities. Because diversity issues are generally experienced first at the grass-roots level, that is the place to initiate firmwide change.

The practice offices plant the action seeds. Offices with immediate needs not covered by a clear policy—such as a valued employee leaving the organization unless some unusual form of work schedule flexibility can be arranged—are encouraged to create a pilot program. To be a part of a pilot means the practice office designs a response to (1) meet the specific needs of the individual(s) and the practice office, and (2) meet the more general learning needs of the firm as a whole.

A current example of an initiative is taking place in conjunction with the needs of a major East coast office. At the invitation of the regional vice chairman and office managing partner, the firm's chief human resources officer and the regional human resources officer conducted a 1-day meeting with representatives of the Women's Forum in that office. The purpose of the meeting was to discuss the need for more formalized alternative work arrangements and to develop an approach to a local concept statement and operational guideline.

In the intervening 6 months, the office and national staff have formed a close working relationship to develop what will soon be introduced as a pilot for the office. The national staff has served as both content and process consultants to the practice office, has provided legal and policy reviews, and has provided a "legitimacy" to the pilot. The practice office has drafted the pilot response to the need for alternative arrangements, based on its perceived needs and local business considerations.

As part of the process, the team has determined expectations and outcome measures to be applied in evaluating the pilot, and has refined the "strategic grass-roots approach" based on this initial actual experience. The regional vice chairman expects to use the experience of this effort to respond to other offices in the region that have expressed similar needs.

Many different types of grass-roots efforts can exist. If one office has particularly pressing cultural diversity issues, it can, without waiting for a firmwide effort, set up its own approach to these issues as a pilot program for the firm. If another office has a high percentage of older workers, it can create its own response to their needs as a pilot program. Pilot programs can be set up in response to needs ranging from those of a single individual to those of an entire practice office. The intent of these grass-roots pilot programs is to allow the field offices to take initiative quickly and be responsive to local needs. Leveraging local initiatives forms the basis of the strategic grass-roots approach.

Prune

Local responsiveness does not inherently mean firmwide adaptability. If it were not a part of a pilot program, a local initiative would represent an exception to firm policy rather than a stage in policy development. A large organization could soon be overgrown with exceptions. The pruning stage acts to prevent program overload and to channel local programmatic responses into uncovering larger policy issues for the firm.

Pruning means that as the seed effort evolves, the practice office and the headquarters staff jointly evaluate it (see Table 10.1). Some initiatives will be allowed to continue and others will be cut. Through careful pruning, growth in the number and diversity of new programs can be managed.

Dialogue between the local practice offices and headquarters is the major conduit for change in the firm. Unique local actions are eventually grown into unified organizational policy through this process. Every participant in the pruning stage guides the growth of policy in the firm. To be successful, each participant in the dialogue must value the other's expertise and perspective. There is no room for either headquarters elitism or local turfism. The firm's teamwork values are particularly important to success in this stage of the change approach.

Negotiating the parameters of a pilot program sets the conditions of learning for the firm. Legal issues and existing policies are checked for applicability to the identified need. Where clear policy is lacking, the participants develop the pilot program to meet the needs of the affected individuals and the firm as a whole. For example, a local need for several individuals to stay home in order to care for temporarily disabled parents

TABLE 10.1. Pilot Program Co-Evaluation Process

Major components	Primary responsibilities		
	Participants	Practice office	Firm
1. Need identification	X	X	
2. Negotiation of pilot programs		X	X
A. Desired outcomes (effectiveness measures)			
Participants	X		
Practice office		X	
Firm			X
B. Time frame	X	X	X
C. Resources		X	X
3. Co-evaluation checkpoint(s)		X	X
A. Participant interviews		X	
B. Comparisons with desired outcomes			X
C. Pilot disposition		X	X
Continue			
Renegotiate			
Conclude			
4. Pilot conclusion		X	X
A. Participant interviews		X	
B. Comparisons with desired outcomes			X
C. Report to firm management		X	X

can be set up as a telecommuting pilot (rather than handled as a leave of absence). After a specified time, results would be co-evaluated.

One objective of program co-evaluation is to promote controlled growth. Another is to prevent abuse of the pilot process. Mutual negotiation and evaluation encourage legitimate workforce diversity initiatives and discourage individuals from creating policy variances for purely personal advantage. In this way, possible perceptions of inequity are minimized.

During the co-evaluation, progress is examined against mutually agreed upon effectiveness measures. Lessons learned are documented. From here the pilot can take one of several directions. First, if all is going well, the pilot can be continued as planned. If all is not going well, the program can be concluded early, or, alternatively, the lessons learned in the first phase of the pilot can be used to redirect it.

When a pilot program reaches completion, participants are debriefed and findings are consolidated. Participants will be interviewed to record their personal experience. The practice office will summarize its experience in conducting the pilot. The actual outcomes will be compared with desired outcomes, and possible reasons for differences will be hypothesized. The ultimate purpose of the pruning stage is to capture the learning from local initiatives in ways useful to the entire firm. Even unsuccessful initiatives provide valuable information. Lessons from such efforts help other initiatives grow successfully. If, for example, a telecommuting pilot was unsuccessful and findings indicated that managers had difficulties with the nontraditional control involved, then future telecommuting efforts might start a training phase for both managers and subordinates that covers new forms of control. Until some efforts try and fail, it won't be clear what factors are actually critical for success in our organization.

The general orientation guiding the strategic grass-roots approach is to act locally and learn globally. As various pilot programs demonstrate local success, the proliferation stage of the change process becomes important.

Proliferate

Once an initiative has shown promise at one practice office, then further testing at other offices is desirable. Only when an initiative demonstrates that it is transplantable elsewhere in the organization does change in firmwide policy become practical. For several well-documented reasons, diffusing innovation in large organizations is often difficult. Traditional hierarchies are designed more to foster communication up and down the organization than across functions and business units. The "not-invented-here" syndrome can also slow awareness of what is happening in other parts of the organization. Therefore, the firm's strategic grass-roots approach fosters proliferation in a variety of ways.

The groundwork for future proliferation is laid at the very beginning of a pilot program. The initiating office is put in touch with other offices known to be addressing the issue. These contacts increase the probability of success for the pilot through cross fertilization of ideas; they also help to identify likely transplant sites for successful initiatives.

At the firmwide level, another mechanism is designed to stimulate proliferation. In conjunction with the firm's existing Coopers & Lybrand Commitment awards process, which recognizes individuals who particularly demonstrate the firm's core values, practice offices that develop innovative solutions to workforce diversity issues will receive firmwide recognition.

The recognition process encourages proliferation in several ways. First, in order to provide recognition, the firm must first evaluate initiatives throughout the firm. This data collection activity, in itself, increases awareness of diversity issues and practices in the firm. Second, besides recognizing success, the process will give firmwide visibility to the initiatives of local offices. The visibility should help other offices learn about these "best practices" in a positive light. Third, in determining which offices to recognize, internal deliberations will occur that will likely raise issues directly related to the forming of firmwide policy. These issues will be based on the firm's first-hand experience with its own workforce innovations rather than trying to infer from other organization's experiences. Policy outcomes will facilitate what were originally grass-roots pilots to spread across the organization.

In addition, national headquarters will facilitate proliferation by stimulating overall awareness of workforce diversity issues. For example, we have recently conducted a systematic survey of professionals who left the firm. Initial data highlight changing workforce priorities. Of 15 turnover factors that included compensation, job challenge, and opportunity for advancement, the ones cited most often as important reasons for leaving were issues associated with balancing one's personal and professional life. We are now designing an ongoing process for surveying our current employees to further understand and highlight workforce issues.

We are also developing a clearinghouse function that will collect, summarize, and distribute information on a wide range of diversity issues occurring both inside and outside the firm. Resources to assist those initiating pilots will be identified, and methods for possible joint funding of these efforts will be developed.

Plant, prune, and proliferate are the major stages in the strategic grass-roots approach to managing workforce diversity. The approach is grass-roots in the sense that change is initiated more from the field based on actual need rather than from headquarters based on abstract analysis. The approach is strategic in the sense that local change is designed to occur in a way that benefits the whole.

In terms of building an organizational change approach, the plant and prune stages represent a vertical link. That is, they deal primarily with the link between headquarters and the field. The proliferation stage adds a horizontal link. It is designed to connect change across the practice offices. Together these stages can create an overall set of connections that allow the firm to tap resources throughout the organization.

In implementing the strategic grass-roots approach, both the local practice offices and the national headquarters function will play vital roles. Next, we sketch the basic elements of each role. These roles will become more "fleshed out" as we gain experience with this approach.

Local Practice Office Responsibilities

Each practice office must stay in touch with the needs of its clients, the economic needs of the practice office, and the needs of the office employees. Each office has significant autonomy in how it achieves these responsibilities.

In terms of workforce diversity, as particular needs arise that are not addressed by traditional firm policy, practice offices (1) develop an initiative they believe will be responsive to those needs, (2) work with headquarters to create the parameters of a local firm pilot, (3) participate in evaluating the initiative after a specified period of time and decide whether to continue it, (4) cooperate with other practice offices working on similar issues, and (5) participate in the firmwide recognition process.

National Headquarters Responsibilities

Besides overall management responsibility, national headquarters (1) develops annual status reports (e.g., see Table 10.2) on workforce diversity issues in the firm; (2) solicits input from the workforce on diversity and

TABLE 10.2. Workforce Diversity Progress: Gender Issues Annual Report Summary[a]

	Male	Female	Expected difference	Actual difference
PRINCIPLE CAREER/REWARD SYSTEMS				
Recruitment	___	___	0	___
Compensation	___	___	0	___
Advancement rates	___	___	0	___
Development	___	___	0	___
Work assignments	___	___	0	___
Mentoring	___	___	0	___
Internal programs	___	___	0	___
External programs	___	___	0	___
Turnover	___	___	0	___
NONSEXIST WORK ENVIRONMENT				
Overtime	___	___	0	___
Required overtime	___	___	0	___
Available paid overtime	___	___	0	___
Harassment	___	___	0	___
Major incidents	___	___	0	___
Minor incidents	___	___	0	___
Language	___	___	0	___
Spoken	___	___	0	___
Written	___	___	0	___
Self-expression	___	___	0	___
Dress expectations	___	___	0	___
Office decor	___	___	0	___
Issue identification and resolution process	___	___	0	___

(continued)

TABLE 10.2. *(continued)*

	Male	Female	Expected difference	Actual difference
BALANCED WORK AND PERSONAL LIFE				
Planned time off	——	——	0	——
Advance notice for unexpected overtime	——	——	0	——
Vacation	——	——	0	——
Overtime taken	——	——	0	——
Flexible work arrangements	——	——	0	——
Flextime: daily, weekly, monthly, annually	——	——	0	——
Part-time	——	——	0	——
Work at home	——	——	0	——
Benefits	——	——	0	——
Comprehensiveness	——	——	0	——
Flexibility	——	——	0	——
Child-care assistance	——	——	0	——
Informational/educational programs (i.e., stress management, personal financial management)	——	——	0	——

[a]Data represent objective quantities or subjective approval percentages. They are obtained through the human resources Information System, a biannual survey of employees, focus groups, and interviews.

Table 10.2 displays a proposed summary of an annual report addressing gender issues. It represents an expansion of the more formal EEO plans and compliance reporting. The structure of this summary is based upon the goal of zero differences between males and females in key areas.

Some of the information will come from existing data systems. Other information will come from data systems currently under development such as a biannual employee survey and a quarterly focus group mechanism. The first section addresses the firm's principal career reward systems. If strong systems bias exists it would likely show up in areas such as pay and career advancement rates. These and the other systems listed represent areas where basic equity is expected across the firm.

The next section, nonsexist work environment, addresses areas where more subtle forms of bias can exist. As large organizations shift from being male dominated to a more balanced gender mix the formal and informal processes should reflect this balance. There is no inherent reason why overtime should be different for men and women even though it can differ greatly between individuals depending upon their unique circumstances. All forms of harassment must be eliminated and the language and self-expression practices should not be gender based. Data for these areas will come from objective measures such as overtime statistics as well as from subjective measures such as focus group discussions on self-expression norms.

The third section of the report addresses issues related to a balanced life. The influx of female professionals into the firm has helped raise these issues for the entire workforce. The report will track both the objective numbers and types of programs available as well as subjective employee perceptions related to these programs.

Although the report focuses on differences, it will also show absolute magnitudes. For example, average time to advance and satisfaction with benefits flexibility percentages will be reported. Absolute values provide an overall assessment of each area and allow longer-term trends to be identified.

TABLE 10.3. Sample of Flexible Work Arrangements (FWA) and Their Relationship to Traditional Work Arrangements

Type of FWA programs		Similar to traditional work arrangements?					
		Work day	Work week	Work year	Work career	Work location	Comp & benefits
Flextime:	Daily schedule to fit personal and office needs; overlapping hours with others in office	No	Yes	Yes	Yes	Yes	Yes
Part-time:	Reduced hours	No	No	No	No	Yes	No
Telecommuting:	Work completed out of office via computer; certain days required in office	Yes	Yes	Yes	Yes	No	Yes
Compressed work week:	Work week completed in less than 5 days	No	No	Yes	Yes	Yes	Yes
Job sharing:	Two employees share same job with half pay and benefits	No	No	No	No	Yes	No
Term positions:	Job is for a specified number of years	Yes	Yes	Yes	No	Yes	Yes
Managed time on:	Yearly number of hours distributed based on office and individual needs	No	No	Yes	Yes	Yes	Yes
Contract:	Work negotiated for a fee	No	No	No	No	No	No
Sabbatical:	Paid period off: 3 mo. - 1 yr.; available every 3-10 yrs	Yes	Yes	Yes	No	Yes	Yes
Phased retirement:	Decreasing work week on a scheduled basis	Yes	No	No	No	Yes	No

Note. Beneath the diversity of programs, all FWAs are simply negotiated variations of work time and place. Within legal, firm policy, and administrative constraints, unique types of FWAs can be tailored to office and individual needs.

There is great diversity in existing forms of flexible work arrangements. New forms are constantly emerging, each with their own advocates. Before choosing any one form it seems prudent to look for an underlying basis for the diversity of forms. A wide range of alternative work arrangements such as the sample displayed above were examined. Although each has its own unique features, they all seem to be variations of three basic factors: work time, work place, and rewards. Instead of adopting specific programs and administering each separately, it may be more practical to develop a simple approach for negotiating work time, place, and rewards based on office and individual needs. Using an approach that flexibly blends these three factors allows a much broader array of flexible work arrangements that may fit specific needs better than existing popularized programs. Working out the legal, policy, cost, and administrative issues may require larger initial investment of resources. However, such efforts should reduce the long-term costs of administering each program as a completely separate entity, and they should increase the fit with specific office and employee needs.

From the perspective of this approach, the traditional work arrangement can be viewed as merely one variation (certainly the most common) of time, place, and reward factors with its own advantages and disadvantages.

other issues biannually through a firmwide employee survey; (3) researches workforce diversity issues and looks for ways to apply the principle of flexible simplicity to aid practice offices in their individual initiatives (e.g., see Table 10.3); (4) connects the local practice office proposing an initiative with other offices known to be addressing that issue, as well as to external resources with relevant expertise; (5) works with the practice office to design the parameters of the pilot program; (6) co-evaluates the pilot program after a specified amount of time; (7) designs and facilitates the workplace innovations recognition process; and (8) codifies the experience of the firm into workforce diversity policies.

SUMMARY

Managing diversity is a broad and complex issue. It goes far beyond cultural diversity. Together, business, organization, and workforce diversity challenge the one-size-fits-all era of management. To manage diversity strategically may require a shift from an efficiency mindset. Organizations that see diversity as an opportunity to be seized rather than as a problem to be avoided will have a better chance to excel in future business environments.

Applying this perspective to workforce diversity makes a programmatic response from headquarters insufficient. Therefore, Coopers & Lybrand is approaching the issue aggressively by establishing mechanisms of change such as the strategic grass-roots approach. The firm recognizes that there are no easy answers to workforce diversity issues, and it will need to modify its own approach as it gains experience. However, the opportunities are too great to wait for others to develop solutions. The firm knows that its motto "Solutions for Business" starts at home.

REFERENCES

DeLuca, J. M. (1988). Strategic career management in non-growing volatile business environments. *Human Resource Planning, 11*(1), 49–62.

Handy, C. (1989). *The age of unreason.* Cambridge, MA: Harvard Business School Press.

Mills, D. Q. (1991). *The rebirth of the corporation.* New York: Wiley.

Toffler, A. (1990). *Power shift: Knowledge, wealth, and violence at the edge of the 21st century.* New York: Bantam Books.

Weick, K. E. (1986, December). The concept of loose coupling: An assessment. *AERA Organizational Theory Dialogue,* pp. 8–11.

CHAPTER 11

Managing Worldwide Diversity at Pepsi-Cola International

JOHN R. FULKERSON
RANDALL S. SCHULER

INTRODUCTION AND COMPANY BACKGROUND

Pepsi-Cola International is the international beverage division (outside of North America) of PepsiCo, Inc. Pepsi-Cola International sells its brands in over 150 countries and faces the challenge of matching the demand for high standards of individual performance with the needs of a globally diverse workforce in a highly decentralized organization that can be most successful when its activities are coordinated on a worldwide basis. Pepsi-Cola International meets this challenge by providing a foundation of human resources (HR) practices that are modified to meet country-specific requirements. The base assumption from which the design of human resources practices starts is that the improvement of individual and organization performance, along with a coordinated, yet decentralized firm is the important desired outcome. This chapter describes some of the challenges encountered when attempting to build a globally applicable set of human resources practices for high levels of individual and organizational performance that also meets the needs of a decentralized organization operating in a highly competitive and rapidly changing international business environment.

Before describing the human resources practices and the challenges encountered in tailoring them to local conditions, it is useful to briefly describe the business context. This includes its products and sales, business objectives, organizational structure, and its shared culture and values. From these flow the human resources practices that help meld its worldwide diversity: selection, performance appraisal, compensation, training, leadership, career management, and human resources planning.

PepsiCo, the parent organization, is a multinational corporation operating in over 150 countries with over a quarter of a million employees. As illustrated in Figure 11.1, PepsiCo's three major business groups include snack foods (Frito-lay), restaurants (KFC, Pizza Hut, Taco Bell), and soft drinks (Pepsi-Cola). Total PepsiCo sales for 1990 were $17.8 billion. Although soft drinks represents the largest segment of PepsiCo's business with sales of $6.5 billion in 1990, restaurants and snack foods are close behind with sales of $6.2 and $5.1 billion, respectively. All three business groups operate internationally, but this chapter focuses on the international (non-North American) soft drinks segment. More specifically, the chapter focuses on Pepsi-Cola International, which employs approximately 5,000 people.

The U.S. soft drink market is more developed than the international market. However, the international market is growing faster and has the larger growth potential. In international markets, soft drink volume for 1990 was estimated at 14 billion cases, which is double the volume for the U.S. market. Per capita consumption internationally is still relatively low but is growing rapidly as soft drinks become more widely promoted worldwide. For example, soft drink consumption in the United States is more than 700, 8-ounce servings per year per individual, whereas consumption in the United Kingdom is less than 300, 8-ounce servings per year. This translates into significant potential for growth in worldwide per capita consumption.

Pepsi-Cola International's human resources plays a key role in helping drive the growth of Pepsi brands (which includes 7-Up outside of the United States). The key human resources challenge is to assist in the

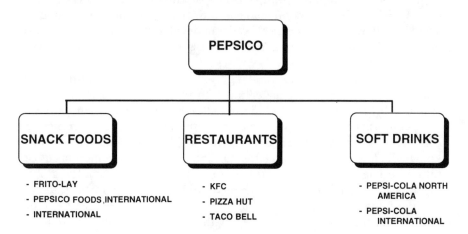

FIGURE 11.1. Breakdown of Pepsico's major business groups.

development of the talent and skills needed to support the rapid growth expected over the coming decade. To fully understand how Pepsi-Cola International's human resources practices meet the needs of the business requires an understanding of Pepsi-Cola International's business objectives, organization structure, and global values. These are described next.

BUSINESS OBJECTIVES

Committed Bottling Organization

At Pepsi-Cola International, the overall business goal is to accelerate growth ahead of global market growth. To achieve this overall growth objective, there are five strategic business goals. Each of these business goals has human resources implications. The human resources actions that support the business goals are designed to assist in aligning employee actions with the business goals. This alignment is accomplished with the assistance of some of the specific human resources practices discussed in this chapter.

The first business goal is to build a bottling organization that is committed to the business, to Pepsi brands and to excellence. The majority of Pepsi-Cola International's business is conducted by franchise bottlers who have an exclusive agreement to produce Pepsi brands in a specific market. In some cases, bottlers may have a local flavor such as an orange-flavored soft drink or perhaps a tea product. The objective is to assure that the local bottler places the highest priority on Pepsi brands. This means that the local Pepsi employees, nonmanagers and managers alike, must understand how to work with the local bottler to develop a strong focus on Pepsi brands and to provide value-added business advice on how to succeed in a given market.

To add value, there are some highly diverse working conditions and requirements the Pepsi manager must be prepared to address. For example, a British manager working in Saudi Arabia must be sure advertising conforms to local laws, which may prohibit the use of women in commercials. An Austrian manager working in the Soviet Union must know which government ministries to contact for transportation needs or to assure sugar availability. To successfully operate in complex global markets, personal flexibility and creative problem solving are required of the individual Pepsi manager. Human resources practices must help the local manager to compete effectively with an ever-changing and complex business environment.

Dedication to Quality

The second business objective is to maintain an uncompromising dedication to the quality of Pepsi products. That appears to be a simple requirement: to make sure all the Pepsi tastes the same and has the same high quality. But when one considers that every country in the world has different food preparation and selling laws, the magnitude of the challenge becomes clear. Diversity of standards within countries around the world requires the individual Pepsi-Cola International quality manager to understand how to get to the same end point in a variety of ways. Human resources practices must help assure that an individual manager focuses more on the result produced than on the way that result is produced. This requires, for example, a performance appraisal process that places a great deal of emphasis on measuring whether accountabilities were satisfied rather than evaluating the personal characteristics or problem-solving style of the individual manager.

Development of Talented People

The development of talented people to drive the growth in Pepsi brands is the third general business objective. The human resources implications of this objective are focused on selection and development. The human resources practitioner must find ways to select, train, and move people around the world. With Pepsi brands being sold in 150 countries, the scale of this challenge is enormous. For example, do you select individuals for employment in only one country or do you select for the ability to work in a multicountry region of the world, like Latin America? Or do you select with a view toward an individual working anywhere in the world? What are the compensation implications of moving people around the world? What are the implications of delivering training in 150 countries on a cost-effective basis? What language do you use? What are the appropriate characteristics for the trainer? And finally and perhaps most importantly, how do you communicate standards of high performance in the variety of cultures?

These are all important questions that Pepsi-Cola International and other global firms are addressing. As they are addressed, however, it becomes clear that there are neither single nor correct answers. Indeed, the answers may not even surface immediately. Rather, the answers evolve through continuous discussions, trial-and-error experiences, and within the context of changing political and economic conditions worldwide. Of the questions raised above, the one that has received the most attention at

Pepsi-Cola International is communicating high standards of performance. And as described later, the answer to this question involves developing a common vocabulary, allowing adaptation to local conditions, and retaining accountability for results at headquarters.

To meet the objective of developing talented people, the fundamental question the human resources function must address is how to develop people and establish performance standards in countries where the use of development and standards is a well-accepted practice (Europe), just becoming accepted (Eastern Europe), or nonexistent (China). Whereas doing this in Europe is similar to the United States, it is less similar in Eastern Europe and China. The real challenge here is getting the individuals in Eastern Europe and China to change their mindset about individual behavior and organizational success. Basically, they need to move away from thinking about just meeting the quota (and then taking the day off) to thinking about how output can be increased and how that output can be produced more efficiently. As many U.S. multinational firms are finding, it takes time and constant discussion to attain this mindset change.

Focus on Growth

The fourth business objective states that Pepsi-Cola International will focus on those markets where the greatest potential for growth exists. This is also a human resources allocation issue. Where should the effort and energy be spent? Do resources go to India or China, and who decides? Additionally, what kinds of skills are required in a given market, and can they be developed locally or do they need to be imported? If a technology does not exist in Nigeria, can it be developed locally or must it be imported? The management of global diversity requires an understanding of the trade-offs that are required to provide the greatest return on investment in human capital. This means that the ideal human resources decision simply may not be possible to implement because of practical business considerations. For example, the importing of an individual with skills in sales may be an ideal business solution, but it may be too costly to relocate a qualified individual and his or her family.

Quality Business Plans

The fifth business objective is to provide continuous improvement in strategic planning. The human resources component of strategic planning is assuring that adequate and skilled personnel are available to implement the business strategies. In a global business, this challenge is always significant. If a tremendous business opportunity exists, it may be easier to decide that this particular opportunity should be pursued than to figure out how to provide the diversity of talent required to fully realize the opportunity. Managing global diversity means sourcing, training, moving, and developing people for an organization that is growing and changing rapidly. In other words, managing global diversity means doing all the traditional human resources actions but doing them across cultures and countries. It means doing this in a decentralized organization that can be responsive to local needs, yet benefits from worldwide integration. It means finding ways to sustain high levels of performance in a competitive, changing world where changing business propositions may make today's solutions obsolete tomorrow.

In summary, the five business objectives of Pepsi-Cola International are an important part of the context that shapes and challenges human resources practices. A similarly important feature of the context is the organization structure.

ORGANIZATION STRUCTURE

In a globally diverse organization, the logistics of how a training program gets delivered or how a performance appraisal is reviewed are critical. An understanding of the difficulties associated with basic communication between field and headquarters puts human resources practices in context. Without clear communication and understanding of the intent of human resources programs, the opportunities for misinterpretation are significant.

The basic organization structure of Pepsi-Cola International is shown in Figure 11.2. The field organization is essentially decentralized. This means that the field is free to pursue local opportunities, but it also means that a prudent manager (either business or human resources) will look for advice and counsel at every opportunity. For purposes of our discussion, this is called mature decentralization. Mature decentralization does not mean total freedom to do whatever the local manager wants; it means constantly sharing ideas and looking for ways to improve. This, in turn, means that local managers are constantly talking to their counterparts around the world.

The concept of mature decentralization is a key to success in global markets. It is essential that as many decisions as possible be made in the field as close to the consumer as possible. The intent is to put decision makers where the action is. The human resources challenge is to assure that a level of trust and open communication prevails so that needed resources, regardless of their source, can be brought to bear on a given

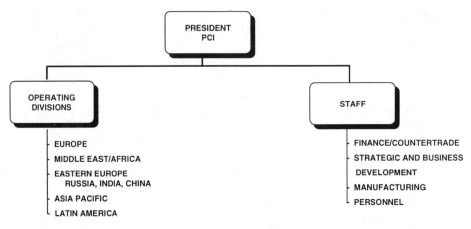

FIGURE 11.2. Pepsi-Cola International (PCI) organization structure.

problem. At the end of the day, a certain amount of consistency is needed to maintain operating efficiencies. The business objectives outlined at the beginning of the chapter cannot be implemented in 150 different ways. Marketing and brand advertising should not, for example, look entirely different around the world. Mature decentralization also means that a manager in Nigeria must be willing and rewarded for talking to a manager in Singapore when they share common operating problems. That is, mature decentralization means cooperation as well as consistency; and it means adaptation to local conditions. Thus, mature decentralization also results in the appropriate level of worldwide consistency. It makes it easier to find cost savings, identify efficiencies, and share advances in manufacturing technology.

From a human resources management perspective, mature decentralization means trusting your counterpart halfway around the world to give you good information even if you both may be competing for the same advancement opportunity. It means understanding that, in the end, you are both on the same team and are focused against the same competitor. It means getting everyone focused on improving performance. To reach this level of cooperation and maturity, Pepsi-Cola International has identified a success factor called "Executive Maturity." At every opportunity, this concept is reinforced through leadership training programs, in functional meetings, and in the performance appraisal process (described later in this chapter). From an organizational perspective this means that cumbersome control and review systems are minimized. It means that the decentralized Pepsi-Cola International organization can work at maximum efficiency because there is a free flow of information and fewer surprises. This sharing and free flow of information increase both individual and organization performance. It also means that senior management must communicate consistent business objectives.

In sum, having the right organizational structure is important in the success of the business. But the success of the structure may depend upon its fit with the business objectives and the human resources practices. It also helps if shared values exist so that global diversity is channeled toward the accomplishment of the single goal, such as doing better than the competition. The development of shared values is discussed next.

DEVELOPING SHARED VALUES

Although the structure of Pepsi-Cola International places emphasis on decentralization, the intent is for the operating units to be globally integrated and cooperative. Common business objectives and human resources practices are certainly critical in this. But in the face of diversity, global cooperation is also accomplished by the following:

1. Identifying values that support the objectives of the business, the organizational structure, and the needs of the individual employee.
2. Developing a set of shared understandings concerning individual performance that flow from the values that shape the human resources practices.

Ongoing Communications and Data Gathering Efforts

As Pepsi-Cola International has grown, senior business and human resources management executives from headquarters and local field operations have met regularly and traveled extensively to understand how the organization's performance can be improved. Thus, both formal and informal meetings and discussions have brought to light needs and stimulated a search for solutions. Indeed, many of the efforts described in this chapter are based on data gathered by the first author, compliments of more frequent flyer mileage than anyone would ever want to redeem.

Whether formally or informally generated, the data used to develop and drive the development of human resources practices generally come from the individuals who are conducting the business. Thus, regular climate surveys are conducted by the local operating units for periodic improvements in their practices. Surveys are also conducted as a regular part of managerial and leadership training programs. Individuals are regularly asked to comment on the needs of the business, on the organization, and on how to improve the performance of individual managers. And because this is done at the local level, the surveys can be translated into the local language and modified to fit local conditions. The actions taken on the basis of the results are also left up to the local HR staff to decide. Survey results in the United Kingdom are likely to be different from those in China. Thus, their actions will be different. But even if the results were the same, the actions they stimulate might be different. For example, if the survey results revealed a need for more entry-level workers, the operation in the United Kingdom would begin an advertising campaign in the local newspaper. In China, the local operation would first go to the local government and discuss the matter.

The philosophy of asking employees and localizing management is a cornerstone of the development of Pepsi-Cola International's human resources practices. It only stands to reason that in a truly diverse work environment, the local manager is the most knowledgeable person regarding what will or will not work. As an example, when it was necessary to redesign the human resources planning process, over 70 managers from across the world were interviewed to gather suggestions on what would help them run their unit more effectively from a human resources planning perspective. (The human resources planning process will be discussed later in this chapter.) It was these same managers who initially suggested that the human resources planning process needed to be more focused on individual and organization development. With an outside consultant, an internal team of both HR and business managers, and senior management involvement, a general consensus was built that preserved local human resources decision making while retaining a common framework for all of Pepsi-Cola International. Thus, although it was agreed that all units would embrace the philosophy of performance improvement and instant feedback, they could adapt this to their own local conditions.

Such data gathering encourages critical input from a variety of diverse sources, yet it leads to a common approach to issues. It also encourages close and continuing communication between field operating units and headquarters, which assures the construction of shared values for a wide range of issues that go well beyond just human resources management. Without going into how each component is developed, Figure 11.3 outlines the most common values that make up the mindset of Pepsi-Cola International. The values outlined are collated from business objectives, climate survey data, and a content analysis of current human resources practices.

Although these values may capture the spirit of Pepsi-Cola International human resources practices, they are not useful unless they enhance organization success. Programs and initiatives must flow from the shared values. Programs may be developed by headquarters, but the field must participate in the design and testing before implementation. The field's involvement in program development helps assure that every program

BUSINESS	To be the world's leading soft drink company
HR FOCUS	To be a world-class company where business results and career satisfaction are synonymous
BUSINESS OBJECTIVES	• Committed bottling organization • Uncompromising dedication to quality • Development of talented people • Focus on growth • Quality business plans
SHARED VALUES	• Leadership • High standards of personal performance • Career/skill development • Balancing teamwork and individual achievement

FIGURE 11.3. The most common values making up the mindset at Pepsi-Cola International.

meets a legitimate business need and that the program will be implemented at the local level. From this perspective, human resources programs are viewed as business building programs as opposed to personnel initiatives. This is illustrated in the Success Study which follows.

The Success Study

Pepsi-Cola International's Success Study is one example of a human resources program that turned out to have much more power to establish common values than anyone predicted. Common values must start with defining how to measure and evaluate individual performance standards. Managerial behavior is difficult enough to measure in a single culture, but the chore is much more difficult internationally with many cultures involved, to say nothing of numerous political and economic systems and time zones.

In 1985, there was some confusion about what it took to be individually successful in Pepsi-Cola International. There was no shared value system or vocabulary for describing individual performance. For example, in the socialist countries the concept of individual performance was practically nonexistent, whereas in Germany it carried the same meaning as it does in the United States. The business was beginning to develop and grow at a rapid rate, and the pressures on individual managers were considerable. As a consequence, the Success Study was launched.

With the full support of the division president, a study was initiated, in cooperation with the Center for Creative Leadership, to determine if there were some factors that might be associated with individual performance success across many markets and nationalities. The study team looked at 100 successful and 100 not-so-successful managers from different functional specialties and different nationalities. The factors that emerged from the study are shown in Figure 11.4.

The impact of the study on building common values was remarkable. The greatest impact was to focus people for the first time on a common vocabulary for discussing individual performance and development. Prior to the study, it had been difficult to articulate dimensions of performance in a consistent, globally acceptable way.

Through the study, Pepsi-Cola International developed a multinational vocabulary that could be used to unite people from many different cultures and countries. For example, "handling business complexity" might have different translations in China and France. In China it might mean that you get a product produced and to the loading dock. By contrast, in France it might mean being concerned with marketing, distribution, and merchandising in addition to getting a product produced and to the loading dock. Although different in meaning, the outcome is the same: generating sales in the local environment. Thus, although "handling business complexity" translates differently, the intent or behavioral outcome remains the same regardless of the language or culture. The business issue addressed by the success factor "handling business complexity" is getting an individual to figure out what needs to be done, regardless of country, and chart a course of action. This turned out to be the most important success factor, and one that could be universally understood from behavioral and business perspectives. Although the Success Study provided some much-needed focus on describing performance and development issues, it also pointed out the need for revision in many of the other specific HR programs and processes being used at Pepsi-Cola International to mold the globally diverse operation.

Handling business complexity: Figuring out what needs to be done and charting a course of action

Drives/results orientation: Focusing on an outcome and driving for completion.

Leads/manages people: Directing the work of and motivating others.

Executional excellence: Putting ideas into action.

Organization savvy: Knowing how the organization works and how to maximize it.

Composure under pressure: Staying focused in the international pressure cooker and still getting things done.

Executive maturity: Always acting with maturity and good judgment.

Technical knowledge: Understanding and applying technical knowledge.

Recruits/develops good people: Making the organization and individuals better.

Positive people skills: Knowing how to get along with people from all cultures.

Effective communication: Knowing how to communicate cross-culturally.

Impact/influence: Being able to get things done when faced with obstacles.

FIGURE 11.4. Pepsi-Cola International success factors.

The HR programs and processes described in the remainder of this chapter represent those revisions made to better knit together a globally diverse company. What follows is a description of those HR programs and processes thought to have the most significant impact on managing the diversity of the worldwide operations at Pepsi-Cola International. It is also a description of what the HR function at Pepsi-Cola International did to better serve its customers—the business managers around the world—and to more closely align itself to the needs of the business. Today, the HR executives around the world have a better understanding of the business and the needs of the people running the business.

In the process of serving the customer and gaining a better understanding of the business, the main HR programs and processes that were reconstituted included leadership, personal performance, and career and skill development. These HR programs and processes were changed with an eye toward satisfying one of PepsiCo's stated human resources objectives of being the employer of choice around the world. This meant Pepsi-Cola International had to install human resources practices that have as much universal applicability as practical and that are, in a sense, culturally neutral. The HR programs and processes that are described here also meet the shared value requirements of PepsiCo and Pepsi-Cola International. For each HR program or practice, issues related to managing cultural diversity will be explored.

LEADERSHIP

At the apex of developing an interconnected yet globally mature decentralized operation and shared mindset is the concept of leadership. At PepsiCo and Pepsi-Cola International today, the idea that everyone can lead even small components of the business is critical. Employees are encouraged to find ways to improve in small as well as large ways. In this mature decentralized organization, leadership in the form of new ideas and innovation are valued and encouraged at all levels.

To build the kind of global organization needed in the year 2000, Pepsi-Cola International embraces the selection and development of leaders from many different cultures. Discussions among the senior staff of Pepsi-Cola International led to the conclusion that a leadership program should be designed for all senior executives. The result was the Executive Leadership Program, which has been modified twice and now uses the leadership model developed by John Kotter of Harvard University. Kotter's model divides leadership into the activities associated with leadership and the activities associated with managing.

In developing this leadership program, an outside consultant and the management development staff of Pepsi-Cola International compiled a list of 33 leadership practices that reflect the actions leaders and managers are expected to take in running their businesses. Now, at least every 18 months, the top 100 officers of Pepsi-Cola International have their performance against these leadership practices reviewed anonymously by their subordinates. The results of this review are fed back to senior staff during the Executive Leadership Program. Examples of some of the practices that are reviewed are: To what extent does the executive regularly share business results and plans? To what extent does the executive articulate a vision for the business? To what extent does the executive value cultural diversity? A sample of the topics included in the Executive Leadership Program is shown in Table 11.1.

The Executive Leadership Program is targeted against improving personal leadership behaviors as well as solving practical leadership questions such as starting a new bottling plant or dealing with the career development concerns of a specific work unit. During the program, each senior executive receives confidential counseling about specific behaviors that need to change to manage a particular work group more effectively. In addition, each executive is expected to share his or her survey results with the work group that provided the data and ask for input as to how the effectiveness of the work group could be improved if he or she did things differently. In general terms, the leadership program is seen as culturally neutral. Although cultural differences are discussed, the focus is on how best to demonstrate the practice regardless of the country of application. Once again, however, typical survey results are likely to vary. For example, the executive in Eastern Europe (where the concept of competition is just starting) is less likely than the executive in Japan to hear

TABLE 11.1. Pepsi-Cola International Executive Leadership Program

	Leadership			Management	
Module	Establishing a vision for the business	Aligning people to accomplish the vision	Motivating and inspiring people	Performance management	Skill transfer
Practice examples	Communicating an exciting vision of the future for our business	Communicating priorities in clear and simple terms	Communicating high personal standards	Establishing clear, specific performance goals and standards	Communicating the importance of developing strong functional skills
	Integrating PCI's cultural priorities into a vision for our business	Encouraging an open discussion of business problems and issues	Valuing individual and cultural diversity	Demonstrating a commitment to long-term career development	Helping subordinates learn new skills

about goals, targets, and the need to beat the competition. Thus, although there are cultural differences, the practice of doing the survey is common.

When this program was initially installed there were some significant misgivings about the confidentiality of the data. An outside consultant was used to assure confidentiality. The program has now passed the confidentiality hurdle, and many participants are eager to attend and find out how they can improve their personal performance. In general, the program provides an intense forum for the discussion of leadership and management issues; these discussions, in turn, provide data about needed human resources practices and interventions.

Whereas the Executive Leadership Program is for the top senior managers, a different program called Excellence in Management is used for mid-level managers. The use of questionnaires (translated at local discretion) and the feedback process are again used, as in the Executive program. This mid-level program focuses primarily on basic managerial skills such as delegating, managing conflict, and being more effective in a mature decentralized international organization. The midlevel program is designed more around executional issues.

In summary, the two leadership programs focus on improving personal effectiveness and providing a forum for exploring ways to improve executive and managerial effectiveness in an international, culturally diverse organization. It would not be uncommon for a half dozen different nationalities to be attending either the executive or managerial program. This provides a unique opportunity to practice problem sharing and problem solving with a diverse group of colleagues. In doing so, it serves as a forum whereby the HR manager from Sweden can learn about the needs of the HR manager from Thailand. Here these two can also discuss how they might solve similar types of human resources issues related to the needs of the business. Another important benefit of these development programs is that the managers get to know each other personally. This can be critical to a global operation that, although decentralized, benefits from interconnectedness. The time may come when the HR manager from Sweden needs to discuss a solution to a problem the HR manager from Thailand talked about in the last development program. Being able to connect a name with a face, and having spoken with the person before, will facilitate the process of making a telephone call. Although international telephone calling is easier than ever, for these two it becomes an issue of when to call when there is more than a 10-hour difference in local time. It also becomes an issue of what to do when the HR manager (who speaks the official company language of English) has his secretary (who does not speak English) answer the telephone.

Each company needs to find its own solution, but one solution used is a form of Bitnet. Here the executive (or an assistant) sends a message in

English anytime that is convenient. The other executive can respond when convenient. This overcomes not only the time barrier, but also the language barrier: The method gives both executives time to think about and compose their messages in what is for them a second language. They can even use a spelling and grammar checker to avoid errors that might be a source of embarrassment. In this way, high standards of personal performance are more likely to be attained.

HIGH STANDARDS OF PERSONAL PERFORMANCE

Communication in an international environment is difficult under the best of circumstances. There are ample opportunities for misunderstanding in terms of language and, as any diplomat knows, in terms of intent. The overlay of 150 potentially different cultures makes it likely that some level of misunderstanding on almost any topic will occur on a regular basis. The problem of understanding what is expected from an individual performance perspective cannot be left solely to a statement of values.

In the early 1980s, it was clear to almost every manager in Pepsi-Cola International that expectations for individual performance standards varied from country to country, and all too often they were dependent on an individual manager's good intentions. For example, in Eastern Europe it was acceptable for a manager to meet the quota and essentially take the rest of the day off, but in Germany continuous improvement in output and efficiency was expected. Thus, a simple yet direct and culturally flexible tool was needed to develop more consistency in managing performance. The answer turned out to be something that any sophisticated human resources executive would have called too simple and not sufficiently structured to work globally. Under the direction of the Pepsi-Cola International president, the answer turned out to be something called Instant Feedback.

Instant Feedback

Instant Feedback is at the base of a chain of feedback systems designed to improve and maintain high levels of personal performance. This chain of performance feedback mechanisms is shown in Table 11.2.

Pepsi-Cola International is fundamentally a feedback-driven organization. This feedback is mirrored in every tool used to measure and improve performance. The need for feedback is also captured in the success factors Executive Maturity and Leads/Manages People. Stated simply, the principle of instant feedback says that if you have a problem or an idea

TABLE 11.2. Feedback Basics

What	Frequency
Instant feedback	Daily
Coaching (performance management)	Event
Accountability-based performance appraisals	Yearly
Development feedback	Yearly
Human resource plan	Yearly

about any aspect of the business or about an individual's performance, then the organization demands that you raise the issue appropriately and discuss it maturely.

The original vehicle that delivered this message was a twenty-minute video tape on Instant Feedback. The tape used dramatizations and explanations to explain how Instant Feedback was to be used in an international environment. Instant Feedback is now a part of the everyday vocabulary of Pepsi-Cola International. It is heard when someone with an issue or problem says to another individual, "Let me give you some Instant Feedback." With travel schedules, and frequent phone contact, and constant time pressure, Instant Feedback has become a shorthand for getting to the point and communicating clearly.

But perhaps the most fascinating aspect of Instant Feedback is that it has worked in every culture. There are differences, but Instant Feedback can be modified to fit any country. The successful delivery of Instant Feedback requires some fitting to local cultures. Americans use it because it fits the fast-paced way we do business. In most Asian cultures, feedback may be tough and direct but it should never be given in public. Canadians will say that Americans are too direct, and some Europeans will say that Americans are too demanding and critical. In some Asian cultures, there is a lot of head nodding during Instant Feedback as if signifying agreement, but it really only signifies that the message has been heard. Some Latins will argue very strongly if they do not agree with the feedback, and some nationalities (e.g., India) will insist on a great deal of specificity.

Forgetting about the cultural context for a moment, in Instant Feedback the performance message still gets delivered and a healthy debate may ensue. The important point is that the Instant Feedback message can be delivered in any culture. The focus of Instant Feedback is always how to improve business performance and is not directed against cultural styles. Some would argue that this method is nothing more than effective communication, but that is only partially correct. It is communication directed at solving performance problems. Although total cultural neutrality is not possible, Instant Feedback says that it does not really matter how you do it as long as you do it.

In addition to feedback, five other individual performance management tools Pepsi-Cola International employs are listed in Table 11.2. In all cases, the intent of each tool is to improve individual performance vis-à-vis business objectives. For example, Pepsi-Cola International has a workshop on performance management that is designed to help managers and employees understand how and why performance management is a competitive advantage and why it can help assure individual success. This performance management workshop, delivered by local staff, takes the concept of Instant Feedback as a starting point and links the feedback tools together. The intent is to assure that performance management occurs in a manner that is as culturally neutral as possible. The performance management workshop may be delivered in the local language, and attendees are encouraged to find ways to apply the principles in concert with local customs and culture.

Coaching

Coaching differs from Instant Feedback in that coaching is a series of Instant Feedbacks designed to improve a large chunk of behavior. Coaching can be scripted to improve larger chunks of knowledge that cannot be learned in one trial. Both Instant Feedback and Coaching are then combined to provide data points that are used in preparing the annual written performance appraisal.

Pay Linked to Performance

Pepsi-Cola International is a pay-for-performance company. This means that compensation is always tied to individual results. A written performance appraisal is required before any compensation adjustments can be made. The appraisal may be written in the local language, but no matter where or how it is done, the language of appraisal is focused on the individual's performance against assigned accountabilities. The appraisal form also requires a specification of areas for improvement within each separate accountability. To make the appraisal as culturally neutral as possible, accountabilities are specified in terms of what must be accomplished. For example, a good accountability statement might read: "Achieve a 15% sales growth for the year." The accountability does not specify the methods by which the accountability is achieved. That is left up to the judgment of local management. The performance management system requires that an appraisal must be done and that it must be very specific in terms of what was good and what needs improvement. Beyond that, local operating conditions dictate the content. To provide guidance and consistency, the headquarters develops models that the local field locations can adopt and adapt. For example, the Pepsi-Cola International headquarters staff has developed models for performance management, selection, and management development. The local operations are expected to adopt and adapt these models, knowing that they are held accountable for accomplishment of the business objectives.

Finally, there is common people management accountability in every managerial appraisal. This linkage and reinforcement assures that people management is part of individual compensation and is constant across the Pepsi-Cola International system. The components of the people management accountability and the behaviors that can be adapted to local conditions associated with each component are as follows:

1. *Conducting performance appraisals.* Managing a diverse organization requires that a manager do a thorough job of evaluating performance. A manager's personal compensation is dependent on doing a good job of evaluating the performance of others in a culturally neutral manner.

2. *Conducting personal development discussion.* Development of skills is a cornerstone of a pay-for-performance organization. Managers must seek ways to develop their subordinates using available performance management tools and have regular feedback discussions.

3. *Implementing development plans.* It is not sufficient simply to have had a discussion about development issues, a manager must follow-up to be certain the plans have been implemented and have the desired outcome.

4. *Attracting/hiring superior talent.* The growth of local country talent is critical to future business growth. It does not matter if the search is for a Chinese or a Nigerian; the manager has the responsibility for attracting and bringing talent into the organization. Of course, in some countries the open market is used, whereas in others, the local government is used as a source of applicants.

5. *Providing instant feedback/coaching.* These are an integral part of a manager's responsibilities, regardless of location. Once again, however, adaptation to local culture is recognized.

6. *Fostering teamwork.* This aspect of managerial behavior helps to build the cooperation and sharing of knowledge that is a key part of Pepsi-Cola International's management style. A manager must share the credit for accomplishments and find ways to energize the cultural synergies that exist.

7. *Building bench* (succession development). The ultimate objective of bringing talented individuals into the organization is not satisfied unless

they are developed and prepared for greater responsibility. In a performance driven organization, there must always be a payoff, and Bench Building is one of those payoffs. Without a bench of talented individuals there is no organization continuity. In a sense, each manager has a continuing responsibility to leave behind even better and more capable people.

8. *Managing/building executional excellence.* At the bottom line of maintaining high standards is a relentless focus on delivering results. All the management in the world counts for nothing unless the results are delivered. It is this constant focus on getting things done that helps minimize cultural differences.

The culture of Pepsico and Pepsi-Cola International is action oriented. Managers within the system believe that national cultural differences can be used as a force for strength if producing results is always the shared goal. Maintaining high standards means that managers understand that Arabs attack a problem in a slightly different manner from Americans or Japanese. However, the focus on high standards produces a mindset that says, "Let me hear what you think or how you believe this should get done and then we will combine the best of both our ideas to produce a culturally creative way of solving our mutual business problems."

CAREER AND SKILL DEVELOPMENT

Perhaps the biggest challenge any organization faces is to assure the continuity of a skilled and long-tenured (career-focused) workforce. Pepsi-Cola International recognizes that career-focused employees provide a competitive advantage. Again, the driving forces of individual performance and a keen focus on the needs of the business have been behind the development of several human resources programs. In this section, four widely varying career/skill development programs and their impact are described briefly. These include development feedback, human resources planning, the Pepsi-Cola International Management Institute, and the Designate program. Basically, these programs touch all of the employees, although the managers may be the primary beneficiaries.

Development Feedback

With the advent of a pay-for-performance appraisal system, it was apparent to all managers using the system that specifying areas for improvement would drive development. It is one thing to tell someone that something needs improvement and quite another to explain how that improvement can and should be accomplished. Pepsi-Cola International and a number of other PepsiCo divisions employ a development feedback process to aid in driving development.

Basically, the process requires individual employees to complete a rating form to assess how well they believe they are doing against the 12 success factors. After the self-ratings have been completed, the employee's supervisor rates each employee on the same success factors. The employee and supervisor then have a development discussion that is relatively free of accountability content. In effect, the pay increase decision has been completed, and the purpose of this discussion is to focus on personal development issues. Put another way, the performance appraisal is focused on what has happened in the past, whereas the development feedback discussion is focused on the future. The content of the discussion revolves around the skills that need to be improved or gained to assure continued success on an individual basis. From this discussion, a development plan is crafted and future career prospects are discussed. For example, if technical knowledge needs development, then the specific knowledge and skills that need improvement are specified and programs for improvement may be suggested.

This entire development feedback effort can be conducted in any language and in any culture. The development action plans can be implemented in the context of the country or business where the employee works. The completion of the development feedback discussion serves to meet the continuing goal of building a feedback-driven culture. The discussion with the employee is open and candid, regardless of nationality, and is free to include a wide range of development issues. The objective is to improve careers and performance in the most culturally acceptable manner possible. Culturally, differences are reflected in career development activities. For example, in Japan career progression generally follows from seniority, with performance being a lagging variable. In the United States and, to a lesser extent, Western Europe, performance seems to matter most and seniority, unless reflective of job-related experience, is the lagging variable. Thus, these cultural differences get reflected in the career activities as the local field operations are left to adapt the common HR practices to their conditions.

Human Resources Planning

The development feedback process also serves another goal: The results of that feedback become the primary document for the human resources planning process.

The human resources planning process is a business tool that is used to plan organizational and individual growth. The organization side of the process drives and defines the human resources actions needed to achieve business plans. From an individual perspective, the human resources planning process is focused on assuring individual development and providing yet another opportunity for feedback to the individual employee on personal growth issues. The same document used for the development feedback process is used in the human resources planning process, and the same performance rating used in the performance appraisal is used in the human resources plan. The linkage is very tight and the communication process is open. The intent is to open up the process to the individuals involved to build trust and to allow the process to be used as a development tool as opposed to a judgment device. Development and personal growth would appear to be universal human needs, and when a human resources system taps into those needs and is relatively uncomplicated, it stands a better chance of working across cultures. Again, there are differences. In Asian cultures, where relationships between the individual and organization are longer term and seniority based, career development activities are not strongly tied to performance. In contrast, in Western cultures career development activities are determined mostly by performance. Thus, career advancement in Western nations is more rapid than in Asian nations.

Pepsi-Cola International Management Institute

Another example of career/skill development is found in the Pepsi-Cola International Management Institute (PCIMI). This umbrella delivery system is the primary vehicle for delivering training programs around the world. It is used to deliver programs to both Pepsi-Cola employees and to franchise bottlers. For example, PCIMI delivers programs on sales force management as well as production techniques for the manufacturing of Pepsi brands. For both types of programs, the business standards are set on a global basis but the program that carries the business message may be done in any language or cultural style that is appropriate at the local level.

Within the framework of PCIMI, employees can request specific programs. Experience has shown that requests for development programs in the Pepsi-Cola International environment fall into the following three major categories:

1. *Individual programs.* These include requests for individual development programs such as writing or presentation skills. These requests are driven by the feedback mechanisms previously described and are usually characterized as unique to the individual, who may need to improve some aspect of performance, business skills, and knowledge. These programs are generally offered by outside vendors or training houses and may be

specifically focused against local language needs or business requirements. The local operating division is generally free to set up these programs on an as-needed basis. The Pepsi-Cola International headquarters
role is to do quality checks on the programs or perhaps to assist on the
inclusion of a particular subject matter. Generally, however, these programs are locally driven and initiated. For example, the Eastern European
nations are currently more likely to be seeking assistance in becoming
competitive and what it means to operate in a market economy, and the
Western European nations are more likely to be seeking assistance on
efficient distribution and marketing information systems.

2. *Managerial/organizational programs.* These are programs designed to
drive cultural themes or initiatives. They are generally designed by the
headquarters staff in response to a need identified by the field divisions or
by the feedback mechanisms identified earlier in this chapter. Examples of
these programs would include the Executive Leadership Program, performance management workshops, and the Excellence in Management Program. The intent of these programs, aside from delivering specific skill
training, is to provide common threads for the Pepsi-Cola International
culture. Put another way, the essence of leadership and management is the
same around the world. Leadership is the same in that people need to be
motivated and aligned with the strategic business vision. Management is
the same in that it always involves planning, organizing, controlling, and
coordinating. Again, the exact application of the skills taught in these
programs may be different, but the outcome (improved business performance) is the same. These programs are generally taught by outside consultants and may be taught in any language.

3. *Business programs.* These are programs designed to improve specific
business knowledges and skills, such as quality control, sales-force management, and merchandising. These programs are developed in partnership with internal Pepsi-Cola International staff and external consultants.
In all cases, the programs are developed to meet a very specific need in the
business as identified by either the franchise bottler or Pepsi-Cola International field managers. These programs may be delivered in local language and by local trainers as long as the standards for the outcomes of
concern do not vary. For example, the look of Pepsi advertising and signs
around the world should not vary. The color and placement of these signs
should meet the same standards regardless of the country. Similarly, the
display and merchandising of Pepsi brands should not vary.

Designate Program

A final example of career/skill development initiatives taken by Pepsi-
Cola International is the Designate Program. This program brings non-U.S.

citizens to the United States for a period of specialized training in the domestic U.S. Pepsi system. The program was developed to provide in-depth experiential training that would build a skill base in overseas markets. The key criterion for being in the Designate Program is that the individual must speak English and must be seen as having potential for significant future growth. Candidates for the program are both internal employees as well as new hires. Each individual must agree before starting the program that he or she will return to the home country or a mutually agreed upon location upon completion of the assignment. The key outcome of the Designate Program is the individual's return to an overseas market and transferring of the skills he or she has learned while in the United States.

Individuals are selected for the program by their sponsoring division. The role of headquarters is to make certain the individuals selected meet the standards of having future potential and have a successful learning experience while in the United States. This requires close collaboration between Pepsi-Cola International and Pepsi-Cola North America. Although all the details of how the program works are beyond the scope of this chapter, the driving principle to assure successful learning is to individualize the experience. Factors such as skills needed, family needs, degree of familiarity with the United States, language skills, and stage of career are all considered when tailoring the Designate experience. To date, some 28 nationalities are participating in the program. The sample sizes for each nationality make it difficult to make generalizations about either the successes of the program or the impact on individuals of different nationalities, but a balance between meeting individual learning needs and helping with cultural adjustment seems to make the program successful.

SUMMARY OF LEARNING POINTS

Pepsi-Cola International is a unique business and a part of a significant, growing global corporation. This is both a challenge and a significant opportunity from a human resources management perspective. Wayne Calloway, the chairman of PepsiCo, has repeatedly said the key to future growth is talented people. This is doubly so on a global scale. International markets are exploding with opportunities for individuals and businesses. The challenge for the human resources practitioner is to find ways to help people succeed in very complex, changing environments. This requires a combination of human resources technology and intuition for working through diversity.

A starting point for Pepsi-Cola International has been to focus on the key values that seem to have struck a resonant cord with international employees. Building the culture is the single biggest challenge to have a successful global corporation. This means articulating principles that will ensure success across markets and business functions, setting and maintaining the highest standards possible, helping people develop the skills necessary for their success, offering jobs with big challenges, and encouraging the building of careers. Doing all this in a global context where the rules are now being written is the challenge. Human resources programs must aid in providing an environment where people can do their best work and then must ensure that they are empowered across cultures.

In an international environment, learning comes fast and furious. This is particularly true in a growing business and in a corporation that places such a high value on driving change and being competitive. The human resources practices described in this chapter have produced some learning points that may be of assistance to the applied human resources practitioner working internationally. A partial list of these includes:

1. *Values drive everything.* As in diplomacy, words and meaning are critical. Meaning is derived from shared values and shared values need to be understood and articulated in a simple and concise manner. Shared values, such as teamwork, are the basis for human resources actions and development (see Table 11.3).

2. *Feedback works.* Feedback related to expectations for performance seems to have universal applicability. People need standards by which to judge their efforts and business-related, objective feedback can be used in most cultures.

3. *Individuals are important.* No program, no matter how well designed, will work unless it helps individuals one at a time. This means each program participant must figure out how to apply what he or she has learned. Every program must have a back-home implementation component that requires specific action steps to be identified and implemented.

4. *Data, sometimes anecdotal, drive programs.* Top-down programs have value, but at the end of the day, if a program does not serve the needs of an individual in a country in a business setting, that program will fail. The

TABLE 11.3. Pepsi-Cola International Teamwork Practices

Content	Understanding others	Driving toward results	Making a contribution
Practice examples	Listening carefully to what others have to say	Focusing on issues rather than personalized	Being willing to share resources under your control
	Giving credit to or sharing credit with others	Openly confronting problems and different points of view	Being a person who delivers what is promised

action step is for the human resources practitioner to look constantly for data and ask people on a local country or market basis what they need to succeed.

5. *Cultural differences may be exaggerated.* This is not to say that culture is unimportant, but knowing how to impact the business is more important. A focus on business outcomes forces greater emphasis on solving problems than worrying about cultural differences.

6. *People are fundamentally the same.* In general, business people want to succeed and to achieve. They may get there in different ways but they are still trying to get to the same place. Human resources programs must aid in that success or they are of limited utility in the international business world.

7. *Patience and flexibility are critical.* No program is likely to have the full, desired, and planned outcome. When it does not, make changes quickly and listen to the feedback coming from the recipients. Pride of authorship may lead to undesirable consequences.

8. *Overcommunicate intentions and expectations.* At every opportunity and at every turn find an opportunity to share expectations and intent. Never take even the most simple communication for granted. Managing worldwide diversity successfully means the human resources practitioner must start with an understanding of the desired business results, gather data, and then install the programs required. The starting mindset for the international human resources practitioner should be a common set of values that may be used to drive interventions with a common focus of improving performance. Initial program designs should seek a common denominator that also allows modification to fit local operating conditions.

9. *Develop a culture that transcends.* The culture being created at Pepsi-Cola International transcends international boundaries. It cuts across differences in language and customs. It unites diversity while recognizing the importance of differences. This culture helps unify and link diverse global operations by unifying the management of human resources against a criterion of improving performance.

STAFFING INTERNATIONAL HUMAN RESOURCES TO MANAGE DIVERSITY

In this international arena where business flourishes only with sharing and coordinating across units worldwide, it is important that local initiative is matched with headquarters input and facilitation. This is attained by explicit value statements regarding local authority and by shared values and a constantly traveling headquarters staff that literally threads together a culturally diverse global operation.

While the human resources practictioner needs to start with an understanding of the desired business results, the individual need not necessarily be out of a line management position. In fact, at Pepsi-Cola International most of the headquarters and local HR staff have degrees in human resources management or industrial relations. A few have general business degrees. The first author of this chapter is the only one in HR at Pepsi-Cola International with a doctorate, it being in industrial/organizational psychology. Regardless of degree type, however, almost all are trained as generalists, thus giving each one of them greater opportunity to serve all the human resources–related business needs of the operations. This, of course, helps the human resources function to operate as efficiently and effectively as the rest of the business.

COMPARING INTERNATIONAL AND DOMESTIC HUMAN RESOURCES

Perhaps a final point here for the HR practitioner is that going global is more than just thinking more broadly or having the opportunity to travel more. Although beyond the scope of this chapter to discuss extensively, it might be useful to highlight some differences between domestic HR operations and international HR operations. Briefly, the factors that differentiate international from domestic HR include:

- More functions and activities
- Broader perspective
- More involvement in employees' personal lives
- Changes in emphasis as the workforce mix of parent country nationals (PCNs) and host-country nationals (HCNs) varies
- Risk exposure
- More external influences

Below, these factors are discussed and illustrated in more detail.

More Functions and Activities

To operate in an international environment, a human resources department must engage in a number of activities that would not be necessary in a domestic environment: international taxation, international relocation and orientation, administrative services for expatriates, host government relations, and language translation services. The HR department also has to deal with three additional categories of employees: those assigned from the parent firm to work in the foreign subsidiary, the expatriate, or parent country nationals; those employed by the parent firm but native to the host country, host country nationals; and those employed to work in the foreign subsidiary but from another country, third country nationals.

Broader Perspective

Domestic HR managers generally administer programs for a single national group of employees who are covered by a uniform compensation policy and taxed by a single government. Because international HR managers face the problem of designing and administering programs for more than one national group of employees (e.g., PCN, HCN, and TCN employees who may work together at the regional headquarters of an overseas subsidiary), they need to take a more global view of issues. For example, a broader, more international perspective on expatriate benefits would endorse the view that all expatriate employees, regardless of nationality, should receive a foreign service or expatriate premium.

More Involvement in Employees' Lives

A greater degree of involvement in employees' personal lives is necessary for the selection, training, and effective management of expatriate employees and TCNs. The international HR department needs to ensure that the expatriate employee understands housing arrangements, health care, and all aspects of the compensation package provided for the assignment (cost-of-living allowances, premiums, taxes, etc.). Many international companies have an international personnel services branch that coordinates administration of the above programs and provides services for the expatriate employees and TCNs such as handling their banking, investments, and home rental while on assignment, and coordinating home visits and final repatriation.

Changes in Emphasis as the Workforce Mix of Parent- and Host-Country Nationals Varies

As foreign operations mature, the emphases put on various human resources functions change. For example, as the need for expatriates declines and more trained HCNs become available, resources previously allocated to areas such as expatriate taxation, relocation, and orientation are transferred to activities such as HCN selection, training, and development. The last activity may require establishment of a program to bring high-potential HCNs to corporate headquarters for developmental assignments. This need to change emphasis in personal operations as a foreign subsidiary matures is clearly a factor that would broaden the responsibilities of functions such as human resources planning, staffing, compensation, and training and development.

Risk Exposure

Frequently, the human and financial consequences of failure in the international arena are more severe than in domestic business. For example, expatriate failure (the premature return of an expatriate from an international assignment) is a persistent, high-cost problem for international companies. Another aspect of risk exposure that is relevant to international human resources management is terrorism. Most major multinational companies must now consider this factor when planning international meetings and assignments.

More External Influences

The major external factors that influence international HR management are the type of government, the state of the economy, and the generally accepted practices of doing business in each of the various host countries in which the business enterprise operates. In developed countries, labor is more expensive and better organized than in less developed countries, and governments require compliance with guidelines on issues such as labor relations, taxation, and health and safety. These factors shape the activities of the international HR manager to a considerable extent. In less developed countries, labor tends to be cheaper and less organized, and government regulation is less pervasive, so these factors take less time. The HR manager must spend more time, however, learning and interpreting the local ways of doing business and the general code of conduct regarding activities such as bribery and gift giving. The HR manager may also become more involved in administering company-provided or company-financed housing, education, and other facilities not readily available in the local economy.

CONCLUSIONS

This brief description of the differences between doing domestic HR versus doing international HR suggests the greater complexity and challenge for the HR manager with international responsibilities. Add to these differences the additional need to mold the diversity of globally dispersed locations and you have even more complexity and challenge. Consequently, the firm is more likely to benefit when those in international HR positions know not only the business well but also the field of human resources management, especially within the international context.

The firm is also likely to benefit from the quality of its international HR staffing to the extent the globally dispersed units operate as one global firm rather than several independent (multidomestic) companies that happen to share the same name. Increasingly, firms such as Pepsi-Cola International find themselves in global markets with global competitors where the activities in one part of the world impact those in another. Discoveries for better production, management, or merchandising made in one part of the world must be shared with operations in other parts of the world. Without this, the firm will not be competitive. But doing this successfully is easier said than done. Doubtless, critical to the entire process is an HR staff that views this situation as one of global diversity that needs to be, and can be, brought together by human resources practices.

Although the use of "managing diversity" in this chapter may be somewhat broader than in the others, its concept has the same implications for the profession of human resources management: Identify the nature of the diversity in the organization that needs to be effectively coordinated and unified and design and implement human resources practices capable of bringing about this coordination and unification. As stated above, easier said than done. Fortunately, HR professionals love challenge!

SUGGESTIONS FOR FURTHER READING

Dowling, P., & R. S. Schuler. (1990). *International dimensions of human resources management*. Boston: PWS-Kent.

Kotter, J. P. (1990). *A force for change*. New York: Macmillan.

Kotter, J. P. (1991). *Developing effective global managers for the 1990s*. New York: Business International Corporation.

PART V

PERSPECTIVES FOR VIEWING THE CHALLENGES OF DIVERSITY IN THE WORKPLACE

The preceding cases illustrated many of the issues organizations face as they create workforce diversity and develop their approaches for working through that diversity. In this closing section, three authors analyze several of the key issues raised, and offer commentaries regarding the many approaches represented by the cases. These last three chapters highlight the recurrent themes underlying much of the public discussion concerning the implications of workplace diversity and appropriate responses to it.

Chapter 12 begins by describing the typical aims and activities of the different strategies being used by organizations to address workplace diversity. This summary includes the approaches described in the cases in this volume as well as strategies being adopted by organizations not represented in this volume. The author then discusses several dilemmas inherent in these activities. These dilemmas force managers to consider carefully whether it is best to emphasize equal treatment or equal outcomes, whether to focus on commonalities or differences, and the tension between candor and sensitivity. These dilemmas are discussed in the context of both the Civil Rights movement and current concerns over workforce diversity. This historical comparison reveals the presence of fundamental differences in the social philosophies that serve as the foundations for alternative routes to creating social change. As Chapter 12 shows, the differing philosophies can result in disagreements about the most appropriate methods for eliminating race- and gender-based workplace discrimination against individuals. Principles for improving the management of diversity while at the same time avoiding some of the negative side effects that might be associated with new initiatives are offered.

Chapter 13 also recognizes the relationship between current concerns related to the diversity of the workforce and the affirmative action programs adopted by organizations during the past two decades. The author provides a detailed description of how the traditional affirmative action approach to working through diversity contrast with two more recent approaches: Understanding Diversity and Managing Diversity. These three approaches are shown to have different goals and to rely on different methods, and ultimately they are likely to have different consequences. Affirmative action initiatives are viewed as artificial efforts to assure equal opportunity for members of some sectors of the workforce. The objective of initiatives directed at Understanding Diversity is to foster awareness and appreciaiton of differences that exist among employees from different backgrounds, in hopes of improving workgroup relations. In contrast, Managing Diversity requires reevaluating basic approaches to human resources management in order to take into account diversity of all types. The benefits of the Managing Diversity approach are highlighted in this discussion. Then the key features of this approach are reviewed as a guide for helping those who wish to move in the direction of Managing Diversity.

Finally, Chapter 14 reviews several issues related to the process of organizational change. The chapter begins by discussing a series of questions that need to be answered by those who wish to consider whether to change a particular organization's current approach to working through diversity. The questions include the following:

What objectives could be served by changing the organization's current model for dealing with diversity?

What is the historical context?

What is the time frame for creating change?

Should change be introduced globally or locally?

Will change efforts stop at the organization's borders or reach beyond?

The cases presented in this volume are used to illustrate how different answers to such questions can impact the nature of initiatives an organization might adopt for working through diversity. The discussion of these questions illustrates the many options available for creating organizational change and emphasizes the value of tailoring responses to workplace diversity to specific organization contexts and objectives. Although tailored responses are encouraged, it is also recognized that a few basic principles are likely to apply to almost all workplace diversity initiatives. Chapter 14 closes by briefly reviewing these principles. Thus, this final chapter is intended to provide general guidance to those who wish to evaluate the implications of workplace diversity for a variety of human resources management activities.

CHAPTER 12

Dilemmas in Developing Diversity Programs

LINDA S. GOTTFREDSON

There is broad agreement that the nation must work harder to help all workers develop themselves to their fullest. Such efforts are required not only in the interest of social justice, but also to maintain competitiveness in the global marketplace. The myriad programs for "managing diversity" now mushrooming throughout corporate America purport to pursue such ends. However, the meaning of "diversity" adopted by various organizations and the goals they actually pursue differ widely. What are the specific aims and outcomes of the various diversity activities? How do they differ from affirmative action and earlier efforts to integrate the workforce? Will they become as controversial and divisive as the affirmative action activities they sometimes supersede? Or will they enable the nation, finally, to fulfill its promise of equal opportunity and become more productive in the process?

The case studies in this book provide partial answers to these questions. They represent some of the best and oldest diversity programs in organizations, and they provide valuable insight into the process of implementing various kinds of diversity initiatives. They also provide a glimpse of the forces that propel the diversity movement and the dilemmas shaping it.

The time is propitious for taking stock of the diversity movement because it is at a critical juncture. The movement can become a powerful force for improving management practice. But it also has the potential to polarize different social groups and harm productivity. This fate can be avoided by closely examining the positive and negative side effects of current efforts to create, manage, and value diversity. By allowing such examination, the detailed and sometimes very candid case studies in this volume can help enhance management practice while preventing further polarization in the name of diversity.

In this chapter, I use the case studies to illustrate the major features of the current diversity movement. The movement originated in the limitations of affirmative action, but has become broader in scope as a result of dramatic changes in the composition of the labor force. Many programs for managing diversity focus on achieving ethnic and gender balance throughout corporate life, but others are designed to promote personal development and teamwork among employees, whatever their ethnicity or gender. Organizations face common dilemmas in how to conceptualize and respond to individual and group differences, but they have approached them differently.

I next show how the diversity movement in organizations emerged from the broader civil rights debate. From that perspective, it becomes apparent that the diversity movement is a new arena in the nation's continuing struggle over the meaning of its most fundamental principles— equal opportunity, individual rights, and merit. The more recent struggles over guiding principles can be traced, in turn, to the problematic fact that two major principles of fairness conflict: "nondiscriminatory treatment" does not guarantee "nondiscriminatory results." To the extent that the diversity movement fails to acknowledge and address the source of this conflict, it will generate many of the same negative side effects associated with parity-oriented affirmative action activities. It will breed cynicism and resentment, heighten intergroup tensions, and lower productivity— just the opposite of what managing diversity is intended to accomplish.

I conclude by providing nine principles for managing diversity so that the process advances organizational goals and benefits all employees. More generally, I argue that diversity initiatives promote productivity and true social equality only when they adhere to the principle of the primacy of the individual over the group in the allocation of rights, responsibilities, and opportunities.

DIMENSIONS OF THE MOVEMENT TO MANAGE DIVERSITY

Origins of the Diversity Movement

Many companies trace their diversity initiatives to *Workforce 2000* (Johnston & Packer, 1987). That report greatly intensified concern for the effective utilization of an increasingly diverse workforce. However, the movement now referred to as "managing diversity" predates that report and has it origins in affirmative action. As the Xerox, Pacific Bell, and XYZ Corporation (a pseudonym) case studies clearly illustrate (see also Thomas, 1990), the movement to manage diversity first arose in response to the limitations of affirmative action.

Beyond the Limits of Affirmative Action

Voluntary affirmative action began as an effort primarily to enlarge the pool of qualified minority and female job applicants. The goal was eventually to achieve ethnic and gender parity in hiring. Pacific Bell doubly illustrates this early approach because it works with high schools, colleges, and community organizations both to locate more of the qualified Hispanics and other minorities in its region and to increase their number. Xerox's Step-Up Program, initiated in 1965 to recruit, train, and place minority workers, is another example.

From the beginning, affirmative action also frequently involved closely scrutinizing hiring standards in order to determine whether they were unfairly exclusionary and whether there existed less exclusionary alternatives. Pacific Bell also illustrates the spirit of this affirmative action strategy. Minorities disproportionately lack the educational degrees necessary for being hired directly into its management jobs, so Pacific Bell focused for some time on getting minorities into management primarily through a less direct but more accessible route already in place in the company.

Affirmative action efforts became more pervasive and more aggressive in the late 1960s and early 1970s as the federal government began holding employers accountable for eliminating ethnic and gender imbalances in hiring. Executive Order 11246, issued by President Johnson in 1965, required companies to set parity-oriented staffing goals and timetables as a condition for receiving federal contracts. Then, in 1971, the Supreme Court ruled in *Griggs v. Duke Power Co.* that plaintiffs could use "disparate impact" (unequal results across groups) as evidence for alleging employment discrimination. No longer was it necessary to show "disparate treatment" (unequal treatment).

Affirmative action opened jobs to qualified women and minorities that had been completely shut to them before. However, some of the more aggressive affirmative action programs began to hire unqualified or less qualified minorities and women in order to meet their goals. This, in turn, generated anxiety and resentment in organizations, particularly among white males. On the other hand, many minorities became dissatisfied because of what they perceived as slow progress and white resistance. Consequently, many organizations began to hire "race relations" consultants and conduct sensitivity training. These activities were designed to improve race relations among employees and thereby ease the organization's compliance with federal equal employment opportunity guidelines. XYZ Corporation's race relations program, begun in 1976, represents one of the most systematic and long-standing of such efforts.

Affirmative action and the related race relations programs have done much to integrate women and minorities more fully into the economy. But they have fallen short of expectations. Affirmative action dramatically increased the hiring of women and minorities, but it has done less to ensure their promotion or retention. It has also created some new problems. For example, Pacific Bell relates that the AT&T consent decree, which required strict hiring goals and racial preferences at Pacific Bell, created the presumption among many employees that affirmative action means lower standards for preferred groups. And as the experiences of Xerox and others have indicated, the targeting of minorities or women for assistance has frequently led white males to feel neglected or disadvantaged.

The diversity movement addresses the newer concerns over low promotion rates and inhospitable organizational climates by broadening the scope of earlier affirmative action activities. It does this in two ways. First, diversity initiatives often seek ethnic and gender balance, not just in hiring, but in promotions, transfers, and other working conditions throughout the organization. Xerox, for example, instituted its Balanced Work Force strategy in 1984, which sets very specific numerical goals for hiring and promotion at all levels and for which it holds managers accountable. Similarly, Coopers & Lybrand has recently set "zero [gender] differences" as its goal in everything from amount of overtime and vacation to compensation, turnover, and promotion rates.

Second, compared to affirmative action programs, diversity programs tend to have broader goals and means for improving the organizational climate. As described further below, diversity proponents often argue that women and minorities will never be able to crack the "glass ceiling" and feel welcome until organizations come to value, not merely tolerate, them. Thus, sensitivity training and race relations seminars are being superseded by the now-popular activities to "celebrate diversity." Their aim is to create supportive, not neutral, environments within which minorities and women will flourish.

The Force of Demographic Change

As the foregoing account reveals, affirmative action activities are being enfolded into the newer diversity programs to which they gave life. In other words, the older affirmative action programs are now a key component of the newer diversity initiatives. However, the diversity movement is not simply affirmative action by another name. It also reflects attempts to deal more effectively with important demographic changes in the workforce.

Although *Workforce 2000* never uses the term *diversity*, it points out that the workforce will increasingly include more females, minorities, and immigrants; it will grow more slowly; the skill demands of jobs are rising; and average skill levels among new entrants to the workforce are falling.

In short, employers face a big human resources challenge. They must maintain or increase productivity with fewer, less skilled, and less traditional entrants to the labor market at a time when the skill demands of jobs are rising and international competition is increasing. *Workforce 2000* led American Express Travel Related Services (TRS), for instance, to become particularly concerned about its ability to attract and retain qualified workers in a shrinking and increasingly diverse labor pool. As Chapter 2 of this volume describes, no longer do organizations have the luxury of picking applicants who fit the organization. Instead, they must change the organization to fit available workers. Good business sense absolutely requires this. Hence, for example, TRS has developed plans to change job structures in order to reduce conflicts between family and work for its more than 70% female workforce.

Proponents of diversity programs tend to evaluate the demographic trends more positively than does *Workforce 2000*. Changes in the composition of the workforce should be seen, they argue, as an opportunity and not as a burden. Specifically, the more diverse a workforce, the more dynamic, creative, and productive it is likely to be. Like much of the diversity literature in the popular press, for example, Digital Equipment Corporation and Coopers & Lybrand suggest that women and minorities bring different perspectives, new ways of doing things, and special knowledge about important markets. In other words, they are especially valuable employees, and the diversity they represent promotes the corporation's own most basic objective, whether that be profit or effective services.

But whatever their interpretations of the demographic trends, many organizations are remodeling themselves in response to them. The remodeling may be designed to improve the organization's ability to compete for the most qualified job applicants or to promote the fuller development and productivity of the individuals it already employs.

Typical Aims and Activities

Trade magazines and the popular press apply the term *managing diversity* to programs intended either to eliminate ethnic and gender differences in promotion and retention rates or else to make the organizational climate more hospitable to women and minorities. This dual set of goals seems to be the defining characteristic of diversity for some proponents: Eliminate group differences in career outcomes but generate respect for group differences in attitudes, values, and behavior.

This volume provides a broader perspective on diversity because it examines diversity programs targeted to ethnicity or gender in the context of two other types of workforce diversity: differences in cultures across organizations and across nations. This breadth of perspective is valuable for management practice. By revealing the similarity of problems and challenges cutting across different kinds of workforce diversity, it suggests that there may be general principles for dealing with them.

Most diversity activities can be grouped into one of the following five categories. Diversity programs commonly include several of these strategies.

Procedures to Reduce Ethnic and Gender Differences in Career Outcomes

Some companies, like TRS, are beginning to restructure jobs and benefits packages in order to reduce conflicts between work and family. The purpose is primarily to attract and retain more women and, secondarily, to increase the satisfaction and productivity of all workers.

Other companies focus their diversity programs on increasing minority representation. Pacific Bell, for example, seeks to expand its minority (primarily Hispanic) applicant pool for management jobs through a variety of means. For example, it offers summer internships and scholarships to minority college students in order to increase the number of minority applicants with the 4-year degrees necessary for direct entry into management jobs. It has also sought to increase the number of its minority managers by hiring minority candidates without the 4-year degree into nonmanagement positions that can lead to management jobs.

A related set of activities might be referred to as guided career development. These activities are intended to increase the promotion chances of minorities and women already employed in the organization. For example, Pacific Bell provides 6-day Efficacy Seminars, which are designed to help minority employees become more competitive for promotion. It has also established a 2-year accelerated development track for minority managers. This program provides minority managers special training opportunities and assistance from supervisors and senior mentors who help guide their career development. And Xerox Corporation expands its pool of promotable women and minorities by assigning women and minorities to pivotal jobs where they will gain the experience that is essential for later promotion. Xerox also supports minority and female Caucus Groups, which assist the professional development of their members through training, networking, and the like.

The foregoing activities represent companywide implementation of specific methods for attaining ethnic or gender balance in the workforce. Another common strategy for achieving representativeness has simply been to tie executives' or managers' evaluations and compensation to their success in meeting diversity goals. This is one element, for example, of

Xerox's Balanced Work Force process. Up to 15% of a manager's performance appraisal is based on his or her efforts to increase minority and female representation.

Procedures to Accommodate Immigrants
to the United States

Immigration is concentrated in the Southwest and coastal areas, and some companies in those regions are now taking more concerted steps to train and otherwise effectively utilize the large number of immigrants. This book does not include any such case studies, so the following examples are drawn from elsewhere. Company-sponsored language instruction is probably most typical. For example, one subsidiary of H. J. Heinz Company sponsors voluntary classes in English as a second language after work hours (Branson, 1988). Another subsidiary has a tuition reimbursement program that allows, among other things, supervisors to take classes in Spanish as a second language. One subsidiary also assigns bilingual employees to be "buddy" translators for Hispanics who speak little or no English. Like H. J. Heinz Company, some companies also provide referrals to social service agencies and other sources of assistance for obtaining work permits, housing, and the like.

Changes in Organizational Climate to Value and Utilize
Ethnic and Gender Differences

Diversity programs that attempt to create more sensitive and appreciative attitudes toward women and minorities are often referred to as valuing or celebrating diversity. They generally rely on films, seminars, and small-group activities, as did the ubiquitous and equally popular race relations training activities of the 1960s and 1970s. The Race Relations Competence Workshops at XYZ Corporation stem from this era. The aims of valuing-diversity activities encompass those of the earlier race relations activities: defuse tensions over affirmative action, foster interracial (and now cross-gender) understanding, and promote better teamwork in mixed settings.

Valuing-diversity programs are more ambitious, however. They seek not just to promote understanding and ease intergroup tensions, and not just to hire, promote, and retain more women and minorities, but also to make women and minorities feel valued. They seek not to fit women and minorities into the existing corporate culture, but to change the culture to encompass styles of behavior and thought presumed to be more typical of women and minorities than of white men. Such programs do not seek that differences merely be tolerated, but actively celebrated and embraced. These include, for example, Digital Equipment Corporation's Celebrating Differences Events and its 2-day Understanding the Dynamics of Differences course. Efforts to change the climate for women and minorities also include the creation or support of groups in which employees explore diversity issues or provide advice on them to higher management.

Changes in Procedures or Climate to Accommodate
Individual Differences among Employees

Some companies sponsor activities intended to promote the personal and professional development of employees regardless of ethnicity or gender. One example is Digital Equipment Corporation's Core Groups, where employees of all kinds meet voluntarily to discuss and learn more about their various similarities and differences as individuals, whether in values, life-style, learning styles, personality, or the like. The aim is to increase knowledge and respect of self and others, both as members of groups and as unique individuals, which in turn is expected to enhance employee satisfaction and performance.

Another example is Xerox's Management Resources Process. This process provides feedback on job performance and assistance in career planning for middle-level managers. A similar example is Xerox's Management Practices Program (MPP), which teaches managers how to manage employees more effectively. That program teaches managers listening and communication skills, coaching and counseling, and how to work with employees on compensation, performance improvement, and career development.

The foregoing sorts of activities often originate as efforts intended to improve attitudes or sensitivity to women and minorities or to promote their career development. The broadening of focus to include all employees often results from the limitations or side effects of the narrower focus. Xerox, for example, implemented its MPP, a basic people-management skills program, when it found that its earlier Awareness Seminars for sensitizing managers to their biases failed to equip them with the means to deal with those biases.

The broadening of focus can also result from efforts to stall or reverse the divisive "us versus them" mentality that can develop when only women or minorities appear to be targeted as program beneficiaries. It can result as well from the realization that all individuals can benefit from activities originally designed to promote the personal and professional development of women and minorities, and that majority males are more likely to accept diversity programs when they too benefit. For example,

Digital Equipment Corporation gives these reasons for the change in focus of its Core Groups over time. First they emphasized ethnic and gender differences, then nonethnic and nongender differences, and finally all differences among individuals.

Other personal development programs are but one tool in a broader effort to create a common, inclusive corporate culture for culturally disparate employees. Pepsi-Cola International, a multinational corporation, has sought to unify its workforce across 150 countries by developing a task-oriented, culture-neutral organizational climate that stresses excellence in individual and team performance. It has set clear performance standards, provided leadership training, and encouraged an ethic whereby employees freely consult with and provide "instant feedback" to one another.

The merger between Harris Semiconductor Sector and General Electric Solid State represents another effort to create a common culture, but one that did not originate in concerns over ethnicity or gender. It illustrates that differences in values, expertise, and cultures across two merging companies can be as divisive and difficult to accommodate as differences in ethnicity and gender.

Harris faced numerous problems in creating a common corporate culture that would embrace both organizations. These problems included distrust, stereotyping, inadequate communication across units, and employee resentment with attempts at "balancing" the composition of management regardless of competence. These problems, in fact, mimic many of the tensions across ethnic and gender lines that diversity programs seek to ameliorate. Ethnic and gender differences will no doubt remain especially sensitive in this country. However, Harris Corporation's experiences in managing nonethnic and nongender diversity reveal that many problems in managing diversity cut across all kinds of workforce diversity.

The more that diversity programs encompass all individual differences and are directed to all employees, the more they can be characterized as general management practice. However, it appears that unless they accompany or originate from concerns related to ethnicity and gender, they are not likely to be labeled as diversity efforts.

Decentralized Problem Solving to Accommodate Local Conditions

Companies like Coopers & Lybrand and Pepsi-Cola International provide services or products to quite different and fast-changing markets around the nation and the world. They therefore cannot impose companywide solutions to all problems. In order to meet companywide production goals under such diverse conditions, they encourage high-quality local problem solving. Pepsi-Cola International, as just discussed, encourages managers to consult with counterparts in other countries to find ways of meeting common production and quality goals under different local conditions. Coopers & Lybrand supports local pilot programs to meet the varying needs for employee benefits of workers at different sites. It then carefully monitors and evaluates the pilots and disseminates effective practices for possible adoption by other sites.

Although these two case studies deal specifically with gender and culture differences among employees, the problem-solving strategies they describe may be useful for dealing with all kinds of diversity in the workplace or local markets.

Major Dilemmas

Like other interventions, diversity programs have had both positive and negative side effects. On the negative side, for example, they have sometimes led to resentment and dissatisfaction among some or all groups of employees and, consequently, to polarization across groups. On the positive side, diversity programs have sometimes led to major improvements in broader management practice; for example, in promoting the personal development and productivity of all workers in an organization. Whether diversity initiatives represent net gains or losses in productivity and fairness depends to a large degree on their handling of the dilemmas inherent in managing diversity.

The five following questions suffuse the diversity movement. These somewhat overlapping issues represent dilemmas, because both courses of action in each case have their advantages and disadvantages. The final section of this chapter suggests some principles for resolving these dilemmas in ways that minimize negative side effects.

Equal Treatment or Differential Treatment?

In the decade or two preceding the diversity movement, equal treatment had been the accepted principle, even if not always standard practice. Antidiscrimination laws forbade employers from treating applicants or employees differently on the basis of race, color, religion, sex, or national origin. Nor could employers even inquire into family status, sexual orientation, and certain other characteristics when interviewing applicants.

Equal opportunity would be achieved only when color and gender ceased being relevant to employers.

Some people now argue that the principle of equal treatment is misguided (Braham, 1989). Equal treatment is not fair and does not provide equal opportunity, they say, because individuals have different needs, backgrounds, ways of doing things, and skills to contribute. Perhaps employees could all be treated the same when the workforce consisted primarily of white men, but that is not true today. White male corporate cultures automatically disadvantage women and minorities in a variety of ways, some people now argue. If women and minorities fail to conform to that culture, they are viewed as incompetent. If they try to conform, they may be viewed as deviant, say, as too aggressive. In other words, they can neither act like white men nor act unlike them. Nor have women and minorities had access to the informal white male networks that help one succeed and climb the corporate ladder. It is neither fair nor sensible, the argument continues, to expect women to separate family and work to the extent that most men have been able to in the past. Nor is it fair or sensible to ignore the fact that many minorities come to the labor market saddled with disadvantages that many white men have escaped.

Treating all people the same, it is said, leaves many of the old barriers in place. It also suppresses the talents of women and minorities and thus hobbles them. Thus, some people argue that good human resources policies recognize differences across groups and tailor treatment accordingly. Sometimes fairness requires color-consciousness or gender-consciousness (Schachter, 1988; Ansberry & Swasy, 1989). Besides, organizations may be vulnerable to employment discrimination lawsuits unless they make good progress toward workforce balance, which may require differential treatment by ethnicity or gender.

The counterargument is that treating people differently on the basis of group membership is unjust and sows the seeds of resentment, thereby creating additional barriers between groups and corroding the morale that is necessary for high levels of performance. Even when it is well intentioned, differential treatment in scholarships, internships, training, career assistance, and job placement is preferential treatment nonetheless. Differential treatment is corrosive, people argue, because it creates resentment among all parties. Many members of nonpreferred groups resent what they perceive to be reverse discrimination and come to believe that members of preferred groups cannot succeed without preferences. On the other hand, members of the preferred groups resent the implication that they cannot compete on their merits and do not deserve their successes (Nazario, 1989). Intergroup tensions rise, not fall (Short, 1988; Sowell, 1990). Conversely, performance standards fall, not rise, because the implementation of "nonexclusionary" employment policies often means the lowering of standards, at least for the preferred groups (Gordon, 1988). Accordingly, by this view, good management practice requires that individuals be treated strictly on the basis of their individual merits, not on the basis of their group membership. Besides, organizations may be vulnerable to reverse discrimination lawsuits if they treat employees differently on the basis of ethnicity or other proscribed characteristics.

The struggle over what constitutes fair and effective treatment is evident, for example, in the evolution of Digital's Core Groups. A focus on group differences left white males feeling neglected, whereas an emphasis on strictly individual differences left women and minorities feeling neglected. Contrasting choices are evident in the comparison between Xerox and Pacific Bell, on the one hand, and Pepsi-Cola and American Express TRS, on the other. For example, Xerox opted to risk a reverse discrimination lawsuit (as too did Pacific Bell and Digital, perhaps) when it reduced the number of whites relative to minorities in management jobs during its downsizing in the early 1980s. By contrast, Pepsi-Cola argues for the importance of a culture-neutral climate in developing human resources. And Coopers & Lybrand opted not to establish special programs for women, partly because it wanted to avoid perceptions of favoritism and the backlash to which such perceptions might give rise.

Commonality or Differences?

Historically, the United States has viewed itself as a melting pot in which diverse groups become assimilated to a common American culture. It was likewise assumed that new entrants to an organization would become assimilated to that organization's culture. Some people now argue that the melting pot is an inappropriate metaphor for the nation and organizations (Kilborn, 1990). They argue that corporate culture, like American culture in general, reflects the values and interests of white males of Western European ancestry. Assimilation therefore represents the domination of one culture over others, not the melding of many. A salad is the more appropriate metaphor because the whole is enhanced by the diversity of its ingredients.

Ethnic and gender differences in values and behavior are not inferiorities to be corrected, as many managers have assumed. Rather, the argument continues, differences should be understood as valid alternative ways of thinking and acting that can lend vitality to teams and organizations. Accordingly, employees should be led to understand the diversity and to see that it can enrich the organization. Rather than ignore or minimize differences, as was once advocated, organizations should recognize, celebrate, and capitalize on them. Understanding differences can break down the old barriers to cross-group communication and cooperation.

Some diversity proponents are uneasy with valuing-diversity programs that explore ethnic and gender differences, as most do. Such programs may reinforce stereotyping. Discussing the negative stereotypes of different groups may ingrain them further rather than root them out. Acknowledging and celebrating average ethnic and gender differences may only replace one set of stereotypes and barriers with others. Rather than unite, the attention to differences may divide and polarize. Stereotypes, favorable or not, deny people recognition as unique individuals.

The dilemma of how to discuss ethnic and gender differences appears repeatedly in the popular literature (e.g., Schachter, 1988; Solomon, 1990). It is also evident in the case studies. Digital's Core Groups struggled with the issue. Coopers & Lybrand expected its female employees to resist the formation of women's discussion groups, should the company try to establish them, because many had worked hard not to appear different from their male counterparts. Some of the case studies either have in place or plan to implement valuing-diversity activities, but others, like Pepsi-Cola, argue that too much is made of cultural differences. Instead, an organization can create a common organizational culture that incorporates and uses but does not highlight cultural differences.

Equals or Victims?

A less explicit but very important dilemma relates to whether minorities and women should be treated as victims or as equals. They were frequently victimized by discrimination in the past and still are to some extent today. Equal opportunity cannot exist, some people therefore argue, until the systematic harm suffered by women and minorities is recognized and redressed.

The persons compensated through preferential treatment or other means of redress (as in the AT&T consent decree establishing strict hiring goals and preferential hiring) are not necessarily the persons who were directly harmed by the discrimination being redressed. However, the harm suffered by some members of a group is shared by all, it is argued, because the others are denied role models, access to networks of opportunity, and the like. Besides, it should be understood, the argument often continues, that harm is not always obvious and thus is more pervasive than usually realized. Everyone harbors unconscious but harmful prejudices (Castelli, 1990; Geber, 1990). In short, most if not all women and minorities face barriers because of their gender or ethnicity, whether they realize it or not.

Counterarguments to the victimization perspective stress its negative side effects for one or more of the parties involved. If minorities and women are viewed as suffering collective harm, then white males become collectively guilty of oppression, regardless of their individual guilt or innocence. Resentment grows as putative "victims" and "oppressors" accuse each other of injustice in the pursuit of self-interest. Worse yet, some critics (e.g., Steele, 1988) argue that relying on the status of victim to obtain rights or favors is demeaning and self-destructive. It creates a stake in poverty, dependence, and impotence, not in developing strengths, talents, and initiative. Rather, minorities and women must move ahead despite past disadvantages and recognize that partial compensation is feasible but full redress probably is not. The only way to become social and economic equals is to act like and demand treatment as equals. This means building skills, showing initiative, and persevering despite real and sometimes unfair obstacles.

Oppression theories are common in the popular diversity literature and are evident to some extent in case studies such as that of XYZ Corporation. By contrast, Pacific Bell rejects "chid[ing]" and "sham[ing]." It also has fought the presumption that its minority candidates are less qualified by concretely demonstrating their skills to prospective supervisors. Similarly, some employee caucus groups seem to focus on monitoring victimization or broadening its definition, whereas others are clearly devoted to developing their members' skills.

Volunteerism or Strong Leadership?

This dilemma is endemic to all programs of organizational change. Real and lasting change is more likely to occur when members "own" the change in some sense—they initiate the change, it meets their own needs, or they are committed to it for some other reason. Relying on voluntary change, however, is a slow and uncertain process. Any significant resistance can stall, redirect, or abort the desired change. Relying only on voluntary commitment to diversity goals may also be perceived as lack of real organizational commitment to those goals, as mere "window dressing."

Strong leadership from the top is more likely to compel compliance. Good examples can be set, directives issued, and reward systems modified in order to redirect employees' behavior. But the more such leadership produces forced rather than voluntary compliance, the more likely it is to generate unintended side effects that can subvert the original goals for change. Coerced change can create cynicism, harm morale, and produce covert but counterproductive resistance. And it may lead to complaints that the organization is engaging in "social engineering."

The organizations described in this book, once again, adopted different strategies in this regard. Digital Equipment executives, for example, first established their own Core Groups in order to improve their understanding of group differences and to promote effective communication and team building. They then encouraged the subsequent growth of other Core Groups through voluntary employee participation. By contrast, Xerox ties its managers' evaluations and compensation to their success in achieving workforce balance rather than first attempting to change attitudes.

Candor or Sensitivity?

The diversity movement is also ambivalent about the need for candor versus sensitivity about group differences. Insensitivity toward minorities and women is strongly condemned today. Race relations seminars and the newer valuing-diversity activities are designed to make employees more sensitive to the needs and feelings of persons different from themselves. This, in turn, requires a new social etiquette that is sometimes formalized in organizational policies. For instance, ethnic jokes and demeaning comments about women violate many new harassment policies.

However, commentary about diversity programs frequently mentions the need for candor in breaking down old barriers. Participants in discussions of diversity typically report that it is difficult to be candid about their feelings on such emotionally charged issues as ethnicity and gender. Accordingly, organizations such as Digital will often require confidentiality or otherwise structure activities to make participants feel "safe." Unless participants are candid, they argue, misunderstanding and stereotypes will bar effective communication and teamwork on the job and will continue to restrict the career opportunities of minorities and women.

Candor has its problems, however. Some critics argue that candor is treated as acceptable only when employees are prepared to renounce beliefs that others deem to be insensitive or otherwise "politically incorrect." Moreover, candor may raise new barriers if the tension it typically produces is not resolved. And as Lucky Stores Inc. recently discovered (Stevens, 1991), the otherwise healthy process of exposing employees' biases can also expose the organization to employment discrimination lawsuits. Similarly, Xerox points out that it puts itself at legal risk when it formally gives negative feedback to managers who have failed to meet the company's Balanced Work Force goals.

DIVERSITY MOVEMENT AS AN EXTENSION
OF THE CIVIL RIGHTS DEBATE

The nature and importance of the social issues and dilemmas shaping the diversity movement are clarified by showing how that movement represents a new direction in the nation's debate over civil rights.

Early Civil Rights Movement

Thirty years ago there was broad consensus among civil rights advocates over principles and goals. The goal was to promote equal opportunity. Everyone should be judged according to his or her individual merits, not according to race, sex, religion, or social class. Martin Luther King, Jr., symbolized this stance when he argued that people should be judged by the content of their character, not the color of their skin. Treating people differently on the basis of such characteristics was discrimination, and such behavior should be illegal. Indeed, it became so with the enactment of the Civil Rights Act of 1964. Color barriers in housing, education, transportation, and employment fell quickly. Doors to education and jobs also opened to women.

This early civil rights stance conformed with the most fundamental of American principles, thus shaming Americans all the more for their mistreatment of blacks and other minorities. Through color-blindness blacks would finally be able to exercise their full rights as U.S. citizens. Treating people according to their individual merits, hiring the best qualified regardless of race or sex, would promote fairness and productivity simultaneously. Women, blacks, and other minorities would no longer have to be better qualified to be treated as equals. The promise of our pluralistic society might finally be realized, for individuals of all origins would be treated with equal respect and with equal rights under the law. No longer would the arbitrary conditions of one's birth determine one's fate.

The Unrecognized Dilemma

The consensus characterizing the early civil rights movement was eroded and eventually shattered by one mistaken assumption. Many civil rights advocates assumed that equal treatment would lead to equal outcomes by ethnicity. The social programs necessary for integrating minorities into the mainstream might be expensive and require time to work. But there was little doubt that blacks and other minorities would make steady and substantial progress toward socioeconomic equality as the new educational programs of Lyndon Johnson's Great Society lifted them out of poverty.

It was recognized, of course, that the eradication of illegal discrimination would not obliterate the disadvantages created by earlier discrimination. A race is not fair when one party is forced to compete with a broken leg. Thus, a panoply of compensatory programs was implemented, particularly in education. Schools began to take more responsibility for remediating the disadvantages that children brought with them into the classroom, for example, by providing free meals or social services.

Compensatory education and similar efforts to "level the playing field" were accepted in principle by many people, especially by those most eager to atone for past inequities. The disadvantaged should receive special resources, they agreed, although just which was not always clear.

The effort to equalize real opportunities continued. Begun in the 1970s, state equalization plans reduced disparities in funding across school districts. Busing for racial balance and the elimination of ability-based grouping helped to reduce differences in school experiences across the races in many districts. But the expected equalization of school outcomes never materialized. For example, busing, Head Start, and similar programs to reduce racial inequalities had some positive effects, but they failed to meet a central goal—to reduce the black–white gap in achievement test scores.

As a stubborn reality mocked the promises of the Great Society, philosophies of equality began to shift. Criticizing the educational system and employment practices became popular among academics. No longer was schooling a gateway to opportunity, critics argued, but a barrier erected by elites to keep the poor in their place (Bowles & Gintis, 1976). Practices that produced unequal results by ethnicity or social class were attacked as barriers to equal opportunity, including ability grouping, tracking, special education classes, disciplinary procedures, and the use of tests, college admissions criteria, and even educational credentials.

For many critics, the old signs of merit became signs of past social advantage, not character or promise. Ability tests were accused of measuring social class and race, not competence. Achievement tests were charged with measuring past opportunities, not achievements. The City University of New York instituted open admissions on the premise that, when given the opportunity, disadvantaged students would achieve at higher levels than predicted on the basis of their past performance. The same premise underlay the special procedures adopted by many colleges for evaluating and admitting minority students. Lower grades and lower test scores did not necessarily mean lesser promise for disadvantaged students or job applicants, it was argued.

No longer was there consensus that the measure of equal opportunity was equal treatment. A more meaningful measure of equal opportunity, some began to argue, was equal results. Tests that showed group differences were, ipso facto, biased. Schools with lower average test scores were automatically assumed to be worse schools. Racial disproportions in hiring, said the Supreme Court in its 1971 *Griggs v. Duke Power Co.* decision, were presumptive evidence of racial discrimination, which the employer then bore the burden of disproving.

With the traditional meaning of both merit and equal opportunity unsettled, the traditional concept of fairness was challenged as well. For many it remained the long-standing principle of nondiscriminatory treatment of individuals. But for others it became equal outcomes across groups of individuals. Where once civil rights advocates stood together, they were now split.

Late Civil Rights Movement

The failure of minorities to progress as much as expected under antidiscrimination policies clearly indicated that basic assumptions underlying those policies were mistaken or that the issue was more complex than previously realized. Of the possible explanations for this unexpected result, one in particular became popular: Discrimination must be subtle and hard to detect. One could not point to it directly, but it suffused all social institutions. Although overt discrimination had become relatively infrequent by past standards, most people unknowingly harbored harmful unconscious prejudices that shaped their behavior.

This new theory of hidden racial oppression reinforced the argument that equal opportunity had to be judged by results, not by observable treatment or conscious intentions. Accordingly, fairness was best judged by the fate of groups, not of individuals. Thus, the term *discrimination* is applied today mostly to inequalities in outcome: "discriminatory results" (unequal results).

Simultaneously, "discriminatory treatment" has been reconceptualized by some people to make it more consistent with "discriminatory results." Specifically, in the early civil rights movement, nondiscriminatory treatment meant color-blindness and gender-blindness in the objective assessment of merit. Now the advocates of equal results often argue that such treatment is an obstacle to social progress. The principle of fairness requires that treatment differ by ethnicity or gender, for reasons discussed earlier. The principle of merit, some would add, also requires differential treatment; specifically, they argue, ethnicity and gender are themselves aspects of merit because they have value on the job or in educational settings.

A new moral philosophy has been developed in the past 10 years to justify the preferential treatment that is usually necessary for obtaining equal results by ethnicity. This philosophy posits "group rights," which take precedence over traditional (individual) rights (Havighurst, 1983; Shapard, 1990; Young, 1989). These group rights are usually seen to emerge from prior victimization of one group by another. Consequently, they inhere only in previously oppressed groups, which excludes white males. The group rights philosophy assigns rights and responsibilities on the basis of group membership—something that the early civil rights movement sought to eliminate.

The controversial practice of "race-norming" employment tests, for example, arises from the same forces that led to the emergence of this new group rights philosophy, and it is consistent with it (Blits & Gottfredson, 1990). Unbiased, job-related employment tests typically have considerable adverse impact against blacks and Hispanics because, as groups, they possess lower average skill levels than whites and Asians. Race norming seeks to overcome this barrier to equal results by grading blacks, Hispanics, and others (primarily whites and Asians) on different racial curves in order to produce equal test results across the three groups.

The practice of race norming (also called "within-group score adjustment") reflects the direction of the late civil rights movement. It was instituted in 1981 by the U.S. Department of Labor's Employment Service solely in order to eliminate adverse impact when using its job-related and unbiased General Aptitude Test Battery (GATB), and thus to equalize the employment chances of minorities. The practice was used by state employment agencies in at least 38 states by the end of 1986 (Hartigan & Wigdor, 1989), at which point expansion of the practice was halted by the U.S. Justice Department's threat to sue the Labor Department for reverse discrimination (Delahunty, 1988). Race norming's chief advocate today is the Lawyers Committee for Civil Right Under Law (Seymour, 1988), which is the major litigator of employment discrimination suits in the country.

The Dilemma of Diversity in Skills and Interests

Like the civil rights movement from which it inherited the dilemmas of diversity, the diversity movement tends to assume that equal outcomes in employment would occur in the absence of discriminatory treatment. Therefore, by this view, the continued existence of unequal results requires further adjustments in how women and minorities are treated. In practice, for the reasons explained below, this has often meant exercising preferential treatment. This, in turn, has created pressure for redefining "merit" and "fairness" so that they are no longer inconsistent with preferential treatment.

The most fundamental dilemma confronting the civil rights and diversity movements is that groups differ on the average in job-related skills, interests, and abilities. On the average, for example, women differ from men in physical strength, which limits their opportunities in some fields of work. Likewise, despite some dramatic changes, women's vocational interests and career orientation continue to differ substantially from men's overall (Gottfredson, 1986b). Data from the National Center for Education Statistics (1989) show that between 1971 and 1986, the percentage of degrees awarded to women increased somewhat and reached parity at the bachelor's level (from 43% to 51%) and the master's level (from 40% to 50%). Women's representation more than doubled at the doctoral level (from 14% to 35%), but remained far below parity. Women increased their representation at all degree levels in all fields where they had been underrepresented, often increasing it by a factor of 10 in the two fields in which they had been least well represented—engineering (from 1% to 12%) and business and management (from 4% to 31%).

Nonetheless, women still differed substantially from men in 1986 in the fields in which they obtained their degrees. Women still tended to greatly predominate in education (76%, 73%, and 53%, respectively, at the bachelor's, master's, and doctoral levels) and to be underrepresented in engineering (13%, 12%, and 7%), the physical sciences (27%, 24%, and 17%), mathematics (46%, 35%, and 17%), and business and management (46%, 31%, and 22%).

More flexible job structures and benefits packages will go a long way toward reducing work-family conflicts. However, the foregoing data indicate that the availability of women can still be expected to differ substantially across different fields and levels of work for some time to come.

Ethnic differences in academic achievement and job skills have been a matter of grave national concern, as is clear in *Workforce 2000*. Minority skill deficits are still relatively large, especially for blacks, and clearly limit employment opportunities. The proportions of blacks and Hispanics who are qualified for particular jobs are often smaller than the proportions of whites and Asians. They are often woefully smaller for higher-level jobs (Gottfredson, 1986a, 1986b).

Only from one-third to two-thirds as many blacks and Hispanics as whites and Asians, proportionately, obtain bachelor's, master's, or doctoral degrees (Berryman, 1983). National Center for Education Statistics (1989) data for 1985 show that the fields of those degrees are fairly similar for whites and Hispanics, although Hispanics tend to be more highly represented in education and the social sciences at the bachelor's and master's levels but proportionately more highly represented than whites in engineering at the doctoral level. The patterns for blacks and Asians depart markedly from those of whites. Blacks are highly overrepresented and Asians underrepresented in education compared to whites at the master's level (42% and 10% of blacks and Asians versus 28% of whites) and doctoral level (45% and 8% of blacks and Asians versus 24% of whites). The converse is true for engineering at all degree levels: 6% and 20% of blacks and Asians versus 9% of whites at the bachelor's level; 3% and 20% versus 6% at the master's level; and 4% and 24% versus 6% at the doctoral level.

More aggressive recruitment and extensive provision of scholarships and training will help to reduce such gaps in qualification, but employers will be faced by divergent applicant pools for the foreseeable future unless education and social policies change fundamentally.

These ethnic differences mean that adverse impact is the rule, not the exception, when hiring and promotion procedures are job related and when they predict job performance equally well for all groups (Schmidt, 1988; Sharf, 1988). On the other hand, substantially reducing or eliminating adverse impact by ethnicity often entails introducing racial bias (against whites and Asians) into procedures and otherwise reducing their validity. This, in turn, leads to losses in productivity as well as violating the principles of merit and fairness as traditionally defined. Adverse impact can usually be reduced substantially only by lowering standards for the less qualified groups (say, through race norming) or by lowering standards for all groups of job applicants (say, by setting low cut-off scores on employment tests). The first strategy, preferential treatment, lowers productivity somewhat in the short run, and the disaffection it generates is likely to erode productivity yet further in the long run. The second strategy, lowering entry or performance standards for all groups, avoids preferential treatment but at the cost of large immediate losses in productivity (Hunter, Schmidt, & Rauschenberger, 1984).

Nonetheless, employers are expected to attain workforce balance in a nondiscriminatory way. On the one hand, they must satisfy the Office of Federal Contract Compliance Programs, which requires goals and timetables in producing workforce balance. Unless employers show progress toward workforce balance, they risk not only losing their government contracts but also being sued for discrimination. On the other hand, they must not violate Title VII of the Civil Rights Act of 1964, which forbids discrimination on the basis of race as well as sex, religion, or national origin. If employers use quotas or preferential treatment to attain workforce balance, as they often must do, they can be sued for reverse discrimination.

Personnel selection research predicted another consequence of the differential skills dilemma that diversity programs now address: low minority promotion rates. Preferential hiring can eliminate adverse impact at the hiring stage. However, it often does so only at the cost of bumping it up to where there might have been none otherwise—in performance appraisals and promotion rates. Avoiding adverse impact further up the ladder then requires instituting preferential treatment at those levels, too. Diversity managers have inherited the dilemma that personnel managers have been tackling with little success for over two decades now—the same dilemma that fractured the civil rights movement.

DIVERSITY PRINCIPLES TO ENHANCE MANAGEMENT PRACTICE

The verdict is still out on the diversity movement in business. The movement can mobilize more of the productive capacity of all workers—especially women, native minorities, and immigrants—while at the same time creating common bonds across social groups. Or it can sap national productivity and increase intergroup tensions.

The following principles are offered in the spirit of promoting what is most constructive in the diversity movement and avoiding that which seems counterproductive. These principles are drawn from the experiences recounted in this volume and elsewhere and from analyses of the dilemmas discussed above.

Develop Individuals, Not Groups

It is a truism in management that employees should be helped to develop as individuals. This principle remains valid in the face of group differences. A concerted effort to develop individual employees as unique individuals will at the same time address the particular characteristics or disadvantages found disproportionately in some ethnic or gender groups. Singling out particular ethnic or gender groups for special treatment may be perceived as preferential treatment and generate its negative side effects.

Stress Variance, Not Just Average Differences

There are differences among ethnic and gender groups along a variety of dimensions, including values, interests, skills, abilities, and experience. Executives and managers should be aware of the average differences they are likely to encounter between different groups of job applicants and employees so that they can better plan organizational policy and evaluate its effects. The failure to appreciate the sometimes large job-related differences by ethnicity and gender can have far-reaching consequences, as the contentious history of the civil rights movement illustrates.

However, knowledge of average differences is less important for the general employee. Stereotyping may, in fact, be reinforced if employees are taught only about average differences; for example, about "how women think," "how Native Americans feel about competition," and the like. Rather, they should be impressed with the variance, or diversity, of individuals within any social group and the consequent fact that no individual can automatically be assumed to be representative of his or her group. Becoming more aware of the wide range of differences among individuals to which they should be alert helps employees to avoid misunderstanding and miscommunication. That range of differences may be far greater than they realized, and it may become even greater as the workforce becomes more diverse.

Cultural differences across nations are generally much larger than the cultural differences across groups in the United States. Chances for miscommunication are myriad, especially because superficial similarities, such as speaking English, may lead one to underestimate more fundamental differences in values and behavior. Consequently, instruction in group differences is essential for all employees. However, appreciation of the variance within other cultures is still important. For instance, nationals who choose to work or associate with Americans or other foreigners should not be assumed to be typical members of their culture.

Treat Group Differences as Important, but Not Special

Ethnic and gender differences in beliefs, backgrounds, skills, and the like are important and should be respected. However, employers should not elevate them as "special" or more important than other differences among employees. There is no doubt that issues of ethnicity and gender may be especially difficult for employees to work through. But that is different from the organization itself elevating them to special status. An emphasis on group differences rather individual differences can divide the workforce, invite blame and resentment, and risk the development of an "us versus them" mentality. Group differences should be attended to as factors in meeting business objectives, but not as ends in themselves.

Tailor Treatment to Individuals, Not Groups

It follows, then, that programs to assist, train, appraise, promote, and consult employees should not be conditioned on group status per se unless there is a compelling reason to do so. Rather, programs should be targeted to the specific strengths and weaknesses, advantages and disadvantages of individuals, some of which may be presumed to differ across groups. For example, special career tracks for only blacks or women are demeaning to blacks and women and they arouse resentment among others. By contrast, flexible jobs or benefits packages may be especially important to women, but they are generally available to all employees at a site who need or want them. Compensatory treatment to overcome past disadvantages may sometimes be needed, but it should be provided on the basis of individual, not group, characteristics. Conditioning rights, responsibilities, and opportunities on ethnicity or gender as a first, not a last, resort constitutes an implicit endorsement of "group rights."

Find the Common Ground

Common ground among employees should be found and common bonds created when employees are quite diverse. For example, an organization might foster an overarching, group-neutral performance goal or ethic to which members of diverse groups can subscribe and work toward together. Group differences may be respected and effectively utilized, but they should be subservient to the common goal, not vice versa.

Reexamine but Maintain High Standards

Employers should ensure that their hiring and performance standards are as clear and job related as possible. The clearer and more job related they are, the more they will enhance employee productivity and perceptions of fairness. To be perceived as fair, those standards must also be common across groups. Preferential treatment corrodes morale and thus productivity. In the absence of a convincing rationale, treating ethnicity or gender per se as a job qualification or an aspect of merit constitutes differential standards. Unfortunately, improvements in workforce parity and workforce productivity do not always go hand-in-hand. Where the two conflict, productivity should take priority. Sacrificing high standards for parity is a burden that neither the organization nor its employees can bear in the long run.

Test Assumptions and Support Claims

Employers should test the assumptions undergirding their personnel policies and support the claims they make about the effects of those programs. For example, if ethnicity or gender per se is presumed to be an asset (say, in certain markets), that assumption should be tested. If it is not tested, it may be viewed as mere ideology and a pretext for reverse discrimination. Likewise, claims that a program has succeeded should be accompanied by evidence, and the kinds of evidence presented should match the kinds of claims being made.

Solicit Negative as Well as Positive Feedback

Employers should solicit broad feedback on the negative as well as the positive side effects of their programs. For example, praise from one constituency must be balanced against the reactions of others who may have become disaffected. Ignoring or discounting a program's unwanted side effects only squanders opportunities for improving the program and allows problems to fester. In view of the dilemmas in dealing with diversity, organizations should expect their programs to have unwanted side effects, especially at first.

Set High but Realistic Goals

The dilemmas in dealing with diversity should not dissuade employers from tackling the issue aggressively. There is much to be gained from good managing-diversity programs and much to be lost if workforce diversity is mismanaged. But employers should also be realistic, and they should be careful not to generate inflated expectations among employees. As the authors in this volume repeatedly argue, progress is slow and incremental. Neither managers nor employees should expect a "quick fix." Most programs are extensively refined in the light of experience, and some are judged unsuccessful and then are terminated. Enduring improvement in the management of diversity requires people and programs that recognize the complexity of organizational change and that confront the hard choices it sometimes requires.

REFERENCES

Ansberry, C., & Swasy, A. (February 10, 1989). Minority job applicants say slurs often surface. *Wall Street Journal*, p. B1.

Berryman, S. E. (1983). *Who will do science?* New York: Rockefeller Foundation.

Blits, J. H., & Gottfredson, L. S. (1990). Equality or lasting inequality? *TRANSAC-TION/Society*, 27(3), 4–11.

Bowles, S., & Gintis, H. (1976). *Schooling in capitalist America.* New York: Basic Books.

Braham, J. (1989, February 6). No, you don't manage everyone the same. *Industry Week,* pp. 28–32, 34–35.

Branson, H. (1988). Hispanics in the workplace. *Supervision, 50,* 12–13.

Castelli, J. (1990). Education forms common bond. *HR Magazine, 35*(6), 46–49.

Delahunty, R. J. (1988). Perspectives on within-group scoring. *Journal of Vocational Behavior, 33,* 463–477.

Geber, B. (1990). Managing diversity. *Training, 27*(7), 23–30.

Gordon, R. A. (1988). Thunder from the Left. *Academic Questions, 1,* 74–92.

Gottfredson, L. S. (1986a). The societal consequences of the *g* factor in employment. *Journal of Vocational Behavior, 29*(3), 379–410.

Gottfredson, L. S. (1986b). Special groups and the beneficial use of vocational interest inventories. In W. B. Walsh & S. H. Osipow (Eds.), *Advances in vocational psychology: Vol 1. The assessment of interests* (pp. 127–198). Hillsdale, NJ: Erlbaum.

Hartigan, J. A., & Wigdor, A. K. (Eds.). (1989). *Fairness in employment testing.*Washington, DC: National Academy Press.

Havighurst, R. J. (1983). Individual and group rights in a democracy. In J. R. Howard (Ed.), *Minorities: Continuity and change* (2nd ed., pp. 17–24). New Brunswick, NJ: Transaction Press.

Hunter, J. E., Schmidt, F. L., & Rauchenberger, J. (1984). Methodological, statistical, and ethical issues in the study of bias in psychologist tests. In L. R. Reynolds & R. T. Brown (Eds.), *Perspectives on bias in mental testing* (pp. 41–99). New York: Plenum Press.

Johnston, W. B., & Packer, A. E. (1987). *Workforce 2000: Work and workers for the 21st century.* Indianapolis, IN: Hudson Institute.

Kilborn, P. T. (October 4, 1990). A company recasts itself to erase decades of bias. *New York Times,* pp. A1, D21.

National Center for Education Statistics. (1989). *The condition of education, 1989: Vol. 2. Postsecondary education.* Washington, DC: U.S. Department of Education, Office of Educational Research and Improvement.

Nazario, S. L. (1989, June 27). Policy predicament: Many minorities feel torn by experience of affirmative action. *Wall Street Journal,* pp. A1, A10.

Schachter, J. (1988, April 17). Firms begin to embrace diversity. *Los Angeles Times,* Sec. I, pp. 1, 14, 17, 18.

Schmidt, F. L. (1988). The problem of group differences in ability test scores in employment selection. *Journal of Vocational Behavior, 33,* 272–292.

Seymour, R. T. (1988). Why plaintiffs' counsel challenge tests, and how they can successfully challenge the theory of "validity generalization." *Journal of Vocational Behavior, 33,* 331–364.

Shapard, L. R. (1990). Group rights. *Public Affairs Quarterly, 4*(3), 299–308.

Sharf, J. C. (1988). Litigating personnel measurement policy. *Journal of Vocational Behavior, 33,* 235–271.

Short, T. (1988). A "new racism" on campus? *Commentary, 86*(2), 46–50.

Solomon, J. (September 12, 1990). As cultural diversity of workers grows, experts urge appreciation of differences. *Wall Street Journal,* pp. B1, B13.

Sowell, T. (1990). *Preferential policies: An international perspective.* New York: William Morrow.

Steele, S. (1988, June). I'm black, you're white, who's innocent? *Harper's Magazine,* pp. 45–53.

Stevens, A. (July 31, 1991). Anti-discrimination training haunts employer in bias suit. *Wall Street Journal,* pp. B1, B5.

Thomas, R. R., Jr. (1990). From affirmative action to affirming diversity. *Harvard Business Review, 68*(2), 107–117.

Young, I. M. (1989). Polity and group difference: A critique of the ideal of universal citizenship. *Ethics, 99,* 250–274.

CHAPTER 13

Managing Diversity:
A Conceptual Framework

R. ROOSEVELT THOMAS, JR.

Seven years ago when launching the American Institute for Managing Diversity, I noted the lack of research available to the manager wishing to develop and implement diversity strategies. Unfortunately, these practitioners either had to reinvent the wheel or they informally had to seek information on what was working or not working for other corporations. Often, these informed accounts offered incomplete data and provided a less than adequate foundation on which to base major diversity initiatives.

The cases in this book represent a major step toward the creation of an empirical data base that can guide managers in moving forward with diversity initiatives. These reports, interestingly, vary significantly in terms of their implicit and explicit definitions of diversity, the levels of organization on which they focus, and the specifics of the interventions themselves. All, however, deal with the process of change.

The cases reflect the variety of thinking in the world of work about diversity. Individuals use labels like managing diversity, multiculturalism, affirmative action, equal opportunity, pluralism, valuing differences, valuing diversity, and diversity to describe diversity phenomena. Some see these labels referring to very different realities, whereas others view them all as being synonymous with affirmative action.

Disagreements over what diversity involves, combined with the diversity of case studies presented, may make it difficult for the reader to glean maximum learning from the articles. As a way of facilitating the reader's digestion of these materials, I offer a conceptual framework for approaching the case studies.

DEFINING DIVERSITY

In everyday usage, people tend to use the word diversity to refer to anyone who is not a white male. I define diversity as being much broader and

306

including an infinite variety of possible dimensions other than race or gender. Selected examples would be age, tenure with the organization, functional background, educational background, sexual preference, physical status, life-style, acquisition/merger diversity, exempt versus nonexempt, union versus nonunion, and religion.

This definition suggests that the white male is part of what I am calling diversity. Also suggested is that even if organizational participants are homogeneous with respect to race and gender, diversity can still exist in significant ways along other dimensions.

An alternative and compatible definition is that diversity is a *multidimensional mixture*. Stated differently, diversity refers to the total mixture. In this context, you might think of diversity as a forest with a number of trees (dimensions). Up to this point, corporate America has focused primarily on the trees of race and gender, and has devoted relatively little—if any—attention to the forest.

Another appropriate analogy would be that of a container of relatively homogeneous balls. Assume you are injecting balls of different hues and shapes. Contemporary and traditional practices call the balls being injected diversity, whereas the definition I am proposing refers to the *mixture* resulting from the infection as diversity.

Multiculturalism, in the context of this definition, means *one* culture reflecting the mixture of diversity in an organization, rather than *several* minicultures reflecting the different elements in the mixture.

Given this mixture definition and the reality that managers addressing diversity have focused on the last balls added, you can conclude that corporate America has not failed in managing or understanding diversity, but rather that it simply has not had these tasks on its agenda.

EXPLORING MORE DEFINITIONS: AFFIRMATIVE ACTION, UNDERSTANDING DIVERSITY AND MANAGING DIVERSITY

There are three fundamental approaches to diversity: affirmative action (traditional), Understanding Diversity (sometimes referred to as Valuing Differences or Valuing Diversity), and Managing Diversity. Although elaborations of these approaches follow below, it is appropriate here to offer brief definitions.

Affirmative Action

Affirmative action initiatives refer to artificial efforts to assure that selected elements of the societal and organizational diversity mixture receive equal opportunity as participants in a given organizational setting. Included here would be "special" efforts to foster the recruitment, development, promotion, and retention of women and "disadvantaged" groups. In practice, these efforts often center on numerical targets as indicators of progress. The governing assumption appeared to be they would assimilate. Historically, the affirmative action option has not called for permanent organizational changes. The adjustment burden has been on these individuals. Conceptually, despite commonly held perceptions to the contrary, affirmative action does not require a lowering of quality selection, performance or promotion standards.

Understanding Diversity

Understanding Diversity initiatives are efforts to foster among organizational members an acceptance, understanding, and ideally an appreciation for the differences that exist among them, with the objective of fostering more harmonious and productive work relationships. (As noted above, practitioners often call these efforts Valuing Differences or Valuing Diversity. However, because I believe that the most significant result of these activities is enhanced understanding, not valuing of diversity, I prefer the term Understanding Diversity.) Commonly included here are multicultural days celebrating diversity, or special days highlighting the culture of a particular racial or ethnic group.

Managing Diversity

Managing Diversity initiatives are efforts to create an environment that works naturally for the *total* diversity mixture. Here, the focus is on the mixture, and managing is defined as empowering or enabling employees. The fundamental question is:

> *As a manager goes about empowering or enabling his or her workforce, and as that workforce becomes more diverse, are there some things that have to be done differently with this evolving diverse workforce (where diversity is defined broadly)?*

Until recently, this question has seldom been asked, primarily because human resources (HR) practitioners have been focusing on *creating* a diverse workforce, on including people who traditionally have had limited participation in corporate America.

MOVING FROM THE TRADITIONAL

As I move through the business sector, I observe that managers increasingly are asking for supplements to their more established affirmative action and Understanding Diversity practices. Why does this restlessness exist? Several factors can be cited.

Diversity Is Becoming More Prevalent in Today's Corporations

Interestingly, this circumstance comes not so much from the changing workforce demographics, but rather from the growing tendency of people who are "different" to celebrate their differences. Many new employees are bringing their differences with them into organizations, as opposed to shedding them at the door. They are less eager to be mainstreamed at the cost of their differences. This celebration of differences is a recent phenomenon. Traditionally, managers and employees have viewed differences as being negative and something to suppress or shed as quickly as possible. For example, often when conducting a seminar on Managing Diversity, I will ask participants what makes them different from this group of individuals. Reflecting the practice of suppressing differences, respondents frequently have difficulty identifying how they differ.

The Traditional Approach Is Declining in Effectiveness

Assimilation has characterized the traditional approach. Although corporate America has welcomed diversity, its managers have also insisted that people "fit in." Specifically, they say to new participants:

> *We are glad to have you. You should know, however, that we do have a way of doing things here and that people who fit a certain mold do best here. We're prepared to help you adjust to the mold—to help you fit in. Your fitting in enhances the likelihood that you will be a success and that we will get our return on our investment in recruiting and selecting you.*

Although this approach may have worked in the past, three factors are now compromising it:

1. The more people celebrate being different, the less willing they are to assimilate to the extent earlier organizational participants did. The new tendency to celebrate differences will call for the management of "un-

assimilated diversity" (people who differ on the surface and below), rather than "assimilated diversity" (people who differ on the surface, but are predictable below as a result of assimilation).

2. An increasingly popular hypothesis is that diversity can give you a "richness" that cannot be provided by the homogeneous workforce. Although concrete data are scarce and the meaning of richness is not well defined, some managers believe that a diverse workforce can outperform a homogeneous one of comparable talent. To the extent a manager buys-in to this belief, he or she will be reluctant to have individuals assimilate more than is absolutely necessary.

3. There is a growing recognition that some factors are beyond assimilation. If assimilation prescribes, for example, ideally assuming the traits of an organization's white males, these requirements respectively could be difficult—or even impossible—for women and minorities. As a consequence, they would have difficulty fitting in to the extent required, regardless of how willing they might be to do so.

The question often arises as to whether the reluctance to assimilate will mean a diminished sense of cohesiveness and common purpose. The answer is a definite no—cohesiveness will still be possible and necessary.

Diversity does not mean that anything goes or that no assimilation will be required; instead, it calls for assimilation only where absolutely necessary. This assimilation in turn will foster the required level of cohesiveness of purpose while allowing for diversity where possible. Unnecessary fitting-in would not be required.

Managers must continue to insist that participants assimilate around the absolute requirements for the enterprise's success. The trick becomes that of identifying requirements as opposed to preferences, conveniences, or traditions. For example, a manager might prescribe "no mustaches" only after determining that it is an absolute requirement for the organization's success and not a personal preference. Under current practices, these distinctions are not being made. *Corporations remain in the costly affirmative action cycle.* The cycle begins with recognition of a problem, which might be inadequate representation, lack of upward mobility, or excessive turnover for a given group. In any event, the next phase is a burst of solution activity. Typically, the solution phase at a minimum includes efforts to enhance the quality of individuals recruited. Other solutions would be special upward mobility or retention programs for the particular employee group.

With these solutions implemented, the cycle moves to the celebration of apparent progress. Progress means programs are in place and results (better recruits, increases in promotions, reductions in turnover rates) are beginning to appear.

Following celebration, the managers relax and await additional fruits of their solution labor. Regrettably, they are typically not forthcoming, largely because affirmative action is artificial and requires continuous attention and effort. The apparent progress comes undone, the number of promotions declines, and new recruits leave or stagnate. And once again, the problem is recognized and the cycle begins anew.

Regardless of the quality of a corporation's affirmative action program, I have yet to see one not caught up in this cycle. Further, the more competitive the corporate environment becomes, the greater the cost of the cycle. Competitive realities are forcing managers to look for escapes from the cycle.

Diversity Is Now a Business Issue

All of the above reasons for moving beyond the traditional approach now mean that diversity is a business or viability issue. Contrary to the traditional view of diversity as a legal or social responsibility or moral issue, contemporary realities now make it a business issue. A corporation's success will increasingly be determined by its managers' ability to naturally tap the full potential of a diverse workforce.

To say that diversity is a business or viability issue is to say that moving forward with progress is a managerial issue as well. This means that dealing with diversity is not about civil rights or women's rights; it is not about leveling the playing field or making amends for past wrongs; it is not about eliminating racism or sexism; and it is not about doing something special for minorities and women. Rather it is about enhancing the manager's capability to tap the potential of a diverse group of employees.

The issue is whether a corporation's managers will have sufficient managerial capability to draw upon the talents of *all* employees. Any weaknesses here will be harmful to the corporation's viability.

ELABORATION OF THE APPROACHES TO DIVERSITY

For the past 6 years, I have been leading an effort to determine how the traditional approach to diversity might be supplemented. The concept resulting from this activity has been labeled Managing Diversity. In this section I detail how Managing Diversity differs from affirmative action and Understanding Diversity.

My thinking is that in the short run, Managing Diversity will not make affirmative action and Understanding Diversity unnecessary, but all these can function as a parallel set of efforts. In the long run, however, effective implementation of Managing Diversity will make the other two unnecessary. Long-run, at the present rate, change will require 15 or 20 years for most organizations. Below are major aspects of what I and my colleagues call Managing Diversity.

Managing Diversity Differs from Affirmative Action

Four major features differentiate Managing Diversity from affirmative action. These are described first.

Affirmative Action Assumes Assimilation

If the individual-organization fit is lacking, affirmative action presumes that the employee who is "different" will adapt. Affirmative action places the burden on the individual; Managing Diversity relaxes the assumption of assimilation and assumes that managers will be open to the possibility of changing organizational culture and systems.

The Focus of Affirmative Action Is Different

Affirmative action focuses directly on recruitment, upward mobility and retention, while Managing Diversity places priority on creating an environment that naturally will tap the full potential of individuals. The Managing Diversity model assumes that if the manager taps an individual's potential naturally, upward mobility and retention will follow in due course.

Affirmative Action Does Not Address Root Causes

Affirmative action provides relief from undesirable circumstances as expeditiously as possible, even if through artificial and temporary means, whereas Managing Diversity calls for a problem-solving approach aimed at addressing root causes. Managing Diversity assumes that if you address root causes, the desired circumstances will evolve naturally.

The Target Employee Is Different

Affirmative action seeks to help individuals who are disadvantaged in some way, whereas Managing Diversity works to help the manager enhance his or her managerial capability. Managing Diversity focuses primarily on the manager.

Affirmative action was never intended to be a permanent managerial tool, but rather a means to the end of equal opportunity. It was *as if* the government said to corporations:

> *We have looked at the results of your people systems, and they cause us to wonder about your commitment to equal opportunity. Further, we think it will take a while for you to bring about the desired changes naturally, so we are prescribing something called affirmative action—something that is temporary, transitional and artificial. It will give us relief from your practices and allow you to take corrective action.*

Unfortunately, managers have fixated on affirmative action and have not moved to take corrective action, in part, because they have assumed that affirmative action is corrective action. Affirmative action is not necessarily corrective action. Corrective action calls for identifying and addressing root causal factors, whereas affirmative action seeks to create circumstances that affirm a commitment to equal opportunity.

As illustration, consider the following case. Media in a southwestern city accused banks of discriminating in their loan practices; specifically, reporters contended that the banks disproportionately rejected loan applications in minority neighborhoods. Bank officials responded by saying *if* they were guilty of discrimination, it was not intentional. As an act of good faith and commitment, the banks set aside a pot of money for minority loans. This act pacified the media and the community.

This provides a good example of a failure even to look for root causes, not to mention addressing them. Never did any bank official ask why the appearance of discrimination existed or how steps might be taken to prevent a reoccurrence. Instead, the focus was on affirming a commitment. They left the factors contributing to the undesired circumstances in place. Corrective action raises the possibility of changing basic cultural assumptions and also modifying people systems. Affirmative action, on the other hand, has not called for these kinds of activities, but rather has placed a premium on adding appendages (special arrangements) to the existing organizational and managerial structures. Examples of such appendages are:

- Special recruitment programs for minorities and women to increase their numbers in the organizations
- Special developmental efforts (such as mentoring) for minorities and women to assure their development

- Special promotional (upward mobility) programs for minorities and women to ensure their advancement

These special programs testify to two facts: "regular" systems are not working for minorities and women, and substantial change is not being sought within the regular arrangements. Accordingly, the label "appendages" fits these "special" efforts.

This focus on "relief from undesirable results" can probably be traced backed to the legal sources of affirmative action. In the context of the law, offenders give priority to compliance, or at least the appearance of compliance, as opposed to getting at root causes.

Managing Diversity Differs from Understanding Differences

By Understanding Differences I refer to generic programs aimed at enhancing acceptance, understanding, and appreciation of differences among people. The objective here calls for helping people to understand where they are individually with respect to diversity, so that they can establish harmonious and productive relationships. End results should include minimization of blatant racism and sexism. Examples of Understanding Differences include the following:

- Establishment of caucuses that support the individual and foster understanding of the given group's culture. Examples would be caucuses for women, blacks, Asian-Americans, and Hispanics, where the group members network and support one another, as well as sponsor events to generate greater understanding of their cultures by others in the corporation.
- Designation of cultural days, where specific cultures are highlighted. On Hispanic Awareness Day, for example, the cafeteria may feature Hispanic food and the Hispanic caucus may present an exhibit and a formal program reflecting the Hispanic culture.
- Presentation of educational and training programs to enhance participants' awareness of "cultural differences" and recognition of their personal feelings regarding individual differences.

Although Understanding Differences can produce some very desirable and helpful ends, it does not necessarily bring about Managing Diversity capability. You can accept, understand, and appreciate differences, even be free of racism and sexism, and still not know how to manage diversity— how to create an environment that naturally taps the potential of a diverse group of people in pursuit of organizational objectives.

Managing Diversity requires a *managerial* capability. When one asks how a corporation is doing with Managing Diversity, the focus is not on how the company is doing with improving relationships or eliminating racism or sexism, but rather how it is doing with creating a *managerial-*capability that will lead to the development of an organizational environment that works naturally for everyone. Implicit here is the reality that some managers will have difficulty managing people who are diverse not because the managers are racist or sexist, but because they lack managerial competence.

What Does Managing Diversity Mean?

Managing Diversity Defines Diversity Broadly

The Managing Diversity model assumes that you cannot make progress with one or two dimensions of diversity and ignore all others without having the dimensions you are ignoring come back and compromise your efforts. Managing Diversity prescribes that your approach has to be philosophically broad enough to encompass all dimensions of diversity.

This breadth of approach suggests that Managing Diversity is not a program or an initiative, but rather a way of life. Not only are changes in behavior required, but also modifications of the basic assumptions that drive individuals and organizations. Managers, therefore, desiring to move forward with Managing Diversity are essentially opting to move forward with a major change. Organizational participants are willing to accept change of this magnitude only if the potential benefits are clear and worthwhile.

Managing Diversity Presumes that an Awareness of the Business (Viability) Rationale for Moving Forward Exists

After more than 6 years of focus on Managing Diversity, I am convinced that progress is most difficult if the business (viability) motive is not present. For many organizations, Managing Diversity is a viability issue in at least six ways:

- *Organizational workforces are diverse and will become even more diverse.* The organization that utilizes these resources more efficiently and effectively will gain a competitive advantage.
- *Some companies are pursuing Total Quality.* All approaches to quality that I have experienced call for empowering the total workforce.

Assuming a diverse workforce, this requires Managing Diversity capability.

- *Independent of Total Quality, some corporations are seeking greater employee involvement and more participatory decision making.* In the context of a diverse workforce, this cannot be done without Managing Diversity capability.
- *Other corporations are implementing "high commitment work teams."* Given a diverse workforce, the desired level of commitment cannot be achieved without Managing Diversity capability.
- *Others are running as lean as possible, thereby placing a premium on tapping the potential of all resources.* With respect to human resources and with a diverse workforce, Managing Diversity capability is required.
- *Corporate external environments are also becoming more diverse.* Effective management of internal diversity will facilitate management of external diversity.

To say that diversity is a business issue does not mean that it no longer has legal, moral, or social responsibility implications, but rather that awareness of the business implications, is necessary for sufficient motivation to implement Managing Diversity.

Managing Diversity Calls for Working the Individual, Interpersonal, and Organization Levels

Traditionally, much effort has been devoted to helping individuals come to grips with their personal predispositions toward diversity, and also learn how to build and maintain quality interpersonal relationships across diverse groups. Managing Diversity calls for the continuation of these efforts, but also recognizes the need to work at it on the organization level.

Managers have ignored the organizational level, primarily because they have assumed that the individual employee would adjust. Under this assumption, the manager experienced no need to explore the possibility of change at the organizational level. With the relaxation of the assimilation assumption, managers implementing Managing Diversity must work organizational culture and system issues.

Managing Diversity Addresses Organizational Cultures and Systems

Managing Diversity calls for assessments of organizational culture and systems, and for modifications where required to foster creation of an environment that will work naturally for all participants. Culture is defined as the basic assumptions underlying all activity in a corporation. They tend to be few in number and not immediately visible. These assumptions can be viewed as analogous to the roots of a tree. A key principle is that the roots control the branches. Nothing can be sustained naturally in the branches unless it is congruent with the roots.

Given that the roots of most corporations were put in place when the workforce was relatively homogeneous, now that the work force is increasingly diverse, Managing Diversity suggests that it is managerially prudent to at least ask whether the old roots will work for the new circumstances. This explains, at least in part, the affirmative action cycle experienced by corporations. Mangers have not taken care to assure that the corporate roots (assumptions) are congruent with their diversity aspirations.

Managers implementing affirmative action have not assessed and modified roots as necessary to make certain they support affirmative action initiatives. The reality of the frustrating affirmative action cycle suggests that practitioners are encountering roots that are incongruent with the desired changes.

This same type of diagnostic analysis has to be made with formal *and* informal systems. Managers must examine these systems to determine whether they have the capability to work naturally for all participants.

I stress that attention must be given to the formal *and* the informal. One example of an informal system is sponsoring. A corporate president discussed this informal process within his company:

"Above a certain level, we require more than written performance appraisals. Someone has to vouch for the candidate for promotion. Someone has to stand up for the individual and push. Without that sponsorship, we by-pass individuals who might otherwise appear qualified."

The task with respect to the informal process described is to assure that it works for all organizational participants. All employees must have an equal opportunity to qualify for sponsoring. Such systems must be surfaced, monitored, and corrected as necessary to ensure an environment that works for all.

Managing Diversity Requires a Long-Term Perspective

Given the magnitude of the change required, for most organizations institutionalization of Managing Diversity as a way of life will require at least 15 to 20 years. Progress, of course, can be seen more quickly, but the institutionalization process will be lengthy. So a major requirement of Managing Diversity is avoidance of the quick fix mentality.

CHAPTER 14

Stepping into the Future: Guidelines for Action

SUSAN E. JACKSON

The territory covered by the preceding cases and commentaries spreads far and wide. The focus of the chapters has been narrow in some instances, such as the case of Pacific Bell's efforts to recruit Hispanic managerial talent, and broad in others, such as the case of Pepsi-Cola International's approach to managing the diversity of a global workforce. Some cases described initiatives that are just beginning, whereas others described activities stretching across two or more decades. Sometimes the primary impetus for change in these cases was a desire to enact socially responsible programs, and other times economic necessity drove the engine of change.

Having traversed this territory, readers may now feel as if they have journeyed into the middle of a forest. Although the path leading into the forest seemed easy enough to follow, the path leading out of the forest to a new destination may be difficult to discern. For readers who wish to continue forward on this journey, this chapter offers some additional guidance.

The foregoing material points to several questions that need to be addressed by anyone considering new human resources initiatives for working through diversity. These questions are briefly discussed in this chapter. The questions posed do not have right or wrong answers. Instead, they simply identify forks in the road. The purpose of considering these questions is to help those who design and implement change to adapt initiatives to their organization's particular needs and context. Following the discussion of these questions is a short list of basic principles that apply to most, if not all, change efforts for working through diversity.

QUESTIONS TO CONSIDER BEFORE INITIATING CHANGE

What Objectives Could Be Served by Changing the Organization's Current Model for Dealing with Diversity?

As this question implies, every organization's management processes and culture include a subtext for dealing with diversity. In many organizations, this subtext has probably not been consciously attended to, at least not until very recently. Before change efforts for working through diversity are initiated, this subtext must be fully understood.

How is Diversity Currently Addressed, and Why?

As described in Chapter 10 (the case of Coopers & Lybrand's strategic grass-roots approach), an emphasis on efficiency and mass production characterizes the traditional model for running business and government organizations. Generally, the traditional model considers diversity to be a condition that should be avoided because it creates uncertainty, which interferes with smooth, predictable, and low-cost operations.

Within the realm of human resources management, the traditional organizational model minimizes diversity among employees in a number of ways: Recruiting practices emphasize finding candidates from sources that have proven to be "reliable" in the past; selection processes emphasize filling positions with candidates who are similar to those who have succeeded in the past and screen out entry-level applicants and promotion candidates who appear to not "fit" the organization's style; socialization and training programs produce uniform ways of thinking and behaving; attendance policies standardize and regulate the scheduling of work; and, more generally, by relying on a centralized, bureaucratic approach to managing the workforce, the traditional model intentionally limits the discretionary latitude given to supervisors and managers for handling the special needs of individual employees.

Presumably, human resources management practices such as these evolved over time because they fit the needs of many organizations. Before embarking on new initiatives to support greater diversity, the system currently in place needs to be fully understood. Otherwise, it will be difficult to accurately foresee all of the consequences likely to follow changes in that system. As a precursor to considering new initiatives, therefore, would-be change agents should analyze the organization's current practices for the purposes of (1) evaluating whether they encourage or limit diversity, (2) understanding the forces that support use of the organization's present system of management, and (3) assessing which aspects of the current system are consistent with the organization's current needs. In other words, any consideration of change should include analyzing *why* things are the way they are, and which things should *stay* the way they are.

Traditional human resources management practices may be consistent with the needs of some organizations. If this is the case, then any new initiatives intended to create and/or support greater diversity are likely to meet with especially strong resistance unless those new initiatives are designed to mesh with the organization's traditional needs.

However, as suggested by Chapters 2 and 10, the traditional bureaucratic model may not fit the new production and service activities of many organizations. In some new-style organizations, diversity can be an asset that supports the valued attributes of creativity and flexibility. Numerous scientific studies document the fact that some types of diversity can enhance creative problem solving (e.g., see Jackson, 1991). Many managers seem to understand this fact; they accept it without scientific documentation because it is consistent with their own experiences. Many managers also realize that creative problem solving and flexibility are required of any organization that must continually adapt to a changing environment, and for this reason, executives intentionally design some types of diversity into their top management teams.

In organizations that value creativity and flexibility over bureaucratic efficiency, it seems reasonable to expect that initiatives aimed at supporting workforce diversity may meet relatively less resistance. But this assumes that the organization's intact system of human resources management practices has already been adapted to fit a new-style mode of conducting business. Unfortunately, this is often not the case. Instead, it is not uncommon to find traditional human resources management practices being used even where they do not effectively support business needs. Traditional practices are used simply because that is the way things have always been done in the past, or because that is the way other organizations do things. Situations such as these call for fundamental changes in the mindset of the human resources organization. Until this is achieved, implementation of new diversity initiatives is likely to be quite difficult because the new initiatives will be incongruent with an existing system that suppresses diversity. For this reason, the next step in the change process—specifying objectives—should be tackled only after the extant system of human resources management has been fully analyzed in terms of its relationship to the needs of the business and its implicit or explicit stance regarding diversity.

What Can Be Achieved by Changing the Organization's Approach to Dealing with Diversity?

Defining clear objectives is a fundamental prerequisite to meaningful change efforts. Whether large or small, change requires time, financial and human resources, and commitment. Time, resources, and commitment are more likely to be forthcoming when everyone touched by a change effort understands what they are attempting to accomplish, and why. This happens only when objectives are clearly specified up front.

Often, change interventions are initiated by organizations simply because they seem popular with competitors or because they have been marketed effectively by an unsolicited vendor. In order to keep up a reputation for being *au courant*, programs may be adopted with little pretense that they are fundamental to the organization's core identity, its productive capacity, or its long-term survival. To some extent, change efforts such as these are low-risk ventures in the short term. With no expectations to be met, the programs' consequences may not be monitored, so there is little chance of failure. The occasional program with positive benefits is welcomed, and may even reinforce the organization's willingness to adopt other new programs under similar circumstances in the future.

The cases in this volume suggest two fundamentally different objectives for change efforts related to workforce diversity. One objective is living up to a view of what it means to be socially responsible in today's society. This objective is most salient in the Digital Equipment Corporation and Xerox Corporation cases; it was probably also important for the XYZ Corporation.

In organizations with strong cultures based on values that transcend changes in leadership, significant change efforts pursued in the interest of social responsibility may be sustainable. However, as is highlighted by the data from XYZ Corporation and the commentary offered in Chapter 12, differing philosophies and perspectives inform people's views of what constitutes socially responsible action vis-à-vis workforce diversity. Differences in opinion run deep and are not easily reconciled. Consequently, full consensus about what constitutes socially responsible action is not likely in most corporations. It may be easier to achieve in some nonprofit organizations, however, for these are often founded on clearly defined values that are shared by most members.

Another objective for change efforts—one that is not inconsistent with being a socially responsible employer—is maintaining the economic viability of the corporate enterprise. To survive long term, corporations must be facile in responding to changes in their environments—dodging threats and seizing opportunities as they arise. As described in Chapter 2, the business environment is changing rapidly along many dimensions, and many of these changes will require new human resources management policies and practices to support diversity. For organizations whose effectiveness depends heavily on their ability to attract and retain a qualified workforce, the impending labor shortage offers clear economic objectives to be achieved by initiatives for responding to the diverse needs of the labor force. For other organizations, the availability of labor may generate less concern than the ability of diverse employees to work together effectively either in face-to-face teams or as partners operating in different parts of the world. Finally, for some organizations, a key determinant of economic viability may be maintaining a workforce capable of spanning the boundary between the internal organization and/or its external markets. As markets diversify, some organizations are finding they must diversify their workforces in order to ensure their ability to communicate effectively with clients and customers.

Each of these objectives—social responsibility, attracting and retaining a qualified workforce, facilitating teamwork, creating synergy between members of geographically dispersed units, and spanning the boundary between the organization and its markets—justifies the investment of time, resources, and personal commitment in initiatives targeted at working through diversity. Which objectives are top priorities for an organization will influence the types of initiatives that are most appropriate.

What Is the Historical Context?

When setting objectives for a change effort, it is necessary to consider the current state of the organization and the desired future state. Although it is sometimes overlooked, it is also important to understand the history behind the current situation. Previous organizational history may ultimately determine whether a change effort fails or succeeds.

Organizations with a history of following the latest fads are usually filled with cynical managers. Knowing that new programs come and go without anyone important ever taking them very seriously, managers tend to yawn at the mention of new initiatives and look forward to seeing the latest fad fade away. Even when new initiatives are taken seriously, organizations may find there is a limit to how many new initiatives can be absorbed over a span of a few years. There is a danger of having constituencies feel "programmed out," as noted in the Coopers & Lybrand case. The design of change strategies needs to take this reality into account.

An organization's general experience with change efforts is one aspect of the historical context to be taken into consideration, but it is not the only one. Also important are experiences more directly related to the topic of diversity. For example, Xerox has a long history of dealing with issues related to the ethnic mix of the workforce. The persistence of its efforts and the specific nature of those efforts has surely shaped the attitudes and expectations of many employees. Employees in organizations without similar historical experiences may respond quite differently from Xerox employees to the same new initiative. When Xerox employees watch the skits now being presented to them as live theater (see Chapter 3), they are likely to find it easy to relate to the situations portrayed and easy to see a variety of nuances in behavior. As an analogy, a Xerox employee would be like a movie buff watching a spoof of old Hollywood films. The movie buff would "see" a much different film from what could be seen by someone with only a casual knowledge of old Hollywood films.

As Chapters 12 and 13 both make clear, an organization's historical experiences with affirmative action and other equal employment opportunity initiatives will influence employees' reactions to new initiatives for working through diversity. In organizations that have (mis)interpreted "affirmative action" to mean preferential treatment for women or members of ethnic minority groups regardless of their qualificiations, reactions to new initiatives for working through diversity may be quite negative. A prevailing perception that "different" means "less qualified" would probably dampen enthusiasm for new initiatives related to working through demographic workforce diversity. In such organizations, initiatives that tackle this perception and its root causes may be mandatory before the organization can begin to move toward a state of genuinely valuing and effectively managing diversity. However, in organizations where affirmative action programs have been used to recruit and develop highly qualified talent, as has occurred at Pacific Bell and many other organizations, new initiatives may be welcomed. By considering the historical context, change agents can more accurately anticipate how initiatives are likely to be received and plan accordingly.

What Is the Time Frame for Creating Change?

In the organizational sciences literature, two types of change are identified: evolutionary change and revolutionary change. As their labels imply, evolutionary change occurs gradually. Each step forward follows in a direct progression from changes achieved in the past. Revolutionary change occurs suddenly. A quantum leap may be achieved almost instantaneously, leaving no artifacts that connect the new order to its predecessor.

Organizational change usually follows a path of evolutionary change—true revolution is rare. Most of the initiatives for working through diversity described in this volume followed the evolutionary model. The evolution of Pepsi-Cola International's global human resources management system and the evolution of Xerox Corporation's current corporate culture are two clear examples of evolutionary change. Evolutionary change is also evident in cases where modest initiatives were introduced first to a small portion of the workforce, and were then amplified subsequently, after the organization adjusted to or absorbed the initial changes. With this approach, which is illustrated well in the cases of Digital Equipment Corporation and XYZ Corporation, progress becomes visible only after a period of years. As discovered by the XYZ Corporation, sensitive measurement tools may be able to document the path of evolutionary change, but those who live through it may barely detect it. In the XYZ case, this led one consultant to comment, "I see it on paper and it looks good. Why don't I feel good?"

Although deep change in corporate culture is accomplished slowly, it would be a mistake to conclude that all useful initiatives require decades to implement. For example, even when deep, evolutionary change is the ultimate goal, an organization's management may elect to make a few relatively revolutionary changes in order to signal its commitment to a new vision that will ultimately require a longer time frame to implement. Furthermore, deep changes in corporate culture are not always needed to address diversity-related issues successfully. Some objectives can be achieved more easily.

Many initiatives for working through workforce diversity are capable of creating meaningful change rapidly. For example, some initiatives for helping employees meet their obligations outside of work can be implemented in a nearly revolutionary fashion (e.g., within a time frame of 1 or 2 years). These include new financial benefits, such as the KidsCheque and FamilyCheque benefits offered at American Express Travel Related Services, and temporary leaves that are likely to affect only a small portion of the workforce at any particular time, such as dependent care leaves.

Similarly, educational initiatives can often be implemented quickly. Included here are Valuing Differences programs designed to increase employees' awareness of differences in the histories and perspectives of various cultural groups; programs for teaching new languages (including alternative technical languages and profession-based jargon) to employees who need to communicate with members of other "cultures;" training in group problem-solving and conflict management skills; and orientation programs for socializing organizational newcomers. Depending on one's objectives, such initiatives may be both feasible and highly effective.

Finally, it is worth noting that the experimental learning model adopted at Coopers & Lybrand is consistent with an intermediate time-frame for creating organizationwide change. The Coopers & Lybrand initiative is likely to stimulate some organizational subunits to experiment with making revolutionary changes that would be considered too risky to try on a larger scale. Many of these small experiments may "fail" the first time they are tried, but these "failures" will be highly instructive for the organization because they will permit fine-tuning to occur before revolutionary changes are introduced on a larger scale. This approach lowers the amount of risk (which is typically quite high) for organizations considering large-scale changes.

Time is a key parameter to consider when planning any change effort. It is one of our most precious and scarce resources, so those who waste it are rightfully chastized in most organizations. One mistake that leads to wasting time is misjudging the amount required to carry a change effort through to a successful conclusion, because unrealistic expectations for fast results may mean potentially useful change efforts are prematurely shut down. To avoid this mistake, the time requirements of new initiatives should be analyzed. Then a decision must be made about whether the time required is affordable and fits the stated objectives.

Should Change Be Introduced Globally or Locally?

As indicated by the discussion above, this question is related to how much time a change effort is likely to require to achieve its intended effects. This section discusses conditions that might influence whether change should be introduced locally or globally.

Global changes refer to those that are introduced simultaneously to everyone throughout the entire organization. The new benefits package offered by American Express Travel Related Services is one example of a global change that could not have been introduced locally without creating inequities among employees. It is interesting to note here that Xerox partially avoided the potential problem of perceived inequities by supporting independent caucus groups that offered their members valued benefits such as special training and career counseling. By offering these benefits, the caucus groups helped Xerox achieve some of its objectives, and at the same time the corporation was shielded from complaints that it was showing favoritism to some subgroups.

Whereas some changes require global introduction, others may be effectively introduced locally to a subsection of the organization, and then gradually spread throughout the organization, as appropriate. The cases in this volume offer several examples of initiatives that were introduced locally and then gradually disseminated. In the case of Coopers & Lybrand, local introduction of change is an explicit and fundamental design aspect of its strategic grass-roots perspective. Although perhaps not as explicitly designed into the other case examples, a similar principle appears in most of the cases in this volume. For example, at Pacific Bell, the learnings about effective recruitment strategies were localized within the Management Recruitment District at first, but were later disseminated when the district was merged with the Management Employment Office. At Digital, XYZ, and Harris Semiconductor, top-level executives were the first to experience the new initiative, followed by their subordinates, and then lower-level employees, each in succession. In the federal government's Quality Assessment Program, the logistics of working within a huge organization requires localized participation. For example, each year only a few occupational groups will contribute data to the longitudinal studies data base.

The decision to introduce an initiative globally or locally is likely to be influenced by several factors: the nature of the initiative, the design of the human resources organization (centralized or decentralized), and how similarities and differences are distributed throughout the organization.

The Nature of the Initiative

The nature of an initiative would include any characteristics that might raise equity issues. Global change may be preferred if inequities would arise by introducing change in a piecemeal manner. Perceived inequity is likely whenever employees are being offered any valued resource, such as financial benefits or special training that will improve eligibility for promotions or special assignments.

Even when inequity is not a consideration, some features of an initiative might limit the feasibility of having all employees participate at the same time. For example, the financial costs of global introduction may be too great to incur in a single year. Or the amount of time employees must be away from their jobs might be so great that it would make it difficult for the organization to function if everyone participated concurrently. In such cases, initiatives might be offered "locally" in the sense that they are offered only to a portion of employees. The subset of employees offered the initiative could be defined by geographic location, by location in the organizational hierarchy, by seniority, or on some other basis.

Organization Structure

Organizational structure may also influence the decision to implement change locally or globally. Several cases highlight the important role that organization structure plays in the design and implementation of human resources initiatives. Centralized structures are common in small companies. Larger companies that offer single products to a single market and/or that operate in very stable environments may also rely on centralized structures. However, for a variety of technological and competitive reasons, many medium and large firms are now moving in the direction of decentralizing their operations.

The global introduction of new initiatives is likely to be easier in organizations with centralized structures, other things being equal. Decentralization makes global change more difficult because it requires cooperation and agreement among dispersed, and often dissimilar, organizational units. These business units may have differing strategies for competing in their particular product and service markets; they may face differing labor markets; and the companies they compete against in the labor market may require them to adopt a variety of different human resources management practices. Such variations among business units mean that any particular initiative is likely to mesh better with the top priorities of some units than others.

The Distribution of Diversity in the Organization

Finally, the distribution of diversity in the organization is an important factor in deciding whether to introduce changes locally or globally. Diversity may exist throughout the entire organization, or it may be localized. Many large U.S. corporations have little gender and ethnic diversity at the top, although most have a great deal of these types of diversity at the lower levels. On the other hand, for occupation-based diversity, the opposite is true. Teams of lower-level employees often include people with relatively similar skills and knowledge, but teams of managers are likely to include people whose areas of specialized knowledge are dissimilar (e.g., accounting, law, marketing, operations).

When the objective is creating diversity, the logical starting places for new initiatives are areas where little diversity currently exists. For example, initiatives intended to increase the number of management positions held by women and members of nonmajority ethnic groups often begin with training for the upper-level managers who serve as gatekeepers to the managerial ranks. On the other hand, when the objective is working through diversity more effectively, both support for new initiatives and associated payoffs are likely to be greater when the initiatives are targeted to locations where diversity currently exists. For example, if the objective is to help ethnically mixed work groups improve their problem-solving skills, it may make more sense to introduce initiatives first among the front-line production and service employees (assuming these groups are more ethnically integrated), rather than beginning with top management.

Will Change Efforts Stop at the Organization's Borders or Reach Beyond?

As described in Chapter 2, many organizations are actively participating in new alliances with their suppliers, customers, and even their competitors. As a consequence, organizational boundaries have become more blurred. Most human resources management activities have been limited in the past to policies, programs, and practices for employees on the organization's payroll. However, as interorganization alliances become more common, so do the pressures to extend human resources management practices beyond the organization's formal boundaries. For example, some organizations already offer training programs to their suppliers in order to improve the quality of suppliers' products. Customers too may receive training, as part of a marketing strategy. Because the success of an organization is partly dependent upon the success of both suppliers and customers, there are good business reasons for offering them services—including human resources initiatives for working through diversity—that strengthen their organizations (see Schuler & MacMillan, 1984). For example, after a company develops an effective training program designed to help work teams use their diversity to support effective problem solving, it may find it can improve the quality of goods and services it receives from suppliers by teaching suppliers how to use the same training program for their employees.

However, alliances with other organizations are not the only reason to extend initiatives for working through diversity beyond organizational borders. As the case of Pacific Bell illustrated, recruiting initiatives can be highly effective when they involve establishing meaningful and sustained relationships with schools and community groups (notice that these are the suppliers of human resources). Schools and community groups can also help organizations design and deliver a wide variety of training programs.

Similarly, when initiatives involve helping employees manage aspects of their personal lives, such as child care, involvement with external organizations may be beneficial. For example, when child-care subsidies are offered to employees, it is important that usable child-care services be available in the local community. "Usable" implies that they are open during the hours when employees need them, that they are affordable given the size of the employer's subsidies, and that employees feel they can easily communicate with the facilities during the workday. Therefore, employers who offer child-care subsidies should consider negotiating with child-care suppliers to ensure that the services they offer fit employees' needs.

Summary: Fitting the Initiatives to the Objectives

In order to design and implement new initiatives for improving an organization's effectiveness in working through diversity, a number of questions should be considered. In particular, before asking the question "What should we do?" it is advisable to begin by analyzing the organization's current stance regarding issues of diversity. This analysis should uncover both formal and informal controls that stifle or nourish diversity, the reason for the existence of such controls, and the appropriateness of diversity-management methods given the organization's current objectives. New initiatives are called for if this analysis suggests that the organization's current objectives could be facilitated by a new approach to managing workforce diversity. In order to develop initiatives that fit the organization's particular situation, several additional issues should then be considered. These include the issue of the organization's past experiences with change programs, the history of affirmative action/equal employment opportunity programs and results, the time frame within which change efforts will be pursued, the forces that will impact whether changes should be introduced locally or globally, and the benefits that might be gained by extending the change effort beyond the organization's formal boundaries. Consideration of these issues will help ensure that new initiatives are developed to fit the specific objectives and constraints faced by each unique organization.

BASIC PRINCIPLES

There are many options and choices to be made when introducing initiatives for working through diversity, but there are also a few basic principles that seem to apply for all circumstances. These are briefly described next. The objective here is not to offer a complete lesson in organizational change, but rather to highlight principles of particular relevance to initiatives for working through diversity.

Develop a Comprehensive Understanding of the Many Types of Diversity in the Organization and Decide Which Are Most Important to Address

Several cases in this volume have alluded to the fact that diversity comes in many forms. Certainly, it is far too simplistic to think of the world in terms of only "them" and "us," a dichotomy automatically invoked whenever "women and minorities" are contrasted either implicitly or explicitly to white males. As the data from the XYZ Corporation reveal, white men differ from black men, who differ from black women, who differ from white women. Similarly, black women differ from Hispanic women, and Hispanic women differ from Hispanic men. Furthermore, there are many cultural differences within some of the general ethnic categories. For example, "Asian-American" lumps together Filipinos, Chinese, Japanese, Koreans, Vietnamese, Asian (East) Indians, and numerous other distinct cultural groups. Similarly, "Hispanic-American" lumps together Puerto Ricans, Mexican-Americans, and others. Add to the many ethnic-gender combinations such basic characteristics as age, family situation, education level, occupational specialty, tenure with the organization, level in the hierarchy, geographical location, and employment status (e.g., full time or part time, temporary or permanent, exempt or nonexempt, etc,), and the true amount of diversity that exists in most organizations soon seems almost overwhelming.

When embarking on change efforts related to diversity, it is important to first understand the many dimensions of diversity that exist in an organization. There are several aspects to the task of developing understanding about workforce diversity. The first task is to develop awareness of the many possible types of diversity that exist in organizations. This book has pointed out many of these, but others might be suggested through an analysis of any particular organization. Having identified the types of diversity likely to be present in an organization, the next step is to learn the facts about the relevant aspects of diversity.

One type of fact relates to information about the nature of the organization's workforce. What do the numbers indicate to you about the backgrounds of people in the organization and the way diversity is distributed throughout the organization? Do people with diverse backgrounds work closely together, or are they segregated into homogeneous subgroups based on occupations, hierarchical level, or geographic location? Facts such as these may be readily available in the data base of the organization's human resources information system, but if not, then some basic research may be needed to answer these questions.

A second type of fact is information about how the backgrounds of people relate to their attitudes and behaviors. For example: Are some subgroups of employees more likely to report dissatisfaction with their co-workers or the type of supervision they receive? Are turnover patterns different among different groups of employees? Do promotion rates differ among subgroups? Is everyone equally satisfied with the career opportunities they see? Valid answers to questions such as these may be easy to obtain in organizations that routinely conduct scientifically designed employee surveys to assess attitudes. In organizations without such ready information, however, systematic research may be needed in the organization.

In addition, change agents should take responsibility for becoming educated on the topic of workforce diversity more generally. This education process may include reading several available books like this one, attending conferences on the topic of workforce diversity, taking courses at local universities, and/or inviting speakers to present special seminars to staff members. Regardless of the format used, the objectives should include learning the facts about the local labor force and projected changes in the local labor force; learning the facts from psychology and sociology research regarding cultural differences, gender differences, age differences, intergroup relations, and teamwork; and, finally, learning about how other organizations are addressing the issue of diversity. The important point here is to be sure that new initiatives are chosen *after* the *facts* about the workforce are known.

With this learning task accomplished, the next task is to prioritize the dimensions of diversity that are important for the organization to address. This prioritization task should go hand in hand with a discussion of the objectives for any new initiatives. The results of the prioritized list of dimensions of diversity that are important should subsequently be used throughout all phases of planning, implementing, and evaluating programs for working through diversity.

When Designing Change, Stay Close to the Customers

Most change efforts have some impact on almost everyone in the organization; often they impact people outside the organization, also. To be effective, new initiatives require buy-in from all the relevant constituencies. In this sense, the constituencies are appropriately thought of as customers.

The customer metaphor emphasizes the importance of designing and delivering initiatives that customers (all customers) see as valuable, are aware of, and evaluate positively. In order to achieve these objectives, close contact with customers is essential. This includes contact with both primary customers, who are targeted as the direct users of a product or service, as well as secondary customers, who may not use the product directly themselves but who are in a position to encourage or discourage direct customers' use of a product or service. For example, if flexible work schedules are the "product," primary customers would be those employees whose work schedules would be made more flexible. Secondary customers would include the managers and supervisors of these employees, and in some cases, the co-workers. Note here that in many cases a particular individual may be both a primary and secondary customer, so it is important to specify which viewpoint you wish a customer to take when discussing a proposed new initiative.

The Design Phase

During the design phase, customers can provide valuable information about their needs, as they conceptualize them; the conditions under which they would "buy" the product or service; constraints that might interfere with their ability to use particular products or services; alternatives that they view as competition for the proposed product or service; and, ultimately, suggestions for how to modify a proposed product or service prototype to make it most appealing. Without this input, well-intentioned change agents are likely to develop initiatives that are never bought by the customers of interest. This problem was illustrated by Xerox's first attempt to introduce caucus groups for women, who turned out to be uninterested in this product, at least in the context and form it was offered at that time.

When customers participate actively in designing a new initiative, a side effect is that the design phase also serves as the first stage of the marketing phase. If the design phase is handled well, the side effects should be positive. But there is the potential for negative side effects, as well. If primary customers are asked to describe their image of the ideal product or service (e.g., the ideal benefits package or the ideal training program), they are likely to conjure up images of something that will never be offered to them. Whatever the features of the final product, they are unlikely to meet the ideal, leading to feelings of disappointment. For this same reason, if secondary customers will ultimately have the power to reject or radically alter an initiative, their input should be sought early in the design process. This will ensure that discussions with primary customers are conducted with full knowledge of any constraints secondary customers might impose.

Several of the cases in this volume illustrate how change agents involved their customers during the design phase. In some cases, the inclusion of customers was both very broad and very formalized. For example, the federal government's Quality Assessment Program was designed with input from both government managers and a committee of representatives from the private sector, various government and congressional agencies, academics, unions, and professional human resources management associations. Pepsi-Cola International also relies on a broad base of customer input as it designs its human resources management system, although the input is solicited more through personal meetings and one-on-one discussions. As a third example, American Express solicited input by conducting a formal survey of employees and through discussions held during an intensive 2-day planning session with senior-line human resources managers. Intensive planning sessions with executives were also used at Harris Semiconductor as a means for ensuring that top-line managers had substantial input in designing their new postmerger organization.

The Marketing Phase

Marketing efforts can begin during the design phase of a new initiative, but they do not end there. Applying the customer metaphor is as useful for planning a marketing strategy as it is for designing the initiative. This is not the place for a full discussion of basic marketing principles; nevertheless, the fact that marketing can play an important role in determining the success of new initiatives should not be overlooked. Recognizing this, American Express hired a consultant specifically to assist with the roll-out phase of the change efforts that it hopes will make it "the best place to work." At Harris Semiconductor, meetings with the president kept top-level managers informed of new initiatives, and the company's internal newsletter was used for informing most other employees. At Coopers & Lybrand, two important vehicles for marketing new initiatives are the corporate office's clearing house and networking activities for putting field offices in touch with one another and the company's internal awards program. As these examples highlight, marketing involves more than simply informing employees about new initiatives. Successful marketing efforts stimulate employees to participate in new intitiatives and to share their experiences with others.

The Evaluation Phase(s)

When a company offers a product to the external marketplace, it is almost certain to monitor the success of that product using some type of objective indicator. On the other hand, often the success of products and services offered in the company's internal marketplace is not monitored closely. Unfortunately, many human resources departments are particularly guilty of not rigorously evaluating the products and services they offer.

Occasionally, there may be justifiable reasons for not investing time and resources to monitor customers' early reactions to initiatives for working through diversity. For example, there may be reasons to expect some negative reactions, which if documented could be used as ammunition to squelch an effort to which mixed reactions are likely. Or if changes are expected to occur very slowly, the argument might be made that the evaluation phase should not begin for several years into the future, when it is more likely that positive results can be shown.

Arguments such as these reflect a legitimate concern about how evaluation results might be used to shut down an initiative, perhaps prematurely. However, if no evaluation data are obtained, then it is also true that supporters of an initiative will have no ammunition to use in fighting the critics. Equally troublesome is that they are shutting themselves off from feedback that might be productively used to make improvements and adjustments in the initiatives.

Implicit in the advice, "stay close to the customer" is the assertion that customers' evaluations are valuable and should be aggressively sought out. Concerns about how data might be misused should not be addressed by not collecting the data. One alternative for handling the problem would be to collect relevant evaluation data on a regular basis and then store them in their raw, unanalyzed form until sufficient time has passed to give an initiative time to "take." Often, a less drastic solution is simply to ensure that the types of evaluation data collected are consistent with the intended objectives of the initiative. For example, if personal self-development is the only objective one hopes to achieve, then asking employees whether an experience was valuable may be the only data that should be collected. However, when large investments are made for the purposes of reducing turnover, attracting new or different employees to the firm, and/or improving team functioning, then data relevant to these objectives should be examined. This is precisely the objective behind the co-evaluation studies that Coopers & Lybrand conducts with field offices that participate in company-approved pilot programs. This evaluation phase will enable the company to assess whether objectives are being met by an experimental program before deciding whether to support the "proliferation" of that initiative. Hopefully, planned evaluations such as these will become more feasible and more common as more and more organizations install computer-based human resources information systems.

Anticipate Possible Problems and Be Prepared to Deal with Them

Any new initiative can run into unanticipated problems, and diversity interventions are no exception. Even the most thorough planning process will not completely prevent problems from arising. Because of the sensitive nature of some types of diversity initiatives, such as awareness training and group discussions that focus of understanding differences, it is particularly important to be prepared for the consequences. For example, if employees are suddenly convinced that the organization really wants to know about incidents of racism, sexism, or any other kind of "ism," there may be several such complaints that suddenly surface. These may implicate an employee who had never been identified as creating problems in the past. In such a circumstance, procedures should be in place for investigating the complaints and resolving the situation fairly.

As another example of a problem that might not be anticipated, employees who attend a training program may feel that the program itself perpetuates destructive stereotyping. "Awareness training" programs and special skills programs such as assertiveness training can easily backfire if they seem to highlight differences that employees have worked hard to obliterate because the differences are devalued by the organization's culture. There is a fine line that must be walked in programs that attempt to both acknowledge some of the differences that characterize members of different demographic groups *on average* and reduce the tendency we all have to rely on stereotypes. Even the most experienced trainer may offend a few participants, so it is desirable to have a mechanism for handling employees' complaints. This may even involve spending extra time counseling distressed employees to ensure they have not misunderstood the intent and content of a particular training experience.

As noted earlier, new initiatives may not be well received if they appear to be directed at meeting the needs of one group while ignoring the equally pressing needs of another group. The American Express and federal government cases provide several guidelines to follow when conducting a thorough needs analysis, which should lessen the risk of accidentally setting off booby traps.

Finally, when organizations announce that they value differences and support diversity, they should be prepared to have employees point out contradictions between words and actions. For example, all printed materials will come under scrutiny, from annual reports to announcements for company-sponsored social events. Of course, the company's own advertising materials will also be examined from a new perspective. Other examples of organizational activities that may suddenly be criticized more openly include the types of clubs frequented by top-level executives, the types of community events and programs supported by company donations (as well as the ones that are not supported), and the types of awards and gift certificates offered to employees as incentives or bonuses. An organization that intends to be serious about supporting diversity should be prepared, even eager, to make adjustments in many spheres of activity, including those not directly linked to a specific human resources initiative.

Institutionalize New Learning

Initiatives for creating organizational changes are likely to involve may different people working on many different specific projects in many different places over a long period of time. Throughout this process, a tremendous about of qualitative and quantitative data will be generated. A lot of these data will be gathered systematically during the planning and evaluation phases of a new initiative. Typically, standard operating procedures ensure that such systematically collected data are summarized and recorded in the form of a report. When this information is subsequently used in making decisions about how to proceed with the initiative of interest, the learning becomes institutionalized. That is, the official policies and practices of the organization change to reflect the new information.

Recording what has been learned is an important first step for institutionalizing what has been learned. But it is unfortunate that this most basic step of recording what has been learned is often conducted only for information obtained through formal, planned channels—such as surveys, workshops, and focus group discussions. A useful improvement on this standard operating procedure would be to encourage the recording of all learnings that occurs on a daily or weekly basis. For example, those with central responsibility for designing and implementing initiatives could keep a diary or log that records new insights. In addition, employees throughout the organization could occasionally be polled anonymously in order to generate information about what they have learned recently. Such polling could be conducted using standard "suggestion" boxes or electronic bulletin boards. Contests might even be conducted periodically to encourage employees to document their learnings in essays, live skits, songs, or video productions. Such steps would ensure that more of the informal, unplanned learnings are recorded.

Recording what has been learned is an important first step toward institutionalizing what has been learned, but more is needed. The second step involves disseminating the learning throughout the organization. Dissemination of learning can be achieved in numerous ways. Redesigning formal policies and practices is perhaps the most fundamental method, but it is also the most difficult and complex. Training programs are another popular vehicle for disseminating learning, but these often reach only a few employees. Therefore, other methods to disseminate learning should be constantly sought with the objective of creating a continuous stream of learning that immerses all employees. Such methods could include scheduled times for sharing log notes during staff meetings, "hotlines" that people can call when they have questions or when they wish to add new information to an available resource, special features in company newsletters (e.g., a monthly listing of "new lessons" submitted by employees), informative anecdotes incorporated into speeches given by higher-level executives, memorable quotes posted on bulletin boards, short essays published in company-sponsored literary forums, and so on. Methods such as these can be quite effective for institutionalizing new learnings and ensuring they have a lasting impact of the organizational culture.

CONCLUSION

To summarize, four simple principles should guide change processes related to working through diversity: (1) Develop a comprehensive understanding of the issue of diversity, (2) stay close to the customers throughout all phases of the process, (3) be prepared to deal with the possible problems that may arise as new initiatives are introduced, and (4) institutionalize the organizational learning that occurs. Although these principles could easily apply to any organizational change efforts, they are particularly relevant to attend to when considering new initiatives for working through diversity.

Diversity is a complex and potentially "hot" issue with many facets, yet relatively little is known about the most effective ways to work through diversity in organizations. Furthermore, the most effective approach is likely to differ from one organization to the next. Therefore, those who wish to improve an organization's effectiveness must be willing to learn as they go. Inevitably, the learning process will be jolting at times, as change agents, supervisors, subordinates, and co-workers realize the need for changes within themselves, in their organization's culture, and in the basic human resources management systems of the organization. Some jolts may be beneficial for the change process, but too many jolts and the process may screech to a halt. For those who learn as much as possible before initiating change, work closely with customers, anticipate problems, and institutionalize what is learned along the way, the path to change may be a bit smoother. More importantly, those on the journey are more likely to reach their desired destination.

REFERENCES

Jackson, S. E. (1991). Team composition in organizational settings: Issues in managing an increasingly diverse workforce. In S. Worchel, W. Wood, & J. A. Simpson, (Eds.), *Group process and productivity*. Newbury Park, CA: Sage.

Schuler, R. S., & MacMillan, I. C. (1984). Gaining competitive advantage through human resources management practices. *Human Resource Management, 23,* 241–155.

SUGGESTED ADDITIONAL READING

Coates, J. F., Jarratt, J., & Mahaffie, J. B. (1990). *Future work: Seven critical forces reshaping work and the work force in North America.* San Francisco: Jossey-Bass.

Fernandez, J. P. (1991). *Managing a diverse workforce: Regaining the competitive edge.* Lexington, MA: Lexington Books.

Fyock, C. D. (1990). *America's workforce is coming of age.* Lexington, MA: Lexington Books.

Jamieson, D., & O'Mara, J. (1991). *Managing workforce 2000: Gaining the diversity advantage.* San Francisco: Jossey-Bass.

Kanter, R. M., Stein, B. A., & Jick, T. (1991). *The challenge of organizational change: How people experience it and manage it.* New York: Free Press.

Katz, P. A., & Taylor, D. A. (1988). *Eliminating racism: Profiles in controversy.* New York: Plenum Press.

Kessler, L. I. (1990). *Managing diversity in an equal opportunity workplace.* Washington, DC: National Foundation for the Study of Employment Policy.

Loden, M., & Rosener, J. B. (1991). *Workforce America! Managing employee diversity as a vital resource.* Homewood, IL: Business One Irwin.

Offermann, L. R., & Gowing, M. K. (1990). Special Issue: Organizational psychology. *American Psychologist, 45*(2), entire issue.

Ridgeway, C. L. (Ed.) (Forthcoming) *Gender, interaction and inequality.* New York: Springer-Verlag.

Thiederman, S. B. (1991). *Bridging cultural barriers for corporate success.* Lexington, MA: Lexington Books.

Thomas, R. R., Jr. (1991). *Beyond race and gender: Unleashing the power of your total workforce by managing diversity.* New York: AMACOM.

Tjosvold, D. (1991). *The conflict-positive organization: Stimulate diversity and create unity.* Reading, MA: Addison-Wesley.

Worchel, S., Wood, W., & Simpson, J. A. (1991). *Productivity and process in groups.* Newbury Park, CA: Sage.

Index